# Journal of the American Revolution

# EDITORIAL BOARD

# JOURNAL

*OF THE*

# AMERICAN REVOLUTION

ANNUAL VOLUME 2024

WESTHOLME
Yardley

Westholme Publishing, LLC
904 Edgewood Road
Yardley, Pennsylvania 19067
Visit our Web site at www.westholmepublishing.com

ISBN: 978-1-59416-427-9

Printed in the United States of America.

# CONTENTS

# EDITOR'S INTRODUCTION

Each year since its inception in 2013, *Journal of the American Revolution* has published hundreds of articles on all aspects of America's founding. Our contributors touch on details of laws and politics, economics, military campaigns and operations, material culture, and a host of other things. But more than anything else, the articles are about people. That focus on people is especially clear in this, our tenth annual printed compilation of selected articles from the online journal.

Most of this year's articles are centered on people, from the famous to the forgotten. George Washington looms large in this collection, as is fitting for one of history's most influential, and most-studied individuals. Did he really write the Rules of Civility that have been widely reprinted and sold in gift shops at historic sites? Why did he choose to attend a meeting of the Continental Congress dressed in a military uniform? How did information from newspapers influence his military planning? And what was the significance of the wooden box sent to Washington from a Scottish lord during his presidency?

Other famous figures from the era had attributes and activities that are not what they are remembered for, such as the redoubtable Charles Lee as an essayist and renowned historiographer Mercy Otis Warren as a propagandist. The famous Paul Revere's interactions with an infamous – and largely forgotten – British spy, John Adams' and Nathanael Greene's correspondence discussion about the purpose of an army, John Hancock's thoughts and personality as revealed in a selection of his quotes, Thomas Paine's changing thoughts on popular government, and Thomas Jefferson's perspectives on how history should be written. All of these things are covered in this volume.

Often more interesting than the famous are the exploits of those whose names are seldom heard, but who were among the multitudes who made contributions, however small, to the events of the era. A mysterious man named Samuel Dyer scheming in Boston. A New York army officer named Rosewell Beebe, and a Connecticut adventurer named Remember Baker, both of whom met untimely deaths. The exploits of James Morris, a Connecticut military officer who typified the company-level leaders of the Continental Army. An unfortunate river crossing by William Walker, a soldier from Massachusetts. Reassessment of a fabled journey by South Carolina's Emily Geiger. These and several other stories of the not-so-famous have been brought to light, some for the first time, by JAR contributors and are included here, giving a feel for the wide range of people involved in founding a nation.

Of course, there are also articles about other aspects of the era, the battles, the politics, the geography. But even those come down to people, to groups and individuals, and their struggles, successes and failures. They made the history happen, and they make it live today.

# George Washington's "Rules of Civility": An Early American Literary Mystery

✺ SHAWN DAVID MCGHEE ✺

Tucked away in George Washington's papers rests a thirty-five-page handwritten folio labeled "Forms of Writing."[1] In Washington's neat and ornate cursive, the first roughly two-thirds of this artifact are comprised of carefully copied examples of legal mechanisms such as promissory notes, bills of exchange, short- and long-form wills, and, ominously, a "Form of a Servants Indenture."[2] Clearly whoever directed the young Virginian to transcribe this legalese felt it to the boy's advantage to have a working understanding of the litigious environment he would likely soon enter. Also included are two poems, "On Christmas Day" and "True Happiness."[3] Historians once attributed these compositions to Washington; more recent scholarship definitively traced them to 1743 and 1734 editions, respectively, of *Gentleman's Magazine*, a London periodical.[4]

This collection of Washington's papers dates to early in his life: in the upper-right hand corner of the twenty-first page, another writer

---

1. This paper stems from *Journal of the American Revolution* editor Don N. Hagist's curiosity into this subject. Any flaws in these pages are mine alone; any valuable insights resulted from his initial query. George Washington, *George Washington Papers, Series 1, Exercise Books, Diaries, and Surveys-99, Subseries 1A, Exercise Books -1747: Forms of Writing, and The Rules of Civility and Decent Behavior in Company and Conversation, ante 1747*. Ante 1747. Manuscript/Mixed Material. *The Washington Papers*, www.loc.gov/item/mgw1a.001/.

2. Ibid.
3. Ibid.
4. *Gentleman's Magazine*, February 1743, February 1734; See also Kevin J. Hayes, *George Washington: A Life in Books* (New York: Oxford University Press, 2017).

scribbled "Geo. Washington's handwriting in 1744 at the age of 12."[5] Within the text of one passage, Washington copied the year "1741," while on the seventh page, he wrote "my hand and seal this Day of April, Anno Dom 1743."[6] Since these dates are within passages he was transcribing, however, they are likely less reliable than the year recorded in the foreign hand for dating these papers with any degree of certainty. It is the final ten pages of this manuscript, however, that have piqued the interest of some scholars. George Washington's "Notes of Civility and Decent Behaviour in Company and Conversation," a compilation of 110 instructions in etiquette and ethics, remains something of a literary mystery.[7] Just where the maxims originated, how they ended up before Washington and what purpose(s) they served, is not entirely clear. The circumstances that produced these papers, however, moved Washington to sponsor educational initiatives at the provincial and national levels both privately and publicly. Scholastic cultivation, Washington came to appreciate, promoted private achievement and the public good, vital contributions to both individual and national success. Taken together, Washington's own acknowledged academic shortcomings led him to identify equitable access to education as a fundamental component for promoting civic virtue, American identity and national security.

I

Washington's earliest biographers took little to no notice of his "Notes of Civility." John Marshall's multi-volume adulatory survey (1804-1807) fails to recognize the maxims, with the chief justice summarizing Washington's education as simply "limited to subjects strictly useful."[8] Mason Weems, in a book one early editor described as an "absurd" contribution to American historiography, made no mention of them in his 1808 publication.[9] In 1842, Jared Sparks, that ambitious if less-than-meticulous scholar, determined the notes originated from various

5. George Washington, *Washington Papers, Series 1, Exercise Books, Forms of Writing*, www.loc.gov/item/mgw1a.001/.
6. Ibid.
7. George Washington, "Rules of Civility and Decent Behaviour in Company and Conversation," Manuscript, *The Washington Papers*, washingtonpapers.org/documents_gw/civility/civil_01.html.
8. John Marshall, *The Life of George Washington*, 5 vols. (1804; reis., Philadelphia: J. Crissy, 1838), 1:3.
9. Mason Weems, *A History of the Life and Death, Virtue and Exploits of General George Washington*, ed. Mark Van Doren (1808; reis., New York: Macy-Masius, 1927), 5.

sources that an adolescent Washington ultimately failed to cite.[10] Washington Irving theorized the young Virginian composed the rules himself to assimilate into the refined household of the Fairfax family his older half-brother Lawrence had married into.[11] In 1888, Dr. J. M. Toner transcribed and published the first full transcription of "Rules of Civility" with limited editorial amendments. He only noted, through use of several ellipses, where lost text from the original pages had been eaten away by mice. After fruitlessly searching the Library of Congress for any books and/or treatises on manners and morality dated 1745 or earlier, Toner determined the maxims "were compiled by George Washington himself when a school-boy." Toner also recognized that Washington's compositions embodied the spirit of Europe's polite society while simultaneously claiming the rules remained "especially applicable" to British North America.[12] How a struggling Virginia boy might have learned of and valued Old World cosmopolitanism the scholar left unanswered. Even as thorough a historian as Paul Leicester Ford simply offered, in passing, that Washington's biographers credited the Virginian with composing "Notes of Civility."[13] Uncharacteristically, the scrupulous Ford provided no further analysis. It was not until eccentric Virginia scholar Moncure D. Conway grew curious about these papers that this mystery began revealing its secrets.[14]

Toner's short treatise sparked Conway's interest in exploring further the origins of "Notes of Civility." When Conway began researching a domestic biography of Washington he scoured the municipal records of Fredericksburg, Virginia, a village the Washingtons had moved within the vicinage of when George was about six. Conway discovered that French settlers had founded that town's first school and Rector James Marye, also an emigrant from France, had presided over St. George's Church, the first such institution in Fredericksburg. This led

---

10. Jared Sparks, *The Life of George Washington* (Boston: Tappen and Dennet, 1842), 6, 513.

11. Washington Irving, *Life of George Washington*, 5 vols. (New York: G. P. Putnam & Company, 1855-59), 1:54.

12. J. M. Toner, ed., *Rules of Civility and Decent Behavior in Company and Conversation: A Paper Found Among the Early Writings of George Washington: Copied from the Original with Literal Exactness, and Edited with Notes* (Washington, D.C. W.H. Morrison, 1888), 5-9.

13. Paul Leicester Ford, *The True George Washington* (Philadelphia: J.B. Lippincott Company, 1896), 74.

14. For a recent survey of Moncure D. Conway, see Dwayne Eutsey, "Devil-Lore and Avatars: Moncure Conway's Likely Influence on 'No. 44, the Mysterious Stranger,'" *Mark Twain Journal* 54, no. 1 (2016): 95-115.

Conway to reasonably suspect that Marye had taught Washington at St. George's and the rules were likely French in origin. Conway divulged these suspicions to a friend at the British Museum who subsequently directed the scholar to an old manuscript written in both French and Latin. Within that archaic tome Conway located most of Washington's rules. Incredibly, this discovery marked just the beginning of Conway's investigation.[15]

Conway uncovered a complicated cultural tale that stretched back into late sixteenth-century France. In 1595, the College of La Fleché, a Jesuit institute of higher learning, sent neighboring College at Pont-á-Mousson a treatise entitled "Bienseance de la Conversation entre les Hommes," which translates roughly to "Good Manners in Conversation Between Men."[16] This brief manuscript contained loose French versions of ninety-two of Washington's hitherto elusive "Rules of Civility." It is not clear why La Fleché sent this work to Pont-á-Mousson, but a local bishop next ordered "Bienseance de la Conversation" translated into Latin. In 1617, Pont-á-Mousson reproduced the work and these French directives underwent subsequent printings in both Paris and Rouen. Scholars eventually translated the treatise "into Spanish, German, and Bohemian," initiatives expressive of the wider European application and polite universality this collection of maxims held. Conway determined that educators had copied this manuscript for the exclusive use of university students where it made its way into print.[17] Both the spiritual and secular themes suggest the author(s) designed these directives to indoctrinate upper-class boys with the appropriate piety and performative virtue with which to aspire.

Conway proved a careful scholar, discovering that eighteen of Washington's rules were not from the pages of "Bienseance de la Conversation." Fortuitously, he learned of an English translation that contained all of the missing maxims. In 1640, eight-year-old Francis Hawkins, according to the publication, translated and published the French instructions as *Youth's Behavior, or Decency in Conversation Amongst Men*. Conway remained unconvinced of the author's proposed age, which, according to a later scholar, clouded the Virginian's judgment and estimation of Hawkins's work.[18] That aside, by 1646 the book had gone

15. Moncure D. Conway, ed., *George Washington's Rules of Civility Traced to their Sources and Restored* (New York: United States Book Company, 1890), 10-12.
16. I am indebted to my colleague Keith Kesten of the Foreign Languages Department at Cinnaminson High School, New Jersey, for providing this translation.
17. Conway, *Washington's Rules*, 12-14.
18. Francis Hawkins, *Youth's Behavior, or Decency in Conversation Amongst Men*, rev. ed. (London: W. Wilson, 1646).

through four editions; by 1663, a mysterious "counsellor of the Middle Temple" had added twenty-five new rules. Conway found that this edition actually included thirty-one new maxims, six more than its title page boasted.[19]

Conway connected these disparate times, tongues, and towns into a plausible synthesis. According to the historian, after James Marye converted from Catholicism to Protestantism in 1726, his family disowned him. This familial ostracism compelled Marye to relocate to England where he met and married Letitia Maria Anne Staige. Incredibly, Staige's brother presided over St. George's church in Virginia, prompting the couple to emigrate to the Old Dominion. In 1735 Marye became minister at St. George's, a position he maintained until 1767. Conway reasoned that Marye had established and taught at a small country school, surmising the intrepid Frenchman had brought a copy of "Bienseance de la Conversation" to England and then purchased *Youth's Behavior* before departing for Virginia.[20] In his final analysis, Conway doubted "whether the Virginia boy used the work of the London boy." He concluded Washington had likely written these maxims down as oral exercises administered by Marye, who used both the French and English versions to craft an amalgamation of both treatises.[21]

In 1926, Charles Moore, head of the Division of Manuscripts for the Library of Congress, published a new transcription of Washington's "Rules of Civility" and included a convenient comparison with the 1663 edition of *Youth's Behavior*.[22] Surveying the available literature, Moore remarked of the shadowy maxims, "much has been written and little is known." He also addressed Conway's reluctance in believing that eight-year-old Francis Hawkins had personally translated the French rules into English. The Hawkins family, Moore uncovered, descended from an old and learned aristocratic family and Francis's father John had already published five books before his talented young son translated "Bienseance" into English. John, proud of his son's advanced linguistic abilities, delivered the work to printer William Lee, who published it as *Youth's Behavior* in 1640. The chaos of the English civil wars prevented a second edition from being printed until 1646, after which the book rapidly ran through numerous editions. Unknown English writ-

---

19. Conway, *Washington's Rules*, 20.
20. Ibid.
21. Ibid., 23, 28.
22. Charles Moore, ed., *George Washington's Rules of Civility and Decent Behaviour in Company and Conversation* (Boston: Houghton Mifflin Company, 1926).

ers, explained Moore, added more maxims over subsequent printings;
the 1663 copy, however, contains every rule found in Washington's
manuscript. This indicates that under whatever circumstances Washington produced his version, he must have had access to the contents
of either the 1663 edition of Hawkins's work or a later form of the
same. Moore concluded that a comparison of Washington's manuscript
"furnishes proof positive" that the maxims came from *Youth's Behavior*
and not "Bienseance." Moore further theorized that some unknown
figure selected, synthesized and situated the specific 110 rules for professional or private purposes. This unique composite found its way into
Washington's possession and the boy copied them, Moore conjectured,
as "exercises in handwriting."[23]

Modern scholars have spilled less ink on Washington's "Rules of Civility." John Ferling offered only that the maxims, which he claimed
Washington "found somewhere," helped the Virginian develop his
courtly manners and modesty.[24] According to Joseph Ellis, Washington
likely used them more for penmanship exercises than moral
instruction.[25] Over two volumes on Washington, Peter R. Henriques
mentioned the rules just once. Contradicting Ellis, he argued that at
least the final maxim, which urges readers to "keep alive in your Breast
that Little Spark of Celestial fire Called Conscience," played a greater
role in settling Washington's own conscience than did any "ministers,
priests, prophets, or holy books."[26] Gordon Wood connected Washington's rules to the Virginian's desire of becoming a liberal gentleman
"aware of the conventions of civility."[27] In addition to embodying the
social etiquette required to navigate virtually any polite environment,
Wood explained that eighteenth-century gentlemen continually refined
their penmanship, grammar, and spelling. And unlike Old World gentlemen, who were effectively rewarded by birth and rank, American cosmopolitanism flowered from individual merit and effort.[28] No doubt all
of the preceding observations fit into the social context of this mystery.

23. Ibid., ix, xi, xii.
24. John Ferling, *The Ascent of George Washington: The Hidden Political Genius of an
American Icon* (New York: Bloomsbury Press, 2009), 11.
25. Joseph Ellis, *His Excellency: George Washington* (New York: Alfred Knopf, 2004), 9.
26. Peter R. Henriques, *Realistic Visionary: A Portrait of George Washington* (Charlottesville: University of Virginia Press, 2006), 182; Peter R. Henriques, *First and Always:
A New Portrait of George Washington* (Charlottesville: University of Virginia Press, 2020),
this book makes no mention of Washington's "Rules of Civility."
27. Gordon S. Wood, "The Greatness of George Washington," in *Revolutionary Characters: What Made the Founders Different* (New York: Penguin Books, 2006), 36.
28. Gordon S. Wood, "The Founders and the Enlightenment," in ibid., 11-15.

Despite some anomalies, Washington almost certainly referenced the 1663 edition of *Youth's Behavior* while drafting his own "Notes of Civility." Hawkins's work is divided into seven chapters, each beginning at rule one and totaling 173 maxims.[29] The chapters are organized by theme: the appropriate behavior among men; conversational protocol; addressing persons of various ranks; clothing maintenance and personal hygiene; walking alone or in company; body language during discourse; and dining etiquette.[30] Washington's copybook, on the other hand, advertises no such topical divisions, begins at maxim one and continues to 110, never again starting at maxim one as Hawkins's chapters do. The Virginian's version also omits fifty rules outright while combining several others into single instructions.[31] Additionally, Washington copied three directives from the unnumbered additions included in the 1663 edition of *Youth's Behavior*. Yet even considering these omissions and combinations, Washington's manuscript follows Hawkins's work faithfully in terms of sequence. For example, Washington began with *Youth's Behavior*, chapter one, rule one, but omitted Hawkins's second rule and skipped to the third. Thus the Virginian's second maxim, as it were, reflected the Englishman's third. Washington's copy does not bounce between chapters or ever go out of order; though he ignored or joined some maxims, what he copied follows perfectly the general chronology of Hawkins's work. This alone is powerful evidence that the Virginia boy worked exclusively with some version of *Youth's Behavior*.

Curiously, not a single rule in Washington's version is copied identically from the Hawkins folio. Each maxim is recognizable to the degree that scholars can confidently identify *Youth's Behavior* as the source material, but nearly every directive in the Washington manuscript is considerably shorter than its seventeenth-century counterpart.[32]

29. Francis Hawkins, *Youth's Behavior, or Decency in Conversation Amongst Men*, rev. ed. (London: W. Wilson, 1663).

30. Moore, *Washington's Rules of Civility*.

31. For example, Washington's Rule 5 combines Hawkins's Chapter 1, numbers 8 and 9; Rule 8 combines chapter 1, numbers 15 and 16; Rule 11 combines Chapter 1, numbers 19 and 20; Rule 87 combines chapter 6, numbers 35 and 39; Rule 92 combines chapter 7, numbers 2, 3, 4, and 7. See Moore's helpful compilation of both the Washington and Hawkins works in Moore, *Washington's Rules of Civility*.

32. There is but a single exception to this claim; Washington's thirty-second rule contains several more words than Hawkins's chapter two, maxim ten. Other than this outlier, Washington's maxims are shorter and more direct than the seventeenth-century English translation. See Moore, *Washington's Rules of Civility*, 38.

Below are three examples representative of this observation:

WASHINGTON, RULE 1:
Every Action done in Company, ought to be with Some Sign of Respect, to those that are Present.

HAWKINS, CHAPTER I, NUMBER 1:
Every Action done in the view of the world, ought to be accompanied with some sign of reverence, which one beareth to all who are present.

WASHINGTON, RULE 25:
Superfluous Complements and all Affection of Ceremonie are to be avoided, yet where due they are not to be neglected.

HAWKINS, CHAPTER 2, NUMBER 1:
Although superfluous Complements, and all affectation in Ceremonies are to be eschewed, yet thou oughtest not to leave them which are due, otherwise thou displeasest the person with whom thou dost converse.

WASHINGTON, RULE 28:
If any one come to Speak to you while you are Sitting Stand up tho he be your Inferiour, and when you Present Seats let it be to every one according to his Degree.

HAWKINS, CHAPTER 2, NUMBER 5:
If any one come to speak with thee whilst thou sittest; stand up, especially if the person do merit it, be it that he be greater than thy self; or for that he is not familiar, or though for the rest he were thy equal, or thy inferior: and if there be any thing for one to sit on, be it a chair, be it a stool, give to each one his due.[33]

It is unlikely that a school-aged Washington took it upon himself to synthesize the meandering language of *Youth's Behavior* into the cleaner, clearer prose reflected in his copybook; his typical dense verbiage conspicuously supports this observation. It is equally unlikely that James Marye, a native French speaker, rearranged the convoluted seventeenth-century maxims into the more condensed English instructions found in Washington's manuscript.[34] Of course this complicates the matter at hand and leaves open some limited possibilities as to how Washington created his "Rules of Civility." Either some unknown person: A) selected and copied the 110 rules they felt most valuable for ingraining a cultural acumen among students and Washington had these drafts before him or attended training under this person; or B) some unknown person had the Hawkins copy and verbally dictated im-

---

33. Moore, *Washington's Rules of Civility*, 27, 35, 36, 37.
34. For James Mayre's native tongue and Jesuit education in France, see "Washington Guided By Jesuit Rules," *American Catholic Historical Researches* 21, no. 4 (1904): 151-53.

provised abridgements to his students as recitation and memory exercises, which may explain why Washington followed *Youth's Behavior* sequentially despite omitting and combining certain maxims. The purpose(s) of these papers is equally unknown. Moncure D. Conway melodramatically declared these directives provided "the art and mystery of moral education" to a man who once dictated the future of "the New World, — in a sense, human destiny." The maxims, he remarked, "celebrate self-restraint, modesty, habitual consideration of others, and, to a large extent, living for others."[35] For Dr. J. M Toner, the rules contained the essential "habits, morals, and manners" that shaped Washington's "noble character."[36] As noted above, Charles Moore and Joseph Ellis viewed the rules as nothing more than mundane handwriting exercises. Instead of considering these written directives as *either* vital for instilling morality *or* critical for perfecting penmanship, it is perhaps more useful to combine these potential intentions. A young eighteenth-century gentleman, after all, would have absorbed the behavioral instructions he was copying while simultaneously perfecting his letters in an effort to realize his maximum potential as a budding intellectual.

Literature promoting model behavior and conversational decorum enjoyed a wide audience in Europe during the sixteenth and seventeenth centuries and in British North America during the eighteenth century.[37] This genre of writing is perhaps most famously exemplified by Baldassare Castiglione's 1528 *Book of the Courtier*, which may have inspired the original authors of "Bienseance de la Conversation" to write that French treatise in the first place.[38] Much of this literature, moreover, advocated the mastery of intellectual, moral and physical qualities. These instructions in gentility, contained in a manuscript like Washington's "Rules," ultimately extended to the tangible advantages of copying them.

Historians may never identify the person(s) responsible for educating Washington. There are, however, several suspects scholars may rea-

35. Conway, *Washington's Rules*, 45, 46.
36. Toner, *Rules of Civility*, 9.
37. Stefan Ehrenpreis, "Reformed Education in Early Modern Europe: A Survey," *Dutch Review of Church History* 85 (2005): 39-51; Lowell C. Green, "The Bible in Sixteenth-Century Humanist Education," *Studies in the Renaissance* 19, (1972): 112-134; Sheldon Rothblatt, *Tradition and Change in English Liberal Education: An Essay in History and Culture* (London: Faber and Faber, 1976); Wood, "The Founders and the Enlightenment," in *Revolutionary Characters*, 11-15.
38. Baldesar Castiglione, *The Book of the Courtier*, trans. Leonard Eckstein Opdycke (New York: Charles Scribner's Sons, 1902).

sonably entertain. Washington's father Augustine received a partial education at the Appleby Grammar School in England during his brief
childhood stay in the metropole.[39] Obviously satisfied with his experience, he made certain that elder sons Lawrence and Augustine, Jr., each
received their schooling at the same institution.[40] Additionally, according to Virginia Rev. Jonathan Boucher, an indentured servant provided
at least part of George's education.[41] Any of the four individuals listed
above could have become familiar with the Hawkins maxims and, either in an English classroom or private quarters, copied the rules while
updating the language. It is also possible that Lawrence, Augustine, Jr.,
or the aforementioned unknown teacher dictated a personal synthesis
of the 110 maxims to an adolescent George. The record as it stands
simply does not allow for definitive closure regarding this matter.

## II

During Washington's long career, he mixed with some of the most educated and creative minds in public life. In comparison with these associates, Washington identified his own education as quite basic,
leaving him underinformed or even ignorant on a range of subjects.
Lacking command of a foreign language, for instance, offered no small
degree of discomfort to him.[42] Washington's sensitivity over his academic shortcomings also caused him to agonize over his public correspondence. When Lt. Gov. Robert Dinwiddie read Major
Washington's account of his 1753 expedition to Fort Le Boeuf, for example, the governor demanded its immediate publication. This left the
young officer with but a single day to craft his minutes into a readable
synthesis. Unnerved by what he considered an unpolished final draft,
Washington opened his treatise with a brief disclaimer, explaining he
could only "apologize . . . for the numberless Imperfections" contained
in his journal. Washington quite reasonably explained he had no time
to "correct or amend" his narrative under the circumstances.[43] As gen-

39. T. Pape, "Appleby Grammar School and Its Washington Pupils," *William and Mary
Quarterly* 20, no. 4 (1940): 498-501.
40. Peter R. Henriques, "Major Lawrence Washington versus the Reverend Charles Green:
A Case Study of the Squire and Parson," *Virginia Magazine of History and Biography*100,
no. 2 (1992): 233-64; Pape, "Appleby Grammar School," 498-501.
41. Jonathan Boucher, *Reminiscences of an American Loyalist, 1738-1789, Being the Autobiography of the Revd. Jonathan Boucher, Rector of Annapolis in Maryland and afterward Vicar of Epsom, Surrey, England* (1797; reis., Boston: Houghton Mifflin Company,
1925), 49.
42. Ford, *True Washington*, 65.
43. George Washington, *The Journal of Major George Washington* (Williamsburg: William
Hunter, 1754), 2.

eral of the Continental forces, he left much of his military correspondence to secretaries. Otherwise, according to Timothy Pickering, he would spend hours correcting the mistakes of a single letter.[44] Indeed, early in the war Washington requested a "good Writer, and a Methodical Man" for a clerk. He claimed the demands on his time prevented him from keeping up with his correspondence, making "it is absolutely necessary . . . for me to have person's that can think for me."[45] As president, he hounded cabinet members to help him write his formal addresses to Congress and further pestered other confidants to proofread them.[46] Public perception remained important to Washington and he aimed to disguise his personal vulnerabilities whenever possible. He proceeded with additional caution when his public letters might potentially expose his country education.

After the American War for Independence, Washington's secretary David Humphreys expressed his "ardent desire to see a good history of the Revolution" personally written by the commander in chief.[47] "I am conscious of a defective education," Washington responded, "and want of capacity to fit me for such an undertaking." The general declared Humphreys uniquely positioned for the task and offered his former secretary an apartment, access to his papers and "any oral information of circumstances . . . that my memory will furnish."[48] Humphreys rose to the occasion and wrote *Life of General Washington* with the Virginian's close cooperation.[49] In response to the manuscript, Washington scribbled comments and criticisms to correct or complete various passages with which he took issue. One passage that escaped any such remarks, tellingly, involved the general's mysterious education;

44. Timothy Pickering as quoted in Ford, *True Washington*, 66; George Washington to David Humphreys, July 25, 1785, in W.W. Abbot, et al., eds., *The Papers of George Washington: Confederation Period*, 6 vols. (Charlottesville: University of Virginia, 1992-), 2:148-51.

45. Washington to Joseph Reed, January 23, 1776, in Philander D. Chase, et al., eds., *The Papers of George Washington: Revolutionary War Series*, 28 vols. (Charlottesville: University Press of Virginia, 1985-), 3:172-75.

46. John Adams to Benjamin Rush, April 22, 1812, founders.archives.gov/documents/Adams/99-02-02-5777.

47. Humphreys to Washington, January 15, 1785, in W.W. Abbot, et al., *Papers of Washington*, 2:268-69.

48. Washington to Humphreys, July 25, 1785, in ibid., 2:148-51.

49. David Humphreys, *Life of Washington with George Washington's Remarks*, ed. Rosemarie Zagarri (Athens: University of Georgia Press, 1991). Humphreys actually did not publish his work though he allowed part of it to be printed in Jedidiah Morse's *American Geography* in 1789. The manuscript vanished until its 1960s discovery by historian James Thomas Flexner.

Humphreys credited Washington's limited schooling simply to a "domestic tutor."[50] The master of Mount Vernon, apparently comfortable
with this description, offered no further direction.
   Washington's self-described "defective education" drove him to help
others avoid the academic inferiority he felt so deeply.[51] After learning
a friend's son wished to attend the College of New Jersey (now Princeton), Washington pledged a £25 annual stipend to help defray the boy's
tuition. He rationalized that a good education would "not only promote
[the young student's] happiness, but the future welfare of others" as
well.[52] When strategizing son-in-law John Parke's continued education,
Washington wrote to prospective tutor Jonathan Boucher that he
wanted the boy to learn French to "become part of polite Education."
The acquisition of that Romance language, he wrote, was vital for anyone hoping to attend to public affairs. "The principles of Philosophy,"
he added, also remained "very desirable knowledge for a Gentleman."[53]
When the Maryland legislature chartered Washington College in 1782,
the general pledged that institution fifty guineas and joined its Board
of Visitors and Governors.[54] Washington likewise gifted Liberty Hall
Academy (now Washington and Lee University) one-hundred shares
of the James River Company to underwrite prospective students' tuition. This generous contribution equated to about $20,000 in eigh-
teenth-century currency and is still providing a modest subsidy to
students in the twenty-first century.[55]
   As president of the United States, Washington began connecting
education with the future security and stability of the nascent nation.
On January 8, 1790, he delivered before the House and Senate his
"First Annual Message to Congress." Surveying the state of the union,
the president advised legislators to provide for the common defense of
America by investing in public education and the production of military

50. Humphreys, *Life of Washington*, 6.
51. Washington to Humphreys, July 25, 1785, in Abbot, et al., *Papers of Washington*, 2:148-51.
52. Washington to William Ramsey, January 29, 1769 in ibid., 8:167-68.
53. Washington to Jonathan Boucher, January 2, 1771 in ibid., 8:425-26.
54. Washington to William Smith, August 18, 1782, founders.archives.gov/documents/
Washington/99-01-02-09173.
55. "Act Giving Canal Company Shares to General Washington," January 4-5, 1785, in
William T. Hutchinson, et al., eds., *The Papers of James Madison: Confederation Period*,
17 vols. (Chicago: University of Chicago Press, 1962-91), 8: 215-16; Betty Ruth Kon-
dayan, "The Library of Liberty Hall Academy," *Virginia Magazine of History and Biography* 86, no. 4 (1978): 432-46; James T. Flexner, *George Washington and the New Nation,
1783-1793* (Boston: Little, Brown, and Company, 1970).

hardware. "Knowledge is in every country," the president proclaimed, "the surest basis of public happiness." Informed Americans, he lectured, bolstered "the security of a free Constitution," as citizens knowledgeable of their rights transformed into vigilant sentries better able to "discriminate the spirit of Liberty from that of licentiousness."[56] In a letter published in the *Gazette of the United States*, one observer encouraged Congress to support Washington's educational patronage by promoting literature rather than attempting to "controul and shackle it." Congress might achieve this, he offered, by establishing federal professorships for history, civics and law at every American university. This observer suggested that the president of the United States should personally appoint all federal professors. He expected these trusted academics to educate citizens about their liberties, "the grand American revolution" and the mechanics of the federal republic. The writer reasoned that graduates exposed to this form of virtuous curriculum would mix with all levels of society and disseminate their wisdom to the benefit of the entire political community.[57]

In Washington's final annual message to Congress, he again stressed the relationship between national security and education. The federal government, he declared, must promote civic cultivation to accelerate "the assimilation of the principles, opinions and manners" of all Americans. "The more homogeneous our Citizens can be made," thundered the president, "the greater will be our prospect of permanent Union." To accomplish this, he again urged Congress to support and fund educational initiatives focusing on civic virtue. He asked, "In a Republic, what species of knowledge is more important . . . to those, who are to be the future guardians of the liberties of the Country?"[58]

President Washington likely expected his carefully crafted "Farewell Address" to be the final time he commanded a public audience to engage with his vision of the republic's future. In that message, he warned Americans that virtue remained the "necessary spring of popular government." In order to preserve the constitution and guarantee the nation's future, Washington asked Americans to support institutions that promoted the general diffusion of knowledge. "In proportion as the structure of government gives force to public opinion," he advised, "it

56. "First Annual Message to Congress," *Gazette of the United States*, January 9, 1790.
57. "The Tablet," *Gazette of the United States*, January 30, 1790.
58. George Washington to the U.S. Senate and House of Representatives, December 7, 1797, in Dorothy Twohig, et al., eds., *The Papers of George Washington: Presidential Series*, 21 vols. (Charlottesville: University of Virginia Press, 1987-2020) 21:317-35.

is essential that public opinion should be enlightened."[59] Washington clearly felt the nation's survival depended on an informed citizenry. He grew concerned that if the political community did not share similar civic values, the social fabric of American life would fray and the republic would descend into something reminiscent of the chaotic 1780s.

Despite George Washington's heroic private and public support of education, his peers often remarked in less-than-favorable terms about his intellectual abilities. According to Rev. Jonathan Boucher, once a close friend of the American general, Washington "had no other education than reading, writing and accounts, which he was taught by a convict servant whom his father bought for a schoolmaster."[60] Aaron Burr condemned Washington as a "Man of no Talents . . . who could not spell a Sentence of common English."[61] Despite offering some kind words, Thomas Jefferson claimed Washington possessed "neither copiousness of ideas, nor fluency of words" and if called on suddenly "was unready, short, and embarrassed."[62] Timothy Pickering cast Washington off as "So ignorant, that he had never read any Thing . . . [and] could not write A Sentence of Grammar, nor Spell his words." John Adams offered an even less flattering picture, claiming Washington "was too illiterate, unlearned, [and] unread, for his Station and reputation."[63] These isolated remarks, of course, only draw out the origins of Washington's educational activism and speak little of its results.

What motivated Washington to promote education evolved over the course of his long career. He harbored a deep sensitivity to his own limited academic exposure, of which crafting "Notes of Civility" was a result. This experience compelled Washington to actively advocate liberal access to education. Following the rise of the republic, his support for civic instruction took the form of a public-spirited crusade. Washington determined that only an educated people could sustain the re-

59. George Washington, "Farewell Address," in Philadelphia *Daily American Advertiser*, September 19, 1796; For a careful study of the drafts of the address as well as the mystery of authorship, see Jeffrey J. Malanson, "If I Had It in His Hand-Writing I Would Burn It": Federalists and the Authorship Controversy Over George Washington's Farewell Address, 1808-1859," *Journal of the Early Republic* 34, no. 2 (2014): 219-42.
60. Boucher, *Reminiscences of an American Loyalist,* 49.
61. Adams to Rush, August 23, 1805, founders.archives.gov/documents/Adams/99-02-02-5096.
62. Thomas Jefferson to Walter Jones, January 2, 1814, in J. Jefferson Looney, et al., eds., *The Papers of Thomas Jefferson: Retirement Series*, 17 vols. (Princeton: Princeton University Press, 2004-20), 7:100-4.
63. Adams to Rush, April 22, 1812, January 5, 2023, founders.archives.gov/documents/Adams/99-02-02-5777.

publican empire of liberty. Any political community dependent upon robust civic participation for its survival, the old revolutionary came to realize, must be certain its participants are politically informed, intellectually engaged and cognizant of their shared future. In short, republicanism depended on academic cultivation; anarchy and tyranny thrived in ignorance and fear. Washington put forth a sustained and herculean effort to entice the political nation to choose the former path. If Americans chose the latter, the president feared, they would become the architects of their own destruction.

# The Perfidious Benjamin Church and Paul Revere

**LOUIS ARTHUR NORTON**

For many years Paul Revere was not prominent in the history of the Revolutionary War. Extremely versatile, he was a Massachusetts militia officer and artillery commander, a skilled artist and engraver, a caster of bells, an esteemed silversmith, and an industrialized coppersmith.[1] He also was a prosthodontist and at one point a forensic dentist.[2] Revere was the principal messenger of the patriot leaders, carrying messages to patriots in New York and Philadelphia on several occasions. Later, he wrote three accounts of his ride to Lexington. Despite these firsthand accounts, Revere did not appear prominently in histories that dealt in the period until after his death in 1818. After the fiftieth anniversary of the April 19 event he began to acquire notoriety largely through Henry Wadsworth Longfellow's poem "Paul Revere's Ride," published in *Tales of a Wayside Inn* in 1863.

Although multitalented, reportage and handwriting were not among Revere's strengths. He made two undated depositions that contain his version of his messenger ride on April 19. He subsequently witnessed the renowned battle on Lexington Green from "a house at the bottom of the street," one that largely blocked his view of the militia. The rambling depositions had been thought not worthy of including with those of other witnesses in the history of the event prepared by Congress. Revere prepared a third account some years after the other two. Also not dated, this account was penned at the request by Jeremy Belknap, the then corresponding secretary of the Massachusetts Historical So-

1. Louis Arthur Norton, "Coppering the Fleet and an American Entrepreneur," *Nautical Research Journal*, vol. 59. no. 2 (2014), 120-28.
2. Mike F. Nola, *"Paul Revere and Forensic Dentistry," Military Medicine*, vol. 181, no.7 (July 2016), 714–715.

ciety. Revere's text, edited by Belknap in 1798, did not differ materially from the earlier versions, but for the first time Revere focused upon the activities of Doctor Benjamin Church.[3]

As I have mentioned Dr. church, perhaps it might not be disagreeable to mention some Matters of my own knowledge, respecting Him. He appeared to be a high son of liberty. He frequented all places where they met, Was encouraged by all the leaders of the Sons of Liberty, and it appeared he was respected by them, though I knew that Dr. [Joseph] Warren, had not the greatest affection for him. He was esteemed as a very capable writer, especially in verse: and as the Whig party needed every Strenght, they feared, as well as quoted him. But it was known that the Sons of Liberty Songs, which we composed, were parodized by him, in favor of the British, yet none dare charge him with it. I was a constant and critical observer of him, and I must say, that I never thought Him a man of Principle; And I doubted much in my own mind, whether He was a real Whig. I knew that He kept company with a Capt. Price, a half-pay British officer, and that He frequently dined with him and Robinson, one of the commissioners. I know that one of his intimate acquaintances asked him why he so often was with Robinson and Price? His answer was He kept company with them for the purpose of finding out their plans. The day after the Battle of Lexington, I met him in Cambridge, when He shew me some blood on his stocking, which he said spurted on him from a Man who was killed near him, and that he was urging the Militia on. I well remember that I argued with myself if a Man will risque his life in A Cause, he must be a Friend to that cause; and I never suspected him after, till he was charged with being a Traytor.

Revere's account also related an incident that involved Dr. Warren.

Church told Warren: I am determined to go to Boston tomorrow— Dr. Warren replied, are you serious Dr. Church? They will hang you if they catch you in Boston. He replied, I am serious and I am determined to go at all adventures. After considerable conversation, Dr. Warren said if you are determined, let us make some business for you. They agreed that he should go to get medicine for their and our Wounded officers. He went the next morning; and I think he came back on Sunday evening. After he had told the Committee how things were, I took him aside, and inquired particularly how they treated him? He said that as soon as he got to their lines on Boston Neck, they made him a pris-

3. Edmund S. Morgan, *Paul Revere's Three Accounts of his Famous Ride* (Boston, MA: Massachusetts Historical Society, 2000).

oner and carried him to General [Thomas] Gage, where He was examined and then he was sent to Gould's Barracks, and was not suffered to go home but once. After He was taken up, for holding a Correspondence with the British, I came a Cross Deacon Caleb Davis;—we entered into conversation about him; He told me that the morning Church went to Boston, He (Davis) received a Bilet from General Gage—(he then did not know that Church was in Town)—When he got to the General's House, he was told the General could not be spoken with, that He was in private with a Gentleman; that He waited near half an hour,—When General Gage and Dr. Church came out of a Room, discoursing together, like persons who had been long acquainted. He appeared to be quite surprised at seeing Deacon Davis there; that he (Church) went where he pleased while in Boston only a Major Caine [Cane], one of Gage's aids went with him. I was told by another person whom I could depend upon, that he saw Church go to General Gage's House at the above time and then He got out of the Chaise and went up the steps more like a Man that was acquainted, than a prisoner.

Sometime after, perhaps a Year or two, I fell in company with a Gentleman who studied with Church—in this coursing about him I related what I have mentioned above; He said he did not doubt that He was in the Interest of the Brittish; and that it was He who informed General Gage that he knew for certain, that a Short time before the Battle of Lexington, (for He then lived with Him, and took Care of his Business and Books) He had no money by him, and was much drove for money; that all at once, he had several Hundred New British Guineas: and that He thought at the time, where they came from.

Benjamin Church was born in Newport, Rhode Island, and graduated from Harvard College in 1754, decades before its medical school was founded. He studied medicine as an apprentice with Joseph Pynchon and later continued his studies in London. He returned to Boston and became a well-regarded physician and surgeon. Among his patients was John Adams.[4]

As friction intensified between the colonies and Britain, church wrote in colonial publications in support of the Whigs. During this time, he was considered an ardent patriot and yet a clandestine Tory sympathizer. He treated some of the wounded of the Boston Massacre,

4. Christopher T. Leffler; Stephen G. Schwartz, Ricardo D. Wainsztein, Adam Pflugrath, and Eric Peterson, "Ophthalmology in North America: Early Stories (1491–1801)," *Ophthalmology and Eye Diseases* Vol. 9 (2017), www.ncbi.nlm.nih.gov/pmc/articles/PMC 5533269/.

and in 1773 he delivered the Massacre Day oration which marked him as an eloquent orator.

In 1774, Church became active in Massachusetts provincial politics and was made a member of the colony's Committee of Safety, a body that was charged to prepare for an armed conflict. About this time, Gen. Thomas Gage began receiving intelligence concerning the Provincial Congress's activities. On February 21, 1775, the Provincial Congress appointed Church and Joseph Warren to conduct an inventory of medical supplies that were on hand for the army and to purchase supplemental supplies that they deemed were needed.

On May 8, 1775, shortly after revolutionary conflict began, Church became a member of an examining board for the army's surgeons. In effect Church was the first Surgeon General of the United States with the title of "Chief Physician and Director General" of the Continental Army's medical service. He held this post only from July 27, 1775, to October 17, 1775. Church attempted to standardize the quality of care and establish general hospitals. As troops from around the colonies descended upon the area around Boston however, the other army doctors, now overwhelmed with patients, largely ignored Church's efforts. When regimental surgeons objected to the director general's commands, he retaliated by withholding supplies. In time, tempers flared between the army surgeons and Church. General Washington was called upon to calm the medical tempest.[5] During this inquiry Church was formally accused of providing intelligence to the British, "aid or comfort" to the enemy.[6]

Evidence was presented that Church had sent an encrypted letter addressed to a British officer in Boston by way of a former mistress. The letter was intercepted and found to contain an account of the American forces situated around Boston. The disclosure proved to be of not great importance, but it did ask for directions for continuing the correspondence thus providing evidence of Church's devotion to the crown. The matter was placed before a court of inquiry made-up of general officers, Gen. George Washington presiding. Church admitted authorship of the letter, but he attempted to explain the purpose of the communication by stating it was written to impress the enemy with the Continental Army's strength and position. He had hoped that this

5. Justin McHenry, "John Morgan versus Henry Shippen: The Battle that Defined the Continental Medical Department," *The Journal of the American Revolution*, January 28, 2020.

6. John A. Nagy, *Dr. Benjamin Church, Spy: A Case of Espionage on the Eve of the American Revolution* (Yardley, Pa.: Westholme, 2013).

"The Rescinders." (*The Life of Paul Revere by Elbridge Henry Goss, 1891, 60.*)

knowledge might prevent an attack while the army was still short of ammunition. The court decided that because Church had ongoing correspondence with the enemy it was recommended that the matter be referred to the Continental Congress for its action.[7]

Church was briefly incarcerated in Cambridge. The Massachusetts provincial Congress arraigned Church on November 2. Despite a powerful defense appeal, he was expelled as a member of the legislative body, an important outcome because Church was a member of the patriot inner circle. The doctor was then incarcerated in Norwich, Connecticut, ironically the birthplace of Benedict Arnold. While in jail he was not allowed pen, ink, or blank paper. During pleasant weather he was permitted outside, but only under guard. He was not allowed to converse with anyone except in the presence and hearing of a town magistrate or the sheriff of the county. Church became ill and in time was returned to Massachusetts under bond and remained imprisoned until 1778. He was named in the *Massachusetts Banishment Act* of that year and was deported from Boston; his status as a prisoner ended because he was exchanged for a captured American doctor. But the boat

7. "Dr Benjamin Church and the Dilemma of Treason in Revolutionary Massachusetts," *The New England Quarterly* 70, no. 3 (1997): 443-462.

on which he sailed from Boston bound to the West Indies never arrived at any port. "Many pious patriots thought God had been more just in his treatment of the traitor than had man."[8]

Some years earlier the Son of Liberty Revere was engaged in etching a political image in his shop. Entitled "A Warm Place—Hell", it was a representation of a violent entrance to an imagined hell through a pair of monstrous open jaws resembling those of a shark from which flames ensued. A satanic image with a large pitchfork was depicted driving seventeen "Rescinders" into the flames. From the devil's cartoon-balloon mouth were the words, "Now I've got you! A fine haul, by Jove!" Those members of the General Court of Massachusetts who voted not to rescind a resolution (sort of political double entendre) were, in essence, disapproved the king's imposition of the Stamp Act.

By chance Benjamin Church stopped by Revere's workshop and, after seeing the nearly completed engraving, he authored the following lines to be included beneath the complex image:

> On brave Rescinders orders! To yon yawning cell!
> Seventeen such miscreants there will startle hell;
> These puny *Villains*, damned for petty sin,
> On such distinguished *Scoundrels* gaze and grin;
> The outdone *Devil* will resign his sway;
> He never curst his *millions* in a day.[9]

Perhaps Church was prescient that day. Paradoxically may have penned an epigram that prophesized his own "Warm Place—Hell" for Paul Revere.

8. Esther Forbes, *Paul Revere and the World He lived In* (New York, NY: The American Past Book of the Month Club, 1942), 304.

9. Eldridge Henry Goss, *The Life of Colonel Paul Revere* (Boston, MAS: Plympton Press, 1891), 62.

# The Return of Samuel Dyer: An Attemped Assassination in Revolutionary Boston

&#xFE;&#xFE; J. L. BELL &#xFE;&#xFE;

On October 10, 1774, the brigantine *Charlotte* arrived at Newport, Rhode Island, from London. On board was a sailor named Samuel Dyer, and he told a shocking story, soon reported in the local newspapers. Three months earlier, on July 6, soldiers of the 4th (King's Own) Regiment of Foot had grabbed him off the streets of Boston and kept him "confin'd in irons" in their camp.[1] And that was just the start of his harrowing tale.

According to Samuel Dyer, the 4th Regiment's commander, Lt. Col. George Maddison, had asked Dyer "who gave him orders to destroy the Tea" tossed into the harbor the previous December. Dyer insisted no one had told him to do that. Maddison replied, "he was a lyar, it was King Hancock, and the damn'd Sons of Liberty"! The officer told Dyer that "he should be hung like a dog" in London, and advised him "to prepare a good story" for the royal governor, Gen. Thomas Gage. Then the sailor, still in chains, was loaded onto Adm. John Montagu's flagship, the *Captain*, to await Gage.

But the governor never came, Dyer said. Instead, after three or four days the ship sailed out of Boston harbor, taking Montagu home. Once the *Captain* arrived in Portsmouth, in the south of England, Dyer "was sent up to London in irons, and examined three times before Lord North, Sandwich and the Earl of Dartmouth, respecting the destruction of the Tea." The men he named were the British Prime Minister, the First Lord of the Admiralty, and the Secretary of State in charge of North America—three of the most powerful officials in

---

1. "confin'd in irons": This text from the *Essex Gazette*, October 25, 1774.

the imperial government. Since Dyer still had nothing to say about the Tea Party, however, they sent him back to Portsmouth, still chained up.

And then, Dyer's complaint continued, the Royal Navy simply set him free as if he were an ordinary sailor, but "without receiving one farthing of wages." Dissatisfied, the seaman "travell'd up to London, 70 miles, (*having but six coppers in his Pocket*) and made his complaint to the Lord Mayor," Frederick Bull. The city government, dominated by merchants concerned in the colonial trade, was often at odds with the imperial government, and the Lord Mayor greeted Dyer "with great Humanity." Other men, Dyer said, offered him "purses of guineas" if he would "accuse certain gentlemen in Boston with ordering him to help to destroy the tea," but he remained adamant.

Dyer received the most support from two London sheriffs, William Lee and Stephen Sayre. Those men were Americans—Lee born in Virginia and Sayre in New York. They promised Dyer that they "and many other gentlemen" would "supply him with any sum of money to carry on a suit against those governmental Kidnappers in Boston," assuming he could "prove his charge." A later American newspaper report said those sheriffs had "generously supplied him with Money, and procured him a Passage" home.[2] When he arrived in Rhode Island, the sailor brought sealed letters from William Lee addressed to the Massachusetts political leaders Samuel Adams and John Hancock.

Among the Patriots in Newport was Dr. Thomas Young. From 1768 on, he had been one of the most prominent protest leaders in Boston, able to lead large crowds despite also being known for his unorthodox ideas on democracy and deism. Young had first come to the royal authorities' attention by supporting people trying to keep British troops out of the government-owned Manufactory building. Just before the Boston Massacre in 1770, the doctor was out on the streets, and a year later he returned to the Manufactory to deliver the first oration commemorating that Massacre. During the Boston Tea Party, Young delivered another speech about the bad medical effects of tea—probably a ploy to keep the audience inside the Old South Meeting House, providing alibis for almost all the Whig leaders, while other men got to work destroying the East India Company's cargo without interference. In the spring of 1774 British regiments returned to Boston. Doctor Young and his wife feared he might be attacked or arrested, so in September the family had suddenly left for Rhode Island.

On October 10, Doctor Young heard the "prodigious noise" kicked up by Samuel Dyer's story. He hurried to the office of Rhode Island

2. "generously supplied him": *Boston Post-Boy*, October 24, 1774.

Secretary Henry Ward to learn more. There he spotted Dyer and "instantly knew" him. Back in Boston, Young had a habit of getting into vituperative newspaper arguments not only about politics but also about religion and medicine. Even his political ally Dr. Joseph Warren had complained of enthusiastic "youngism."[3] In 1767 Young's public dispute with a rival doctor named Miles Whitworth became so heated that Whitworth's teenaged son had slapped Young around on the street. When in the middle of 1773 two other men attacked Young one night, he still blamed Whitworth, rightly or not. But on that occasion, Young recalled, there had been a "sailor who rescued me out of the hands of Whitworth's mob": Samuel Dyer.[4]

Doctor Young told his Newport friends that he could vouch for this new arrival. Some of those gentlemen were still dubious about the connection, so to satisfy them Young walked by Dyer on the street. The sailor recognized the doctor "at first sight." Young then had this exchange with Dyer, as he described to Samuel Adams:

> He told me he had letters from Mr. Sheriff Lee to yourself and Mr. Hancock, which on going into Mr. Southwick's office he shewed me, and I knew the handwriting. I told him you were absent at the [First Continental] Congress at Philadelphia, and desired the Letter to transmit to you there. He returned that Sheriff Lee had enjoined him to carry both letters to Boston, and in case of the death or absence of either of you to deliver the letters to the present gentlemen and in case both were dead to burn them unopened or never come to him again. In this dilemma I took your letter home to my house & carefully cut the cover preserving the seal and having transcribed the deposition and perused the attending letter closed them up and in another cover committed them to him again, informing him however of the freedom I had taken with them and entering my apology for it within the covers.

Always enthusiastic and unbound by convention, Young saw no problem in breaking open the envelope that Dyer was supposed to protect so carefully.

The Rev. Ezra Stiles of Newport was often a sucker for wild rumors and false claims that fit his political thinking. But he used some uncharacteristically skeptical language in describing Dyer's story: "If it should appear to be a real Seizure of an American & carrying him

---

3. "youngism": *Boston Gazette*, July 6, 1767. For a thorough analysis of this debate, see Samuel A. Forman, *Dr. Joseph Warren: The Boston Tea Party, Bunker Hill, and the Birth of American Liberty* (Baton Rouge: Pelican, 2011), 70–87.
4. "sailor who rescued me": Young to Samuel Adams, October 11, 1774, Samuel Adams Papers, New York Public Library (NYPL).

home in Irons for a Trial, it will rouse the Continent—if he was in fact carried to London in Irons and examined by any of the Ministry, as he says."[5] The minister looked for reasons to believe Dyer. He wrote, "About the time he was taken there was an account in the Boston prints of a Man of his Name missing & supposed to have been drowned." In fact, while the July 4 *Boston Evening-Post* had reported about a body found floating in Boston harbor, no newspaper had identified that man as Samuel Dyer or said Dyer was missing.[6] Stiles, not for the first time, ended up selecting his facts to fit his convictions.

The minister also recalled hearing reports that an army officer passing through Newport to New York had "seemingly accidentally mixt in with some of the Mechanics & robust Tradesmen warm for Liberty, & said in their Hearing that one of the Rebels was lately taken at Boston & sent home in Irons." Young wrote that he had heard the same whispers:

> his being kidnapped is confirmed by the information of two officers given here at sundry times, presently after the affair. One of them was so circumstantial as to mention his being confined in the common and then being put on board the Captain, where he saw him in irons. This was said in a barber's shop, where many now remember they heard it.

If these memories were accurate, these army officers were trying to make Dyer's fate into a warning for other workingmen "warm for Liberty."[7]

Unfortunately, Samuel Dyer himself is a mystery. His own statements and others' say that he was from Boston and had a wife and children there, but no one mentioned his age or those relatives' names. As an ordinary sailor, he was very unlikely to own property, advertise in newspapers, or formally join a church. And the name Samuel Dyer was relatively common. In the 1770s there was a Boston office-holder named Samuel Dyer, and a Newport merchant. (The latter spelled his last name "Dyre," and the Rhode Island newspapers sometimes

---

5. "If it should appear": Ezra Stiles, *The Literary Diary of Ezra Stiles, D.D., Ll.D.*, Franklin Bowditch Dexter, editor (New York: Scribner's, 1901), 1:462-3.

6. Drowned men: The *Evening-Post* said of the drowned man, "by some Articles found in his Pockets, it is supposed that he was a Taylor; But as his Face was greatly disfigured, . . . the Jury was obliged to give a Verdict, that he was a Person unknown, and drowned by Accident." *Boston Evening-Post*, July 4, 1774. The *Essex Gazette* had also reported a drowned man that summer up in Marblehead harbor, someone whose shoe buckles bore the initials "B G"; *Essex Gazette*, June 28, 1774.

7. "his being kidnapped": Young to Adams, October 11, 1774, Samuel Adams Papers, NYPL.

rendered the sailor's surname the same way.) Further afield, the radical British politician John Wilkes had a valet named Samuel Dyer a few years before.[8] Doctor Young's recollection about the fight in Boston is the only solid clue to this Samuel Dyer's activity before the fall of 1774.

On October 11, the Newport committee of correspondence examined Dyer. He swore to an affidavit about his horrendous experience. The Rhode Islanders decided to send the sailor on to Massachusetts with their endorsement, as well as ten or twelve dollars for his expenses—a "genteel viaticum," wrote Young, who rarely ended letters without tossing in some classical phrases and allusions to demonstrate how well he had educated himself.

In sending Samuel Dyer back to Boston, the Newport Patriots risked striking a spark inside a powder house. In late summer Parliament's Massachusetts Government Act, coming on the heels of the Boston Port Bill, had pushed the province into turmoil. Crowds were forcing the county courts not to open, starting in the western counties. On September 2, a militia uprising culminated in thousands of men ringing Lt. Gov. Thomas Oliver's house in Cambridge and forcing him to sign a resignation. General Gage had responded by mounting cannon on Boston Neck, pointing out at the people he was supposed to govern. With British regiments stationed in Boston, and more being summoned from other parts of the continent by Gage, that town became a refuge for royal appointees who no longer felt safe in their home towns. But most locals seethed about the military occupation. Among other covert acts, they spirited away their militia's four cannon before the Royal Artillery could confiscate them.[9]

Outside Boston, Patriots felt safe enough to convene a Massachusetts Provincial Congress in direct defiance of Parliament's new law. This was the equivalent of the lower house of the colony's regular legislature, which Gage had refused to meet with. These elected delegates first gathered on October 7 in Salem, choosing John Hancock to preside over their sessions. On October 11–14, the body convened in Concord. Those days were taken up in getting organized, writing a critical report on the state of the province, and calling on towns not to send tax revenues to the royal government's treasurer. Then the men agreed to meet in Cambridge on October 17.

8. Wilkes's valet: Arthur H. Cash, *John Wilkes: The Scandalous Father of Civil Liberty* (New Haven: Yale University Press, 2006), 218, 273.

9. "their militia regiment's cannon": For the full story, see J. L. Bell, *The Road to Concord: How Four Stolen Cannon Ignited the Revolutionary War* (Yardley, PA: Westholme, 2016).

Samuel Dyer reportedly planned to travel from Newport to Concord to deliver his letter to John Hancock. It is not clear if the sailor reached that town before the Provincial Congress adjourned on the afternoon of Friday, October 14. In any event, Dyer's main business lay in Boston. Stiles wrote that the sailor planned to "take Evidences & return to London, where he intends to eat his Xmas Dinner."[10] Young agreed that "a prosecution may be carried on against those dignified scoundrels to the satisfaction of the immediate sufferer and advantage of the public."[11]

Dyer was in Boston by Sunday, October 16. On that day, the Patriot publisher Joseph Greenleaf wrote to his brother-in-law Robert Treat Paine, then at the Congress in Philadelphia, about the sailor's story. According to Greenleaf, General Gage had promised Dyer "that there shall be an examination of the affair" the next day.[12] The Patriot-leaning merchant John Andrews wrote that the sailor's story of being kidnapped was widely believed and causing "much speculation" in Boston.[13] Nonetheless, he cast some blame on Dyer himself for his trouble: "he having said that he knew all about and who were concern'd in the destruction of tea—being an artfull fellow and one who pretends to know every thing—in consequence of which, he was seiz'd by two soldiers."

On October 17, Andrews reported hearing that Hancock and Lieutenant Colonel Maddison "had an interview" about the sailor's allegation that the regimental commander had tried to make him accuse "King Hancock" of being behind the Tea Party. Andrew heard that "the latter has fully satisfied the former that what the fellow has alledged is *absolutely* false." General Gage might have hoped that the agreement between those gentlemen would lay the whole affair to rest.

Dyer himself clearly was not satisfied. He had reportedly come to Boston to "take Evidences" and start a "prosecution" against Lieutenant Colonel Maddison. But he could not file a lawsuit for damages because the Patriots had shut down all the provincial courts as a protest against Parliament's Massachusetts Government Act. According to Andrews, Dyer "declar'd since he came home, that if he could not have public satisfaction for his *extraordinary* treatment, he would take it personally."[14] The aggrieved sailor decided to act on his own.

10. "take Evidences": Stiles, *Literary Diary*, 1:462–3.

11. "a prosecution": Young to Adams, October 11, 1774, Samuel Adams Papers, NYPL.

12. "that there shall be an examination": Greenleaf to Paine, October 16, 1774, *Papers of Robert Treat Paine*, Stephen T. Riley and Edward W. Hanson, editors (Boston: Massachusetts Historical Society, 2005), 3:11.

13. "much speculation": Andrews, October 17, 1774, *Massachusetts Historical Society Proceedings* (MHSP), 8:377.

About noon on Tuesday, October 18, Dyer spotted two British army officers "returning together from the Neck" at the southern tip of Boston, where General Gage had ordered new fortifications and artillery.[15] Those military men were Lt. Col. Samuel Cleaveland, the head of the Royal Artillery in North America, and the army's chief engineer, Capt. John Montresor. Cleaveland was around age fifty-eight, no longer young but spry enough to take one of the twentysomething daughters of the South Latin School's master as his mistress.[16] At thirty-eight, Montresor had served in America for years. As for mistresses, Montresor had had at least three in America and would inspire the roué who seduced the title character in *Charlotte Temple*, America's first best-selling novel.[17] These two officers "were standing together in the main Street, just above *Liberty tree*."

Dyer came up and asked Captain Montresor "if his name was Collonel Maddison." Montresor's Royal Engineers uniform in bright red cloth with blue facings was similar to the coats of officers in the 4th Regiment. However, given that the sailor had repeatedly and loudly identified Maddison as the officer who had interrogated him at length three months before, he should have been able to recognize that man.

The two officers had reason to be wary about strangers. According to Lt. Ashton Shuttleworth of the Royal Artillery, a local had "cut a running Centry on his Post with a Cutlass in the middle of the day, and cut one of his Ears off," and Bostonians would "get in Bodys about the Dusk of the Evenings, and whenever they get one or two Officers by themselves, they will abuse and knock them down, if they can."[18] But this encounter was taking place at midday on the town's busiest street, so Cleaveland and Montresor did not have their guard up. They told Dyer that neither of them was Maddison and sent him on his way.

---

14. "declar'd since he came home": Andrews, October 18, 1774, MHSP, 8:377.

15. Dyer's attack: This account is based on reports in the *Boston Post-Boy*, October 24, 1774; Lt. Ashton Shuttleworth to John Spencer, November 2, 1774, in "Letters by British Officers from Boston in 1774 and 1775 to John Spencer," *Bostonian Society Proceedings*, 38 (1919), 12–3; and Andrews, October 18, 1774, MHSP, 8:377–8. Those three accounts do not agree completely on the sequence and details of the action.

16. Samuel Cleaveland: Richard Frothingham, *History of the Siege of Boston, and of the Battles of Lexington, Concord, and Bunker Hill*, 4th edition (Boston: Little, Brown, 1873), 140. Francis Duncan, *History of the Royal Regiment of Artillery* (London: John Murray, 1879), 1:297–318.

17. John Montresor: "The Montresor Journals," G. D. Scull, editor, *Collections of the New-York Historical Society*, 14 (1881). For his fictionalization in *Charlotte Temple*, see Philip Young, *Revolutionary Ladies* (New York: Alfred A. Knopf, 1977), 24–6.

18. "cut a running Centry": Shuttleworth to John Spencer, November 2, 1774, *Bostonian Society Proceedings*, 38:12–3.

The sailor did not accept that answer. He snuck up on Cleaveland's left side, snatched his sword from its scabbard, and "made a back Stroke with it" at the officer's head. Cleaveland ducked. Dyer "drew out a Pistol and directed it at the Colonel, but it missed Fire." Captain Montresor pulled out "a Kind of half Dirk" and moved toward Dyer. The sailor pulled out another pistol and pointed it at the engineer's head "at about three Yards Distance." But that gun "flashed in the Pan." Montresor ducked behind a cart.

Doubly frustrated, Dyer turned back to Colonel Cleaveland and "made two or three Strokes at him" with his own sword.

> The Colonel elevated his arm, and fortunately received the blow upon one of his buttons on the sleve of his coat, which diverted the edge in such a manner, as that the blade glanced down by the side of his head and gave him only a small wound in the neck, and splitt the *favorable* button in two.

Still, those swipes cut through the colonel's hat and "made an Incision behind his Ear." As Dyer went in for another thrust, "a Townsman jump'd in between, and near got his Arm quite cut off."

The sailor decided he had made his point. He ran south down Orange Street to the gates of Boston. One source said he threw his pistols at Montresor, another that he tossed them "into a Shop as he went along." Either way, Captain Montresor picked up those guns while Dyer kept Colonel Cleaveland's sword. Up to three hundred men were reportedly at work nearby, but no one tried to stop the sailor. He passed through the gates of Boston, "even walked by the Guard with the Hanger drawn in his hand." Dyer was not simply escaping—he was seeking a sympathetic audience.

From the narrow Boston Neck, Dyer headed south through Roxbury and then turned onto the road to the first bridge across the Charles River. That route led straight into Cambridge. The Massachusetts Provincial Congress had convened in that town's Congregationalist meetinghouse the previous day. That body was continuing its high-level epistolary exchange with the royal governor about who was doing more to undermine Massachusetts's charter. Since uncharitable observers might consider that debate as treasonous, that morning the delegates had voted "That the galleries be now cleared, and that the doors of the house be kept shut, during the debates of the Congress."[19] The Cambridge delegates recruited a local man to be doorkeeper.

19. "That the galleries be now cleared": *Journals of Each Provincial Congress of Massachusetts in 1774 and 1775*, William Lincoln, editor (Boston: Dutton & Wentworth, 1838), 22.

Dyer apparently refused to be excluded. According to Andrews, the sailor "went into the room where the *provisional Congress* were sitting" and showed them Cleaveland's hanger, possibly colored with a bit of Cleaveland's blood.[20] He told the representatives "he had got one of the swords that Lord North had sent over to kill 'em with." Again, it is not clear whether any of those men had already met Dyer in Concord or Boston. John Hancock was presiding over the meeting; he had evidently heard about the seaman's accusations but may not have met him personally. In any event, the sailor's surprise arrival with a stolen sword surely made a big impression.

But that was not an impression that the Provincial Congress wanted to be part of. The Massachusetts Patriots were trying to portray themselves as aggrieved victims, protesting respectably against the imperial government's oppression and forced to convene this outlawed legislature by that government's intransigence. They painted that self-portrait in words to their neighbors, to the representatives of other colonies at the Continental Congress in Philadelphia, and to sympathetic Whigs in London. Despite all the violence in Boston during the previous ten years, no townsman had yet fired a gun at a royal official or soldier. (As the Patriots were happy to remind people, back in 1770 the Crown's customs officers and soldiers had fatally shot four men and two boys.) An angry sailor snapping pistols at army officers in the street threatened to sully the whole Patriot movement.

Dyer's attempt on the two British officers might even have set off a harsh government crackdown or ignited a war. He had, after all, traveled to Boston with the support, and perhaps the money, of the imperial government's opponents in two other cities, and had been greeted with some enthusiasm by the Patriots there. If he had actually taken one or two officers' lives, the royal government would have had to act against him. The Massachusetts Patriots might have feared that, if they did not repudiate Dyer, General Gage would use his action as an excuse for military intervention. Though the Provincial Congress was already discussing the possibility of war against the king's forces, they knew they were not ready for it; they were still forming committees to decide what further committees they needed to form.

The Patriots in Cambridge therefore concluded that Dyer was dangerous. "When they came to know what he had been doing," Andrews wrote, "they immediately sent for an officer and committed him."[21] Nothing about this disruption went into the congress's official

---

20. "went into the room": Andrews, October 18, 1774, MHSP, 8:378.
21. "When they came to know": Andrews, October 18, 1774, MHSP, 8:378.

record. The next day, wrote merchant John Rowe, the sailor "was brought from Cambridge & committed to our Goal," or jail, in the center of Boston. Rowe deemed Dyer "an audacious Villain."[22] Boston's Patriot newspapers all reported the attempted shooting in one short paragraph, two stating early that Dyer "appears disordered in his senses" and the third concluding, "It is in general imagined that he is insane."[23] The *Boston Post-Boy*, leaning firmly toward the royal government, carried the most detailed report on the violence. With the court system shut down, the angry sailor would stay in the Boston jail indefinitely. Samuel Dyer's attack on British army officers had not made him a hero, and only by a stroke of luck had he not started a larger conflict.

Despite the congress's repudiation, army officers took Dyer to be typical of the New England resistance, probably even directed by its leaders. Capt. William Evelyn of the 4th Regiment wrote home that the sailor was one of "their agents," not just a madman acting on his own.[24] Later Captain Montresor would perceive a wider conspiracy: "This man was sent off by the Sheriffs of London, Messrs. Lee and Sayre, to murther Lt.-Col. Maddison of the 4th. Regiment."[25] Dyer's misfiring pistols had prevented his attack from being fatal, but it still raised tensions. The Patriots might repudiate the angry sailor's actions, and even start to doubt his story of being hauled off to London in the first place, but they still had to deal with how his action had made all of General Gage's defensive actions seem more reasonable.

Meanwhile, in his official residence at the Province House, Gage was secretly dealing with his own Samuel Dyer headache. Because he knew that many of the sailor's wild accusations about royal officials were actually based in fact.

Dyer's attempt at homicide undoubtedly alarmed Governor Gage. Not just because the targets had been two of his top officers, Cleaveland and Montresor. Not just because the attacker had received support from top Whigs in London, Newport, and Boston. Gage had to deal with the uncomfortable knowledge that many of the Samuel Dyer's outrageous accusations were basically true. Just because Dyer might

22. "an audacious Villain": John Rowe diary, October 19, 1774, 11:1918, Massachusetts Historical Society.

23. "appears disordered": *Massachusetts Spy*, October 20, 1774; *Boston Gazette*, October 24, 1774; and *Boston Evening-Post*, October 24, 1774.

24. "their agents": William Glanville Evelyn, *Memoir and Letters of Capt. W. Glanville Evelyn, of the 4th Regiment ("King's Own") from North America, 1774-1776*, G. D. Scull, editor (Oxford: James Parker, 1879), 35.

25. "This man was sent off": "Montresor Journals," *Collections of the New-York Historical Society*, 14:120.

have been crazy didn't mean that royal authorities hadn't been out to get him.

The sailor's first complaint was that the army had taken him prisoner. In Governor Gage's files is the attorney Robert Auchmuty's bill listing work on July 5 for a case labeled "King vs Dyer." Among those tasks were:

> To draft of an Information against Samuel Dyer for seducing James Little & Andrew Hughes private Soldiers in his Majestys 4th Regiment to desert
>
> To Special Warrant to apprehend Dyer & attendance in Camp who was discharg
>
> To attend 3 different Times at ye Province House upon ye same Affair.
>
> To Hearing ye Complaint & three Conferences with Col Maddison upon a point of Law as to ye legality of Dyer Committment in Camp.[26]

In preparing that bill, Auchmuty clarified at the bottom that he had "Received nothing" so far.

Seducing soldiers to desert was a serious crime, but it would have been legally difficult and politically dangerous to prosecute Dyer on that charge in Boston. According to Gage, "Lieutenant Colonel Maddison prevailed with Admiral [John] Montagu, to impress and carry [Dyer] to England."[27] Since Dyer was a sailor, he was subject to a long British tradition, hotly disputed, of naval officers drafting or "impressing" seamen for their ships. In his log entry for on July 7, the captain of the British warship *Captain* wrote: "at 5 came on board General Gage Saluted him with 13 Guns as we did at his leaving the Ship."[28] The next day, the *Captain* weighed anchor, carrying both Montagu and Dyer. When he heard about the sailor's assault on the two officers, Gage's adjutant, Maj. Stephen Kemble, immediately recognized him as the "Man who had been carried from Boston by Admiral Montague to England for Inveigling the Soldiers from their Colours."[29]

---

26. "King vs Dyer": Invoice, July 5, 1774, vol. 123, Thomas Gage Papers, Clements Library, Ann Arbor, Michigan.

27. "Lieutenant Colonel Maddison prevailed": Gage to Dartmouth, October 30, 1774, Colonial Office, Great Britain, *Documents of the American Revolution, 1770–1783*, K. G. Davies, editor (Dublin: Irish University Press, 1975), 8:222.

28. "at 5 came on board": log of H.M.S. *Captain*, July 7, 1774, ADM 51/158, Part VII, National Archives, UK.

29. "Man who had been carried": Stephen Kemble, journal, October 18, 1774, *Collections of the New-York Historical Society*, 16:39.

Furthermore, Dyer was correct in claiming he had been interrogated by British officials, though not men with such high positions in the government. At the same time, however, the sailor was lying to the American Whigs about how he had resisted all those attempts to make him share incriminating information. On July 30, as the *Captain* neared Europe, Admiral Montagu extracted a deposition from him. It said "Samuel Dyer (Seaman now on board His Majs. Ship Captain)" made the following statements under oath:[30]

> • "he has been frequently employed by the said Mr. Samuel Adams & Doctr. Young to go to the Northend of the Town of Boston, to collect Shipwrights & Carpenters &c. together, to certain Public Houses (the Expence of which used to be paid by People who stiled themselves of Liberty, of which the said Adams and Young, generally, were the Heads of the Party) in order that they might be sure of a Number of Men, upon making a Signal, at a Minutes warning, whenever they wished to collect a Mob".
>
> • "some time in June last . . . he received a Letter from Mr. Samuel Adams of Boston, desiring him to come to Town, and meet him at the House of Doctr. Young" to deal with "a Quantity of a Tea being shiped by the East India Company on board Merchants Ships for the Port of Boston". That "Tea was afterwards destroyed by a Number of People in disguise," with the "Captains of the Gang" being "Mr. [blank] Short a Merchant near the Mill Bridge in Boston & Capt. Wood or Hood who commands a Merchant Vessel in Mr. John Hancock's employ." Dyer himself had not been at the Tea Party, however, being "prevented by Sickness."
>
> • "Mr. Samuel Adams did promise him at the House of Doctr. Young in June last," that Dyer would receive £4 sterling for every soldier he could convince to desert, and "every Soldier should receive the like Sum of four pounds, or three hundred Acres of Land, and a Quantity of Provisions so soon as they arrived at a certain part of the Country, provided they would cultivate the said Land."
>
> • Clothing to disguise those deserters was "lodged at proper Places," and "a Boat should always be ready at Hancock's Wharf" to carry them out of town by water. What's more, "Captain Conner, Inn Holder near the Mill Bridge in Boston," had promised horses "to carry the Soldiers off" and "a Room or Store . . . to conceal them in." And the key to that room was in Dyer's possession.

Dyer signed that document with a mark—his initials.

---

30. Dyer's statement to Montagu: Samuel Dyer deposition, July 30, 1774, CO5/120, ff. 251–2, National Archives, UK.

On the same day Admiral Montagu questioned another sailor, Samuel Mouat. He too accused "Mr. John Short Merchant near the Draw Bridge in Boston" of bribing a soldier to desert. Mouat also claimed that Judge Meshach Weare of New Hampshire had offered "393 Acres of Land to any Soldier who would desert." Reportedly, Weare even offered one former soldier confined in the Amherst, New Hampshire, jail for debt "his Fredom and £150 Stg. if he would Head a Regiment of Arm'd Men to attack the Kings Troops at Boston." Other conspirators, Mouat said, were "Mr. Page and Mr. Joseph Buckman Farmers in upper Cohorse" and a New Hampshire magistrate helpfully named "John Smith Esqr." Mouat also signed his deposition with a mark.[31]

When Dyer arrived back in America in Newport, Rhode Island, he had told local Patriots that on the high seas Admiral Montagu had "often threatened" him and "offered him Rewards at Times to accuse Mr. Hankock and other eminent Patriots, [. . . but] Dyre said he knew nothing of the matter."[32] In fact, Dyer had put his initials on a document accusing Hancock, Adams, and other Bostonians of planning the destruction of the East India Company tea even before it was shipped to Boston. That deposition had described Dr. Thomas Young as trying to entice British soldiers to desert, a fact that Dyer neglected to disclose when he met Doctor Young again in Rhode Island. The sailor concealed from the New England Patriots how much he had cooperated with Montagu's inquiry. He might have been under duress aboard the *Captain*, but it appears likely that even before then Dyer had dropped hints of knowing things about the Tea Party that royal officials were anxious to hear.

At the same time, most of the testimony Dyer offered to the admiral was nonsense. As one of the "Captains of the Gang" in destroying the tea he named John Hood, a captain working for Hancock. Newspaper records show that Hood was at sea on the date of the Tea Party.[33]

Dyer said "Captain Conner, Inn Holder near the Mill Bridge in Boston," would provide horses for deserters seeking to sneak out of town. Charles Conner did own a boarding-house and stable near the North End. During the Tea Party he had made himself notorious by trying to make off with some tea for himself, so he was an easy scapegoat.[34] However, putting a deserting soldier on a horse in the

---

31. Mouat's statement to Montagu: Samuel Mouat deposition, July 30, 1774, CO5/120, f. 253, National Archives, UK.

32. "often threatened": Stiles, *Literary Diary*, 1:462.

33. John Hood: *Connecticut Courant*, January 25, 1774.

34. "Captain Conner": Benjamin L. Carp, *Defiance of the Patriots: The Boston Tea Party and the Making of America* (New Haven, Yale University Press, 2010), 128.

middle of town would only have made that man more conspicuous, so that escape method made no sense. Notably, Dyer was careful not to confess to any crimes himself: he had been ill during the Tea Party, he said, and he never claimed to have *succeeded* in bringing off a deserter.

The day after his deposition, as the *Captain* was "Running up Channell," Dyer prepared a different document.[35] In a personal letter to Lord Dartmouth, Secretary of State, written "From On Board His Majestys Ship Captain at Spithead,"[36] Dyer offered to spill many Patriot secrets in exchange for protection:

> Whearas I am Brought Prisoner from Boston In New England, I humbly beg your Lordships to Take my Case into Consideration, whereas I shall be Examined before your Lordships, I will Declare the truth, that shall be required of me, in all Questions, and shall keep nothing Secerit from your Lordships, Whereas I have been Lead away by Gentlemen of Boston, being so unwise, as to take there Counsell, Whareas I have Ruined myself, and Wife and Children, Unless your Lordships will take my Case in hand, and settle me in som Part in England, as I shall never Dare to return to Boston, I must humbly beg your Lordships Clemency; I must humbly Intreat your Lordships to hear me Examined, and I shall relate all affairs from the begining, to the Ending in the town of Boston, and Province, I most humbly Intreat your Lordships to here me Examined me as soone as Possibly, as there is Boston, and Charlestown People, here belonging to this said ship, Captain, that is endeavering to gather all they News the[y] Can, to send Boston People, an account that they truths, I shall revail, will be of Little Use unless the Gentlemen, in Boston that, I shall Mention, be Brought on Tryall for there Misdenavours, as I shall Lay before your Lordships, that Tea affair, and all there Scheems, and Plans Concerning there Troops in they Country, Whereas they a Generall, and Captain and all other Officers to head there, troops at a Minutes Warning, as there is one Evedince in the Ship I should be Glad your Lordships Would Please to Examine him . . .[37]

This document the sailor signed with "Sam. Dyer," not just his initials—he could write his name after all.

---

35. "Running up Channell": log of HMS *Captain*, July 31, 1774, ADM 51/158, Part VII, National Archives, UK.
36. "From On Board": Dyer to Dartmouth, July 31, 1774, CO5/120, f. 255, National Archives, UK. See also "Entry of" Dyer's letter, CO5/247, ff. 210–1.
37. Ibid.

On August 2, the *Captain* "Moored at Spithead," on the south coast of England.[38] In London, the Admiralty Office received Admiral Montagu's report that he had brought over Dyer "by the desire of the Governor and Colonel Maddison, for endeavouring to entice the Soldiers to desert." The Admiralty quickly passed on those depositions, and the legal and political headaches they brought, to Lord Dartmouth at the Colonial Office, asking to know "his Majesty's pleasure, whether the said Dyer should be detained, or set at liberty."[39]

While he was in Newport, Dyer claimed that as soon as his ship arrived in England "he was sent speedily under a strong Guard to London, & carried before Lord North & examined, who said he was a Rebel & should be hanged."[40] Or, according to another report, that he "was sent up to London in irons, and examined three times before Lord North, Sandwich and the Earl of Dartmouth, respecting the destruction of the Tea."[41] Or even that he underwent an "Examination in London before the privy Council."[42] All those claims were false. None of the British ministers wanted anything to do with him.

When the papers arrived from the Admiralty Office, Undersecretary of State John Pownall quickly passed that news up to Lord Dartmouth. Then Dyer's own letter arrived, pleading for support and hinting at further information. On August 4, Pownall twice visited Thomas Hutchinson, former royal governor of Massachusetts, to consult with him on the situation. He brought Dyer's letter, which Hutchinson "thought carried marks of madness."[43] The former governor wrote in his diary:

> Mr. P. seemed in great distress from a prospect of trouble which it was likely he should meet with; for the last accounts are that Dyer informi'g says he has other witnesses on board of treasonable practices by [Samuel] Adams, [William] Molineux, [Dr. Thomas] Young, and what is more strange, Judge Wear of New Hampshire. I thought there was no more difficulty now to get rid of this affair than when they had so many witnesses examined, proving Treason against all but one of the

38. "Moored at Spithead": log of HMS *Captain*, August 2, 1774, ADM 51/158, Part VII, National Archives, UK.

39. "by the desire of the Governor": CO5/120, f. 247, National Archives, UK.

40. "he was sent speedily": Stiles, *Literary Diary*, 1:462.

41. "was sent up to London": *Essex Gazette*, October 25, 1774.

42. "Examination in London": Gage to Dartmouth, October 30, 1774, Colonial Office, *Documents*, 8:222.

43. "thought carried marks of madness": Thomas Hutchinson, *The Diary and Letters of His Excellency, Thomas Hutchinson, Esq.*, Peter Orlando Hutchinson, editor (Boston: Houghton-Mifflin, 1884), 1:205.

same persons in the affair of the Tea, upon which there had been no further proceeding; however, he determined there was no avoiding to send for Dyer.

Contrary to Hutchinson's assessment, back in February the government's top lawyers had decided the available evidence about the Tea Party was too weak for any prosecution.

Pownall also checked in with one of those lawyers that Thursday evening: Attorney General Edward Thurlow. He told the undersecretary that "Dyer's case [was] a foolish unconsidered proceeding on the part of General Gage and Admiral Montagu. No facts are charged on him or others for which they could be tried or prosecuted here. All Dyer says about the destruction of the tea is mere hearsay. He should be immediately released."[44]

At nine o'clock that evening, Dartmouth and his staff at Whitehall happily prepared their response to the Admiralty. "I have not failed to lay before the King Your Lordships Letter to me," the Secretary of State began—though mentioning "the King" might have been only a formula for consideration at high levels of government rather than personally involving George III. Dartmouth told his Admiralty colleagues:

> I am to acquaint Your Lordships, that it appears, upon a full Exam-ination of the Papers inclosed therewith, that there is no reason, from any Facts stated in the said Papers, for detaining the said Dyer on board His Majesty's Ship Captain. There seems, however, to be no objection to his being told, that if he has any thing to communicate to me, relative to public Transactions in the Province of Massachusetts Bay, I shall be ready to receive such Communication.

That letter was sent off to the Admiralty Lords at 8:50 on the morning of August 5.[45]

Though Dartmouth left open the possibility of receiving more testimony from Dyer, he and all those other royal officials seem to have just wanted the man to go away. Montagu no doubt felt he had performed a great service in getting his testimony down on paper. But Gage would later say, "Nobody Supposed that he could give any Material Intelligence of Transactions here,"[46] and Hutchinson judged

---

44. "Dyer's case": Dartmouth, *The Manuscripts of the Earl of Dartmouth: Volume II, American Papers*, Historical Manuscripts Commission, 14th Report, Appendix, Part 10 (London: Her Majesty's Stationery Office, 1895), 220.

45. "I have not failed": CO5/120, f. 257-7a, National Archives, UK. See also entry of Dartmouth's letter to the Admiralty, CO5/250, f. 164.

46. "Nobody Supposed": Gage to Dartmouth, October 30, 1774, Colonial Office, *Documents*, 8:222.

the admiral's deposition "very imprudent."[47] Even before testing Dyer's evidence against the facts in Boston, Thurlow realized that it offered no legal grounds for holding the sailor or pursuing others. American Patriots were loudly accusing royal officials of trampling on people's rights, but those officials strove to adhere to British law.

Dyer probably spoke the truth when he told Newporters that "he was discharged [from the *Captain*] as if he had been only one of the people who were all discharged the ship being paid off & laid up."[48] Indeed, he may have worked as a common sailor during at least part of the passage. Dyer was now free, perhaps with a bit of money in his pocket—though he claimed not to have received "one farthing of wages."[49] Instead of finding a new ship back to America, however, Dyer set out for London. But he never spoke to Lord Dartmouth. Instead the sailor met with Sheriff William Lee, a native of Virginia, and probably other sympathetic officials ready to entertain his story of being kidnapped. Only then did Dyer make plans to return to Boston.

At the end of the month, on August 28, Lord Dartmouth's office was concerned enough about Dyer to send a private letter to General Gage mentioning him. Unfortunately, that document is lost—one of the very few letters between Gage and Dartmouth that does not survive on either side of the correspondence. We have only Gage's reply, dated October 30 and marked "private"—the one surviving letter classified that way in the governor's 1774 missives to the ministry. Gage said that he had received his lordship's letter about Dyer just two days before, long after the sailor had returned. He blandly recounted Dyer's accusations and attack on the army officers before reporting that the would-be assassin had "made off to the Congress sitting at Cambridge where he was apprehended and is now in the jail of this town. He appears to be a vagabond and enthusiastically mad."[50]

General Gage concluded that letter with an explanation for why he was operating so carefully even when his officers were under attack:

> affairs are at such a pitch through a general union of the whole that I am obliged to use more caution than would otherwise be necessary, lest all the continent should unite in hostile proceedings against us, which would bring on a crisis which I apprehend His Majesty would by all means wish to avoid unless drove to it by their own conduct.[51]

47. "very imprudent": Hutchinson, *Diary and Letters*, 1:207.
48. "he was discharged": Stiles, *Literary Diary*, 1:462.
49. "one farthing of wages": *Essex Gazette*, October 25, 1774.
50. "made off to the Congress": Gage to Dartmouth, October 30, 1774, Colonial Office, *Documents*, 8:222.

In other words, the general wanted to avoid giving the Patriots any reason for outrage. Instead, he was waiting for them to go too far so he could strike back from the moral high ground.

Of course, both Gage and Dartmouth understood that if the Patriots had known all that their government had done on this matter, they would have had plenty of grounds for protest. The army really had grabbed a man and put him on board a navy ship to sidestep his right to a trial in Boston. The Samuel Dyer affair had involved the highest levels of the royal government: the governor of Massachusetts and army commander for North America, the navy's ranking rear admiral in America, the Admiralty Board, the Secretary of State and his undersecretaries, the former governor of Massachusetts, and the Crown's Attorney General. At a formal level at least, the matter had been laid "before the King." But Gage was the only person in Boston to learn about any of that business in London, and he kept quiet.

The Massachusetts Patriots decided that Dyer, despite his letter from Sheriff Lee and the endorsement of Dr. Young in Newport, was probably insane and clearly unreliable. They had championed his cause for a few days, and then he had tried to murder two officers in broad daylight. After that, Boston's political leaders decided that Dyer was crazy, and that they were as lucky as Lieutenant Colonel Cleaveland in escaping the effects of his rash actions. The Patriots let the sailor stew in the town jail through the winter, the local courts still shut down.

In April 1775, war broke out with the Battle of Lexington and Concord. Provincial militia regiments besieged Boston and reorganized themselves into a New England army. On June 17, British troops forced that army back off the Charlestown peninsula at the cost of hundreds of dead and several hundred more wounded.

In the wake of that Battle of Bunker Hill, the British military cracked down on potential spies inside Boston. On June 19, sailors detained Peter Edes, the eighteen-year-old son of Benjamin Edes, who was now printing the militant *Boston Gazette* for the Patriots outside Boston. Young Edes was put into Boston's jail, which had come under the control of the military government.[52] Ten days later, the schoolteachers James Lovell and John Leach joined him there. British officers had found a letter containing sensitive information on Dr.

---

51. "affairs are at such a pitch": Gage to Dartmouth, October 30, 1774, Colonial Office, *Documents*, 8:223.

52. Peter Edes arrested: Samuel Lane Boardman, editor, *Peter Edes: Pioneer Printer in Maine* (Bangor: De Burians, 1901), 93–4. Edes's prison diary appears on pages 93–110.

Joseph Warren's corpse after Bunker Hill; evidently it came from a teacher using the initials "J. L.," so the army arrested both Lovell and Leach on suspicion. (Warren's correspondent was Lovell.)[53]

Peter Edes and John Leach kept diaries of their weeks in the Boston jail.[54] Many of their entries are the same, showing they collaborated to record what they saw as abuse rather than to preserve their individual personal thoughts and experiences. Samuel Dyer resurfaces in those journals—and he was once again cooperating with his captors.

The provost martial in charge of the British military's prisoners was a man from New York, William Cunningham. He had been one of the Sons of Liberty a few years before, but by 1775 he was a fervent Loyalist, brawling with his former comrades. In June he was attacked and run out of the city. Cunningham would work for the king's army throughout the war before becoming a prison warden in Gloucestershire.[55] On August 9, Edes's diary complained: "a poor painter, an inhabitant, was put in the dungeon and very ill used by the provost, and his deputy, Samuel Dyer; then the provost turned him out and made him get down on his knees in the yard and say, God bless the King."[56]

In less than a year, Samuel Dyer had moved from attacking Crown officers to working for one, from complaining about being mistreated as a prisoner to lording over prisoners (even as he technically remained a jail inmate himself). No doubt the sailor had felt betrayed by the Massachusetts Provincial Congress after those Patriots turned him over to the authorities. But he also had a pattern of shifting allegiances, cooperating with whoever in the area appeared to be most powerful. And there is the real possibility, which many people at the time found easy to believe, that Dyer was insane.

Leach and Edes set down two recurring complaints about Dyer, Cunningham, and their guards. The first was profanity. In early July

53. Lovell and Leach arrests: *Papers of John Adams*, Robert J. Taylor, editor (Cambridge, Mass.: Harvard University Press, 1979), 3:69, 76. *The Political Magazine, and Parliamentary, Naval, Military, and Literary Journal*, 1 (1780), 757.

54. John Leach diary: John Leach, "A Journal Kept by John Leach, During His Confinement by the British, in Boston Gaol," *New England Historical and Genealogical Register*, 19 (1864), 255–63. Reprinted in Boardman, *Peter Edes*, 115-25. Leach's entries are often more full and personal than Edes's, but fewer entries survive.

55. William Cunningham: Thomas Jones, *History of New York During the Revolutionary War*, Edward Floyd de Lancey, editor (New York: New-York Historical Society, 1879), 484. Henry B. Dawson, *Reminiscences of the City of New York* (New York: 1855), 39–40. J. R. S. Whiting, *Prison Reform in Gloucestershire, 1776-1820: A Study of the Work of Sir George Onesiphorus Paul, Bart.* (London: Phillimore, 1975), 21.

56. "a poor painter": Boardman, *Peter Edes*, 99.

they stated: "a complicated scene of oaths, curses, debauchery, and the most horrid blasphemy, were committed by the provost martial, his deputy and soldiers who were our guard, soldier prisoners, and sundry soldier women confined for theft &c." On August 13 the prisoners were confined to their rooms with "much swearing and blasphemy close under our window the whole day, by the provost, his deputy, and our guard of soldiers." Leach and Edes wrote: "It appears to be done on purpose, as they knew it was disagreeable to us to hear such language."[57]

The provost and deputy's other sin, according to their captives, was greed. It was common in British and American prisons of the time for inmates to have to pay the jailers certain fees for their upkeep, and those rules were not relaxed in wartime. On August 17 one prisoner was discharged owing a dollar; "he paid a pistareen and left a silver broach in pawn for four more; the provost kept the broach, and gave Dyer the pistareen." Nine days later Dyer "demanded two dollars" of another prisoner. He received one dollar and "a pillow, porringer, &c. pledged for the other."[58]

On August 28, Edes wrote, "We complained about Dyer to the Gen. about ill usage." By this time, General Gage probably sensed that his military and political career was coming to a halt. Samuel Dyer was a loose end from the previous year, still causing headaches. The next day, the British authorities finally brought Dyer to court for assaulting Lieutenant Colonel Cleaveland and Captain Montresor. He was now showing loyalty to the Crown—but he probably also seemed unstable. The upshot: "Dyer tried and acquitted and ordered to depart the province."[59]

Nonetheless, the sailor stuck around the jail. "Dyer in his glory," Edes wrote on September 11; "he is the provost's deputy, and a very bad man." Four days later the new royal sheriff of Suffolk County, Joshua Loring, Jr., oversaw a mock auction of goods taken from Bostonians' houses to the prison, with "the provost, his son and Dyer, the bidders—a most curious piece of equity."[60]

Finally on September 18, Peter Edes could write:

> Dyer discharged, to the great satisfaction of the prisoners. He seemed
> to be a most unhappy, wicked wretch; Lord have mercy on him, for if

57. jailers' profanity: Boardman, *Peter Edes*, 96, 100, 116, 120. There are many more complaints about swearing that don't specifically mention Dyer.
58. jailers' fees: Boardman, *Peter Edes*, 101–2, 104, 121–2.
59. complaint to general and acquittal: Boardman, *Peter Edes*, 105.
60. Dyer at mock auction: Boardman, *Peter Edes*, 107.

we may be allowed to judge agreeably to the word of God, he was ripe for destruction, a most awful state.[61]

Samuel Dyer left the Boston jail. With the town besieged, his best prospect was probably going back to sea, either in the Royal Navy or on one of the private vessels bringing in food and supplies. But Dyer's fate remains his final mystery.

61. Dyer discharged: Boardman, *Peter Edes*, 108.

# "Those Noble Qualities": Classical Pseudonyms as Reflections of Divergent Republican Value Systems

❀ SHAWN DAVID MCGHEE ❀

During the trial years under the Federal Constitution, some political observers contributed to the national discourse by employing one of the period's most ambitious and creative ornaments: the classical pseudonym. Cloaked behind these ancient disguises, commenters added a historically nuanced layer to their arguments that enlisted the ubiquitous gravity of the classical past.[1] These signatures have puzzled generations of scholars since at least the middle of the twentieth century, leaving them scrambling to decode their exact purposes. Douglass Adair, for example, argued that a classically-educated audience integrated the diplomacy of a pseudonym's historical figure into contemporary essays.[2] Mackubin T. Owens, Jr., conjectured the founders "looked to antiquity for their models of greatness" and selected classical masks to emphasize a particular virtue for an eighteenth-century audience.[3] Other scholars determined that ancient *noms de plume* allowed

---

1. Paul A. Rahe, "Cicero and the Classical Legacy in America," in eds. Peter S. Onuf and Nicholas Cole, *Thomas Jefferson, the Classical World, and Early America* (Charlottesville: University of Virginia Press, 2011); Gordon S. Wood, "The Legacy of Rome in the American Revolution," in Gordon S. Wood, *The Idea of America: Reflections on the Birth of the United States* (New York: Penguin, 2011), 57-79.

2. Douglass Adair, "A Note on Certain of Hamilton's Pseudonyms," *William and Mary Quarterly* 12, no. 2 (1955): 282-97.

3. Mackubin T. Owens, Jr., "A Further Note on Certain of Hamilton's Pseudonyms: The 'Love of Fame and the Use of Plutarch,'" *Journal of the Early Republic* 4, no. 3 (1984): 275-86.

elite statesmen to participate in an erudite parlor game or simply behave in a manner unbecoming of their station.[4] Most recently, Eran Shalev argued that the founding generation used these literary devices to connect with and channel the virtue of the past.[5]

Each of these explanations is convincing, but a critical element remains absent from this conversation. During the early 1790s, political contributors used classical pseudonyms to draw on the authority of the ancient world in their contemporary struggle to define the new national order. By reflecting their republican value system through a Greek or Roman prism, these actors sought to legitimize their vision with the sacred wisdom of the classical world. Ultimately, writing under ancient veneers allowed partisans to politicize and weaponize ancient history during the turbulent start of the Federal Republic.

Federalists employed ancient personalities who advocated a patrician worldview and a culture of deference. These American aristocrats resurrected historical and semi-historical actors such as Timoleon, Lycurgus and Marcus to help articulate and cultivate their contemporary republican vision. In contrast, Republicans conjured classical figures who championed plebeian rights and a culture of vigilance. These American activists animated ancient figures such as Caius, Aratus and Lucius to promulgate an opposing value system. In the process, these factions transformed revered heroes of the ancient world into de facto American partisans, channeling their legacies into the national drama.

The following passages examine classical pseudonyms as presented in the two nationally distributed newspapers, the *Gazette of the United States* and the *National Gazette*.[6] Advertisements for titles arriving in American bookstores during the 1790s, as reflected in those papers, reveal Americans' continued fascination with the classical past.[7] For most, John Dryden's translation of Plutarch's *Lives of the Noble Grecians and Romans* remained the most widely available source of ancient history.[8]

4. Marcus Daniel, *Scandal and Civility: Journalism and the Birth of American Democracy* (New York: Oxford University Press, 2009); Jeffrey L. Pasley, *"The Tyranny of Printers": Newspaper Politics in the Early Republic* (Charlottesville: University of Virginia Press, 2001); Donald H. Stewart, *The Opposition Press in the Federalist Era* (New York: State University Press, 1969).

5. Eran Shalev, *Rome Reborn on Western Shores: Historic Imagination and the Creation of the American Republic* (Charlottesville: University of Virginia Press, 2009).

6. Pasley, *Tyranny of Printers*.

7. See for example, *Gazette of the United States*, November 14, 1792; *National Gazette*, November 3, 1791.

8. Carl J. Richard, *The Founders and the Classics: Greece, Rome, and the American Enlightenment* (Cambridge: Harvard University Press, 1994).

Other classical works or classically-themed literature commonly refer-enced by Americans include translations of Homer, Virgil, Tacitus and reprints of Joseph Addison's *Cato: A Tragedy.*[9] This keen interest in the ancient world conditioned the reading republic to think creatively and politically about classical pseudonyms.[10]

Sampling four months of the *Gazette of the United States* reveals that, over thirty-one editions, that paper published thirty-nine pseudony-mous articles. Contributors submitted a full 33 percent of these under a classical *nom de plume.*[11] Within those same months, the *National Gazette* published thirty-three editions with sixty-one articles attrib-uted to a concealed author; 31 percent of these writers obscured them-selves behind a Greek or Roman personality.[12] Taken together, roughly one third of the pseudonymous essays printed in both papers invoked the power of the classical world. While this essay is by no means com-prehensive, the following examples uncover a pattern for how some contemporary contributors engaged ancient figures to articulate their republican order during the first Washington administration.

Shortly after George Washington took the first presidential oath of office under the new constitution, John Fenno established the pro-ad-ministration *Gazette of the United States* to endear the new federal sys-tem to Americans.[13] Below are two examples from that newspaper reflective of how Federalists politicized ancient history through classical pseudonyms before Republicans responded in kind.

Championing elite rule, "Timoleon" educated the public on the nec-essary qualities national figures ought to possess to serve the federal government. Only men of pedigree with character and fortune great enough to resist corruption, he lectured, were fit for higher office. The people, he warned, ought to dismiss outright any man who openly sought public affection. This essayist communicated with an audience

9. For the print availability and general popularity of *Cato: A Tragedy* and the message most colonists received from that work, see Forrest McDonald, "Foreword," in Joseph Ad-dison, *Cato: A Tragedy and Other Selected Essays*, eds. Christine Dunn Henderson and Mark E. Yellin (Indianapolis: Liberty Fund, 2004).

10. Michael Warner, *The Letters of the Republic: Publication and the Public Sphere in Eigh-teenth-Century America* (Cambridge: Harvard University Press, 1990); Robert A. Ferguson, *Reading the Early Republic* (Cambridge: Harvard University Press, 2006).

11. *Gazette of the United States*, February, March, October, November, 1792.

12. *National Gazette*, February, March, October, November, 1792.

13. For an account of George Washington's first inauguration, see *Hartford Courant*, May 4, 1789; John Fenno has no biographer. For a good survey, see Eric Burns, *Infamous Scrib-blers: The Founding Fathers and the Rowdy Beginnings of American Journalism* (New York: Public Affairs, 2006), 262-68.

likely familiar with Plutarch's Timoleon, the Greek warrior who killed his tyrant brother to protect the liberties of the *polis*. Later in life, the people summoned Timoleon from a self-imposed exile to rescue Syracuse from Carthaginian oppression.[14] In the wake of Washington's inauguration, the American Timoleon asked that voters only elevate men similar in character to the president to national positions. Washington, himself a man of virtue and wealth, left public life after vanquishing his British brothers to secure American liberty during the Revolution. And like Timoleon, he returned from this self-imposed exile to rescue the people from popular oppression. Through this pseudonym, the writer wrapped Washington and a patrician worldview in the robes of an ancient Greek to advocate an elite leadership class.

In an equally telling essay, "Lycurgus" urged Americans to instill in their children "a just regard for the ruling and protecting powers." Elites, he recorded, absorbed the political wisdom of the modern world and studied the ancient past before designing the Federal Constitution; that document rescued the republic from the chaos of the 1780s. National figures transformed into "the fathers of a country," this writer claimed, and thus deserved the appropriate degree of deference from the people. These men, he continued, assumed the obligation of modeling exemplary behavior in both their private and public lives to communicate their continued fitness to lead.[15] This essayist's readers likely recalled the pseudo-historical Spartan king, Lycurgus. According to Plutarch, he too traveled beyond the *polis* and recorded the best qualities of each government he encountered, weaving them into Sparta's constitution. Spartans praised Lycurgus for "his eminent virtues" and swore allegiance to his fundamental law.[16] The Oracle at Delphi, explained Plutarch, openly praised Lycurgus for advancing the happiness of his people through the wisdom of his constitution.[17] This writer invited Americans to connect the founding of the new republic with that of Lycurgus's Sparta. And like the mythical king, this contributor asked that citizens respect their virtuous leaders, defer to their superior wisdom and unconditionally adhere to their just laws. By recruiting Lycurgus into the Federalist fold, this essayist conjured the authority of a revered Spartan king to advocate a political culture of deference.

14. Plutarch, *The Lives of the Noble Grecian and Romans*, trans. John Dryden, 2 vols. (New York: Modern Library, 1979), 1:325-55.
15. "Lycurgus," in *Gazette of the United States*, July 10, 1790.
16. Plutarch, *Lives*, 1:55.
17. Ibid., 1:52-80.

The elite vision propagated by the *Gazette of the United States* rattled those of the Republican persuasion. Secretary of State Thomas Jefferson condemned that paper for promoting "pure Toryism" that disseminated "the doctrines of Monarchy [and] aristocracy" while marginalizing the people.[18] He concluded only a "whig-vehicle of intelligence" could combat Federalists' dangerous indoctrination, and ultimately recruited Philip Freneau to publish the *National Gazette*.[19] Republicans, some behind ancient disguises, took to Freneau's paper to condemn the patrician worldview propagandized by Federalists and to offer Americans an alternative vision.

"Aratus" wasted no time condemning enemies of republicanism and described the American and French revolutions as crises in "the affairs of mankind." Though these two regime-toppling uprisings had granted more optimism to the present generation than any before, he urged that resistance actors not imbue a "mistaken confidence." He pleaded with observers to remain vigilant, as reactionary forces actively plotted to regain authority and extinguish the flames of liberty. Aratus next reminded readers that since the days of Herodotus and Thucydides, the greater portion of mankind had groaned under "the scourge of a vigorous despotism."[20] Tyrants would smother hard-earned liberty, he warned, the moment sentinel-citizens eased their guards.[21] Unveiling the historical Aratus unlocks the relevance of this otherwise mysterious pseudonym and adds additional urgency and depth to this writer's message.

Plutarch's Aratus hailed from that den of tyranny, Sicyon. As a boy, Aratus narrowly escaped a murderous political purge and nourished "a vehement burning hatred against tyrants" ever after.[22] As an adult, he liberated his *polis* and kept a watchful gaze over the Peloponnese, vanquishing tyrants who threatened the people's sovereignty. After a lifetime performing as a bulwark of liberty, however, he momentarily relaxed under Philip II. That Macedonian king wasted no time orchestrating Aratus's assassination.[23] This Greek liberator spent a lifetime

---

18. Thomas Jefferson to Thomas Mann Randolph, May 15, 1791, in Julian P. Boyd, et al., eds., *The Papers of Thomas Jefferson*, 44 vols. (Princeton: University of Princeton Press, 1950-2021), 20:416.

19. Thomas Jefferson to James Madison, July 21, 1791, in William T. Hutchinson, et al., eds., *The Papers of James Madison: Congressional Series*, 17 vols. (Charlottesville: University of Virginia Press, 1962-1991), 14:49-51.

20. "Aratus," in *National Gazette*, November 24, 1791.

21. "Aratus," in ibid., November 14, 1791.

22. Plutarch, *Lives*, 2:613.

23. Ibid., 2:612-45.

combating tyranny, yet a single unguarded moment sent him to the grave. The American Aratus offered American readers a dire warning: republican government was fragile and only a vigilant citizenry could sustain it. American and French resistance actors had vanquished the tyranny of their respective kings, but without vigilance, patrician opponents of both revolutions would reclaim their Sicyon.

Over a series of essays, "Caius" howled that Alexander Hamilton's financial plan sacrificed "the *many* to the aggrandizement of the *few*."[24] Elites designed the funded debt, he asserted, to "perpetuate oppression to your remotest posterity."[25] A dangerous cabal of American patricians, he claimed, conspired to "erect a detestable *aristocracy* or *monarchy* on the ruins of republicanism and the independence of our country."[26] The Washington administration, Cauis warned, not only threatened the fundamental principles of the American Revolution; it sought to corrupt a healthy Federal Constitution with "all the weaknesses, vices and infirmities of the decayed and expiring constitution of Great Britain."[27] Expressing faith in American vigilance, he remarked, "The people are not inattentive . . . [They] will unite when this danger is brought to bear."[28] Caius hoped to awaken Americans to the iniquitous plans of what he considered a self-interested elite. Recovering the Roman origins behind this mask adds remarkable historical power to Republicans' pleas for vigilance.

No Federalist would have dared stir the ghost of Caius Gracchus to advocate national elitism. That Roman raised plebeian awareness of patrician greed, advocated for equitable land distribution and demanded voting rights for all peninsular citizens. While making these demands, he did not follow custom and address the comitium. Instead, he spoke directly to the people, his back to that assembly.[29] Plutarch marveled that this slight positional change revolutionized Roman politics, transforming the government "from an aristocracy to a democracy" and engendering public figures to appeal to plebeians rather than patricians. Elites murdered Caius during his crusade against their perceived greed.[30] Advocating vigilance through this radical Roman joined Republicans in a timeless struggle between the privileged few and the vigilant many.

24. "Caius," in *National Gazette*, January 16, 1792.
25. "Caius," ibid., January 26, 1792.
26. "Caius," ibid., February 6, 1792, January 26, 1792.
27. "Caius," ibid., February 6, 1792.
28. "Caius," ibid., February 9, 1792.
29. Plutarch, *Lives*, 2:371-84.
30. Ibid., 2:374.

One of the more dynamic exchanges between these value systems unfolded during the nation's second presidential election. Disguised writers took to the press to either attack or advocate for Vice President John Adams in what became for some a struggle for the soul of the republic.[31] In the *National Gazette*, "Lucius" warned Americans to "guard themselves" from Adams, since the second magistrate remained "attached to a government of kings, lords, and commons." Lucius voiced his support for New York governor George Clinton since Adams aimed to introduce "hereditary orders" to the republic.[32] These remarks prompted a response from "Marcus" in the pages of the *Gazette of the United States*. Marcus advised readers to ignore Lucius, since independent (wealthy) "men of information" supported both Washington *and* Adams. The current national magistrates, he lectured, satisfied "the real republicans of our country." Any literature critical of Adams, he concluded, came from the deranged minds of designing demagogues.[33]

This discourse continued in the pages of the *Gazette of the United States*. "Lucius" again warned that if Americans wished to preserve republican government and the principles "upon which it was founded" they must abandon Adams for Clinton.[34] Assessing the argument, "Antonius" offered his own warning. "Beware my countrymen," he wrote, "of those temporizing politicians, who under the pretense of advancing your interest" served their own. "Though Lucius, like his predecessor among the Romans sacrifice[d] the principles of honor to the gratification of his ambition — like him I trust he will . . . meet a similar fate."[35] Uncovering the source material for this triumvirate exposes an even richer discourse.

For many Americans, the most widely known models for Lucius and Marcus rested in the pages of Joseph Addison's *Cato: A Tragedy*. Lucius stood with Cato in his doomed resistance to the ambitions of Caesar, making this pseudonym a powerful indictment of Adams's alleged monarchical inclinations and designs on an imperial presidency. Unwilling to allow Republicans to cast themselves as heroes in this neo-Roman drama, the Federalist "Marcus" invoked the spirit of Cato's son: Caesar's allies struck down this defender of Roman republicanism dur-

31. Shawn David McGhee, "'Characters Pre-Eminent for Virtue and Ability': The First Partisan Application of the Electoral College," *Journal of the American Revolution* (Yardley, PA: Westholme Publishing, 2023): 289-95.
32. "Lucius," in *National Gazette*, November 17, 1792.
33. "Marcus," in *Gazette of the United States*, November 21, 1792.
34. "Lucius," ibid.
35. "Antonius," ibid., November 28, 1792.

ing Rome's crisis of order.[36] Addison's work clearly held great emotional significance in the American imagination.[37] Both proto-parties linked their cause to Cato while casting Caesar as the villain, a development this essay rationalizes below. First, however, we must address Antonius, who at first glance does not fit neatly into this Addisonian dialogue.

A contextual reconfiguration accommodates Antonius's involvement in the above exchange. Admittedly, the following passage is conjectural, yet it offers a plausible explanation for how "Antonius" effortlessly cast "Lucius" as a villain. It also remains confined to the classical texts eighteenth-century Americans regularly consumed. If Lucius is plucked from Addison's play and returned to the pages of Roman history, he transforms into Lucius Catiline, a "vicious and depraved" popular leader, according to the historian Sallust, motivated only by his "Passion to seize the Commonwealth . . . in his pursuit of Tyranny."[38] The post-Julian historian Plutarch accused him of incest, fratricide and debauching the Roman youth. When Lucius challenged Cicero's consulship, the latter successfully sent Antonius forth to destroy the former and his army.[39] Reframing this debate allowed Antonius to strip Lucius of his republican credentials and recast him as traitor to Rome and America while Antonius debuted as conqueror of Catiline and defender of Adams.

The classical world resonated deeply with this generation of Americans, many of whom were convinced they were living in a transformative moment.[40] Certainly political observers felt a connection with the ancients and sought to capture something of their virtue.[41] They also likely hoped Americans would aim to replicate the character of the classical veneers they ventriloquized through; Plutarch anticipated as much. Even that historian expected his biographical sketches to encourage readers to emulate "those noble qualities" of his virtuous subjects.[42]

36. Addison, *Cato: A Tragedy and Selected Essays*, Henderson and Yellin.

37. McDonald, "Forward," in ibid.

38. Thomas Gordon, ed., *The Works of Sallust, Translated into English with Political Discourses upon that Author: To Which is Added, a Translation of Cicero's Four Orations against Catiline* (London: R. Ware, 1744).

39. Plutarch, *Lives*, 2:415-23.

40. See, for example, John Adams to Abigail Adams, July 3, 1776, in Lyman H. Butterfield, et al., eds., *The Adams Papers: Adams Family Correspondence*, 14 vols. (Cambridge: Harvard University, 1961- ), 2:29-33.

41. Gordon S. Wood, *The Radicalism of the American Revolution* (New York: Vintage Books, 1991), 109.

42. Plutarch, *Lives*, 1:205.

Shortly before the end of the first Washington administration, Alexander Hamilton composed a letter expressive of how naturally the classical rationalized the contemporary world in many eighteenth-century American minds. "No popular government was ever without its Catalines and Caesars," he reasoned to the president. "These are its true enemies."[43] Naturally neither party supported Catiline. Yet both feared Caesar for different reasons. Republicans despised him for his imperial ambitions, Federalists for his popular demagoguery. Strangely, both occupied the obverse and converse sides of the same proverbial coin. And which contemporary version of Caesar threatened the American republic, of course, depended on partisan loyalties.

Reconfiguring classical pseudonyms as partisan tools expressive of a particular republican vision offers a deeper understanding of the hysteria that characterized the 1790s.[44] By animating Greek or Roman leaders, contemporary observers transformed ancient actors into American advocates of divergent worldviews. This multi-dimensional colloquy connected the ancient past with the American present and pitted competing conceptual models of the new republican order in a struggle for the nation's future. Print culture circulated these ideas and helped a classically-literate citizenry make sense of the world around them. During the final decade of the eighteenth century, Americans performed a number of popular rites and rituals that served as political expressions.[45] Deploying ancient signatures only added to the festive nature of the Early Republic's street politics.

43. Enclosure: [Objections and Answers Respecting the Administration], [August 18, 1792], in Harold C. Syrett, ed., *The Papers of Alexander Hamilton* (New York: Columbia University Press, 1961-87), 12:229-58.

44. For the 1790s as a passionate or emotional moment of American politics, see Marshal Smelser, "The Federalist Period as an Age of Passion," *American Quarterly* 10, no. 4 (1958): 391-419.

45. Simon P. Newman, *Parades and the Politics of the Street: Festive Culture in the Early American Republic* (Philadelphia: University of Pennsylvania Press, 1997); David Waldstreicher, *In the Midst of Perpetual Fetes: The Making of American Nationalism* (Chapel Hill: University of North Carolina Press, 1997).

# Algernon Sidney and the American Revolution

## ◆◆ DAVID OTERSEN ◆◆

Algernon Sidney was a seventeenth-century British political theorist, Member of Parliament, and Whig politician who was executed for treason on December 7, 1683, during the reign of Charles II. At his trial, the most incriminating evidence presented by the prosecution was a series of anti-monarchical passages from a seized manuscript of Sidney's reformist treatise, *Discourses Concerning Government*. The *Discourses* were ultimately published ten years after the Glorious Revolution, in 1698, and would subsequently have a profound intellectual and ideological influence on the American Revolution.

Indeed, many leading revolutionary patriots, including Thomas Jefferson, John Adams, Benjamin Franklin, and Stephen Hopkins, had carefully and sedulously studied Sidney's *Discourses*, integrated his principles into their own writings, and admired him greatly. Franklin, in fact, was so enamored of Sidney that he glowingly described him as "the British Brutus, the warm, the steady friend to liberty, who from a defusive love of mankind left them that in-valuable legacy his immortal 'Discourses on Government.'"[1] And Jefferson was equally effusive in his praise for Sidney's tome, which he characterized thusly: "it is probably the best elementary book of the principles of government, as founded in natural right which has ever been published in any language."[2]

Moreover, the Declaration of Independence, the most prominent and definitive text of the Revolution, owes a deep theoretical debt to

---

1. Caroline Robbins, "Algernon Sidney's Discourses Concerning Government: Textbook of Revolution," *William and Mary Quarterly* 3rd ser., 4:4 (1947), 267-296, 269.
2. Edward Dumbauld, "Algernon Sidney on Public Right," *University of Arkansas at Little Rock Law Journal* 10 (1987-88), 318.

Sidney's *Discourses*. To that end, in 1825, as an octogenarian reflecting on the Declaration, Jefferson candidly acknowledged that, as its principal author, he had introduced no innovative doctrines or groundbreaking ideas. Jefferson, in fact, explicitly rejected the notion that he ever had any such intent. The purpose of the Declaration was, he said:

> not to find out new principles, or new arguments, never before thought of . . . but to place before mankind the common sense of the subject; [in] terms so plain and firm, as to command their assent . . . neither aiming at originality of principle or sentiment . . . all it's authority rests then on the harmonising sentiments of the day, whether expressed, in conversns in letters, printed essays or in the elementary books of public right, as Aristotle, Cicero, Locke, Sidney Etc.[3]

Therefore, when Jefferson asserted the Declaration's fundamental principles of natural equality, government by consent, the right of revolution, and God-given, inalienable rights, he relied heavily upon the noetic antecedents advanced by the political philosophers who preceded him, including those of Algernon Sidney. And the principles, which Jefferson articulated in the Declaration, and which had been earnestly argued in the vast body of revolutionary literature by the Continental leadership, thoroughly permeate the pages of Sidney's *Discourses*. Indeed, Bryn Mawr historian Caroline Robbins has even referred to the *Discourses* as a "Textbook of Revolution" for American Independence.[4]

SIDNEY AND NATURAL EQUALITY

The Declaration's self-evident truth that "all men are created equal" is widely recognized as an indispensable value of the document and the revolution at large, although the sentiment it expresses does not, again, originate with Jefferson and the Declaration. The conviction that equality is the natural and essential condition of humanity had been contemplated and advocated well before Jefferson authored the Declaration, and it is thoroughly endogenic to Sidney's political philosophy in the *Discourses*. Arguing the point, Sidney himself draws on the erudition of his predecessors, while also presenting his own enlightened notions, both of which helped guide Jefferson in writing the Declaration. From the *Discourses*:

---

3. Merrill D. Peterson, ed., *Thomas Jefferson, Writings; Autobiography, Notes on the State of Virginia, Public and Private Papers, Addresses, Letters* (New York, NY: Library of America 1984), 1501.
4. Robbins, "Algernon Sidney's Discourses," 267-296, 267.

> By nature all men are equal.[5] Hayward, Blackwood, Barclay, and oth-
> ers . . . do with one consent admit as an unquestionable truth . . . the
> natural liberty and equality of mankind[6] The equality in which men are
> born is so perfect, that no man will suffer his natural liberty to be
> abridged, except others do the like[7]

Sidney referred to, in order, Robert Cardinal Bellarmine's treatment of natural equality from Bellarmine's treatise *De Laicis;* a commentary from Sir Robert Filmer's *Patriarcha* (as Filmer references three prominent seventeenth-century historians and political theorists: John Hayward, Adam Blackwood, and Robert Barclay); and finally, his own interpretation and affirmation of human equality. Accordingly, even a casual consideration of Bellarmine's attributed quote, "by nature all men are equal," joined with Filmer's commentary describing the natural equality of mankind as an "unquestionable truth," reveals a synonymous and theoretical connection between Sidney's *Discourses* and Jefferson's Declaration. And Sidney's explication of natural equality was even more emphatic.

In the *Discourses,* Sidney placed no fewer than eight separate references or discussions asserting, describing, and accentuating the idea that natural equality is the original and rightful condition of humanity. Thomas Jefferson and the Second Continental Congress unmistakably culled from that concept to help advance and justify the cause of American Independence.

### SIDNEY AND GOD-GIVEN UNALIENABLE RIGHTS

In addition to his pronouncement on natural equality, Jefferson's self-evident truths include the axiom that all men are "endowed by their Creator with certain unalienable Rights," principal among them being life and liberty. Here, too, the influence of Sidney is clear and compelling. Doubtless, in the *Discourses,* Sidney addressed the matter extensively and in terms perfectly consistent and almost interchangeable with those written by Jefferson in the Declaration. Sidney wrote:

> I affirm, that the liberty we contend for is granted by God, to every
> man in his own person[8] God is our Lord by right of creation, and our

---

5. Algernon Sidney, *Discourses Concerning Government* (London, Forgotten Books, 2018), 16. Sidney made a slight error here. The quote is indeed from Bellarmine's *De Laicis,* although Bellarmine quoted Pope Gregory I.
6. Ibid., 7.
7. Ibid., 437.
8. Ibid., 78.

only Lord, because he only hath created us[9] Liberty subsists, as arising from the nature of man . . . God only, who confers this right upon us, can deprives us of it[10]

There are, of course, certain contextual distinctions when the quotes are taken in full, and there are many additional relevant excerpts found throughout the work. In fact, the final reference is from a section of the *Discourses* specifically entitled "The liberty of a people is the gift of God and nature."[11] Once more, there exist demonstrable parallels between the *Discourses* and the philosophy of the Declaration's articulation of life and liberty as God-given, unalienable rights.

As to "the pursuit of happiness," Sidney deliberated upon happiness in the *Discourses*, although he considered it in a slightly different sense than Jefferson. More specifically, Sidney considered happiness inclusive of and inseparable from liberty, whereas Jefferson identified and enumerated the "pursuit of happiness" as a separate end in itself. From the *Discourses*:

> A people, in relation to domestic affairs, can desire nothing but liberty, and neither hate or fear any but such as do, or would, as they suspect, deprive them of that happiness.[12]

Whether, in the final analysis, Jefferson's "pursuit of happiness" as an end in itself represents a meaningful deviation from Sidney's definition is improbable, inasmuch as in the absence of liberty, any Jeffersonian "pursuit of happiness" would be rendered chimerical. The consequent implication is that Jefferson and Sidney held identical ideas of happiness, as both must be exclusively based on civil liberty.

## SIDNEY AND GOVERNMENT BY CONSENT

Whereas Sidney presented his convictions in the context of a lengthy philosophical treatise, his treatment of theories, abstractions, and postulates was necessarily more comprehensive and detailed than Jefferson's truncated summary in the Declaration. Accordingly, Sidney's discussion of the evolution and institution of civil government was more nuanced and complete, and it included everything Jefferson also communicated. In particular, the argument expounding upon the establishment and purpose of government is immediately recognizable, as Sidney explained both the progression and meaning of consent as

9. Ibid., 101.
10. Ibid., 406.
11. Ibid.
12. Ibid., 228.

well as the purpose of government in relation to its critical function of protecting life and liberty. Sidney's language of "lives, lands, liberties, and goods" is especially noteworthy. Sidney wrote:

> By this means every number of men, agreeing together, and framing a society, become a complete body, having all power in themselves over themselves, subject to no other human law than their own.[13] I take liberty to say, that whereas there is no form appointed by God or nature, those governments only can be called just, which are established by the consent of nations[14] But if the safety of nations be the end for which governments are instituted, such as take upon them to govern . . . are by the laws of nature bound to procure it; and in order to do this, to preserve the lives, lands, liberties and goods, of every one of their subjects[15] the power which the prince has, be given for the good of the people, and for the defence of every private man's life, liberty, lands, and goods.[16]

Jefferson, of course, argued that government is instituted to secure the God-given, unalienable rights of life and liberty, and that the powers possessed by government are justly exercised only when they emanate and proceed with and by the consent of the people. Sidney advanced identical ideas, although on occasion he preferred the term "nations" (as distinct from the term "nation-state") in place of "the people" or "the governed."

SIDNEY AND THE RIGHT OF REVOLUTION

The right to revolution forms the core of the Declaration, the apotheosis of which is captured by the notion that should government become pernicious or ruinous to its original and designed purposes, "it is the Right of the People to alter or to abolish it." This same right occupies a prominent position in the *Discourses*. Indeed, Sidney considered the right exhaustively, returning to it repeatedly, and was adamant and uncompromising in his advocacy and support of it. From the *Discourses*:

> And we justly conclude, that God having never given the whole world to be governed by one man; nor prescribed any rule for the division of it; nor declared where the right of dividing or subdividing that which every man has should terminate; we may safely affirm, that the whole is forever left to the will and direction of man: we may enter into,

13. Ibid., 76.
14. Ibid., 155.
15. Ibid., 320.
16. Ibid., 351.

form, and continue in, greater or lesser societies, as best please ourselves.[17] If the laws of God and men are therefore of no effect, when the magistracy is left at liberty to break them; and if the lusts of those who are too strong for the tribunals of justice, cannot be otherwise restrained than by sedition, tumults, and war, those seditions, tumults, and wars, are justified by the laws of God and man.[18] Laws and constitutions ought to be weighed, and while all due reverence is paid to such as are good, every nation may not only retain in itself a power of changing or abolishing all such as are not so, but ought to exercise that power according to the best of their understanding, and in the place of what was either at first mistaken or afterwards corrupted, to constitute that which is most conducing to the establishment of justice and liberty.[19] I may justly say, that when nations fall under such princes as are either utterly incapable of making a right use of their power, or do maliciously abuse that authority with which they are entrusted, those nations stand obliged, by the duty they owe to themselves and their posterity, to use the best of their endeavor to remove the evil, whatever danger or difficulties they may meet with in the performance.[20] They who create magistracies, and give to them such name, form, and power as they think fit, do only know, whether the end for which they were created, be performed or not.[21]

Sidney's expositions on the right to revolution were strongly reflected in everything Jefferson wrote in the Declaration on the topic, and were immediately pertinent to the specific historic circumstances of the British American colonies. They also gave Jefferson and the colonists everything they needed in order to morally and intellectually shield themselves against recriminations of treason and rebellion, if not from the British Parliament and Monarchy, then at least from the existing international order.

SIDNEY'S PHRASEOLOGY AND STYLE

There are several noticeable instances in which Jefferson and the Congress appear to have been influenced not only by the substance of Sidney's *Discourses*, but by its style as well. In some cases, it is quite subtle, as when, for example, Sidney wrote, "amend or abolish" and "change or abolish," and Jefferson wrote, "alter or abolish." Other cases are perhaps more pronounced, as when, for example, in the opening paragraph of the Decla-

17. Ibid., 44.
18. Ibid., 174.
19. Ibid., 366.
20. Ibid., 436.
21. Ibid., 438.

ration, Jefferson used the familiar phrase "the Laws of Nature and of Nature's God." By comparison, throughout Sidney's *Discourses*, the closely corresponding phrase "the laws of God and nature" appears repeatedly. In fact, the expression appears on the very first page of the *Discourses*, the very last page, and in a dozen or more instances in between.[22]

There is still another stylistic similarity. In the *Discourses*, the unadorned phrase "the rectitude of their intentions" was used by Sidney, whereas in the Declaration's version it appears as "the rectitude of our intentions." In this instance, it should be noted that this phrase was not used by Jefferson in his original draft, and was included, as with many other edits, at the demand of Congress.[23] And while other members of Congress were certainly familiar with Sidney, it is, of course, entirely possible that that language was simply in common use at the time. Still, the expressions are virtually identical, suggesting the reasonable possibility of Sidney's direct influence.

BEYOND THE DECLARATION

Thomas Jefferson once referred to John Adams as the "Colossus of Independence," and indeed, few of the Founding Fathers were more ardent in their pursuit of American Independence than Adams. Among his more industrious efforts in advancing the cause were the Novanglus essays, written and published in the early months of 1775. In the course of writing thirteen sophisticated political articles advocating the rights of the colonies, Adams referenced Sidney on numerous occasions, and the sixth Novanglus paper quotes lengthy and protracted passages from the *Discourses*. In consequence, and demonstrating his revolutionary zeal, Adams quoted Sidney as follows:

> He that draws his sword against the prince, say the French, ought to throw away the scabbard; for tho' the design be never so just, yet the authors are sure to be ruined if it miscarry. Peace is seldom made, and never kept, unless the subject retain such a power in his hands, as may oblige the prince to stand to what is agreed; and in time some trick is found to deprive them of that benefit.[24]

Adams first became acquainted with Sidney at the youthful age of twenty-four, and never lost his appreciation and admiration for him.

22. Ibid., 3, 462, 46, 73, 75, 81, 87, 127, 128,129, etc.
23. Peterson, *Thomas Jefferson*, 23.
24. John Adams, "To the Inhabitants of the Colony of Massachusetts-Bay," founders.archives.gov/documents/Adams/06-02-02-0072-0007. The quote from Sidney appears on page 173 of the *Discourses*.

In September of 1823, at the age of eighty-eight, Adams wrote to Jefferson:

> I have lately undertaken to read Algernon Sidney on Government there is a great difference in reading a Book at four and twenty, and at Eighty Eight, as often as I have read it; and fumbled it over; it now excites fresh admiration, that this work has excited so little interest in the literary world . . . as for the proof it brings of the bitter sufferings of the advocates of Liberty from that time to this, and to show the slow progress of Moral phylosophical political Illumination in the world ought to be now published in America.[25]

Stephen Hopkins was an esteemed statesman and Founding Father who served as a delegate from Rhode Island in both the First and Second Continental Congresses. He also had a long and distinguished career as both a jurist and a politician, having served as Rhode Island's chief justice and governor. In November of 1764, while serving as governor, he published a twenty-four-page paper opposing the Sugar Act entitled *The Rights of Colonies Examined*. In *The Rights of the Colonies*, Hopkins endeavored to demonstrate the unconstitutionality and severe injustice of Parliament's taxing authority over the colonies by asserting that the colonies, if coerced into obedience, particularly because they were unrepresented in Parliament and therefore could not consent, would be reduced to the condition of slavery. And in making the comparison, he depended on Sidney's definition and theory of liberty and slavery. Hopkins wrote:

> On the contrary, those who are governed at the will of another, or of others, and whose property may be taken from them by taxes, or otherwise, without their own consent, and against their will, are in the miserable condition of slaves: 'For liberty solely consists in an independancy upon the will of another; and by the name of slave, we understand a man who can neither dispose of his person or goods, but enjoys all at the will of his master;' says *Sidney* on government. These things premised; whether the *British American* colonies on the continent, are justly intituled to like privileges and freedom as their fellow-subjects in *Great-Britain* are, shall be the chief point examined.[26]

---

25. John Adams to Thomas Jefferson, September 18, 1823, founders.archives.gov/documents/Adams/99-02-02-7842.

26. Stephen Hopkins, *The Rights of the Colonies Examined*, quod.lib.umich.edu/e/evans/N07846.0001.001/1:2?rgn=div1;view=fulltext(4). The quote from Sidney appears on page 12 of the *Discourses*.

Hopkins, then, a brilliant legal mind in his own right, premised his precepts and protests of the Sugar Act squarely on Sidney's *Discourses*. *The Rights of the Colonies* was an efficacious and distinctively successful pamphlet, and it earned widespread acclaim throughout the colonies, including effusive praise from Thomas Hutchinson, the Lieutenant Governor, and later Governor, of Massachusetts. In point of fact, *The Rights of the Colonies* was so highly regarded that it remained a source of anti-authoritarianism for years and was relied upon extensively by the anti-federalists as a means to impose interpretive control of the taxing authority of the United States Congress under the Constitution.[27]

And to the distinguished list of American Patriots such as Hopkins, Adams, Franklin, and Jefferson, could be added James Otis, Arthur Lee, Johnathan Mayhew, and Josiah Quincy Jr., whose admiration of Sidney was manifest, with Quincy even designating Sidney's works to be bequeathed to his son in his will.[28]

CONCLUSION

When discussions of the ideological influences of the Revolution proceed past American sources and figures, they are most often directed towards John Locke and his *Two Treatises of Government*. Algernon Sidney is sometimes referenced, no doubt; but it is generally far less common to have the particulars and fullness of his contributions examined. This in itself is a curiosity, as while both Locke and Sidney advanced similar reformist ideals and Whiggish ambitions, Sidney's work was more thorough and almost certainly preceded Locke's (although not by date of publication). In the final analysis, however, Algernon Sidney is doubtless well worthy of recognition as one of the true moral, intellectual, and philosophical luminaries of the American Revolution.

27. Bernard Bailyn, *The Ideological Origins of the American Revolution* (Cambridge, MA: Harvard University Press, 1992), 344.
28. Robbins, "Algernon Sidney's Discourses," 267-296, 270.

# Charles Lee: The Continental Army's Most Prolific Essayist General

**GENE PROCKNOW**

Many contemporaries and historians overlooked Maj. Gen. Charles Lee's substantial literary contributions to the American independence movement because he challenged Gen. George Washington for Continental Army leadership and the 1860 discovery of a potentially treasonous document.[1] Initially, Revolutionary Era Americans viewed Charles Lee as a highly accomplished military officer and a learned scholar and admired his ardently-argued republican political beliefs. Don Higginbotham, a twentieth-century historian, asserts that Lee was a "genuinely talented soldier" whose "star shown brighter than Washington" during the first year of the war.[2] However, after his 1778 clash with Washington on the Monmouth battlefield, Lee's reputation nosedived, and Congress cashiered him from the Continental Army. As a result, historians focus on Lee's fall from grace, lack of social manners, and undesirable personal affectations, thereby underestimating his discerning political insights and highly cultivated intellect.

Building upon an English grammar school education, Lee developed into a lifelong reader, amassing an extensive book collection, portions of which traveled with him during his many military campaigns.[3]

---

1. Readers interested in the debate over Lee's Continental Army military career should consult Christian McBurney's *George Washington's Nemesis* and Mark Edward Lender and Garry Wheeler Stone's *Fatal Sunday* for opposing views on Lee's treason but a consistent assessment of his Monmouth battlefield performance.
2. Don Higginbotham, *The War of American Independence Military Attitudes, Policies, and Practice, 1763-1789* (Norwalk, CT: The Easton Press, 1971), 92.
3. Lee biographer John Alden provides the best description of Lee's formal education and reading habits, John Richard Alden, *General Charles Lee Traitor or Patriot?* (Baton Rouge: Louisiana State University Press, 1951), 3–4.

In addition, he possessed a gift for languages and regularly inserted quotes and commentary from Greek and Roman antiquity into his writing. For example, Lee corresponded with the King of Poland, employing classical illusions and receiving replies written in French.[4] A few months before hostilities broke out at Lexington and Concord in April 1775, Lee wrote two prominent "page one" newspaper articles. In the first, he vociferously attacked Gen. Thomas Gage's Boston occupation policies.[5] In the second, he cleverly used the colonial example of the Mediterranean island of Minorca to demonstrate that King George III would unjustly use physical force to subdue American colonists.[6] Additionally, Lee corresponded with prominent politicians and intellectuals, including Edmund Burke, David Hume, Benjamin Franklin, and a wide range of American and British politicians advocating anti-Tory, Whig, or republican views. Lee's artful polemic skills generated a convincing "resistance to tyranny" reputation among the American public.

As a result of his scholarly pursuits, Lee was the most prolific author among the Continental Army generals and the only one to write a pamphlet advocating the Rebel cause before the war.[7] Two political essays stand out as the best examples of Lee's scholarship, bookending his participation in the American Revolutionary War. The first essay, written before the outbreak of hostilities, bolstered American confidence that its soldiers could stand up to and defeat the British military. The second article presented a utopian plan to build a western American military colony late in the war to avoid, in Lee's view, the Rebel government's missteps.

Soon after emigrating to America, Lee wrote the first pamphlet, *Strictures, on a pamphlet, entitled "A friendly address to all reasonable Americans, on the subject of our political confusion:" Addressed to the people of America*.[8] Lee published the essay in response to a pamphlet by Rev. Thomas Bradbury Chandler. The cleric argued that Britain had the

4. Charles Lee, *The Lee Papers*, ed. Henry Edward Bunbury (New York: New York Historical Society, 1872), 1:55-59, 62-4.
5. Charles Lee, "Queries Proposed to General Gage, and Which If He Does Not Think It Consistent with Prudence Publicly, Be It Earnestly Requested to Resolve in His Own Breast," *Pennsylvania Journal, or Weekly Advertiser*, January 18, 1775, 1.
6. Charles Lee, "To Mr. Purdie," *Virginia Gazette* (Purdie), February 24, 1775, 1.
7. For example, Charles Lee is the only Continental Army General who authored an essay in Gordon Wood's voluminous compendium of Revolutionary Era pamphlets. Gordon S. Wood, ed., *The American Revolution: Writings from the Pamphlet Debate* (New York: Library of America, 2015), 2:379-410.
8. Lee, *The Lee Papers*, 1:151-66.

power to tax tea and warned that the total weight of the mighty British Empire would fall upon any violent dissent.[9] Loyalist printer James Rivington first advertised Chandler's essay for sale on November 10, 1774, sparking notoriety and vocal outrage.[10]

While the responding *Strictures* pamphlet was unsigned, Lee made it known that he was the author. For example, in a letter to Dr. Benjamin Rush Lee expressed indignation "that the miscreant Rivington is suffer'd to heap insult on the Congress with impunity" for publishing Chandler's loyalist missive.[11] One ad for a *Strictures* reprint identified the author as "a celebrated MILITARY OFFICER, who is a regular Soldier."[12] Another advertisement characterized Lee as "a certain regular officer of Distinction, who has approved himself a warm Advocate for the Liberties of America."[13] As a result of Lee's growing reputation, many in the general public recognized Lee's authorship.

In his essay, Lee demonstrated his Whiggish republican political beliefs by allying with those Americans opposing the Coercive Acts and arbitrary rule by the Tory-dominated Parliament over the American colonies. Initially focusing on Chandler's ecclesiastical connections, Lee railed against the priest, who possessed "a zeal of arbitrary power" and "has a want of candour and truth" as a "high part of the Church of England." In addition, Lee criticized the pecuniary-minded Anglican leaders who "wallow in sinecures and benefices helped from the fruits of your labor." Finally, he countered Chandler's political arguments for American subservience and counseled the Americans that their cause was just. Lee characterized Parliament's right to impose a duty on tea based on "audaciously false assertions and "monstrous absurdities."[14]

Lee spied an opening to display his soldierly skills by asserting that the colonists should not fear British military might. On the contrary, he believed that British military commanders underestimated American courage. Unlike the British regulars, Lee argued that the Americans knew how to fight in North America's rugged terrain. He estimated

9. Thomas Bradbury Chandler, *A Friendly Address to All Reasonable Americans, on the Subject of Our Political Confusions: In Which the Necessary Consequences of Violently Opposing the King's Troops, and of a General Non-Importation Are Fairly Stated* (Boston, 1774), Evans Early American Imprint Collection, name.umdl.umich.edu/N10432.0001.001.
10. "This Day Is Published, Price Eighteen Pence, A Friendly Address to All Reasonable Americans," *Rivington's New-York Gazetteer*, November 10, 1774, 82, 3.
11. Lee, *The Lee Papers*, 1:143-4.
12. "Just Published, and to Be SOLD, by the Printer Hereof," *Newport Mercury*, January 16, 1775, 4.
13. "Just Published," *Providence Gazette*, January 28, 1775, 4.
14. Lee, *The Lee Papers*, 1:155.

that the Americans could raise two hundred thousand yeoman soldiers who would vastly outnumber any British army sent to put down a rebellion. Also, Lee dismissed any British attempt to supplement their forces by hiring German troops as doomed to fail. He believed that if "ten thousand could possibly be transported to-morrow ... that in less than four months, not two of these ten thousand would remain with their colours."[15]

Further, he reported that the British soldiers were generally unfit for duty and possessed low morale. Similarly, Lee disparagingly observed that the 1775 British Army officers didn't measure up to Gen. James Wolfe, the heroic conqueror of Quebec, whom he viewed as liberal and virtuous. While the Americans lacked trained military officers, he believed that civilians such as "country gentlemen, civilians, lawyers, and farmers" could ably serve just as they did in Parliament's army during the English Civil War. Finally, he advocated that the Americans prepare for armed conflict if the British government did not back down, offering, "to keep the swords of your enemies in their scabbards, you must whet your own."[16] Lee closed with a rhetorical flourish exhorting the Americans as "brave citizens, with invoking the Almighty God, from who all virtues flow, to continue you in that spirit of unanimity and vigor which must insure your success, and immortalize you through all ages, as the champions and patrons of the human race."[17]

Lee made a compelling case that the Americans should not fear British military power as they could field a larger army of better soldiers led by more competent officers. Lee's essay became an immediate publishing success. At least five printers widely advertised its sale as a separate monograph.[18] One publisher observed that the pamphlet "contains particular Military Directions, worthy to be put in Practice by ALL AMERICANS."[19] A Salem, Massachusetts newspaper editor characterized Lee's essay as bringing "honour to the author as a soldier and a writer." To further mass distribution, Massachusetts printer Isaiah Thomas reduced the price to two coppers and even offered gratis to those who could not afford it. Further demonstrating public interest, several New England and Middle Atlantic newspapers reprinted Lee's

---

15. Ibid., 1:158.
16. Ibid., 1:165.
17. Ibid., 1:166.
18. The five publishers are William and Thomas Bradford (Philadelphia), Noel and Hazard (New York City), Isaiah Thomas (Boston), T. Green (New London, CT), and unnamed (Providence, RI).
19. "This Day Published," *Boston Post-Boy*, January 9, 1775, 4.

work in part or whole.[20] As a result of widespread public acceptance, rebellious-minded leaders took notice.

Dr. Benjamin Rush viewed Lee as a "genius" with "great attainment in classical learning and in modern languages" who "was useful in the beginning of the war by inspiring our citizens with military ideas and lessening in our soldiers their superstitious fear of the valor and discipline of the British army."[21] Benjamin Franklin recognized Lee's rhetorical skills and sought to introduce Thomas Paine to Lee as "I know his sentiments are not very different from yours."[22] While there is no evidence that his writing directly influenced Paine, Lee was the first to characterize America as the "asylum of liberty" in a letter to Samuel Adams.[23] Additionally, the revolutionary firebrand asserted that Lee "has heartily espoused the Cause of America" with "integrity" in a letter to James Warren, the President of the Massachusetts Provincial Congress.[24] Abigail Adams summed up Lee's literary abilities but added a knock on his social skills: "The eloquence of his pen far exceeds that of his person."[25] While many contemporaries also pointed out Lee's impolite social manners, political leaders and the general public demonstrated a high regard for his character and intellect.

After composing *Strictures on a pamphlet*, Lee continued to write newspaper articles advocating resistance to the British and became one of the first to advocate for American independence.[26] After the Battle of Bunker Hill, the Continental Congress named Lee the second-highest-ranked major general after Artemas Ward in the first tranche of general officer commissions under George Washington's overall command. While serving under Washington during the Siege of Boston, Lee operated as Congress's troubleshooter and independent com-

---

20. At least four newspapers reprinted Lee's "Strictures" essay including the *Massachusetts Spy, Essex Gazette* (Salem, MA), *Virginia Gazette* (Purdie), and *Connecticut Courant*.

21. Benjamin Rush, *The Autobiography of Benjamin Rush: His Travels through Life Together with His Commonplace Book for 1789-1813*, ed. George Washington Corner (Westport, CT: Greenwood Press, 1970), 155–56.

22. Benjamin Franklin to Charles Lee, February 19, 1776, Lee, *The Lee Papers*, 313.

23. Charles Lee to Samuel Adams, Newport, Rhode Island, July 21, 1774, digitalcollections.nypl.org/items/800441f0-1157-0134-2211-0050568a51c.

24. Samuel Adams to Joseph Warren, June 20, 1775, in *Letters of the Delegates to Congress*, 25 vols., ed. Paul H. Smith (Washington, DC: Library of Congress, 1976–1998), 1:553

25. Abigail Adams to John Adams, July 16, 1775, www.masshist.org/digitaladams/archive/doc?id=L17750716aa&bc=%2Fdigitaladams%2Farchive%2Fbrowse%2Fletters_1774_1777.php.

26. Phillip Papas, *Renegade Revolutionary: The Life of General Charles Lee* (New York: New York University Press, 2014), 105.

mander in Rhode Island, Canada, New York City, and the South. While Lee's military career started well, a British cavalry patrol captured a careless Lee while transiting New Jersey and held him as a high-value captive for over a year. After a prisoner exchange, Lee returned to the Continental Army. However, a public tiff with Washington and subsequent court-martial cut short his military career, and Lee returned to his home in western Virginia.

Dismissal from the Continental Army did not end Lee's literary career. As a private citizen, Lee continued to prepare political essays, albeit to a smaller and less receptive audience. In a letter to his friend and fellow former British officer, Maj. Gen. Horatio Gates Lee attached a quixotic plan to establish an extensive military colony in western America. The settlement would apportion land by rank, with sizeable areas reserved for common use. Land ownership would be limited to a maximum of five thousand acres. He proposed a strong militia backed by small, professional cavalry and artillery units consistent with Lee's previous Continental Army recommendations. Religious practices would be encouraged because "without religion, no warlike community can exist; and with religion, if it is pure and unsophisticated, all immortalities are incompatible." Other features of Lee's liberal community included speech free from government control, personal daily ablutions "as practiced in the religions of the East," simple laws obviating the need for lawyers, and bountiful trade with neighbors, including an annual three-week to a month great fair.[27] Despite extensive interactions with various Native peoples during the French and Indian War, he did not address how to secure the western lands from the current residents.

While Lee's *Strictures* essay received widespread publicity and public acclaim, the military colony proposal never entered the public discourse. The concept of a military colony was the work of a distraught person who suffered from increasing health and financial issues. By considering a new society, Lee continued his search for a community that reflected his political views, which started in Britain, Poland, and Eastern Europe and continued in America. But he never located the political and intellectual home he hunted for, perhaps overly iconoclastically.

In Lee's lifetime of authorship, he presented two consistent themes. First, he opposed autocratic or monarchial power, professing stridently republican rule. In Lee's view, by advocating for these rights in America, he was also fighting for the same rights in Britain. Conversely, Lee viewed that the British people could not enjoy republican rights while

27. Lee, *The Lee Papers*, 3:323–330.

suppressing similar rights in America. Consistent with contemporaries, Lee's definition of republican government excluded many people, such as non-white people and women.

Second, Lee offered warnings of governmental abuses of power, resonating with like-minded Congressional members. For example, he advocated citizen soldiers as he was wary of standing armies and recommended leadership rotation as he opposed long-tenured politicians and generals. Lee's politics almost saved him from dismissal from the army after his court-martial. Lee's congressional support emanated from his republican views shared by the more populous, small national government members such as Samuel Adams, Edward Langworthy, and Benjamin Rush. A Lee biographer and noted American Revolution historian, John Alden, asserts Lee retained significant congressional support and the vote to confirm the court-martial sentence was "far from unanimous." It would have been much closer if all members of Congress voted; several absented themselves on purpose to avoid voting against Washington.[28]

Charles Lee did not live to see a military colony or American independence, passing away in Philadelphia on October 2, 1782. Despite lingering doubts about his loyalty, he died enjoying deep friendships with a broad range of political leaders and military officers. A notable example, writing late in life, John Adams reflected on Lee's Revolutionary era contributions and republican views. He characterized Lee as "a kind of Precursor of Miranda," the enlightened, adventurous, and iconic South American Revolutionary leader. Continuing, Adams concluded that Lee generated "Enthusiasm and made as many Proselytes and Partisans" as patricians John Hancock and George Washington.[29] While Congressional leaders, including John Adams, did not want to replace Washington, Lee retained the durable support of republican-leaning politicians who valued his populist principles.

---

28. Alden, *General Charles Lee Traitor or Patriot?*, 253–54.

29. John Adams to James Lloyd, April 24, 1815, founders.archives.gov/documents/Adams/99-02-026460.

# Reframing George Washington's Clothing at the Second Continental Congress

**SHAWN DAVID MCGHEE**

Dressed in defiance, Col. George Washington arrived at each session of the Second Continental Congress donning a new buff and blue uniform he helped design with fellow Virginian George Mason.[1] Washington, a staunch but cautious Whig, fully embraced the American cause and, incredibly, his military exploits from the French and Indian War roughly two decades earlier thrust him to the crest of public affairs during the Coercive Acts Crisis.[2] As the empire's political turmoil escalated into a military crisis, six Virginia counties sought the colonel's martial leadership in preparation for potential civil conflict.[3] When John Adams endorsed Washington to lead the Continental forces on June 15, 1775, the Virginian exited the room to allow delegates political space to deliberate this touchy but necessary development.[4] The fol-

1. For George Washington's costume at the Second Continental Congress, see John Adams to Abigail Adams, May 29, 1775, in Lyman H. Butterfield, et al., eds., *The Papers of John Adams: Family Correspondence*, 15 vols. (Cambridge: Harvard University Press, 1963-2022), 1:207-8; For the design of the uniform, see George Mason to George Washington, February 6, 1775, in W.W. Abbott and Dorothy Twohig, eds., *The Papers of George Washington: Colonial Series*, 10 vols. (Charlottesville: University of Virginia Press, 1983-95), 10:21.
2. Silas Deane to Mrs. Deane, September 9, 1774, in Edmund C. Burnett, et al., eds., *Letters of the Members of the Continental Congress*, 24 vols. (Washington, D.C.: Carnegie Institute of Washington, 1921-36), 1:28; Joseph Ellis, *His Excellency: George Washington* (New York: Alfred A. Knopf, 2004), 18-35; John Ferling, *The Ascent of George Washington: The Hidden Political Genius of an American Icon* (New York: Bloomsbury Press, 2009), 98-99.
3. David Ammerman, *In the Common Cause: American Response to the Coercive Acts of 1774* (New York: W.W. Norton & Company, 1974), 142-44; Lawrence Delbert Cress, *Citizens in Arms: The Army and Militia in American Society to the War of 1812* (Chapel Hill: University of North Carolina Press, 1982), 49-50.
4. John Adams, Autobiography, in L.H. Butterfield, ed., *The Adams Papers: Diary and Autobiography of John Adams*, 4 vols. (Cambridge: Harvard University Press, 1961), 3:321-24.

lowing day, Washington accepted his unanimous nomination, meta-morphizing from provincial colonel to commander-in-chief of the Continental army. He offered a carefully worded address to Congress, declaring "I do not think myself equal to the Command I am honored with."[5] To the fiddle-playing fire-breather Patrick Henry, Washington predicted his nomination marked "the ruin of my reputation."[6] The newly-minted general next lamented to his wife that, "far from seeking this appointment I have used every endeavor in my power to avoid it."[7] Writing to his brother-in-law, he described his recent promotion as "an honor I by no means aspired to."[8] Historians have yet to adequately reconcile this discordant sequence of events. If Washington did not think himself qualified to lead an army and feared reputational ruin, why did he attend Congress immaculately clad in his war robes?

Some scholars simply write this affair off as disingenuous behavior on Washington's part; others rationalize it as naked ambition followed by calculated damage control.[9] But why have academics yet refused to take Washington at his word? In a broader sense, the British Empire was about to sink into civil war, naturally making this episode appear trivial by comparison.[10] Yet Washington's sartorial choices at Congress reveal a lost mental landscape that helped shape his character, inform his behavior and instill in him a calculated (if cold) shrewdness. This

5. Address to the Continental Congress, June 16, 1775, in Philander D. Chase, ed., *The Papers of George Washington: Revolutionary War Series*, 28 vols. (Charlottesville: University of Virginia Press, 1985- ), 1:1-3.

6. For Patrick Henry's affinity for playing the fiddle, see Thomas Jefferson to William Wirt, August 5, 1815, in J. Jefferson Looney, ed., *The Papers of Thomas Jefferson: Retirement Series*, 16 vols. (Princeton: Princeton University Press, 2004- ), 8:646; See also Richard R. Beeman, "The Democratic Faith of Patrick Henry," *Virginia Magazine of History and Biography* 95, no. 3 (1987): 313; For Washington's conversation with Patrick Henry, see George W. Corner, ed., *The Autobiography of Benjamin Rush* (Princeton, NJ: Princeton University Press, 1948), 113.

7. George Washington to Martha Washington, June 18, 1775, Chase, *Papers of George Washington*, 1:3-6.

8. George Washington to Burrell Basset, June 19, 1775, ibid., 1:12-14.

9. Ellis, *His Excellency*, 67-72; Ferling, *Ascent of Washington*, 85-89; For more nuanced coverage, see Peter Henriques, *Realistic Visionary: A Portrait of George Washington* (Charlottesville: University of Virginia Press, 2006), 39-43.

10. Some standard surveys of the American Revolution include Bernard Bailyn, *The Ideological Origins of the American Revolution* (Cambridge: Harvard University Press, 1967); Pauline Maier, *From Resistance to Revolution: Colonial Radicals and the Development of American Opposition to Britain, 1765-1776* (New York: W. W. Norton & Company, 1972); Robert Middlekauff, *The Glorious Cause: The American Revolution, 1763-1789* (New York: Oxford University Press, 1982); Gordon S. Wood, *The Radicalism of the American Revolution* (New York: Vintage Books, 1991); T. H. Breen, *The Marketplace of Revolution: How Consumer Politics Shaped American Independence* (New York: Oxford, 2004).

landscape formed in the mortal uncertainty of eighteenth-century colonial Virginia and matured on that colony's violent western frontier in the heat of imperial conflict during the 1750s. As a young provincial soldier, Washington came to view military attire as a signal of martial solidarity and military potency. Some twenty years later, this vision translated, however imperfectly, to America's ideological frontier on the eve of the American Revolution. By the time the empire experienced its final convulsion, colonists had already incorporated clothing into their political lexicon. Revolutionary Americans' wardrobes transmitted to observers certain personal details, such as political persuasion, social class and even occupation. Yet military attire alone communicated the aforementioned qualities as well as a preparedness for organized violence. At Congress, Washington revealed his politics, martial proficiency and soldier's temper without having to utter a word; his uniform spoke for him.

George Washington's pursuit of a soldier's life resulted from familial misfortune as much as inspiration. When his father died in 1743, the boy lost access to the English education that helped refine and prepare his older half-brothers, Lawrence and Augustine, for Virginia's deeply hierarchical society.[11] In this environment, where settlers calculated virtually every distinction, this lost opportunity severely limited young George's future career options.[12] Thereafter, eldest sibling Lawrence became the most influential man in George's life and likely roused in him a desire to embark on a military path.[13] The former had served in Admiral Edward Vernon's 1741 attack on Cartagena during the War of Jenkins's Ear, miraculously surviving Britain's devastating casualties. Lawrence returned home with the social currency of a veteran and, perhaps as a result, received from Lt. Gov. William Gooch a commission as major in the Old Dominion's provincial forces.[14] In July 1743, Lawrence married into the powerful Fairfax family, firmly planting himself in the upper crust of Virginia's aristocracy. He next stood for and won election to the House of Burgesses in 1744 from Fairfax County.[15] Lawrence's careful social maneuvering combined with his

11. Rhys Isaac, *The Transformation of Virginia, 1740-1790* (Chapel Hill: University of North Carolina Press, 1982); Peter Henriques, *First and Always: A New Portrait of George Washington* (Charlottesville: University of Virginia Press, 2020), 23.

12. Ferling, *Ascent of Washington*, 9-10.

13. Ibid., 10-12.

14. Peter R. Henriques, "Major Lawrence Washington versus the Reverend Charles Green: A Case Study of the Squire and the Parson," *Virginia Magazine of History and Biography* 100, no. 2 (1992): 233-64.

15. Ibid.

public service credentials advanced the Washingtons to the nexus of Virginia's political and military elite.[16] Twelve-year-old George no doubt absorbed and admired the martial substance and accompanying gravity of consequence, into which his brother and extended family ushered him. He also sought to emulate Lawrence's career path so far as he could.

At fifteen, George hoped to follow in Lawrence's footsteps by enlisting in the British navy.[17] Yet the former's mother, Mary Ball Washington, harbored grave misgivings about this potentiality. More than a little familiar with the staggering death toll suffered under Admiral Vernon, she asked her brother, Joseph Ball, about her son's maritime fantasies. Ball responded in a way that would have caused any white Virginian to recoil in horror, warning that the British navy would corporeally disfigure her son and "use him like a Negro, or rather, like a dog."[18] One can only imagine Mary Washington configuring this bigoted, degrading and horrific conflation onto her first-born child. Needless to say, George's naval career ended before it began.[19] However, after Lawrence's untimely death in 1752, the younger Washington found a home in the Virginia militia.[20]

In February 1753, Washington accepted a commission from Lt. Gov. Robert Dinwiddie as major in the provincial militia.[21] That October, Dinwiddie sent him into the contested western frontier on a sensitive mission to assess French military strength and warn out Louis XV's soldiers from the region.[22] The governor provided Washington a passport demanding all His Majesty's subjects and allies assist the new major with his "Business of great Importance."[23] When the ambitious

16. Ferling, *Ascent of Washington*, 12-13.

17. Ellis, *His Excellency*, 9.

18. Joseph Ball to Mary Ball Washington, May 19, 1747, in Donald Jackson, ed., *The Diaries of George Washington*, 6 vols. (Charlottesville: University of Virginia Press, 1976-79), 1:1-5; Ferling, *Ascent of Washington*, 12.

19. Henriques, *First and Always*, 27-28.

20. Henriques, "Major Lawrence Washington versus the Reverend Charles Green."

21. For Washington's appointment, see founders.archives.gov/documents/Washington/01-01-02-0001-0001; For the socio-political context of this appointment, see Ferling, *Ascent of Washington*, 13.

22. Instructions from Robert Dinwiddie, October 30, 1753 in Abbott and Twohig, *Papers of Washington: Colonial Series*, 1:7, 60-61; See also George Washington, Diary, October 31, 1753, in Dorothy Twohig, ed., *George Washington's Diaries: An Abridgement* (Charlottesville: University of Virginia Press, 1999), 17-18; For political context see Fred Anderson, *Crucible of War: The Seven Years' War and the Fate of Empire in British North America, 1754-1766* (New York: Vintage, 2000), 43.

23. Passport from Robert Dinwiddie, October 30, 1753, in Abbott and Twohig, *Papers of Washington: Colonial Series*, 1:62.

Virginian returned to Williamsburg (narrowly escaping death on at least two occasions), his adventurous account so thoroughly impressed Dinwiddie that the governor had it published and promoted the young major to lieutenant colonel of the new Virginia Regiment.[24] The governor next sent Washington back into the interior to enhance his colony's defense in the face of an encroaching French menace. Drawing out the very real possibility of violent resistance to this mission, Dinwiddie instructed Washington to "kill & destroy" any opposition.[25] Within these dangerous frontier spaces, Washington began to appreciate the critical importance and visual power of costume during moments of profound crisis.

George Washington became aware of the etiquette of clothing at a young age. In his handwritten copy of "Rules of Civility and Decent Behavior in Company and Conversation," for example, he learned to keep his clothes "Brush'd" and "orderly with respect to times and places."[26] Mary Ball Washington's own keen interest in fabrics and fashion also likely influenced her son; whether foxhunting, surveying his plantations on horseback, or dancing, he strategically selected his wardrobe for maximum effect.[27] Washington's adept use of clothes reveals his sensitivity for their social value and performative potential. And as he prepared to lead the Virginia Regiment into contested territory, his appreciation for both the practical and theatrical value of costume evolved further.

After confronting his recruits' material paucity shortly before departing for the frontier, Washington began a frantic exchange with Governor Dinwiddie. Washington agonized over "the great necessity for Cloathing the men," and apprised that few possessed a coat, others needed shoes, and others still wanted for stockings or a shirt. To his dismay, most were "as illy provided as can well be conceiv'd." From a practical perspective, Washington reasoned his regiment's impoverished condition rendered it incapable of military service. Unclothed men "must unavoidably be expos'd to inclement weather in their Marches" and risked encountering "every difficulty that's incident to a Soldier's life."[28] He feared that poorly equipped men subjected to harsh condi-

24. Journey to the French Commandant: Narrative, in Jackson, *Diaries of Washington*, 1:130-61; See also *Maryland Gazette*, March, 21, 1754; *Boston Gazette*, April 16, 1754.

25. Robert Dinwiddie to George Washington, January 1754, in Abbott and Twohig, *Papers of Washington: Colonial Series*, 1:63-67.

26. Charles Moore, ed., *George Washington's Rules of Civility, and Decent Behavior in Company and Conversation* (Boston: Houghton & Mifflin Company, 1926), 11.

27. Henriques, *First and Always*, 26-27, 156-57.

28. George Washington to Robert Dinwiddie, March 9, 1754, in Abbott and Twohig, *Papers of Washington: Colonial Series*, 1:73-75.

Left, portrait of George Washington by Charles Willson Peale, 1772, detail. (*Washington and Lee University*) Right, George Washington at the Battle of Princeton by Charles Willson Peale, 1776, detail. (*Metropolitan Museum of Art*)

tions in an unforgiving environment ran a higher risk of sickness, injury or death. And on the western edge of the British Empire, little relief or asylum awaited provincials exposed to such dangers.[29] After rationalizing the utilitarian benefits of military attire, Washington next offered Dinwiddie a perceptive analysis of its theatrical value.

From Lieutenant Colonel Washington's perspective, uniforms provided soldiers an overlooked psychological advantage. He explained to Governor Dinwiddie that Native Americans judged men by appearance. "It is the Nature of Indians," he lectured the governor, "to be struck with and taken by show." To further bolster his position, Washington claimed Native warriors despised and ridiculed common French soldiers for their "shabby and ragged appearance." In contrast, he reasoned a uniformed Virginia regiment would impress, intimidate and perhaps even shock into submission an otherwise aggressive Indian threat. Men outfitted in the cloaks of war, he theorized, presented "a much higher Conception of . . . Power and Greatness" to potential enemies. He assured Dinwiddie that he had drawn his conclusions about Native Americans from careful "Study of their Tempers," which laid

---

29. Washington and his men were all too aware of this alarming reality. One example is George Washington to John Robinson, August 5, 1756, in ibid., 3:323-33.

bare their "Customs and dispositions." This potential theatrical edge, the lieutenant colonel assured the governor, would outweigh any hardships undertaken in procuring uniforms.[30]

If Dinwiddie had any doubts left about the psychological advantages of military garb, Washington next offered some grizzled frontier wisdom: Uniforms gave men confidence and self-worth and demarcated soldiers from citizens. He desired for each man to wear a "Coat of the Coursest red," since his subordinates likened red to blood and considered either form of that hue as "the distinguishing marks of Warriours and great Men."[31] Standardized costume, Washington argued, telegraphed unity of purpose and a proficiency in organized violence.[32] Dinwiddie agreed, responding, "I have no Objection to the Soldiers being in an uniform Dress, on the Head you propose."[33] Uniforms, then, provided protection from the natural environment and suggested skill in coordinated brutality, a combination of the practical and theatrical.

Whether griping over a need for clothes, recording their relative availability or simply taking inventory, Washington's mind remained firmly engrossed in the functional and psychological advantages of costume on the frontier: Soldiers were safer, more confident and appeared stronger when properly outfitted. Washington rarely lost sight of the value of clothes, though on one occasion he did lose clothes of value on the frontier. In May 1754, the frustrated lieutenant colonel recounted to Col. Joshua Fry a bungled moment of improvised frontier diplomacy. Washington explained that one of his Native rangers refused to continue a reconnaissance mission until the Virginia officer promised him a "shirt . . . and a watch-coat," the latter referring to a military overcoat. An exasperated Washington agreed and begrudgingly withdrew the prized items from his personal wardrobe. He then urged Fry to invest in attractive "treaty goods" since Natives had "come to expect presents." Indian friendship, assessed Washington, "is not so warm" and "must be bought."[34] He strongly advised Fry to keep on hand some disposable gifts or risk losing critical military attire. Shortly afterward, Washington ordered a replacement coat from England fashioned from "rich crimson" and fitted with gold buttons.[35] This expensive purchase,

30. George Washington to Robert Dinwiddie, March 7, 1754, in ibid., 1:71-73.
31. Ibid.
32. Ibid.
33. Robert Dinwiddie to George Washington, March 15, 1754, in ibid., 1:75-77.
34. George Washington to Joshua Fry, May 23, 1754, in ibid., 1:100-102.
35. Invoice, October 23, 1754, in ibid., 1:217.

he no doubt understood, projected his status and capabilities as both soldier and leader.

Washington resigned from his regiment in 1758 and next joined Virginia's House of Burgesses where he emerged as a sharp critic of Parliament's taxation designs during the imperial crisis period.[36] "Americans," he thundered, "will never be tax'd without their own consent," reasoning Parliament had "no more right to put their hands into my pocket, without my consent, than I have to put my hands in your's, for money."[37] His military experience and Whig principles inspired constituents to include him in Virginia's delegation to the "Grand Continental Congress" in 1774.[38] When Washington arrived at Philadelphia for that assembly's convening, his frontier experiences, far from being unknown or forgotten, became the talk of the town. Connecticut delegate Silas Deane, for example, associated Washington with saving the panicked remains of Gen. Edward Braddock's "unfortunate army." He also repeated a circulating tall tale that had Washington volunteering to raise and lead an army at his own expense to liberate the colonies from British oppression.[39] Visiting medical student Solomon Drowne described Washington as "Virginia's Hero" and recorded yet another yarn that claimed Washington "wished to God" the fate of American liberty could be decided by "a single combat between himself" and King George III.[40] Despite his celebrity, delegates did not appoint Washington to any of Congress's special committees and the record is silent on any intellectual contributions he may have offered. Chronically insecure over what he described as "a defective education," he felt more comfortable listening to others' thoughts than divulging his own.[41] When Washington left Mount Vernon to attend the Second Continental Congress, however, he returned to Philadelphia educated in that assembly's deliberative culture.

---

36. Ferling, *Ascent of Washington*, 68-71.
37. George Washington to William Fairfax, June 10, 1774, to Bryan Fairfax, August 24, 1774, in John Rhodehamel, ed., *George Washington: Writings*, 150, 155-56.
38. Enthusiastic colonists referred to the First Continental Congress by this moniker. Some examples include *Newport Mercury*, August 15, 1774; *New-Hampshire Gazette*, August 12, 1774.
39. Silas Deane to Mrs. Deane, September 9, 1774, in Burnett, *Letters of Members*, 1:28.
40. "Solomon Drowne, Jr., to Solomon Drowne, Sr., October 5, 1774," in *Pennsylvania Magazine of History and Biography* 48, no. 3 (1924): 231-33.
41. George Washington to David Humphreys, July 25, 1785, in W.W. Abbot, ed., *The Papers of George Washington: Confederation Series*, 6 vols. (Charlottesville: University of Virginia, 1992-97), 3:148-51.

A large crowd gathered to fete Washington upon his arrival at Philadelphia and the Virginian looked every bit the part of veteran-protector.[42] "Coll. Washington appears at Congress in his Uniform," marveled John Adams, and "by his great Experience and Abilities in military Matters, is of much service to Us."[43] In recognition of both the rapidly deteriorating political circumstances and Washington's obvious strengths, Congress appointed him to its premier military committees.[44] Washington's costume partially helped him circumvent his educational insecurities, as his attire expressed to delegates his willingness to secure American liberty by force if necessary. During every debate, meal and fraternal engagement, Washington said plenty without having to utter as much as a syllable. He did not need to wear his uniform to remind delegates of his military pedigree; clearly few had forgotten his frontier bravery. And he did not wear it to posture for position: His attire simply revealed his uncompromising politics and experience in the military arts. Combined, Washington's costume communicated his readiness to resort to violence to achieve his political objectives.

Historian Peter Henriques correctly described Washington as "a master at lowering and then exceeding expectations."[45] When the Virginian accepted his nomination for commander-in-chief, he skillfully set the conditions for that appointment. He publicized his self-assessed shortcomings and expressed fear his reputation might suffer as a result of them. This new role required him to lead more men, defend more geography and consider more logistical and administrative demands than during his frontier years. And from the doorstep of the Pennsylvania State House, a complete and humiliating American military failure loomed as the most likely outcome of any potential civil conflict. In the face of such grim odds, Washington seized control of the narrative. In the unlikelihood of a hard-earned success, he could claim to have defied the odds. But even in the likelihood of failure, he could declare with verity to have resisted British oppression, in spite of the long odds, to the best of his abilities. And once Washington accepted command, he ordered a new uniform from a Philadelphia tailor to reinforce

---

42. Henriques, *Realistic Visionary*, 37.
43. John Adams to Abigail Adams, May 29, 1775, in Butterfield, et al, *Adams Papers: Family Correspondence*, 1:207-208.
44. Worthington Chauncy Ford, et al, eds., *Journals of the Continental Congress, 1774-1789*, 34 vols. (Washington: Government Printing Office, 1904-37), 2:52-53, 66-67. For example, Washington lists first for both the committee to defend New York and the Ways and Means Committee to supply the colonies with ammunition and military wares.
45. Henriques, *First and Always*, 160.
46. Ibid., 158.

his image as both warrior and great man.[46] He next sent out general orders outlining officers' requisite attire to mark their "Badges of Distinction."[47]

Historians have long recognized the critical role costume and performative politics played in early American discourse.[48] Going back to the Stamp Act Crisis, some American Whigs encouraged colonists to protest Parliament's taxation attempts and project solidarity with other resistance actors by wearing homespun.[49] When Boston radicals tossed 342 chests of the Royal East India Company's tea into the sea, they obscured their faces and dressed in crudely fashioned Native attire.[50] During the Coercive Acts Crisis, Whigs again resorted to material self-denial to express harmony with Boston.[51] And at the Second Continental Congress, George Washington signaled his politics and capability for organized violence through his military garb. Drawing the practical and theatrical power of costume he learned on the western frontier into the Pennsylvania State House, he silently communicated all he had to say. Delegates determined the best man suited for war was the one man *suited* for war. Perhaps it is time scholars take Washington at his word.

47. General Orders, July 14 and July 24, 1775, in Chase, *Papers of Washington: Revolutionary War Series*, 1:114-15, 158-59.
48. David Waldstreicher, *In the Midst of Perpetual Fetes: The Making of American Nationalism* (Chapel Hill: University of North Carolina Press, 1997); Simon P. Newman, *Parades and the Politics of the Street: Festive Culture in the Early American Republic* (Philadelphia: University of Pennsylvania Press, 1997).
49. *Pennsylvania Gazette*, October 10, 1765.
50. Carp, *Defiance of the Patriots*.
51. Ammerman, *In the Common Cause*; Shawn David McGhee, "Suffering in the Common Cause: The Continental Association and the Political Transformation of American Subjects to Citizens during the Coercive Acts Crisis, 1774-1776," PhD diss. (Temple University, 2022).

# By Strategem and Hard Fighting: The Improbable Capture of Eleven British Ships

### 🏵 MARK R. ANDERSON 🏵

On the third day of November 1775, Brig. Gen. Richard Montgomery and his Continental army triumphantly concluded a taxing two-month siege with the surrender of British Fort St. Johns and its 600-man garrison. Their invasion of Canada had finally gained momentum. A week later, the Continentals assembled on the south shore of the St. Lawrence, ready to cross the river and take their next objective, Montreal.

British Governor Guy Carleton had already recognized that Montreal was not tenable. On Thursday, November 7, he ordered his last 150 British regular soldiers, government officials, prominent Loyalists, gunpowder stores, and other military supplies to be loaded aboard eleven sailing ships: the brig HMS *Gaspée*, armed provincial schooners *Isabella*, *Maria*, *Polly*, and *La Providence*, transport schooner *Reine des Anges*, sloops *Brilliant* and *St. Antoine*, and three smaller, unidentified sailing vessels. The governor and his deputy, Brig. Gen. Richard Prescott, embarked on *Gaspée* to lead the mass evacuation downriver (northeast) to Quebec City.[1]

---

1. Christopher Prince, *The Autobiography of a Yankee Mariner: Christopher Prince and the American Revolution*, Michael J. Crawford, ed. (Washington, DC: Brassey's, 2002),53-54; November 14, 1775, Benjamin Trumbull, "A Concise Journal or Minutes of the Principal Movements Towards St. John's," *Collections of the Connecticut Historical Society,* volume 7, (Hartford: Connecticut Historical Society, 1899), 164-65; Return of Provisions on board the several Vessels under the command of Brigadier-General Prescott, November 19, 1775, Peter Force, ed., American Archives. 4th [*AA4*] and 5th [*AA5*] Series (Washington, DC: M. St. Clair Clarke and Peter Force, 1837–53), *AA4* 3:1693. Colonel Prescott was breveted as a brigadier general for North American service.

Once the ships were loaded, however, prevailing winds blew directly from the northeast for several days, hindering departure and making "every British heart tremble" over their fate. The act of sailing a ship directly into the wind on the St. Lawrence was risky—even with the one or two knot current. It required tacking through narrow channels with the risk of grounding on shallows, or having one's ship stuck vulnerably "in irons," with no wind in the sails to maneuver.[2]

On Saturday afternoon, November 11, the days of waiting came to an end as flags and weathervanes turned under a cold northwest wind, with snow flurries. Around three o'clock, a single cannon signaled the governor's flotilla to weigh anchor and set sails for the 170-mile river voyage to Quebec City. The British and Canadian Loyalists fled in the nick of time—Montgomery and his advance guard marched victoriously into Montreal just two days later.[3]

On the first full day underway, the challenges of sailing ships on the river became readily apparent—one of the armed schooners ran aground on a shoal, just a short distance downstream from Montreal. The crew took hours to free the ship and get back underway. Carleton's eleven ships had only put thirty miles between them and Montreal that day before the winds shifted northeast again. "The elements seemed to conspire" against their timely escape. The fleet sat in anchorage off the north shore parish of Lavaltrie for two days, waiting until advantageous winds returned on Tuesday, November 14. The ships resumed their trip downriver, but only managed to sail another dozen miles before contrary winds, "very violent with heavy snow," returned that evening. The fleet anchored a few miles short of Sorel, a fifty-dwelling town at the confluence of the Richelieu River.[4]

Carleton and his captains had good reason to wait for favorable winds before attempting to pass the narrows between Sorel and Isle St. Ignace. Just a week had passed since American artillery forced some of the king's ships away from that very point. Merchant mariner Christo-

2. Prince, *Autobiography*, 54.

3. Guy Carleton to Earl of Dartmouth, November 20, 1775, K. G. Davies, ed., *Documents of the American Revolution, 1770-1783* (Dublin: Irish University Press, 1976), 11:185 (Carleton Account); Aaron Barlow Journal in Charles B. Todd, "The March to Montreal and Quebec, 1775," *American Historical Register* 2 (March 1895): 648; November 11, 1775, Trumbull, "Journal," 162-63.

4. Carleton Account; Prince, *Autobiography*, 54-55; Amable Berthelot, "Extraits d'un Mémoire de M. A. Berthelot sur L'Invasion du Canada en 1775," in Hospice-Anthelme Verreau, ed., *Invasion du Canada: Collection des Mémoires Recueillis et Annotes* (Montréal: Eusèbe Senécal, 1873), 233 (author's translation); November 15, 1775, Trumbull, "Journal," 166-67.

pher Prince, piloting HMS *Gaspée*, observed, "I knew we could not pass the batteries at Sorrel without being sunk by the guns at that fort [battery at Sorel], unless the wind shifted."[5]

The eleven ships faced this looming encounter with considerable limitations. The flotilla leaders had to worry about the lives of one hundred and forty women and children who accompanied soldiers and officials on board various ships. Capt. François Bellette's schooner *La Providence* was a Vesuvian danger of its own, carrying all of Montreal's gunpowder. The captains included some of the most respected St. Lawrence River navigators; yet they must have had doubts about their merchant-mariner crews' abilities to sail close-hauled into the wind while facing enemy fire. The armed schooners were nominally able to fight back, having up to sixteen cannon each, but the provincial sailors' gunnery skills were unproven at best. Even the one proper warship, HMS *Gaspée*, had only a half crew of fifteen navy sailors—augmented by foot-soldier passengers—to man the sails, six cannon, and ten swivel guns. *Gaspée's* captain and the rest of the crew had been detached to Fort St. Johns for Lake Champlain duty before the invasion. These compounding challenges presumably biased Carleton and Prescott toward caution as they approached enemy-held Sorel.[6]

OPPOSITION

The American force awaiting Carleton's fleet consisted of a couple hundred Continentals and Canadian partisans, flushed with recent victories. They were led by Maj. John Brown, intrepid and seemingly omnipresent in the campaign, and his west Massachusetts Regiment commander, Lt. Col. James Easton. In the week before Fort St. Johns surrendered, much of this composite corps had successfully repelled a Canadian Loyalist detachment that marched from Sorel to relieve that beleaguered British fort. The Loyalist corps retreated back to Sorel and embarked on three armed ships, but lingered off the town. On the night of Tuesday, November 7, Brown led a detachment that quietly built a

5. Carleton Account; Prince, *Autobiography*, 50-51, 54.
6. Prince, *Autobiography*, 45, 46, 50, 51, 53; John Brown to Richard Montgomery, November 8, 1775, William B. Clark, ed., *Naval Documents of the American Revolution* [*NDAR*] (Washington, DC: Department of the Navy, 1964-), 2:922; Berthelot, "Mémoire," 233; Return of Ordnance . . . on board the different Vessels, November 20, 1775, and A List of the Officers of His Majesty's Troops on board the Vessels near Montreal, November 21, 1775, *AA4* 3:1693-94. Prince reported fourteen to sixteen guns on the schooners, yet only two each were reported as captured on *Isabella* and *Maria* (none on the others). Most may have been dumped overboard before the surrender. Prince's memory of the numbers might also have been inaccurate and/or included swivel guns.

fascine battery of five 6- to 12-pounder cannon within musket shot of the enemy. When the British ships fired their regular morning gun signal, those aboard were shocked to receive an American reply of "at least 12 Rounds" from the new works. Brown reported that his gunners "plumed" HMS *Fell* "thro' in many Places before she . . . slip[p]ed her Cable." The small British warship fired "briskly" at Sorel as she "made the best of her way down the River out of sight," sailing down to Quebec City.[7]

In the week after that initial ship-and-shore encounter, Easton amassed additional strength with the conclusion of the Fort St. Johns siege. The rest of his regiment and soldiers from Daniel Denton's company, 3rd New York Regiment, joined him. American soldiers also hauled additional artillery to Sorel, so Easton established a second battery of three 12-pounders and a single 9-pounder. He left two 6-pounders in the original works. Lt. Martin Johnson arrived to help direct the guns. Johnson was a recently discharged Royal Artillery man, whose technical expertise and leadership stood out while serving with John Lamb's New York company. Easton also acquired two small armed vessels, brought down the Richelieu after the siege. These were the Continental gondolas *Hancock* and *Schuyler*, each mounting one 12-pounder cannon on the bow and twelve swivel guns along the gunwales. The two sixty-foot flat-bottomed boats were sometimes referred to as row galleys, but were also rigged to sail. Easton, Brown, and their men at Sorel were well prepared for the approaching enemy.[8]

CONTESTED PASSAGE

The first test came on Wednesday morning, November 15. Carleton ordered HMS *Gaspée* and the armed schooner *Polly* to "reconnoitre the fort at Sorrel, and see if it was possible" for the flotilla to safely pass. As *Gaspée* "doubled the point" at Sorel with "starboard tacks on board,"

7. Montgomery to Philip Schuyler, November 3, 1775, and Brown to Montgomery, November 8, 1775, *NDAR* 2:867, 922; Levi Miller S13937 p3-4 and Moses Bartlett S28630 p8, RG15 M804 Pension Records [M804], National Archives and Records Administration [NARA]; "Narrative of Uriah Cross in the Revolutionary War," Vernon Ives, ed., *New York History: Quarterly Journal of the New York State Historical Association* 63, no. 3 (July 1982), 288.

8. November 15, 1775, Trumbull, "Journal," 146, 166-67; Montgomery to Schuyler, November 17, 1775, Schuyler to Benjamin Franklin, August 23, 1775, and November 21, 1775 entry, Journal of Robert Barwick (Berwick), *NDAR* 2:1056, 1:1217, 2:1104; Orasmus Holmes S2621 p8-9, John Williamson S11784 p6, and Garret Reed S14257 p3-4, M804; *Calendar of N.Y. Colonial Manuscripts Indorsed Land Papers*, 1643-1803 (Albany: Weed, Parsons, & Co., 1864), 870; Minutes of the Ordnance, *AA4* 4:534.

the Americans opened fire, striking the brig. Pilot Christopher Prince reported that it "threw us in such confusion not a gun was fired from us." The crew of *Polly*, in trail, heard the thundering blasts and "wore round before she got to the point." Prince immediately heeled *Gaspée* around to reverse course, reaching safety upriver in a few minutes. Easton boasted that a British ship was "greatly Damaged" in this encounter, but Prince recalled that everyone on board was unscathed. In any case, the Americans had provided an intimidating display of their ability to defend the Sorel narrows.[9]

*Gaspée* and *Polly* only worked about a mile back upriver before whiteout snowfall prompted them to anchor for safety. About one o'-clock in the afternoon, the squall abated to reveal that the ships were within a half mile of the southern riverbank. Officers soon spotted men gathering on the shore, but could not determine if they were friend or foe.

That question was answered with a bang as a cannon ball pierced both of *Gaspée*'s bulwarks. General Prescott immediately ordered Prince to "get the brig out of their reach," but a pelting of grapeshot and musket balls drove everyone below decks. Brave sailors and redcoat volunteers ventured topside to adjust the sails and get the ships underway, but were repeatedly driven back to cover. A sergeant received fatal wounds. After several attempts, a party managed to "cut the gaskets" and free the sails. Others frantically cut the anchor cables. *Gaspée* and *Polly* soon drifted behind a snowy veil and turned upriver to rejoin the flotilla. In this engagement, the startling shore fire had come from Canadian partisans that Easton had equipped with two long 9-pounders. The detachment, probably led by Capt. Augustin Loiseau, believed they had stopped a British landing attempt.[10]

The *Gaspée* and *Polly* had just rejoined the other nine ships nearby when a "floating battery" approached. This was one of the Continental gondolas, manned by Easton's soldiers, sent to chase the ships. Carleton

9. Prince, *Autobiography*, 55; November 16, 1775, Trumbull, "Journal," 167-68; Carleton Account; Simon Sanguinet, "Témoin Oculaire de l'Invasion du Canada par les Bastonnois: Journal de M. Sanguinet," in Verreau, *Invasion du Canada*, 87; Berthelot, "Mémoire," 233; Precis of Operations on the Canadian Frontier, CO 5/253, 26-27, MG-11-CO5, Library and Archives Canada. Some accounts mentioned fire from a battery on Isle St. Ignace, opposite Sorel. American accounts do not mention any such works. Perhaps gondola fire near the low island was mistaken for shore fire.

10. Prince, *Autobiography*, 56; Carleton Account; Schuyler to Cornelius Wynkoop, January 7, 1776, *NDAR*3:670; November 16, 1775, Trumbull, "Journal," 168; Levi Miller S13937 p4, M804; Petition of Augustin Loiseau, r158, i147 v3, p410, RG360, M247 Papers of the Continental Congress, NARA.

had already seen enough of his persistent enemy's capabilities that day. He immediately directed his fleet to run with the wind, returning further upstream. The gondola broke off pursuit when the ships took sail.[11]

The next day, General Montgomery issued new orders from Montreal to put the enemy "between two fires." He directed Col. Timothy Bedel to lead his New Hampshire Rangers and the Green Mountain Rangers downriver "to harass the enemy in their retreat, and if possible to get possession of any or all their vessels, especially that with the powder . . . [and] . . . to secure the persons of the Governor [Carleton] and General Prescott." Since all the rangers were at the end of their enlistments, Montgomery added motivation "beyond the letter of the law." He promised that "all public stores, except ammunition and provisions, shall be given to the troops who take them." Even with that enticement, the Green Mountain men declined to participate and headed home; their tattered summer field garb was inadequate for the increasingly hostile Canadian winter. Bedel's men, however, answered the call and marched down the north shore to find the enemy ships anchored off Lavaltrie. By Thursday, November 16, after five days underway, Carleton's fleet was still just thirty miles from its original point of departure—and now faced threats in either direction: Bedel's force gathering near the anchorage, and Easton's at the Sorel narrows.[12]

NEGOTIATIONS AND SURRENDER

On river and shore, everyone endured very stormy, unpleasant winter weather as they waited in suspense on November 16. Finally, about an hour before sunset, a boat approached the ships off Lavaltrie, under a flag of truce. An American envoy—probably Dr. Jonas Fay—was granted permission to board and asked to speak with Carleton. General Prescott appeared topside instead. He said he was "the only one to

---

11. Jonathan Curtis W18986 p12-14, Levi Miller S13937 p4, and Daniel Beeman W17295 p11, M804; Carleton Account; Sanguinet, "Temoin Oculaire," 86-87; Ira Allen, *History of the State of Vermont* (originally *The Natural and Political History of the State of Vermont . . .* [1798]) (Tokyo: Charles E. Tuttle, 1969 reprint), 49-50.

12. Montgomery to Timothy Bedel, November 16, 1775, W. J. R. Saffell, ed., *Records of the Revolutionary War . . .* (Philadelphia: G. G. Evans, 1860), 27-28; Montgomery to Schuyler, December 5, 1775 and November 17, 1775, *NDAR* 2:1277 and 1056; Thomas Ramsey S15609 p8, Nathaniel Eastman W22992 p4, William Greenough S8613 p4, Benjamin Martin S22376 p8, Isaac Stevens S11460 pp 6 and 13, John Waters W25905 p7, Job Moulton W16656 pp 5 and 43, Thomas Spring S3965 p10, 25, M804; "History of 1776," *The Scots Magazine,* October 1777, 521.

transact any business with friends or enemies," deliberately shrouding Carleton's presence in ambiguity.[13]

The American delivered a "spirited letter" from Colonel Easton. His message suggested that the British commander "must be very sensible" that "from the Strength of the United Colonies on both sides," his situation was "Rendered very disagreeable." Easton proposed "That if you will Resign your Fleet to me Immediately without destroying the Effects on Board, you and your men shall be used with due Civility, together with women & Children on Board." Prescott asked for time to consider the proposal and the American envoy left in his boat to carry the general's message to Easton.[14]

About an hour later, a different American officer arrived by boat. It was Maj. John Brown, a more assertive and authoritative agent. Brown and Prescott negotiated in the rapidly fading twilight, agreeing to a truce until the next morning.[15]

Early that night, Carleton summoned his captains to a council aboard *Gaspée*. The governor detailed their predicament and solicited his officers' opinions. They all agreed it was imperative for Carleton to reach Quebec City. Capt. François Bellette boldly suggested that the flotilla should fight through the enemy, even though his gunpowder-laden schooner was the most vulnerable. Capt. Jean-Baptiste Bouchette suggested a more cautious course. He promised to deliver Carleton safely downriver by boat. The council favored this option. Early that night, Carleton left *Gaspée*, joined Bouchette in a whaleboat, and unceremoniously departed the fleet. Bouchette stealthily piloted the boat past the enemy at Sorel in the middle of the night. The Americans failed to capture the governor and remained oblivious to his escape for the next two days. Carleton ultimately reached Quebec City on Sunday, November 19. General Prescott was left to deal with the fleet's dire circumstances.[16]

The timing and nature of discussions between Prescott and the Americans over most of November 17 and 18 remain obscure. Christo-

---

13. Prince, *Autobiography*, 56-57; Allen, *History*, 50; Berthelot, "Mémoire," 234. Ira Allen's account says "the writer" delivered the letter; historians have generally interpreted this to mean Allen, author of the *History*, but in context, it appears to mean Fay, writer of the surrender proposal.

14. Allen, *History*, 50; James Easton to General Carleton or Officer commanding the Fleet in St. Lawrence, November 15, 1775, Historical Section of the General Staff (Canada), ed. *A History of the Organization, Development and Services of the Military and Naval Forces of Canada*, . . . (Quebec: 1919), 2:127.

15. Allen, *History*, 50.

16. Carleton Account; Berthelot, "Mémoire," 233-34; Prince, *Autobiography*, 62.

pher Prince's autobiographical narrative provides some great first-hand detail, but by the time he recorded it, his memory had blended three days of negotiations into one. There is one other contemporary description of an episode that presumably happened over this period.

On a trip to Sorel in late May 1776, six months after the surrender, Continental Commissioner Charles Carroll of Carrollton recorded an account he heard from an unnamed source. The individual explained that during negotiations, Major Brown asked Prescott for a British officer to accompany him ashore and verify the threat posed by the American batteries. Once on land, Brown took the redcoat officer to unoccupied battery works upriver from Sorel. The Continental major allegedly deceived him there, saying "two thirty-two pounders" were about to arrive, and ominously warned: "If you should chance to escape this battery, which is my small battery, I have a grand battery at the mouth of the Sorel, which will infallibly sink all your vessels." By Carroll's story, it was the returning officer's testimony following this exchange that convinced Prescott to surrender.[17]

Carroll further suggested that Brown's threat was entirely a bluff, noting that the Sorel batteries lacked guns of any sort during his visit there, two seasons later. In reality, Continentals had removed the cannon shortly after the surrender and shipped them downriver for the Quebec City siege. Carroll, however, wholeheartedly accepted the account and concluded: "It is difficult to determine which was greatest, the impudence of Brown in demanding a surrender, or the cowardice" of the allegedly hoodwinked officer who persuaded Prescott to capitulate. His assessment has been the most commonly repeated account of the negotiations, effectively dismissing the proven American shore fire capabilities and the fleet's tremendous weather and navigation challenges. Without direct attribution, or primary source records that corroborate or refute the Carroll story, it should be treated with historical caution.[18]

Whether a redcoat officer had been sent to observe American batteries and report back to Prescott or not, the Continental threat to the fleet manifested in another form. The two gondolas "demonstrated"

---

17. *Journal of Charles Carroll of Carrollton, during His Visit to Canada in 1776 . . .*, Brantz Mayer, ed. (Baltimore: Maryland Historical Society, 1844), 97. The story could not have come directly from Brown, who was operating west of Montreal during Carroll's Sorel visit, nor from Easton, who was in Philadelphia. The largest guns reported at Sorel were 12-pounders; the largest American-held guns in Canada at the time were 24-pounders; Minutes of the Ordnance, *AA4* 4:534.

18. Carroll, *Journal*, 97; Robert Barwick Journal, *NDAR* 2:1151-52.

near the fleet off Lavaltrie. They were probably joined by "field artillery mounted in batteaus" sent down from Montreal by General Montgomery. Despite the marginal size disparity between the well-rigged, deep-draft British sailing ships and squat American gondolas, the latter had the maneuvering advantage and actually had larger (if fewer) guns: 12-pounders against the fleet's 6- and 9-pounders. Both sides, however, refrained from initiating a river battle.[19]

Resolution came in final negotiations which must have occurred late on the afternoon of Saturday, November 18. Christopher Prince recorded an eyewitness perspective from *Gaspée*'s deck. Major Brown came shipboard to offer General Prescott the terms one last time. Prescott still said "he could not nor would not sign the proposals." The American major threatened that the ships would be boarded by force if not surrendered that evening. Then the two held quiet discussions, ending with Brown's declaration that he would not accept any alteration of the terms. He embarked on his boat, and as his crew pushed off in the dim gloam, the major proclaimed, "I am going on shore, and I think it my duty to tell you that before tomorrow, many of you will [be] enfolded in the arms of death." The boat had not gone far when Prescott called the American back.[20]

Prescott and Brown re-entered private discussions. After a short while, the American major paced the deck in disapprobation, and began to descend to his boat again. At that point, the forlorn British general finally yielded. Prescott signed the capitulation and agreed to effect the surrender in four hours, at eight o'clock that night. Brown left with a warning: he expected to find the ships and their cargos as he left them.[21]

Prescott, however, had secret guidance from Carleton to follow. The general promptly sent boats to all the ships with orders to "heave overboard all the powder, nearly all the provisions, and a number of other articles." This act served utilitarian military purposes, but dishonorably violated the surrender terms. Most significantly, Captain Belette dumped hundreds of barrels of gunpowder from *La Providence* into the river, denying the powder-poor Americans that precious military commodity. Other captains appear to have complied in varying degrees—HMS *Gaspée*, at one extreme, had only six firkins of butter remaining as provisions, and apparently no ordnance on board, when the Ameri-

19. Berthelot, "Mémoire," 234; Richard Montgomery to Philip Schuyler, Montreal, November 17, 1775, *AA4* 3:1633; Daniel Beeman W17295 p1, M804; "History of 1776," *Scots Magazine*, October 1777, 521.
20. Prince, *Autobiography*, 57-58; Allen, *History*, 50; Berthelot, "Mémoire," 234.
21. Ibid.

cans seized her; *Maria,* on the other hand, still had what seems to have been her full cargo the next day.[22]

The ship crews were probably still busy jettisoning cargo when the capricious weather intervened one last time. A "perfect gale" blew from the northwest, keeping American soldiers from coming to seize the vessels that night as arranged. Prescott sent an officer to deliver new orders to all the ships. With the shift of winds, they were "to make every preparation to get underway and follow the brig *Gaspée* down to Quebec." Prince warned that it was "impossible to get under way without going on shore when it is so dark and such a gale," yet Prescott persisted. Prince then recounted that he and some virtuous redcoats subverted or rejected the general's instructions, refusing to be party to an ignoble violation of accepted capitulation terms. Prescott's orders met a similar response across the fleet. As a Loyalist described it, second-hand, "the pilots on board the vessels mutinied, and refused to conduct them past the batteries." The furious general could not cajole the crews into action.[23]

All eleven ships were still sitting at the Lavaltrie anchorage when American boats finally appeared around dawn on Sunday, November 19. The first Continental officer to board *Gaspée* cursed Prescott for destroying cargo in violation of the surrender terms, having seen the jetsam on his approach. American soldiers took control of the fleet and sealed their remarkable conquest. Gen. Philip Schuyler gave credit to Easton, saying he had "behaved with bravery and much alertness." As gondola crewman John Philips observed, the eleven British vessels had been taken "partly by stratagem & partly by hard fighting."[24]

REPERCUSSIONS

Many contemporaries critiqued Prescott for surrendering without truly testing the American threat. General Montgomery was harshest, writing: "I blushed for His Majesty's troops! such an instance of base poltroonery I have never met with, and all because we had half a dozen cannon on the bank of the river to annoy him in his retreat!" Canadian Loyalists Simon Sanguinet and Henry Caldwell, and Continental Lt. Ira Allen all shared common sentiments that "the ships might have passed the narrows with little loss." These perspectives all align neatly

22. Prince, *Autobiography,* 59; Berthelot, "Mémoire," 234; Return of Ordnance, and Return of Provisions, November 19 and 20, 1775, *AA4* 3:1693.

23. Prince, *Autobiography,* 59-63; Henry Caldwell to [James Murray], June 15, 1776, *The Invasion of Canada in 1775: A Letter Attributed to Major Henry Caldwell* (Quebec, 1887), 4.

24. Prince, *Autobiography,* 63-65; Philip Schuyler to George Washington, November 28, 1775, *AA4* 3:1692; John Philips S9457 p8, M804.

with Charles Carroll's oft-cited contention that John Brown completely bluffed Prescott into an otherwise unwarranted surrender. None of these assessments, however, were directly informed by shipboard perspectives, and Caldwell judiciously conceded: "there must have been some circumstances with which we were unacquainted."[25]

Mariner Christopher Prince's eyewitness account from *Gaspée*—not publicly available until the mid-twentieth century—complicated the traditional interpretation of the affair and surrender. Prince detailed the fleet's manifold challenges: adverse and unpredictable weather, inadequately crewed ships, precious passengers and dangerous cargos, and the repeated American demonstrations of shore fire accuracy. Given this narrative context, the British capitulation seems far more reasonable.

It is also noteworthy that no one at the time seems to have publicly called the governor or general to account for the fleet's capitulation. It certainly helped that the first news to reach London provided scant details, and by the summer of 1776, word of Carleton's obstinate Quebec City defense and the British recovery of Canada swept the Lavaltrie surrender into insignificance. Prescott's military career did not suffer, either. He was promoted to major general (in North America) while still held by the Continentals, and promptly returned to active service after a prisoner exchange.[26]

For the Americans, the fleet capture categorically delivered immediate and substantial operational gains. General Montgomery used the sailing ships to rush hundreds of troops downstream within days, rendezvous with Benedict Arnold's corps, and blockade Carleton at Quebec City early in December. With the ship cargos, Montgomery outfitted Arnold's ragged corps with new redcoat uniforms, fed his men British provisions, and equipped his soldiers with military tools to fortify positions around the enemy-held city.

As a second-order effect, Montgomery's access to river transport helped lure him into strategic overreach. Loyalist Simon Sanguinet was

25. Richard Montgomery to Janet Montgomery, November 24, 1775, in Louise L. Hunt, ed., *Biographical Notes concerning General Richard Montgomery together with Hitherto Unpublished Letters* (Poughkeepsie: News Book and Job Printing House, 1876), 15; Allen, *History*, 50; Sanguinet, "Temoin Oculaire," 86-87 (author's translation); Caldwell to [Murray], June 15, 1776, *The Invasion of Canada in 1775*, 4.

26. J. Almon, *The Remembrancer . . . for the Year 1776*, part 1, (London, 1776): 131, 234; "History of 1776," *The Scots Magazine*, October 1777, 521, also March 1776, 167 and February 1776, 93. Prescott was embroiled in a separate controversy when the Continental Congress kept him in close confinement as retribution for his mistreatment of captive Ethan Allen in the fall of 1775.

"certain that if the eleven ships had not been taken—that [Montgomery] would not have been able to go to Quebec, because he would have lacked everything." Even if Sanguinet exaggerated, an absence of maritime lift would presumably have given the American commander pause to consider before he doubled the length of an already-tenuous supply line between Fort Ticonderoga and his front-line troops. Montgomery, who died in a failed New Year's Eve attempt to take Quebec City, left his men in an unsustainable logistical position. The ships could not operate on the frozen St. Lawrence from December to mid-April, and land transport proved completely inadequate to the task.[27]

The ill-supplied and poorly reinforced army hung on until May 6, 1776, when it collapsed like a house of cards upon the arrival of British reinforcements that relieved Quebec City. In the Americans' chaotic flight, British forces promptly recovered the river navy and returned the ships to their own use. Of particular note, the armed schooner *Maria* and one of the abandoned Continental gondolas—renamed *Loyal Convert*—were transported up the Richelieu to serve on Lake Champlain. They were part of the British fleet at the Battle of Valcour Island that fall.

Surprisingly, the Lavaltrie victory also failed to boost the promising careers of the key American players, but embroiled them in controversy instead. Lt. Col. James Easton, despite having been recognized for his "diligence, activity, and spirit," was imprisoned for debt in April 1776— still awaiting the substantial prize-money payment for the ships' cargos. Maj. John Brown went to join the Quebec City siege, but found himself under Benedict Arnold's command after Montgomery's death. Long-smoldering personal enmities took flame when Arnold publicly accused Brown and Easton of "plundering the Officers Baggage taken at Sorell, Contrary to Articles of Capitulation, and to the great scandal of the American Army." Brown and Arnold exchanged vicious recriminations throughout 1776. Brown resigned from Continental service in early 1777, war-worn and completely exasperated by the unresolved insults to his honor. He did, however, continue to bravely and effectively serve the American Cause as a Massachusetts officer. Easton, unable to get a court of enquiry to officially clear his name from Arnold's accusations, was sidelined as a supernumerary colonel, without command. He remained in this limbo state for three years before ultimately being dismissed. Both Brown and Easton suffered grievously from the bureaucratic incompetence of the Continental confederation, and from

---

27. Sanguinet, "Temoin Oculaire," 88-89.

senior leaders' failure to properly reward their contributions or resolve the Arnold controversy.[28]

The ripples of direct and indirect effects from the capture of "eleven Sail of British vessels" on the St. Lawrence are just one previously-neglected aspect of that affair in the Revolutionary War historiography. Careful re-examination of primary sources complicates the common narrative that victory hinged on an audacious Yankee bluff, especially with the integration of Prince's autobiography. The expanded documentary record reveals that Montgomery, Easton, and Brown skillfully employed Continental forces to exploit the opportunity presented by weather contingencies, pressed their worn and vulnerable British enemy, and secured a significant American victory on the St. Lawrence.[29]

28. Easton to Hancock, May 8, 1776, *AA4* 5:1234; *Journals of the Continental Congress, 1774-1789,* ed. Worthington C. Ford et al. (Washington, D.C., 1904-37), April 26, 1776, July 16, 1779, and August 22, 1786, 4:312, 14:843, 31:553; Benedict Arnold to Hancock, February 1, 1776, *NDAR* 3:1072, 1074; Petition of John Brown, June 26, 1776, *AA5* 1:1219-20. Brown successfully raided British-held Fort Ticonderoga in 1777 and died on the battlefield at Stone Arabia in 1780.
29. Cross, "Narrative," 288-89.

# Smallpox by Inoculation: The Tragedy of New York's Rosewell Beebe

❦ PHILIP D. WEAVER ❧

The day following the legendary taking of Fort Ticonderoga on May 10, 1775, Lt. Col. Ethan Allen reported the successful mission to New York's Albany County Committee of Safety, as well as to plead for their immediate assistance:

> I have the inexpressible satisfaction to acquaint you that at day-break of the tenth instant, pursuant to my directions from sundry leading gentlemen of Massachusetts-Bay and Connecticut, I took the fortress of Ticonderoga, with about one hundred and thirty Green Mountain Boys. Colonel Easton with about forty-seven, valiant soldiers, distinguished themselves in the action, Colonel Arnold entered the fortress with me side by side. The guard was so surprised, that contrary to expectation they did not fire on us, but fled with precipitancy. We immediately entered the fortress, and took the garrison prisoners, without bloodshed, or any opposition. They consisted of one Captain, and a Lieutenant and forty-two men.
>
> Little more need be said. You know Governor Carleton of Canada will exert himself to retake it; and as your County is nearer than any other part of the Colonies, and as your inhabitants have thoroughly manifested their zeal in the cause of their Country, I expect immediate assistance from you both in men and provisions. You cannot exert yourselves too much in so glorious a cause. The number of men need be more at first, till the other Colonies can have time to muster. I am apprensive of a sudden and quick attack. Pray be quick to our relief, and send us five hundred men immediately—fail not.[1]

---

1. Ethan Allen to Abraham Yates, Chairman of the Albany Committee of Safety, May 11, 1775, Peter Force, ed., *American Archives* (Washington, DC: 1837-53), 4th Series, 2:606 (*American Archives*).

The Albany Committee noted on May 12, that

We received a Letter Signed Ethan Allen by the Hands of Mr.
[John] Brown acquainting us of the taking Ticonderoga, upon which
we wrote a Letter to the Committee of New York by Captn. Barent
Ten Eyck express and each of us paid him a Dollar a peice for going—
The Draft of Letter is on fyle.[2]

The following day, the Albany Committee recorded the receipt of
two letters from the New York Committee of Safety, which went into
session when the New York Provincial Congress was out of session.
These letters prompted the Albany Committee to reply to Allen via
John Brown, who was still in town:

We have now received an Answer from our Brethren at New York,
who agree with us to use their own Words, that the Powers invested in
them and us, are too limitted to permit either Body to take an Active
step in the Matters proposed, before we have the Opinion of the
Provincial or Continental Congress.[3]

On May 18, Brown delivered to the Continental Congress a quan-
tity of letters that provided important intelligence. At their request,
Brown also presented his observations regarding "the disposition of the
Canadians, the taking of Ticonderogo and the importance of that post."
The resulting resolution, states in part:

Resolved, Whereas there is indubitable evidence that a design is
formed by the British Ministry of making a cruel invasion from the
province of Quebec, upon these colonies . . . this Congress earnestly
recommend it to the committees of the cities and counties of New York
and Albany, immediately to cause the said cannon and military stores
to be removed from Ticonderogo to the south end and of Lake George;
and if necessary to apply to the colonies of New Hampshire, Massachusetts bay, and Connecticut, for such an additional body of forces as
will be sufficient to establish a strong post at that place and effectually

2. Meeting Minutes, May 12, 1775, *Minutes of the Albany Committee of Correspondence
1775-1778* (Albany, NY: The University of the State of New York, 1923), 1:31 (*Minutes
of the Albany Committee*). John Brown was a Massachusetts attorney who took part in the
taking of Ticonderoga. Known as Major John Brown, he would command the forces that
besieged Fort Chambly in the fall of 1775. He was promoted to lieutenant colonel of
Samuel Elmore's (unnumbered) continental regiment in 1776, but later resigned his commission. He returned to the Massachusetts militia and was later killed at the Battle of
Stone Arabia (New York) in 1780. For more on Barent Ten Eyck see
allthingsliberty.com/2016/10/worthy-troubled-continental-service-capt-barent-j-ten-
eyck/.
3. Meeting Minutes, May 13, 1775, ibid., 1:32.

to secure the sd. cannon and stores or so many of them as it may be judged proper to keep there.[4]

A week later, on May 25, the Albany Committee passed a resolution to send troops to Fort Ticonderoga:

> Agreeable to a recommendation from the Continental Congress— It is resolved that a sufficient Body of Forces be raised and enlisted under the Command of such officers as shall be approved of by this Board and that they with all possible dispatch proceed to Ticonderoga.[5]

Records are sparse, but five companies of the "Albany County Provincials Employed for the Common Defense of the Continent of North America" were raised to aid Allen. Capt. Hezekiah Baldwin commanded one of them. It was regionally recruited in southeastern Albany County, which today is southern Rensselaer County. Second in command was 1st Lt. Nathaniel Rowley, who was backed up by 2nd Lt. Rosewell Beebe. These three officers were commissioned "by authority from the Committee of Albany" on May 25 and ultimately "by Warrant from the Congress" on June 28.[6] It was not until October that the New York Provincial Congress requested the dates of service and the names of the troops who were "raised by the Committee of Albany & went on Service before the 28th of June" in order "that their Commissions may be so dated as to save their pay." The Albany Committee confirmed these men were paid thru June 23 and that Baldwin, Rowley, and Beebe actually went into service on June 3.[7]

4. Congressional Resolution, May 18, 1775, Worthington C. Ford, ed., *Journals of the Continental Congress, 1774-1789* (Washington: Government Printing Office, 1905), 2:55-56 (*Journals of the Continental Congress*). The message delivered by Brown was presumably from either Allen or, perhaps, Philip Schuyler, but that has yet to be determined.

5. Meeting Minutes, May 25, 1775, *Minutes of the Albany Committee*, 1:40.

6. A Muster Roll of Captain Hezekiah Baldwins Company of the Second Regiment of the New York Forces ... at Fort George, October 13, 1775, Revolutionary War Rolls 1775-1783, National Archives Microfilm Publications, M246, War Department Collection of Revolutionary War Records, Records Group 93, Roll 67, Folder 19 (Baldwin's Muster Roll). Commissary receipts, Henry Bogart Papers, Folder 8, New York State Library, Albany, NY. Receipts signed by company officers themselves are the source for this unusual aggregate name. There appears to be no official correspondence, from the Albany Committee, regarding this company until they took the field.

7. Proceedings— October 1775, Entry for October 13, 1775, *Minutes of the Albany Committee*, 1:269-273. Letter from the Albany Committee, enclosing a memorandum of the Officers elected, October 21, 1775, Correspondence of the Provincial Congress, &c., *Journals of the Provincial Congress, Provincial Convention, Committee of Safety and Council of Safety of the State of New-York: 1775-1775-1777* (Albany, NY: Thurlow Weed, 1842), 2:97 (*Journals of the Provincial Congress*).

Meanwhile, in a June 2 letter to the New York Provincial Congress, the Albany Committee noted that they had

> raised several companies to go up to Ticonderoga, &c, two of which are on their way up. This we did in consequence, first, of the resolution of the Continental Congress of the 10th ulto.; secondly, of the letter from the New-York committee enclosing said resolve dated 20th ult.; and thirdly, Col. Arnold's letter to us requiring immediate assistance; but on our receipt of the above letter from Govr. Trumbull, we are in great doubts with respect to our men already raised in this county, and those who stand ready to march up. As we know not the nature of the resolve you have sent to Govr, Trumbull, and his letter contains a clause that these one thousand forces are to continue at Ticonderoga, &c. until relieved by troops from this Colony, &c. We should be extremely glad to have plain explicit instructions from time to time, that we need not wander astray and act counter to your intentions and the general good of the public.[8]

Moses Myer, a private soldier in Capt. Joel Pratt's company, noted that while his company arrived at Albany from Hillsdale, New York, "they were joined by the three companies under the command of Capt Fisher [Visscher], Capt White and Capt Baldwin."[9] These four companies set out for Fort Ticonderoga, but on June 6 were ordered by the Albany Committee to stop their advance at the south end of Lake George until further orders.[10]

Baldwin and Capt. George White were among the officers at a council of war at Crown Point on June 10 who signed a letter to the Continental Congress in Philadelphia reporting how the advance force was doing in the fight against the British.

> We, whose names are prefixed above, do in council approve of and nominate Colonel Ethan Allen, Captain Seth Warmer, and Captain

8. Albany Committee to the Provincial Congress, June 2, 1775, ibid., 1:29.

9. Deposition of Moses Myer, August 22, 1832, S.14002, *Revolutionary War Pension and Bounty Land Warrant Application Files, 1800–1900*, Record Group 15, National Archives Building, Washington, DC (National Archives Microfilm Publication M804, Roll 1798), *(Pensions)*.

10. The Militia, Albany County, *New York in the Revolution*, Berthold Fernow, ed., (Cottonport, LA: Polyanthos, Inc., 1972), 261, previously published as *Documents Relating to the Colonial History of the State of New York* (Albany, NY: Weed, Parsons and Co., 1853–1887), 15:261 (*Documents Relating*). Meeting Minutes, June 6, 1775, *Minutes of the Albany Committee*, 1:66-67. These captains were Joel Pratt (allthingsliberty.com/2019/05/the-court-martial-of-captain-joel-pratt/ and jardispatches.podbean.com/e/e23-philip-d-weaver-the-court-martial-of-captain-joel-pratt/), John Visscher (a.k.a. Fisher), George White, and Hezekiah Baldwin.

Remember Baker, to meet you in Congress, to consult and have your advice upon this move, which we have understood that you have approved; we are now in possession of Ticonderoga and Crown Point. And this day, at five o'clock, our armed sloop and schooners arrived here and furnished us with intelligence, that about three hundred of the Regular forces were at St. John's, fortifying and intrenching upon the Grants, near this place. We think it might be practicable, in case of emergency, to raise about five hundred men, in case (as they are poor) of encouragement. Colonel Allen has behaved, in this affair, very singularly remarkable for his courage, and must, in duty, recommend him to you and the whole Continent.[11]

With the front line pushing the advantage following the taking of Fort Ticonderoga, it seemed illogical to call back the companies, especially Baldwin's and White's who were already there. This is easily discerned in one of three barely legible letters Beebe's wife retained from her husband. He wrote on June 16 that "our Company [Baldwin's] is now encamped in the woods on the East Side of Lake George . . . We have been to Ticonderoga and by orders have returned back again to this place until having orders from the Committee of New York in order for the Yorkers to be in Regiments."[12]

In late June, the New-York Provincial Congress started the process of arranging 3,000 men into four infantry battalions as part of the Continental army establishment of 1775. Each battalion was divided into ten companies recruited regionally. The companies from the Albany area were named the 2nd battalion, whose field officers were to be Col. Goose Van Schaick, Lt. Col. Peter Yates, and Maj. Peter Gansevoort "Jr." Their companies, together with Cornelius Van Dyck's, formed the nucleus of the unit.[13]

11. Letter to the Continental Congress of North America, June 10, 1775, Force, *American Archives*, 4th Series, 2:957-958. Baldwin's name is spelled "Baulding" due to an obvious transcription error. The other Albany captain in the council was George White. Rosewell Beebe's future commanding officer, Samuel Elmore, is listed as president of the council. See also allthingsliberty.com/2021/04/joseph-mccracken-new-yorks-first-revolutionary-captain/ and jardispatches.podbean.com/e/e119-philip-d-weaver-new-york-s-first-revolutionary-captain/.

12. Beebe to his wife Sarah, June 16, 1775, W.16997, *Pensions*, Roll 200.

13. Entries for June 28-30, 1775 and The New York Line on the Continental Establishment of 1775, Fernow, *Documents Relating*, 15:12-13, 527-528. Baldwin's Muster Roll. In rare cases, an infantry regiment might be split into two or more battalions, but during the American Revolution, most regiments were a single battalion. Thus, the terms regiment and battalion became interchangeable.

About a month later, Van Schaick sent an accounting of the number of troops recruited for his regiment to the Provincial Congress. In the report he noted that

> The five first companies on this return, are those raised by the committee of this city and county, who are now on actual service at Lake George and the posts adjacent, from whence General Schuyler has ordered an officer out of each company down the country to complete the levies of those companies. The officers of the last five companies on this return, have but lately received their warrants, and are now raising men in this and the neighbouring counties.
>
> ... It is impossible for me at present to say when my regiment will be ready to take the field, as I cannot determine with what success the recruiting officers will meet.
>
> You may depend upon me that nothing will be wanting on my part to expedite the completing of the Regiment as I am convinced that the circumstances of the country admit of no delay.[14]

The chart included with this report shows that Baldwin's company was comprised of just thirty-two rank and file, plus three sergeants, the two lieutenants, and the captain.[15] As these numbers were roughly half the desired seventy-two for a company in the new 2nd New York, they needed to recruit.

As the junior lieutenant, Rosewell Beebe was likely to be tasked with increasing the number of recruits needed to fill the ranks. There is nothing of this duty in any official records, but one of Beebe's men, Samuel Doty, mentioned a leave that Beebe was on where he would, indeed, do some recruiting afterwards:

> Lieut. Rosewell Beebe, after an absence of some weeks returned home to Kings district with recruiting orders; this deponent having now obtained liberty from his master immediately enlisted as a private in the aforesaid company and on the return of Lieut. Beebe to the Army this Deponent accompanied him and in the regiment commanded by Colo. Goose Van Schaick. Sometime in the month of August at Fort George; at this place this deponent and the aforesaid Lieut. Beebe continued to perform the duties of soldiers until late in the fall when they took the Lakes and went by water to Montreal in Canada.[16]

14. Goose Van Schaick to the Provincial Congress, July 24, 1775, *Journals of the Provincial Congress*, 2:68.
15. Ibid.
16. Samuel Doty's deposition, May 27, 1837, W.16997, *Pensions*, Roll 200 (Doty Deposition). With so many veterans being lost to the ravages of time, Sarah Beebe Frisbee, who re-married to Philip Frisbee in 1779 and survived him as well, was lucky to have an eighty-

Beebe's wife confirmed his recruiting trip to his home district saying that "her husband after being absent for about a month or six weeks returned home with recruiting orders, and did enlist a number of men in the vicinity of New Concord, after remaining with his family and friends for about two weeks he left."[17]

This would not be Beebe's only leave. Baldwin's company muster roll, dated October 13 at Fort George, lists Beebe as being "Absent by Leave" with no explanation.[18]

Beebe himself does not appear again in the documentary record until November 2, when Yates, second in command of the 2nd New York and ranking officer at Fort George, sent him north from there with a parcel of watch coats for the use of the New York forces located between there and Fort Ticonderoga. With five coats to be distributed per company, it had to have been a good-sized parcel.[19]

In addition, Yates wrote to Maj. Gen. Philip Schuyler to inform him of the plan and that he, and apparently Beebe, were open to sending the watch coats to the army to the north. Yates also gave Beebe a nice little compliment in his memo to the general.

> I send in Charge of Lieut Roswell Beebe a parcell of Watch Coats for the use of the New York forces if you think fit to forward them to the army the Bearer Being a Carfull & Deligent officer & deserious of proceeding if you should think proper.[20]

Following the fall of Fort Chambly to the Congressional forces on October 18, the area in and around Montreal became a hotbed of activity. Troop movements between locations were not uncommon. Companies of the 2nd New York regiment could find themselves arriving at one location only to move to another the next day.

four-year-old Samuel Doty available to provide a deposition for her pension application in the name of her late first husband, Rosewell Beebe. This deposition is full of important details and is remarkable for its time. Few men lived to be his age and even fewer had so many details readily at hand.

17. Sarah Beebe Frisbee's deposition, May 3, 1832, W.16997, *Pensions*, Roll 200.

18. Baldwin's Muster Roll. Fort George was a single bastion of an incomplete fort and support buildings located at the south eastern end of Lake George.

19. Yates to Beebe, November 2, 1775, Manuscripts and Archives Division, New York Public Library, Philip Schuyler Papers, MssCol 2701, Box 40, Reel 20, Letters O-Z, courtesy of Donald M. Londahl-Smidt (Schuyler Papers). New York Public Library Digital Collections accessed February 2, 2022. digitalcollections.nypl.org/items/95d3f0d0-d6b3-0134-e6a4-00505686a51c.

20. Yates to Schuyler, November 2, 1775, Schuyler Papers, Box 26, Reel 12, Letters to Schuyler. Source courtesy if Don Londahl-Smidt. New York Public Library Digital Collections accessed February 2, 2022. digitalcollections.nypl.org/items/0edd3e60-4aea-0134-3adb-00505686a51c.

Baldwin's company finally moved north again and arrived at Fort Ticonderoga on November 13, joining White's company which had arrived the day prior. Both companies "imbarked" for St. Jean on November 14.[21]

Brig. Gen. Richard Montgomery's branch of the Continental army's Canadian campaign strategy had not been doing well. Despite the brief and successful siege of Fort Chambly that ended on October 18, the siege of Fort St. Jean took two and a half months. Ending on November 3, the St. Jean siege was an accomplishment that had taken far too long to achieve. The assault on the walled city of Quebec was yet to come and it was getting colder every day. Enlistments were expiring. Exact dates varied, but most of the men would be out of the army by year's end.

In an attempt to combat this, Montgomery made an announcement through his aide-de-camp, James Van Rensselaer:

> The General embraces this happy occasion of making his acknowledgments to the troops, for their patience and perseverance during the course of a fatiguing campaign. They have merited the applause of their grateful countrymen. He is now ready to fulfil the engagements of the publick. Passes, together with boats and provisions, shall be furnished, upon application to commanding officers of Regiments, for such as choose to return home. Yet he entreats the troops not to lay him under the necessity of abandoning Canada; of undoing in one day what has been the work of months, and of restoring to an enraged and hitherto disappointed enemy the means of carrying a cruel war into the very bowels of their Country. Impressed with a just sense of the spirit of the troops, their attachment to the interest of the United Colonies, and of their regard to their own honour, he flatters himself that none will leave him at this critical juncture, but such whose affairs or health absolutely require their return home. He has still hopes, notwithstanding the advanced season of the year, should he be seconded by the generous valour of the troops, hitherto highly favoured by Providence, to reduce Quebeck, in conjunction with the troops which have penetrated by way of the Kennebeck River and thereby deprive the Ministerial Army of all the footing in this important Province.

21. Entries for November 12, 13, and 14, William Yarrington Diary, 1759-1776, MS 2958.11299, The New-York Historical Society's manuscript collection. The New-York Historical Society Digital Collections, accessed April 3, 2022. cdm16694.contentdm. oclc.org/digital/collection/p16124coll1/id/32455 and cdm16694.contentdm.oclc.org/digital/collection/p16124coll1/id/32456. Thank you to Robert Winowitch for providing the digital source originally provided by Alan C. Aimone. The entries refer to "headquarters," not "Fort Ticonderoga," but at this time they were one-in-the-same.

Those who engage in this honourable cause shall be furnished completely with every article of clothing necessary for the rigour of the climate, viz: a blanket coat, coat, vest, breeches, one pair stockings, two shirts, leggins, socks, shoes, mitts, and cap, at the Continental charge, and one dollar bounty. The troops are only requested to engage till the 15th of April. They shall be discharged sooner, if the expected re-enforcements arrive before that time.[22]

Those who did not take Montgomery's offer to extend their enlistments were left to their own devices when their original enlistments expired. One of the officers who missed out on the extension opportunity was Beebe, but instead of going home, he re-engaged on January 1, 1776 for an additional four months with the Connecticut forces. Doty explained that

Their time of engagement and service having expired on the first of January 1776, at this time Captain Hezekiah Baldwin and Lieut. Nathaniel Rowley, having returned home Lieut. Rosewell Beebe was promoted to the Rank of Captain and [Sergeant] Lathrop Allen to a Lieut. Captain Rosewell Beebe raised a company for 4 months to this company, this Deponent immediately enlisted and performed the duties of a private in the aforesaid Rosewell Beebe's Company.[23]

From Montreal on January 1, Beebe wrote to his wife explaining his extended enlistment and his hope for a future with her upon returning home in the spring:

I once more write to let you know that I am well and healthy I was never So fat in my Life as I am at this present time. I am Returned in our morning Reports Present fit for Duty thanks bee to God that I can thus Write with truth and I hope these Lines will find you and our Children in as good a State of health as they Leave me . . . .

I have nothing strange to write at present But what Capt. Baldwin as he is Coming home can Relate. I have Engaged to Serve my Country till the fifteenth of April Next to Be Dismist Sonnor if the Service will admit. I am in hope to come home Some time this winter if the troops arrive which are expected if not I shall return home in April if alive and well. I want to [hear] from you But don't Expect I shall Before I Return as we are a great Distance from Each other[24]

---

22. General Order from Montreal, November 15, 1775, Force, *American Archives*, 4th Series, 3:1683-1684.
23. Doty Deposition.
24. Beebe to his Wife Sarah, January 1, 1776, W.16997, *Pensions*, Roll 200.

Beebe was to command the ninth company of Brig. Gen. David Wooster's new Provisional regiment.[25] This short-term understrength regiment would serve as a landing place for soldiers who wanted to continue serving through the winter, but whose enlistments had expired. It consisted mostly of Connecticut troops, but also some New Yorkers. A number of Baldwin's old company, like Doty, would follow Beebe into the new regiment.[26]

Historians generally agree that the December 31 assault on Quebec City was a complete disaster. Many of the troops under Col. Benedict Arnold's command were killed or captured, while those under Montgomery retreated after he and a number of others were killed by an opening cannon shot.

The newly organized Canadian department of the Continental army, often referred to as the "army in Canada," was in deep trouble after failing to capture Quebec.[27] Their intended commander, Montgomery, who unbeknownst to him had been promoted to major general on December 9, was now dead.[28] The British were expected to send a relief force to break through to the now besieged Quebec and, with many not taking Montgomery's reenlistment offer, most of the troops were leaving the theater.

Even though they were far away in Philadelphia, Congress was fully aware of these issues. On January 8, they resolved to consolidate the rest of the regiments remaining in Canada and to start moving fresh troops into the area. The attempt to hold the line was on.[29]

While Arnold commanded the forward areas surrounding Quebec, the lesser-known Wooster, from Connecticut, was in charge at Montreal. Well into his mid-sixties, Wooster was a bit of an enigma. He

---

25. *Arrangement of Officers in the Regiment rais'd at Montreal 18th Novr 1775 to serve 'till ye 15th April 1776 Commanded by Brigadier Genl. Wooster*, George Washington Papers, Manuscripts Division, Library of Congress. Source courtesy of Donald M. Londahl-Smidt. The undated list was filed at the end of July 1776, but does not reference Beebe's passing. This regiment is often confused with Wooster's old 1st Connecticut from 1775 that had already disbanded. In addition, this regiment and subsequently Samuel Elmore's Connecticut regiment included two additional companies commanded by former 2nd New York officers Israel Spencer and John Tillman, plus Theodore Woodbridge's Connecticut company included a number of former 2nd New Yorkers.

26. Some of these men include federal pensioners Lathrop Allen, S.42898, *Pensions*, Roll 1586; Samuel Doty, S.43351, *Pensions*, Roll 837; Jerimiah Griffith, W.19532, *Pensions*, Roll 1133; and Timothy Lord, S.42898, *Pensions*, Roll 1586; plus non-pensioners Palmer Cady, Asa Chapman, and Josiah Fuller.

27. Congressional Resolution, February 17, 1776, *Journals of the Continental Congress*, 4:156

28. Congressional Resolution, December 9, 1775, ibid., 3:418.

29. Congressional Resolutions, January 8, 1776, ibid., 4:39-40.

was a brigadier in the Continental army, while at the same time a major general of Connecticut's forces. He also simultaneously commanded a regiment, initially the 1st Connecticut regiment in 1775 and then the aforementioned provisional regiment in early 1776.[30]

In the midst of all this, smallpox was spreading through the ranks of the Continental army. This was not an ideal situation for starting a revolution, but concern about a smallpox epidemic was already growing throughout colonial America. Given the limited technology of the day, there were only two options for protecting against the contagion: quarantine and inoculation.

As early as December 1775, the New York Provincial Congress made it clear what option they preferred:

> Ordered, That no person whatsoever do inoculate for the Small-Pox within this Colony, until the further order of this Congress; and that the several Committees in this Colony, within their respective Districts, carefully observe that there be a punctual compliance with this order.[31]

General orders to the Continental troops before Quebec on February 11, probably issued by Arnold, indicated the concern about the spread of smallpox:

> Whereas the repeated orders given to prevent the spreading of that fatal disorder the Small-Pox, have been in a great measure disregarded; it is ordered that the commanding officer of every company immediately send such of his company as are seized with it to the Hospital; and all soldiers who shall know of any persons with that disorder in their private quarters, and do not make immediate complaint thereof to the Barrackmaster, shall be treated as neglecting their duty, and guilty of a breach of orders.[32]

Arnold also submitted a status report to John Hancock, president of the Continental Congress. In this report, he explained that

> We have been reinforced with only one hundred and seventy-five men; our whole force is about eight hundred effective men. We have about two hundred sick and unfit for duty, near fifty of them with the

---

30. Entry for David Wooster, Frances B. Heitman, *Historical Register of Officers of the Continental Army During the War of the Revolution, April, 1775, to December, 1783, Reprint of the New, Revised, and Enlarged Edition of 1914, With Addenda by Robert H. Kelby, 1932* (Baltimore MD: Genealogical Publishing company, 1982), 606 (*Historical Register of Officers*).

31. Congressional order, December 13, 1775, Force, *American Archives*, 4th Series, 4:406.

32. General Orders before Quebec, February 11, 1776, ibid., 5:550.

small-pox. The Canadians, in most of the Parishes, mount for their own safety.[33]

Two weeks later, Arnold sent a similar report to Gen. George Washington who was with the main army outside Boston. In this one, he indicated that the smallpox numbers were quickly changing. He also added his concerns about the command situation.

> I am sorry to inform you, notwithstanding every precaution that could be used, the small-pox has crept in among the troops; we have near one hundred men in the Hospital; in general it is favourable, very few have died. I have moved the inhabitants of the vicinity of Quebeck into the country, and hope to prevent its spreading any further . . . .
>
> As General Schuyler's ill state of health will not permit his coming this way, I was in hopes General Lee, or some experienced officer, would have been sent to take the command here. The service requires a person of greater abilities and experience than I can pretend to. General Wooster writes me his intention of coming down here; I am afraid he will not be able to leave Montreal.
>
> I have the pleasure to inform you my wound is entirely healed, and I am able to hobble about my room, though my leg is a little contracted and weak. I hope soon to be fit for action.[34]

By March 15, things were still changing. Another general order, presumably from Arnold, was issued. This one, however, noted that some of the officers and men were defying orders and getting inoculated.

> As the spreading the Small-Pox at this juncture will probably prove the, entire ruin of the Army, the officers are desired to take all possible care to prevent it, by keeping the men from strolling from their quarters.
>
> The Surgeons of the Army are forbid, under the severest penalty, to inoculate any person. And as many officers and men are preparing for the small-pox, it is said with an intention of taking it by inoculation; to prevent the fatal consequences attending such conduct, those who are found guilty, if officers, will be immediately cashiered; if private soldiers, punished at the discretion of a Court-Martial.[35]

In "A Return of the Troops before Quebeck," dated March 30, Arnold numbered 2,505 men spread among fifteen regiments, with 786 of them sick. At least 501 of them were reported sick from "Small-Pox

33. Arnold to President of Congress, February 12, 1776, ibid., 4:1017.
34. Arnold to Washington, February 27, 1776, ibid., 4:1513-1514.
35. General Orders before Quebec, March 15, 1776, ibid., 5:551.

by inoculation." Clearly someone had not gotten the word from Arnold about only quarantining.[36]

Further investigation will be necessary to determine where these regiments were located at the time, but it is unlikely they were all specifically at Quebec. Since fifty of these men were from Wooster's regiment in Montreal; the suspicion is that some were at, or transferred from, Montreal, and were probably inoculated there. It remains an open question if this was done per orders, doctor's instructions, or by the men themselves.

Beebe was not among the men counted on that list as being sick from "Small-Pox by inoculation." Doty explained that he was

> under his [Beebe's] command till the small pox [illeg.] in the Continental Army, Captain Rosewell Beebe was there [Montreal] inoculated with it and died of the same on or about the 23 day of March 1776. The command then fell on Lieut. Lathrop Allen under him This deponent served until the 2 Day of May 1776 completing his engagement–Lieut. Allen was made Captain and this deponent continued in his Company and Joined Colo. Samuel Elmores Regiment of the Connecticut line some time in the month of June 1776 this Deponet subsequently marched to Fort Stanwix and continued in Lathrop Allen's company and Elmore's Regiment for one year."[37]

Following the campaign, Beebe's name was included in an official document that named the New York officers who were erased from the rolls "either on the account of promotion, resignation or death." The undated list has Beebe twenty-second out of the forty original second lieutenants in the 1775 New York Continental line.[38]

Outside of the information found in his federal pension application and some official documents, there appears to be no recognized record of Beebe's brief service in 1776 and his tragic death. He is listed in Heitman's *Historical Register of Officers of the Continental Army*, but only for his service with the 2nd New York in 1775.[39]

---

36. Arnold to Schuyler, April 20, 1776, ibid., 5:1098-1100. The chart was an enclosure in this letter.

37. Doty Deposition. Muster roll, Capt. Lathrop Allen's company, Col. Samuel Elmore's Battalion, 1777 January 13, *Revolutionary War Rolls 1775–1783*, (National Archives Microfilm Publications, M246), War Department Collection of Revolutionary War Records, Record Group 93, Roll 27, Jacket 206.

38. State of the Rank of the Officers raised in the Colony of New York in the Year 1775, *Calendar of Historical Manuscripts Relating to the War of the Revolution, in the Office of the Secretary of State* (Albany, NY: Weed, Parsons and Company, 1898), 2:42-43.

39. Entry for Rosewell Beebe, *Historical Register of Officers*, 96.

Established in 1783, the Society of the Cincinnati was the first veterans' fraternal organization in the United States. Its original purpose was to facilitate fellowship, friendship, and recognition for veteran officers of the Continental army and navy. They also lobbied Congress for promised benefits such as land-grants and backpay. Veteran infantry and artillery officers were eligible to join if they had served to the end of the war, resigned honorably after a minimum of three-year's service, were downsized out of the army (known as "derangement"), or died in the service. After a member's death, the Society provided for his eldest direct male descendant to replace him. If an officer had no son, they provided for the admission of the closest male relative. The Society also allowed for the admission of "the eldest male branches" of officers who had died in service on the same basis as the children of members.

The Society continues today as a multi-branch not-for-profit organization that supports American history education as well as cultural and literary activities.[40]

Having quietly passed away while serving, Beebe was understandably overlooked for posthumous membership by the Society of Cincinnati. As a New York resident he could have been inducted into the New York branch, or because he was a Connecticut officer at the time of his death, he could have been made a posthumous member of Connecticut's branch. Either way they chose, he deserves recognition by the Society.

EPILOGUE

Shortly after this article was published, Dr. Matthew S. Bowdish, a member of the Committee on Pretensions for the Society of the Cincinnati in the State of Connecticut, contacted the JAR about their desire to determine if Beebe could be included in their Society. Over the next six months, with support documentation provided by Mr. Weaver, Dr. Bowdish was able to get Beebe's propositus approved for membership. Since the Connecticut Society is a lineage-based organization, a male descendant of Beebe should contact them for more information about representing him.[41]

---

40. www.societyofthecincinnati.org/. mountgulian.org/history/the-society-of-the-cincinnati/.
41. Matthew S. Bowdish, personal communication, November 18–24, 2022 and June 17, 2023.

# Burlington, 1776:
# The Forgotten Opportunity

## COLIN ZIMMERMAN

The 1776 campaign season had ended badly for General George Washington and the Continental Army as the dejected Patriots struggled through foul weather over primitive New Jersey roads as they marched toward Trenton in early December. To compound matters, Washington was faced with certain termination of the conflict if the situation did not dramatically improve. The only remedy at this bleak hour would be a bold, almost miracle-like, victory to turn his fortunes around.

True to his character Washington, with his army now safe in Bucks County, Pennsylvania in the first week of December, urgently set out to save his young nation's cause. His enterprise, planning, and innovation ultimately resulted in crossing the Delaware River and the subsequent attack on the isolated Trenton outpost. This event, which occurred on the evening of December 25 and carried into the morning of the 26th has gone down as one of the most singular, recognizable, and critical events in the American national story. This decisive moment, however, was only possible because of a series of independent, yet strategically linked incidents, which individually laid the foundation for Washington's strategic stroke of genius and the rescue of the American cause. Washington understood the necessity of keeping rivercraft out of the hands of the British and securing the ferry systems along the river. There were many key areas along the Delaware River, the most important of which was Burlington, a bustling little town that served as the gateway to Philadelphia.

The small yet commercially prosperous river font town of Burlington, New Jersey, boasted several large ferries, wharves, major road networks, and a military barracks. For British general Sir William Howe's army, Burlington was the first step to taking the rebel capital of

Philadelphia by land in 1776, and, certainly, Washington and other top Continental officers also acknowledged its vital importance for the same reason. On December 8, the day after his army crossed into Pennsylvania, Washington, now roughly twenty miles north of Burlington, seized its critical importance in the larger strategic focus. Col. John Cadwalader, then at Continental Army headquarters at Trenton Ferry, received orders from Washington to "dispatch a party of men from Philadelphia to cut down and destroy the two bridges on the Burlington Road, one on Pensawkin [Pennsauken] and the other on Cooper's Creek, as he is apprehensive the enemy intend to pass to Philadelphia by that route."[1] The reference to the Burlington Road implies that its junction at Burlington was of major significance should Howe opt to use Cooper's Ferry further south in conjunction with the upper ferry.

As the tense situation along the Delaware continued to reveal itself, new strategic initiatives and opportunities forced new decisions to be made. Washington dispatched Virginia Col. Samuel Griffin to organize the Gloucester, Salem, and Cumberland County militias and take them into Burlington County to create a "diversion." While Griffin was gathering his force, other disconnected commands prepared to make their own strikes. The small, undermanned, and ill-equipped Pennsylvania Navy had in the waning days of 1776 performed valuable service. The gunboats and galleys of its fleet had helped cross Washington's dejected army from Trenton on December 7 and had since vigorously patrolled the river, remaining vigilant for what was coming next.[2]

The Pennsylvania Navy was the most significant military obstacle that Howe's forces would have to overcome should the decision be made to cross the Delaware and move on Philadelphia. Commodore Thomas Seymour, in command of the forces in that part of the river, saw fit to dispatch four galleys to protect the area around Burlington. This small squadron had strict orders to cannonade the town should Hessian troops appear within its limits. While the naval forces gathered themselves, the second largest force next to the main Continental Army at Newtown, Pennsylvania was gathering across the river from Burlington in Bristol.

1. John Cadwalader to the Pennsylvania Council of Safety, December 8, 1776, Charles Roberts Autograph Collection, 724, Box 1, HCL.; George Washington to John Hancock, December 9, 1776, founders.archives.gov/documents/Washington/03-07-02-0222; Washington to Hancock, December 8, 1776, founders.archives.gov/documents/Washington/03-07-02-0213.
2. Joseph Reed to Washington, December 22, 1776, founders.archives.gov/documents/Washington/03-07-02-0324; In Council of Safety, December 5, 1776, Minutes of the Pennsylvania Council of Safety, *Colonial Records of Pennsylvania* (Philadelphia: Jo. Severns & Co. 1852), 11:4.

This command consisted of five battalions of the Pennsylvania Associators, the Burlington County militia, and a later addition of New England Continentals.[3] This force was responsible for protecting the area ranging from Bordentown down to Dunks Ferry just south of Burlington. Holding Bristol ensured opposition to any attempt by Howe to cross, but it was soon recognized that any Hessian advance from Bordentown toward Burlington would need to be checked or contested by forces in New Jersey in order to deprive the enemy of its vital usage.

The concept for this aggressive defense was probably formulated by officers in the Pennsylvania Navy. Aside from retaining overall command of the operation, with its officers leading the land force, this novice navy had in the days prior patrolled up and down the river, pulling into the various creeks and streams to confiscate boats and other craft from being used by their enemy. They gained firsthand knowledge of the terrain, and the general road networks, and could by the presence of their boats on the river dictate which route the Hessians would have to march to get to Burlington.[4] Contesting them on the inland route was a way to save Burlington from occupation and thwart Howe's grand strategy.

As would be expected, Philadelphia, the capital of the new United States, was embroiled in panic as the war approached its doorstep. The Council of Safety, eager to provide for the defense of the region, sought Washington's advice. The general responded on December 10 to the Pennsylvania Council of Safety:

> Yours of last Evening reached me at 4 OClock this Morning. I immediately sent Orders to Commodore Seymour to dispatch one of his Gallies down to Dunk's Ferry, and I shall dispose of the Remainder in such Manner, and at such places as will be most likely, not only to annoy the Enemy in their passage, but to give the earliest Information of any Attempt of that kind. Parties of the Enemy have been reconnoitering both up and down the River, and I imagine it has been one of those parties that have appeared near Burlington, for as they have not found the least Opposition from the people of Jersey, they venture very far from their main Body, which from the best Information still lays.[5]

3. Washington to John Hancock, December 10, 1776," founders.archives.gov/documents/Washington/03-07-02-0225; General Orders, December 12, 1776, founders.archives.gov/documents/Washington/03-07-02-0239.
4. Minutes of the Pennsylvania Council of Safety, December 3, and December 5, 1776, *Colonial Records of Pennsylvania*, 11:25, 39, 52.
5. Washington to Thomas Wharton, Jr., December 10, 1776, founders.archives.gov/documents/Washington/03-07-02-0229.

The need for organized bodies of troops to secure New Jersey was paramount, but with the Continental Army securely on the Pennsylvania side of the river, the largely inexperienced New Jersey militia was hard-pressed to take on the bulk of the Crown Forces alone. The Pennsylvania Committee of Safety also recognized that

> whereas, some designing, ill-disposed persons, have spread false reports that the number of troops now in New Jersey is too great; that many are in consequence discharged by the generals; and that there is not any occasion to forward the troops who have not yet been at camp. The Council, therefore, to frustrate the designs of such persons, and to hasten the march of the Associators to the Camp in Jersey. Make known that there is an immediate necessity for the Associators to hasten their march to the said camp with all expedition and pay no regard to any reports which do not come from this Council or other proper authority.[6]

As early as September, the Pennsylvania Navy had been preparing for the war to come to the Philadelphia area, which saw both Pennsylvania and New Jersey militia forces begin preparing the Delaware River for defense. Capt. Thomas Seymour was appointed commodore in September 1776 and was furnished with instructions from his superiors at the Pennsylvania Committee of Safety. The instructions consisted of five necessary guiding principles for the commodore and his fleet. The points elaborated on the need to maintain a disciplined force that remained in constant readiness to meet the enemy. As a final thought, the Committee stressed the need for the fleet to operate as one:

> these being the principal matters that have occurred to the Council, they earnestly recommend to you however, that you endeavour to promote the Utmost Harmony between you and the officers of the fleet, and between one another, on which depends so much the success of every undertaking where men are to act in concert, and mutual assistance required.[7]

With Patriot militia concentrating on the Bristol side of the Delaware in conjunction with the Pennsylvania Navy's vigilant patrolling, it became immediately clear to Col. Carl Emil Ulrich von

6. The Committee of Safety 1775-1776, The Council of Safety 1776-1777, Concerning the Necessity of Troops for New Jersey, *Colonial Records of Pennsylvania*, 10:706.
7. "Instructions to the Commodore of the Fleet, the Council of Safety, September 26, 1776," *Colonial Records of Pennsylvania*, 10:730, 731-32; Pennsylvania Council of Safety to Washington, December 9, 1776, founders.archives.gov/documents/Washington/03-07-02-0224.

Donop, the commander of the Hessian and Scottish forces in the Bordentown area, that there would be some level of resistance. Von Donop was an opportunist and was not fighting in the American rebellion because he was ordered to by his landgrave; he had willingly volunteered and pushed for the assignment, as he hoped it would further his career. His professional eye was set on obtaining an appointment in the Prussian service, the best European army at the time. Action in America afforded him the opportunity to establish a sturdy command and combat record that would make him more marketable to Prussia. Von Donop had served with distinction during the Seven Years' War and afterward as the Landgrave of Hesse-Kassel's personal adjutant prior to coming to America.[8] Von Donop and the Hessians had been in the war since the summer of 1776, and they had already established a fearsome reputation for themselves, fighting fiercely at the battle of Long Island and especially the assault on Fort Washington.[9]

As the last of the Continental troops crossed the Delaware River to safety, Sir William Howe began to reign in his forces. Although he was often criticized by contemporaries and later by scholars, it is fair to point out that putting a temporary halt to operations to regroup was a wholly sound strategic principle, allowing him, in theory, to apply his army's maximum potential in a final stroke on Philadelphia under favorable conditions. The deployment of the Hessians on the left flank of his line of garrisons across New Jersey, aside from symbolically recognizing their excellent performance, also had a calculated propaganda factor. Hessian soldiers were feared, and their concentrated presence in Southern New Jersey may have served to deter the untried local militia from any significant resistance.[10] For a rebellion that seemed very likely to be over in a matter of days if not weeks, this appeared to be a sound strategy.

Von Donop was the senior ranking officer in Southern New Jersey. This, coupled with his desire to advance his reputation, made taking

8. Wilhelm Gottlieb Levin von Donop: The Obermarschall and Drosten Wilhelm Gottlieb Levin von Donop zu Lüdershofen, Maspe Nachricht von dem Geschlecht der von Donop (Paderborn: Herman Leopald Bittneven, 1796), 21.

9. Edward J. Lowell, *The Hessians: And the Other German Auxiliaries of Great Britain in the Revolutionary War* (New York: Harper & Brothers, 1884), 53-54.

10. Sir Henry Clinton, *The American Rebellion: The British Commander -in- Chief's Narrative of his Campaigns, 1775-1782* (New Haven: Yale University Press, 1954), 55-56; Margaret Morris, *Margaret Morris: Her Journal with Biographical Sketch and Notes*, ed. John W. Jackson (Philadelphia: George S. McManus Company, 1949), 6; Johann Ewald, *Diary of the American War: A Hessian Journal*, ed. Joseph P. Tustin (New Haven: Yale University Press, 1979), 30.

Burlington, the principal riverfront city needed to capture Philadelphia by a land campaign, a very tempting target. At his disposal and immediate command, he had roughly 2,500 men. These troops consisted of the Hessian grenadier battalions Linsingen, Block, and Minnigerode; Hessian jägers; and the 42nd Regiment of Foot. The brigade was rounded out with six 3-pound cannons served by Hessian artillery and two 6- and 3-pound guns from the Royal Artillery. Additionally, von Donop had command over the Trenton garrison and was expecting heavy cannons capable of contesting the Delaware River fleet. His plan was simple: once in Bordentown he would stage his men, proceed with a detachment down to Burlington to test its limits, and determine if he could immediately occupy the town or wait for the arrival of the heavy cannon then en route from New York.[11]

The three Hessian Grenadier battalions and the Jäger detachment occupied posts in the immediate vicinity of Bordentown. One important detachment occupied the middle ground between Bordentown and Trenton along Crosswicks Creek and acted as the lifeline for communication between the two larger garrisons. Immediately south of Bordentown, Capt. Johann Ewald and his detachment of Jägers occupied an advanced post at the Lewis family mill situated along Black Creek, a small tributary that emptied into the Delaware River. Although the Lewis family were patriots, Captain Ewald recalled the warm hospitality offered by the family, from which a friendship grew. Ewald's men were ideal for this sort of outpost duty and were the logical choice to act as the vanguard when von Donop chose to make his move on Burlington. The last command associated with the larger Trenton-Bordentown force was comparatively its most unique; the 42nd Regiment of Foot, the Royal Highland Regiment or Black Watch, would hold an isolated outpost in Black Horse several miles east of Bordentown and just north of Mount Holly.[12]

Through one channel or another, word of von Donop's plan was made known to the Patriot forces within the sector. Gathering an appreciation of the lethality of von Donop's command, local commanders understood that the mostly-untried militia forces would likely have a hard time contesting the full might of their enemy in open traditional combat. The decision was made to dispatch the 5th Battalion of the

11. Ewald, *Diary of the American War*, 30-31; William S. Stryker, *The Battles of Trenton and Princeton* (Trenton: Old Barracks Association, 2001), 46; William Howe to Wilhelm von Donop, December 13, 1776, Correspondence and Papers as Commander-in-Chief in the American Colonies, PRO 30/35, the National Archives, UK.
12. Ewald, *Diary of the American War*, 31.

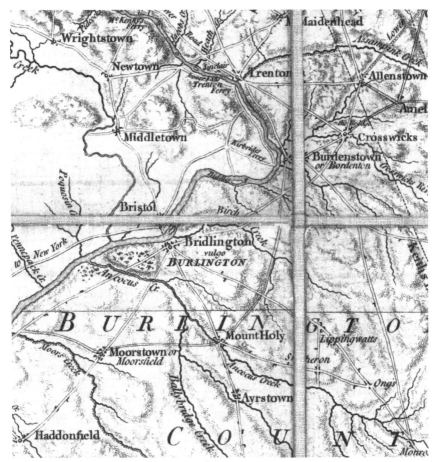

Detail from "The Province of New Jersey," 1778, engraved and published by William Faden. (*Library of Congress*)

Philadelphia Associators, which was designated a rifle battalion. These men in their rudimentary hunting shirts and rifles could in theory obstruct and haunt any movement southward towards Burlington and add a morale boost to the Burlington militia with their presence.

Pennsylvania Navy officers, Capt. Wingate Newman, Capt.-Lt. William Baxter, Lt. John Sober, and 2nd Lt. Nathaniel Wallace had been given temporary army commissions on December 7, and were the officers most likely placed in charge of the coming land portion of the operation. These men, sometime between the 7th and 10th of December, met with the Pennsylvania and New Jersey militia officers to hatch out the details of the plan.[13] This ad-hoc force totaling about 100 men would rendezvous in the early morning hours of December 11 somewhere near modern-day Fieldsboro. From here they would strike the marching Hessians with hit-and-run tactics, and destroy the many small bridges along the way to Burlington.

Almost all of these men had no previous combat experience, and the prospect of facing soldiers rumored to have no respect for Americans must have unnerved them slightly. Nevertheless, the 5th Battalion was in theory suited for the type of fighting they were about to engage in. These riflemen were feared amongst their enemies, and this coupled with the general terrain in the region favored defensive military actions suited for their skillset.[14] There were only several roads that a large military force such as von Donop's could travel on, with the most direct route to Burlington covered by the prowling eyes of the Pennsylvania galleys. Along the inland roads to Burlington, the countryside was generally flat, with small knolls, fence lines, and scattered woodlots interspersed throughout the neatly kept farms and plantations. There were several small bridges along the route, but the bodies of water they spanned were insignificant obstacles for a determined aggressor.[15]

From von Donop's perspective the weather considerations on December 11 were ideal for a movement; there had been no rain since December 5, and the temperature had consistently remained above freezing with mostly overcast and fog dominating the river in the early hours of the day.[16] It was protocol before making a general advance on an objective to reconnoiter it. Whatever rumors on the strength of the Patriot forces filtered into von Donop's headquarters would need to be verified. Three hundred grenadiers along with Ewald's Jägers were selected for the assignment. The only direct road to Burlington protected from the galleys was the York Road (modern Old York Road). With the temperature in the mid-thirties, the Hessian column of 300 grenadiers, jägers, two field pieces, and amusettes, began its reconnaissance in the early morning hours of December 11.[17]

13. Minutes of the Pennsylvania Council of Safety, December 7, 1776, *Colonial Records of Pennsylvania*, 11:36, 37.
14. Silas Deane, *The Deane Papers Vol 1. 1774-1777*, University of Wisconsin - Madison Digitized Aug 4, 2011. 53; Morris, *Margaret Morris: Her Journal*, 6.
15. York Road Property Survey 1775, Mansfield Historical Society.
16. Phineas Pemberton Weather Diary, December 1, 1776 – January 31, 1777, American Philosophical Society, Philadelphia.
17. Ewald, *Diary of the American War*, 30.

It remains unclear when Americans opened fire on the Hessian column. As Captain Ewald noted, the fire was sporadic and intensified closer to the small hamlet of Bustleton, roughly halfway to Burlington. Although no existing sources describe the detail of the fighting that occurred between Bustleton and Burlington, accounts of other similar actions may allow for the most likely scenario of how this fight unfolded. As previously noted, the terrain was generally flat with many intersecting fence lines and walls made of field stone. The roads were all dirt, with only several being large enough to accommodate a marching column of infantry and their field guns. Well to the front and fanned out across either side of the road, the Jägers would have led the advance, constantly looking for an enemy on the horizon. The American riflemen and militia likely formed in small clusters in woodlots, behind fences, and at choke points along York Road. The actions would have been fast and chaotic. Typically, the militia discharged their weapons once and removed to the rear to escape the accuracy of Jaeger rifles. Ewald and his men, although fewer in number than their opponents, were veterans and disciplined, and thrived in this sort of combat. They would have moved in concert with their commanding officers' orders, taking careful aim, all the while moving on the flanks and driving their foe back to the next position.[18]

Bustleton, the largest hamlet along York Road, also was a road junction. While the York Road continued, another smaller road forked off to the west, running down to the north side of the Assiscunk Creek. The Assiscunk, in a strange twist of geography, nearly quadrupled in size after it crossed the York Road. Taking the westerly road at the fork would have brought the command to the widest part of the Assiscunk where it conjoins with the Delaware River and is in direct line of sight of the Pennsylvania galleys. If von Donop had been banking on rebel ships not playing a role in protecting Burlington, he was sorely mistaken. In the stretch of the Delaware that flows south then east of Burlington Island, four galleys from the Pennsylvania Navy, *Hancock, Bull Dog, Dickinson,* and *Effingham,* were cruising in anticipation of engaging the Hessians, and were to bombard Burlington should any enemy troops appear in it. While this might appear harsh, it shows just how valuable Burlington was to the American cause at that moment;

18. This opinion is based on the broader analysis and synthesizing of a wild variety of firsthand accounts that deal with Crown Force actions against New Jersey and surrounding area militia.

the idea that the naval forces would have rather laid waste to the city than let it fall into enemy hands cannot be taken lightly.[19]

Perhaps the man with the most difficult job that day was Burlington's mayor, John Lawrence. His reputation has been linked to his very borderline views on the war, which eventually got him branded a Loyalist and expelled to Canada. On this day, he was faced with being bombarded by Pennsylvanians or occupied by nearly 2,000 German-speaking soldiers. His only immediate option was to try to mediate some sort of solution. Riding to the corner of modern-day High and Federal Streets, Mayor Lawrence caught a glimpse of the retreating militia making their way to the safety of the *Hancock*, then the only galley at Burlington, and understood that he would now have to act. Spurring his horse, Lawrence and a small escort galloped up Federal Street and out onto Jacksonville Road, crossing a small bridge known locally as Yorkshire Bridge, where they met von Donop and his men somewhere between the bridge and the road's intersection with York Road. Here Lawrence sought reason from the Hessian officer, which to his satisfaction he found. Von Donop was a professional, and a man who, like many other military officers of the era, lived by a strict moral code; there was certainly no favor seeing the town destroyed. The Hessian colonel, upon hearing Lawrence's plea to keep the soldiers out of town due to the threat of the navy opening fire, immediately understood that his intended occupation of Burlington was suspended until the large cannon arrived to drive off the rival ships.[20]

Grasping the delicate nature of affairs, and likely wanting a closer look at the town, von Donop, with a small escort, including Captain Ewald, accompanied Mayor Lawrence into Burlington to negotiate with Captain Moore of the *Hancock* who had placed himself on shore to serve as a liaison between the town and Commodore Seymour. Not having the authority to cut terms with von Donop and knowing that Seymour's orders to cannonade the town were firm and from General

19. Minutes of the Pennsylvania Council of Safety, December 5, 1776, *Colonial Records of Pennsylvania*, 11:39, 52; Plan of road from Colonel Shreve's to Black Horse, John Black Dept. Surveyors 1774, Mansfield Historical Society; John W. Jackson, *The Pennsylvania Navy, 1775-1781: The Defense of the Delaware* (New Brunswick, NJ: Rutgers University Press, 1974), 76-77.

20. Morris, *Margaret Morris: Her Journal*, 6; Richard L. Thompson, *Burlington Biographies: A History of Burlington, New Jersey, Told Through the Lives and Times of Its People* (Galloway, NJ: South Jersey Culture & History Center, 2016), 121-126; Ewald, *Diary of the American War*, 31; George Morgan Hills, *History of the church in Burlington, New Jersey; comprising the facts and incidents of nearly two hundred years, from original, contemporaneous sources* (Trenton, N.J., W. S. Sharp, 1876), 315.

Washington, Moore, at the insistent urging of a delegation of towns-people, some of whom accompanied him, agreed to go and confer with Commodore Seymour to find an alternate solution to this imminent problem; both parties agreed to a two-hour ceasefire.[21]

With this temporary agreement, the entire situation in Burlington became docile for the moment. Mayor Lawrence invited von Donop and his escort to his residence for a midday meal. By all accounts the company was enjoyable. Lawrence and von Donop treated each other accordingly and came to find through the course of their conversations, through a Dr. Odell who was able to speak French to Colonel von Donop, that they very much respected each other. Just as the agreed upon two hours was nearing its end, a jäger who had been on guard ran to Lawrence's house to inform them of galleys approaching from the south. Lawrence, accompanied by two other men, made haste down to the riverfront to deliver the arranged signal, the waving of his hat.

As fate would have it, Commodore Seymour, before Captain Moore could reach him, had dispatched the *Effingham*, *Dickinson*, and *Bulldog* to fire on the town upon hearing it was occupied. Captain Moore on board the *Hancock* attempted to inform the approaching squadron about the cease-fire agreement but a dominating wind stole his verbal warnings; the galleys sailed past unaware and arrived at Burlington ready to engage Hessians. Spotting Mayor Lawrence and the other men waving their hats, one of the approaching galleys opened fire on the small group with a swivel gun. Shocked, Lawrence made a second attempt at the signal, only to be answered this time with an 18-pound cannon blast. Similarly, sailors had climbed atop the masts of the gal-leys, and with small arms began to pepper the small detachment of Hessians within the town. Insulted, von Donop and his officers sprang up from the table and dodged fire as they rode out of town back to the Yorkshire Bridge.[22]

Von Donop was understandably irritated; he after all was a profes-sional officer and a gentleman of his word. Opening fire on an enemy while under a temporary truce was a bad move for the Americans. Al-though the Hessian colonel had no way of knowing about the apparent miscommunication, the damage was done and he would seek his re-venge. In a letter days later to his superior, von Donop expressed his desire to make a move on Burlington when he wrote, "I am waiting with impatience the arrival of the Grenadier Battalion Koehler which

---

21. Morris, *Margaret Morris: Her Journal*, 7.
22. Ibid.; Ewald, *Diary of the American War*, 31; Hills, *History of the church in Burlington*.

will bring with them six eighteen pounders, after which I will take possession of Burlington." In another letter he confidently stated that once
the guns arrived, "It will soon appear what resistance these marauders
will make when the six pieces of artillery are discharged at them, for
they will destroy all before them." To ensure this success, von Donop
instructed the 42nd Regiment to construct eight hundred fascines so
that a battery could be constructed overnight and surprise the Pennsylvania Navy by day. Irritating the Hessian officer even further was
the reported influx of militia forces operating from behind the haven
of the Rancocas Creek from which they pushed patrols towards Mount
Holly and Burlington to the north, which had the potential to alter his
designs – and would do so in the coming weeks.[23]

The issue surrounding Burlington, its intended occupation and potential use as a springboard to march on Philadelphia, was eclipsed with
General Washington's bold strike on Trenton and the follow-up victory
at Princeton only a few weeks later. Understandably, the rapid reversal
of events generated a strategic situation that aptly took Burlington off
the table as the center of the conflict moved back into northern New
Jersey. Colonel von Donop's reputation fell under a cloud as a result of
the events that transpired over the course of that December. He would
fall leading his men in battle the following year at Fort Mercer, never
earning the opportunity to clear his name. As the war continued Mayor
Lawrence's fate was also sour. Suspected of being a Loyalist, Lawrence
found himself jailed, only to be released later. His standing ruined,
Lawrence emigrated to Canada after the war for a short time. As for
many of the military elements involved, with the exception of Captain
Ewald's men and the 42nd, none of the units would rise to fame in the
war and collectively faded into memory.

In all fairness, the fighting around Burlington on December 11 was
almost insignificant in terms of scale and tactics. However, historians
and public memory alike should not downplay its importance on the
grand operational scale. Had George Washington not seized the opportunity to strike when he did, one can wholly assume that von Donop
would have carried out his plans for taking Burlington, creating an entirely new set of strategic circumstances that favored the Crown Forces,
which in turn may have created the needed circumstances to officially
end the American Rebellion in favor of the British.[24]

23. von Donop to William Leslie, December 16, 1776, William Stryker, *The Battles of
Trenton and Princeton*, 318-319; von Donop to James Grant, December 16, 1776, ibid.,
320; Hills, *History of the church in Burlington*, 315.
24. Thompson, *Burlington Biographies*, 121-126.

# Remember Baker:
# A Green Mountain Boy's
# Controversial Death and Its
# Consequences

### ⁂ MARK R. ANDERSON ⁂

Despite the imperative nature of his unusual name, Remember Baker has garnered significantly less historical attention than fellow Green Mountain Boys Ethan Allen and Seth Warner. Baker seemed destined for an important role in the Revolutionary War, but his life was cut short in an August 22, 1775 incident across the Quebec border. As a result of this "unhappy affair," Remember Baker's most significant Revolutionary War legacy was the diplomatic crisis caused by his "imprudence" on the very eve of the Canada invasion. Previously neglected documentary material only reinforces Baker's responsibility for the controversial incident that resulted in his death.[1]

Remember Baker had emerged as a Green Mountain Boys leader in the early 1770s, during the land-rights struggle in what is now Vermont. He moved from Connecticut to the disputed New Hampshire Grants region with his cousins, Allen and Warner. Together they settled, speculated, fought, and established de facto control that subverted New York's lawful authority there. Baker was indomitable in this effort, a French and Indian War veteran, "about 5 feet 9 or 10 inches high, pretty well sett, something freckled in his face," who had once killed a bear with only a hatchet. Friends and allies considered him "a Man of

---

1. "Extract of a Letter . . ., Sept. 5," *New-York Gazette,* September 11, 1775; Philip Schuyler to George Washington, August 31, 1775, Peter Force, ed., *American Archives. 4th Series [AA4]* (Washington, DC: M. St. Clair Clarke and Peter Force, 1837–53), 3:467.

Courage and Integrity and well beloved in that Country," but not everyone shared those sentiments.[2]

New Yorkers ranked Remember Baker as "one of the worst men among the Riotors" in the Grants region. He terrorized unwanted settlers with threats, property destruction, and corporal punishment. When a posse tried to arrest and deliver him to New York authorities in 1772, Baker lost a thumb to a sword stroke in the ensuing struggle before being rescued by compatriots. After this incident, he flaunted the missing digit as a badge of honor and authority while enforcing insurgent rule as a judge and militia captain. New York government officials grew increasingly exasperated with the Green Mountain Boys' relentless challenge to their jurisdiction. By March 1774, Gov. William Tryon had formally requested military support and offered £100 rewards for the apprehension of Ethan Allen or Remember Baker. The Grants conflict seemed to be reaching a climax.[3]

The spark of Revolutionary War in 1775 completely recast the region's politics. Shortly after Lexington and Concord, the Green Mountain Boys allied themselves with New England patriots to take British Fort Ticonderoga on May 10. Captain Baker and his militia company arrived too late for that conquest, but helped capture Crown Point a day later. Riding this wave of victory and eager to strengthen their position in the American Cause, the Green Mountain Boys selected Ethan Allen, Seth Warner, and Baker to represent them to the Continental Congress—although Baker does not seem to have joined his cousins on their Philadelphia trip.[4]

The Green Mountain Boys' political reorientation put them in some strange company, especially when Maj. Gen. Philip Schuyler took command of the Continental Northern Army. The general was a major New York landholder and assembly member—someone with clear political interests on his colony's side of the Grants struggle; yet as fellow patriots, Baker and Schuyler apparently overlooked past conflict. By mid-July 1775, the Green Mountain Boys captain was voluntarily

---

2. "100 Dollars Reward," *Connecticut Courant*, April 27, 1773; Ira Allen "Autobiography [1796]," in James B. Wilbur, *Ira Allen, Founder of Vermont: 1751-1814*, vol. 1 (Boston: Houghton and Mifflin, 1928), 9, 11-12.

3. "Account of the Temper of the Rioters . . .," April 15, 1772, *Documentary History of the State of New-York*, E. B. O'Callaghan, ed. (Albany, 1851), 4:776; "William Tryon . . . A Proclamation," [March 9, 1774], *New-York Gazette*, March 28, 1774.

4. Ira Allen, *History of the State of Vermont . . .*, (Tokyo: Charles E. Tuttle, 1969; reprint of *The Natural and Political History of the State of Vermont . . .*, London, 1798), 43-44; Letter from the Officers at Crown Point and Ticonderoga to the Continental Congress, June 10, 1775, *AA4* 2:957-58.

scouting the northern end of Lake Champlain for the general. With his "Bush fighting" skill and initiative, Baker proved to be a valuable intelligence source for military developments in Canada.[5]

In another unexpected twist that summer, New York reluctantly accepted a Continental Congress request to enlist a regiment of Green Mountain Boys. Cautious Grants township leaders, however, did not elect either Ethan Allen or Remember Baker as officers for the unit, which was commanded by Seth Warner. Nevertheless, Baker continued his reconnaissance missions around—and sometimes across—the New York-Quebec province line. Schuyler referred to him as "Captain Baker of the unenlisted Green Mountain Boys," differentiating him from peers in the new Continental regiment.[6]

THE UNHAPPY AFFAIR

The stage for Remember Baker's final act was set on July 27, as he prepared for another Lake Champlain mission. That day, Baker wrote to General Schuyler, proposing an aggressive scheme to ambush enemy forces from Canada, using a light boat to lure them into range of a hidden bateau armed with swivel guns. The general's response was recorded in the Orderly Book of Philip John Schuyler in the Huntington Library collections. Schuyler agreed to send Baker north again, but provided explicit instructions to ensure the captain's actions reflected Continental strategic objectives for Canada.[7]

> you are to proceed down the Lake and scout the coast in quest of any parties of *regular Troops* that may be sent by General Carlton to reconnoiter, if you should fall in with any you will use your Best Endeavours to take or Destroy them . . . *Should you meet with any Canadians or Indians you will Treat them with the greatest Kindness* and Invite them to Come and see me . . . *You will not go beyond the Limits of this province with your party* but as I wish to have Intelligence of what is Doing at St Johns *you are at Liberty with a few of your party to go by Land and reconnoiter that place* . . . You will on all such act with prudence and according to the best of your Judgment. [*author's emphasis*][8]

5. An Account of the voyage of Captain Remember Baker, begun the 13th day of July . . ., July 26, 1775, *AA*42: 1735.
6. Schuyler to Commissioners for Indian Affairs, August 31, 1775, *AA*43:493.
7. Baker to Schuyler, July 27, 1775, Philip Schuyler Papers [PSP], New York Public Library [NYPL], digitalcollections.nypl.org/items/5d144f00-84e2-0134-bce2-00505686a51c.
8. Philip Schuyler Orders to Capt. Remember Baker, July 27, 1775, Orderly Book of Philip John Schuyler, 1775, June 28 – 1776, April 18, Huntington Library [Orderly Book, Huntington Library].

Schuyler's specific restraints and different rules of engagement for British regular troops or Canadians and Indians would prove critical one month later when the general found himself dealing with the undesired consequences of Baker's mission.

The Orderly Book also contained Schuyler's supporting orders for the mission. Captain Baker was authorized to "take as many men of his own chusing" from Crown Point to form a detachment of twenty-five men, and the commander there was directed to issue them twenty days' provisions. The detachment embarked on the Continental schooner *Liberty*, which towed Baker's bateau and light boat north on Lake Champlain.[9]

Patrolling near the province line, *Liberty* served as a mobile base for Baker's reconnaissance forays. By mid-August, Baker and the schooner had been out longer than expected, so officers sent additional provisions from Crown Point. Uriah Cross, a soldier in James Easton's Massachusetts Regiment, was in this resupply party and joined Baker's detachment after their rendezvous.[10]

On August 20, Baker also welcomed Pvt. Peter Griffin aboard *Liberty*. He was another soldier from Easton's Regiment, who had just completed a separate lake scouting operation. Baker decided to send Griffin and a friendly Odanak (St. Francis Abenaki) across the province line by land to reconnoiter British Fort St. Johns, per Schuyler's orders. At dawn the next day, Baker and four men, including Uriah Cross, escorted the scout duo from *Liberty* in the two boats. Griffin and his partner disembarked on the western shore, near modern Rouse's Point, New York, south of the province line. As the scouts set out for a long, swampy trek to the fort, Griffin said that Baker proceeded down the Richelieu River, which flows north out of Lake Champlain, "in a boat to the Isle aux Noix, and Did Determine to Intercept the Scouts of the Regulars there." Ile aux Noix was nine miles north of the province line, indicating that Baker was intent on ignoring Schuyler's orders against operating "beyond the Limits of this province."[11]

There is no record of Baker's activities for the rest of that day. According to the captain's cousin and close associate Ira Allen, "in the

---

9. Schuyler to the Commanding Officer at Crown Point, July 27, 1775, Orderly Book, Huntington Library.

10. Uriah Cross, "Narrative of Uriah Cross in the Revolutionary War," ed. Vernon A. Ives, *New York History: Quarterly Journal of the New York State Historical Association* 63, no. 3 (July 1982): 279-294. 285; Richard Montgomery Examination of Peter Griffin, August 25, 1775, *AA4* 3:670.

11. Examination of Peter Griffin, August 25, 1775, *AA4* 3:671.

silent watch of the night," Baker's party landed on the east shore of the lake. Their camp was back on the New York side of the line, probably near Windmill Point (Vermont). At dawn on August 22, the captain and his four men "secured" the heavy bateau on land before embarking in their light boat. They paddled north to cross the province line.[12]

Around the same time, Lt. Edward Pearee Willington of the 26th Regiment of Foot led a party of eight native allies from British Fort St. Johns on a regular border patrol, accompanied by Indian Department interpreter Claude de Lorimier. They were looking for rebel spies and indications of a coming invasion. Like all of the king's Indian allies, this party was under Gov. Guy Carleton's strict orders not to operate across the province line. Willington took four men in one canoe to scout the west shore; Canadian interpreter Lorimier went east with four Kanesatake warriors in another canoe.[13]

Claude de Lorimier and his party disregarded Carleton's general orders that day and patrolled south of the province line. Concealed among low tree branches and reeds on the shoreline, the Canadian interpreter "saw the famous Captain Baker, but . . . was obliged to come back without attacking the party because we didn't want to start any trouble on the other side of the line." Oblivious to the potential ambush, Baker and his Americans continued north. Lorimier and his warrior companions kept exploring southward until they found Baker's cached bateau on the shore, hidden under branches. The party launched the armed boat and paddled it toward Canada.

Remember Baker, meanwhile, had crossed the province line and landed on the east shore, five miles into Canada. The captain "sat down and sharpened his flint"—he was "a curious marksman" who "always kept his musket in the best order possible." At this most unfortunate moment, the captain spied "a party of Indians . . . approaching the point of land where he was"—and they were in his own armed bateau! Baker ordered his four men to "be concealed and ready."[14]

---

12. Allen, *History of Vermont*, 45.

13. Lorimier said he was "patrolling with five Algonquians." Based on context, they were probably Arundaks, one of three different nations at Kanesatake village, twenty-five miles west of Montreal; Claude de Lorimier, *At War with the Americans: The Journal of Claude-Nicolas-Guillaume de Lorimier*, trans. and ed., Peter Aichinger (Victoria, BC: Press Porcepic, 1987), 28.

14. Allen, *History of Vermont*, 45; Cross, "Narrative," 285. The most precise contemporary description of this site came from "Diary of Captain John Fassett, Jr," in *The Follett-Dewey Fassett-Safford Ancestry* (Columbus, OH: Champlin, 1896), 216.

Details of the fatal affair that followed come from a number of sources.[15] General Schuyler provided the most detailed contemporary reports, undoubtedly informed by American survivors. Participants Claude de Lorimier and Uriah Cross wrote first-hand accounts many years after the fact. The most comprehensive version of the violent encounter came from Baker's cousin Ira Allen in his 1798 *History of Vermont*. This second-hand narrative aligns with details in the various primary sources and offers additional context for the complicated but fleeting encounter:

> when the Indians came near [, Baker] hailed them, and desired them to give up his boat in a friendly manner, there was no war between the Indians and the Americans . . . the Indians showed no signs of giving up the boat, whereupon Baker ordered them to return his boat, or he would fire upon them. An Indian in the boat was preparing to fire on Baker, who attempted to fire before hand with him, but his musket missed fire, owing to the sharpness of his flint, which hitched on the steel; he recover his piece, and levelled it at the Indian, at which Instant the Indian fired at him, one buck shot entered his brains and Baker fell dead on the spot. His men fired on the Indians and wounded some, but the boat was soon out of gun shot.[16]

Baker's spur-of-the-moment decision to fight for his lost boat was a direct contravention of Schuyler's strategically deliberate orders to treat Indians and Canadians "with the greatest Kindness."

After the exchange of volleys, Lorimier reported "all was silent." He and his Kanesatake companions, one wounded in the neck and another in the thigh, left in haste for Fort St. Johns aboard the captured bateau. A contemporary Quebec newspaper account reported, "it being almost dark they could not see whether or not they had killed or wounded any of the Enemy."[17]

The four Americans, jarred by Baker's death, reported seeing just a single Indian paddling off. One of the four survivors may also have been hit by the enemy salvo, since the British later found "a Grass Bed

---

15. Key sources for the Baker engagement are: Lorimier, *At War*, 28; Cross, "Narrative," 285; Allen, *History of Vermont*, 45; Schuyler to Washington, and Schuyler to the Commissioners for Indian Affairs, August 31, 1775, *AA4* 3:467, 493; "A Correspondent has sent us the following Account of a Skirmish happened on Lake Champlain," *Quebec Gazette*, August 31, 1775; "Quebec, August 28," *Northampton Mercury*, October 23, 1775; Journal of Colonel Guy Johnson, E. B. O'Callaghan, ed., *Documents Relative to the Colonial History of the State of New-York*, vol. 8 (Albany: Weed, Parsons and Company, 1857), 660.
16. Allen, *History of Vermont*, 45.
17. Lorimier, *At War*, 28; "A Correspondent . . .," *Quebec Gazette*, August 31, 1775.

had been made for a wounded Man at some Distance from the dead Man." The men left Baker where he had fallen, a single shot between his eyes. They did not linger. American participant Uriah Cross simply recounted, "We returned to our boats & shoved off."[18]

The next day, British Capt. Andrew Gordon led "25 Indians, 33 Soldiers, and 5 or 6 Volunteers" from Fort St. Johns to the skirmish site. They found Baker's body and collected his papers. Native warriors scalped Baker, cut off his head, and removed at least one finger, carrying the severed body parts back to Fort St. Johns. There, the warriors erected Baker's head on a pole before taking it to Montreal. According to Ira Allen, British officers eventually bought the head from their Native allies and had it buried with the body back at the skirmish site.[19]

IMMEDIATE RESPONSES AND LEGACY

Baker's papers provided British government officials with important intelligence on rebel scouting efforts around Fort St. Johns and incriminated several American contacts in Canada. The commander of Fort St. Johns was even ordered to arrest one of Baker's contacts at Lacolle, who had been "very kind & free in telling" the captain "all the proceedings of the Regulars." Loyalists also hoped that this opening act of violence, north of the province line, would inspire Canadians and Indians to decisively commit themselves to the British side of the war. The locals largely remained unaligned though, even as false rumors spread that Baker had orders from Schuyler "to give no quarter to Canadians or Indians."[20]

On the same day that the Baker affair took place, Peter Griffin and his Odanak scout companion completed their Fort St. Johns reconnaissance. When they reached their original landing spot, they did not see Baker. Instead, they "saw Ten Indians Coming in a Canoe from the East side of the River towards them." Griffin and his partner fled into

18. Cross, "Narrative," 285; "A Correspondent . . .," *Quebec Gazette*, August 31, 1775.

19. "A Correspondent . . ., *Quebec Gazette*," August 31, 1775; Lorimier, *At War*, 28; Thérèse Benoist to François Baby, Montreal, August 29, 1775, Hospice-Anthelme J.-B. Verreau, ed. *Invasion du Canada, Collection de Mémoires Recueillis et Annotes* (Montréal: Eusèbe Senecal, 1873), 309; Allen, *History of Vermont*, 45-46.

20. Daniel Claus, "Memorandum of the Rebel Invasion of Canada in 1775," CO 42/36 (microfilm), fol. 38b, Library and Archives Canada; Lorimier, *At War*, 28; Richard Prescott orders, August 31, 1775, Arthur G. Doughty, ed., "Appendix B – Papers Relating to the Surrender of Fort St. John's and Fort Chambly," *Report of the Work of the Public Archives for the Years 1914 and 1915* (Ottawa: J. de L Taché, 1916), 6; "Extract of Another Letter from Quebeck, Dated October 1, 1775," *AA4* 3:926; "Quebec, August 28," *Northampton Mercury*, October 23, 1775.

the woods to avoid capture and spent the night with a friendly settler nearby. The next morning, the Odanak's father found and delivered them back to *Liberty*. Griffin had vital intelligence for General Schuyler—the two British warships at Fort St. Johns were very near completion. American naval superiority on the lake was at risk. The Canada invasion could not begin soon enough. The schooner expeditiously set sail to deliver this time-sensitive information. Everyone aboard was still oblivious to Baker's fate. When Griffin reached Ticonderoga on August 25, General Schuyler was away at a crucial Six Nations Indian treaty conference in Albany. The deputy commander, Brig. Gen. Richard Montgomery, heard Griffin's report and promptly set the invasion into motion.[21]

Schuyler received word of the Baker affair by August 31, after the survivors had made their way back to Crown Point. The captain's unauthorized violence against Natives took place at the very moment when Continental officials were trying to secure the powerful Six Nations' neutrality. Schuyler had to limit the potential political damage. Erroneous information from Canada raised the stakes even further. The general was led to believe that Baker's party had killed two of the British-allied Native scouts—and the dead were reportedly from the village of Kahnawake, the central council fire of the Seven Nations in Canada. The Continentals were desperately hoping that confederacy would also avoid taking sides in the coming invasion. If Baker actually had killed Kahnawakes, Schuyler justifiably feared it might drive their nation to take up arms with the British.[22]

Schuyler shared all of this unfortunate news in letters to George Washington, Connecticut Gov. Jonathan Trumbull, and his fellow Continental Indian commissioners in Albany. Since the commissioners were still conducting treaty business with Six Nations chiefs, they were in the best position to assess and limit the diplomatic damage. Schuyler provided them all available details and emphasized that Baker had acted against express orders. He concluded, "What the consequence of

21. Examination of Peter Griffin, August 25, 1775, *AA4* 3:671; Montgomery to Schuyler, August 25, 1775, PSP, NYPL.
22. Montgomery to Schuyler, August 30, 1775, PSP NYPL; James Livingston to Montgomery, [August 1775], NYPL, digitalcollections.nypl.org/items/bad6720b-4792-a00b-e040-e00a18067aa1.
23. Schuyler to Washington, Schuyler to Jonathan Trumbull, and Schuyler to Commissioners for Indian Affairs, August 31, 1775, *AA43*:467, 469, 493. Biographer (and descendent) Ray S. Baker contended that Schuyler's claim that Remember Baker' went on his fatal mission "without my leave . . . contrary to the most pointed and express orders," was

Baker's imprudence will be is hard to foresee." Without advocating specific actions, Schuyler advised, "It behooves us . . . to attempt to eradicate from the minds of the Indians any evil impressions they may have imbibed from this mortifying circumstance."[23]

Schuyler joined his army for the Canada invasion, but continued working to limit the impact of "the intemperate heat and disobedience of Captain Baker." After crossing the province line and setting up camp at Ile aux Noix on September 5, the general published a circular letter to the Canadians and Indians. It explained that the Americans had come to help, rather than fight them. Specifically addressing Baker's actions and condoling the Seven Nations, Schuyler wrote: "If any of them have lost their lives, I sincerely lament the loss; it was done contrary to orders, and by scoundrels ill-affected to our glorious cause; and I shall take great pleasure in burying the dead, and wiping away the tears of their surviving relations, which you will communicate to them." Following Native protocols, he promised to do this through "an ample present."[24]

Back in Albany, the ink on the Six Nations treaty was barely dry when the Indian commissioners delivered an unvarnished account of the "melancholy news" to the chiefs. This was in accordance with treaty terms that encouraged open and honest communication. Six Nations chiefs were ultimately persuaded that it was "meerly an unfortunate accident." At the commissioners' request, four Oneida warriors agreed to visit Kahnawake to deliver news of the Albany treaty and explain the facts of the Baker incident. In mid-September, the Oneidas reached Canada at a critical point in the invasion. Their messages, reinforced by Schuyler's diplomatic gifts, ensured that the Seven Nations confederacy remained neutral for the rest of the year. With essential Native diplomatic assistance, Continental authorities had managed to avert catastrophic repercussions from the Remember Baker affair.[25]

a matter of diplomatic convenience — disavowing Baker for the greater good — but the clear language of Schuyler's orders show that the biographer was working on incorrect assumptions; Ray S. Baker, "Remember Baker," *The New England Quarterly* 4, no. 4 (October 1931): 627-28.

24. Schuyler to Jonathan Trumbull, August 31, 1775, and Schuyler to the Inhabitants of Canada, September 5, 1775, *AA4*3:469, 671-72.

25. Oliver Wolcott and Volckert P. Douw to Philip Schuyler, September 4, 1775, PSP NYPL; Douw to John Hancock, September 6, 1775 and A Speech to the Chiefs and Warriours of the Six Nations from the Commissioners, August 31, 1775, *AA4*3:494-95; Douw to New York Provincial Congress, October 4, 1775, *AA4*2:1275; Mark R. Anderson, *Down the Warpath to the Cedars: Indians' First Battles in the Revolution* (Norman: University of Oklahoma Press, 2021), 25-27.

In the immediate aftermath, Baker's death received relatively little popular notice. A couple of early articles described what little was known of the engagement. After word spread about the desecration of Baker's corpse, a few more pieces sought to inspire patriotic vengeance for the "base and savage conduct" of the British and their Native allies. Then the story effectively disappeared for twenty-four years. Ira Allen brought it back to light in his 1798 *History of Vermont*, which included the most detailed narrative of the affair. Allen accurately noted that "Captain Baker was the first man killed in the northern department." His conclusion that Baker's "death made more noise in the country than the loss of a thousand men towards the end of the American war" appears to have been a substantial exaggeration, though, based on what is reflected in contemporary written records.[26]

The Baker affair continued to receive scant attention through the 1800s. When the occasional historian or biographers told the story of Baker's death, they most often used it as a concluding point for their more detailed recitations of his Green Mountain Boys exploits. An early twentieth-century surge of patriotic commemoration brought slightly more enduring recognition for the captain's wartime contributions. Initially, Remember Baker's "sacrifices and valor" were honored in a single line on a Lake Champlain Tercentenary memorial plaque at Isle La Motte, Vermont in 1909. Twenty years later, the Vermont Society, Sons of the American Revolution erected a Baker-specific monument in Noyan, Quebec, the product of almost a quarter century of research and cross-border lobbying. Its bronze tablet read: "Captain Remember Baker, Vermont pioneer and leader of the Green Mountain Boys was killed near this spot by Indians while on a scouting expedition in Canada in the War of the American Revolution," and it repeated Allen's hyperbolic quote, "His death made more noise . . ." Overall, Baker's wartime contributions and death remain obscure historical points.[27]

26. Allen, *History of Vermont*, 46; "Extract of a Letter from a Gentleman at Albany, Sept. 2" and "Extract of a Letter . . ., Sept. 5, *New-York Gazette*, September 11, 1775; "Extract of a letter dated at the Carrying Place, near Ticonderoga, September 14, 1775, from an Officer in the New-York Forces," *The Constitutional Gazette* (New York), September 27, 1775; "Reflections on Gage's Letter to General Washington," *The Constitutional Gazette*, October 18, 1775.

27. "Exercises at Isla La Motte Close Celebration," *Bennington Evening Banner*, July 10, 1909; "Remember Baker's Grave," *St. Albans Daily Messenger*, September 16, 1905; *The Minute Man: Official Bulletin, National Society Sons of American Revolution* 24, no. 3 (January 1930): 369; www.vtssar.org/memorials/CPT%20Remember%20Baker.pdf. The Noyan memorial is currently being dismantled and concerned parties are seeking a new home for its bronze plaque.

The story of Remember Baker's fatal "unhappy affair" does serve to illuminate his influence in northern politics to the time of his death. It also shows the dangers that seemingly minor, rash tactical decisions—like fighting to recover a lost boat—can pose to strategic efforts. The captain's Vermont settlement and military contributions are worth remembering; but General Schuyler, the Continental Indian commissioners, and key Native diplomatic partners also deserve considerable credit in this event. By actively averting a strategic political catastrophe, they ensured that Remember Baker did not become a better known, but infamous, figure in American Revolutionary War history.

# Captain James Morris of the Connecticut Light Infantry

◆◆ MARK R. ANDERSON ◆◆

In 1812 when the British attacked the United States for the second time, Captain James Morris of the South Farms District of Litchfield, Connecticut took quill to parchment to capture his six years of experiences during the Revolutionary War as an officer in Connecticut's Light Infantry.[1] The light infantry was the battle-hardened, elite fighting force of Washington's army and was at the front of the battle lines. Over the next several years, when the spirit moved him, he recounted for posterity his many battle experiences, including his heroism during the siege of Yorktown where he helped take redoubt 10 which broke the back of the British defenses and forced their surrender. He also described his survival as a prisoner-of-war for three-and-a-half years. This is Capt. James Morris's story, one of unheralded heroism, patriotism, suffering, and triumph.

The Morris family immigrated from England in 1637 and was one the founding families of New Haven, Connecticut. Several generations prospered in New Haven before James' father, known as Deacon James, married the recently-widowed Phoebe Barnes about 1750 and decided to move north to the South Farms District of Litchfield where they started their family. Litchfield is an, "exceptionally handsome town, founded in 1715 in Connecticut's northwest hills, and is considered one of the most historic locations in the state. During the Revolutionary War years, the village was a center of patriotic activity; and in a subsequent period of cultural flowering, the community earned a national name for its excellent educational institutions, fine houses, and sophisticated residents." Morris's farm was next to a carriage road that con-

---

1. Robert Clark Morris, *Memoirs of James Morris of South Farms in Litchfield* (Yale University Press, 1933), III-IV.

nected South Farms to the town of Bethlehem, located about seven miles south from the center of Litchfield and three miles north of the town of Bethlehem's meeting house.[2]

James Morris was born on January 19, 1752 on a typical Connecticut farm for the times with a house which he described as "40 feet by 30, two stories high, kitchen back, a chimney at each end and a space way through, with a design that I should live in one half of the house." The family attended church in Bethlehem and James was baptized by the famed pastor Doctor Joseph Bellamy in Bethlehem's "old Meeting House." Bellamy was one of New England's leading pastors and social activists in his time.[3] The Morris and Bellamy families became close and remained close for many years. Jonathan Bellamy, Doctor Bellamy's son, was good friends with both James Morris and Aaron Burr throughout his short life.[4]

James was a very bright child, leaning to read at age four. At age six, after he finished reading his father's entire bible, his father honored his achievement by buying him his own bible which he cherished for many years. His youth was spent tending to farm duties, attending church meetings, and reading the bible with zeal. Throughout his life, even at a young age, Morris had an unwavering passion for education, learning, and teaching. In September 1771 at age nineteen he was accepted into Yale College and graduated in July 1775 with a degree in Divinity. He returned home and became a teacher in Litchfield's Grammar School. But the war's opening battle in Lexington, Massachusetts in April 1775 disrupted his career plans. Unsolicited, the Connecticut State Legislature offered Morris the rank of ensign in the Connecticut Light Infantry if he enlisted for six months. After consulting with his father and Doctor Bellamy he accepted the commission. His good friend and fellow Yale classmate, Jonathan Bellamy, received a similar offer and was commissioned at the same time.[5]

On August 27, 1776, under General Washington's command, Ensign Morris's first battle was the Battle of Long Island after which he and the rest of Washington's army safely escaped across the Hudson River. Three weeks later, on September 15, he was in the retreat from

2. Ibid., V-VI, 6; www.litchfieldhistoricalsociety.org/litchfield-the-making-of-a-new-england-town/.

3. Ibid., 1, 6-8.

4. Ibid., 15; en.wikipedia.org/wiki/Joseph_Bellamy; aminoapps.com/c/hamilton/page/item/jonathan-bellamy/8Jel_WdHXIQLlJeeDkBV1pN2Q0WZgwD4p.

5. Morris, *Memoirs*, 4-5, 11-15; aminoapps.com/c/hamilton/page/item/jonathan-bellamy/8Jel_WdHXIQLlJeeDkBV1pN2Q0WZgwD4p.

the city of New York when British troops landed on Manhattan. But his most memorable battle early in the war was the Battle of White Plains on October 28. And it was here his natural leadership skills became apparent. He wrote,

> I was in the battle of White Plains, where sundry of the soldiers, my friends and acquaintances, were killed and where I heard the bitter groans of the wounded. The Captain and Lieutenant of the company were taken sick and were removed from the camp. The command of the company wholly devolved to me. The soldiers universally manifested a great respect for me, for my care of the sick and my attention to their wants, and for my sympathies in their distress.[6]

Near the end of his enlistment the Second Continental Congress offered Morris a promotion to second lieutenant if he reenlisted with the light infantry. With the army moving into winter quarters, and Litchfield being only seventy miles away, Morris returned home to consult with his father and friends before deciding. On January 1, 1777, Congress upped their offer; his rank would be first lieutenant if he reenlisted. He decided to not only reenlist, but he signed up for the duration of the war. His orders for the winter were to recruit soldiers from Litchfield and to oversee the inoculation of soldiers who hadn't already survived small pox. By the end of the May he had recruited "thirty to forty soldiers" and oversaw the inoculation of nearly 200 men. Tragically Morris's fellow officer, classmate, and good friend, Jonathan Bellamy, died of small pox on January 4 while stationed in New Jersey.[7]

At the beginning of June, 1st Lieutenant Morris marched his new recruits to Peekskill, New York where they joined Washington's army.[8] It wasn't long before the army went on the move. By the beginning of August, General Washington had moved his army to Pennsylvania in an effort to protect Philadelphia. British Gen. William Howe's army had sailed out of New York and his ships were spotted in the Chesapeake Bay. In late-August Howe's army landed about fifty-five miles southwest of the city and on September 26 they captured Philadelphia.

A large portion of the General Howe's army encamped outside of Philadelphia in the town of Germantown, and General Washington planned a surprise attack on the British troops. At six o'clock on the evening of October 3, under the cover of darkness, Washington's army

6. Morris, *Memoirs*, 16.
7. Ibid., 16-17; aminoapps.com/c/hamilton/page/item/jonathan-bellamy/8Jel_WdHX-IQLlJeeDkBV1pN2Q0WZgwD4p.
8. Morris, *Memoirs*, 17.

began its twenty-mile march to Germantown. At first light on the 4th Washington's troops fell upon the British. 1st Lieutenant Morris with the light infantry units were at the front of the attack. Despite a heavy fog Washington's troops gained the advantage.[9] But Gen. Adam Stephen, who commanded the Connecticut Light Infantry, became lost in the heavy fog which was made worse by the musket smoke. General Stephen blundered badly when he mistook a group of American troops for British troops and opened fire. The resultant firefight caused both units to break and flee, and the British took advantage of it. This culminated in a near disaster for the Americans. Washington lost hundreds of men on the battlefield and another 500 were captured. General Stephen was found to have been drunk during the battle. Shortly afterwards he was court martialed, stripped of his command, and booted out of the army.[10]

One of the captured men was 1st Lt. James Morris. He was now a prisoner-of-war and would remain one for the next three-and-a-half years. He wrote of his capture:

> But the success of the day, by the misconduct of General Stephen, turned against. Many fell in battle and about five hundred of our men were made prisoners of War, who surrendered at discretion. I being in the first company, at the head of one column that began the attack upon the Enemy, was consequently in the rear of the retreat. Our men, then undisciplined, were scattered. I had marched with a few men nearly ten miles before I was captured, continually harassed by the British Dragoons and the Light Infantry. I finally surrendered, to save life, with the few men under my command, and marched back to Germantown under a guard.[11]

For the first six months he was held captive in Philadelphia's New Jail, a most terrible place:

> At this time and in this jail were confined seven hundred prisoners of War. A few small rooms were sequestered for the officers and each room must contain sixteen men. We fully covered the whole floor when we lay down to sleep, and the poor soldiers were shut into rooms of the same magnitude with double the number. The soldiers were soon seized with the jail fever, as it was called, and it swept off, in the course of three months, four hundred men who were buried in one continuous grave without coffin, lying three deep, one upon another . . . our number

9. Ibid., 18-19.
10. en.wikipedia.org/wiki/Adam_Stephen.
11. Morris, *Memoirs*, 18-19.

being daily decreased by the King of Terrors. Such a scene of mortality
I never witnessed before. Death was so frequent that it ceased to terrify;
it ceased to warn; it ceased to alarm survivors.[12]

By the end of April 1778 Morris had become so weak and ill he was
granted a "parole of pardon" and was able to live outside the prison with
the promise to remain within the city limits of Philadelphia. He lodged
with a kind family who nursed him back to health. Once he regained
some strength he frequented the Library Company of Philadelphia to
read. He'd learned about the library from his jailers who brought him
books from the library during his months in the jail. At the end of May
British forces withdrew from Pennsylvania and moved all the prison-
ers-of-war. Morris and the others were marched onto a ship which
sailed to Long Island, New York.[13]

James Morris was granted another parole and lodged with a Dutch
family in what is now Brooklyn. Compared to the horrors of the
Philadelphia jail, his next three years as a prisoner-of-war were Elysian
Fields. He spent his time gardening and walking, and became friends
with his neighbor, Mr. Clarkson, who "owned the most extensive private library that I had ever known in the United States." Clarkson allowed Morris free access to his collection and he immersed himself in
books on ancient and modern history.[14]

On January 3, 1781, three-and-a-half years less one day after his
capture, Morris was released in Elizabeth, New Jersey in a prisoner exchange. He immediately marched north to New Windsor, New York
and rejoined General Washington's army. He discovered that in his absence he had been promoted to the rank of captain. After a two month's
furlough to visit his family he rejoined the army and was given command of a light infantry company composed of men drawn from several
Connecticut regiments.[15]

During the summer's campaigns around Westchester County, New
York, Morris commanded his company in several battles in which
"numbers fell on both sides. I was personally involved in several severe
actions of which the Light Infantry must always be in front. I then experienced many narrow escapes, but still I was preserved, not a bone
fractured, not even a flesh wound, while others fell by my side."[16]

12. Ibid., 24-25.
13. Ibid., 26-27.
14. Ibid., 27-28.
15. Ibid., 29-32.
16. Ibid., 32.

General Washington and French General Rochambeau received word on August 15, 1781, that the French navy was willing to support a military campaign against British general Charles Cornwallis's forces stationed in Yorktown, Virginia. Washington and Rochambeau quickly devised a plan. They would feign an attack on General Howe's army in New York to hold his army there while secretly marching both of their armies south to Yorktown. If this plan worked Cornwallis's forces would be bottled up with no escape by land or sea. Washington could finally deliver a fatal blow to the British military, one he had worked for for more than six years.

On August 21, Captain Morris and General Washington's army began their long breakneck march to the head of Chesapeake Bay in Virginia. On August 29, they arrived and were sailed to Williamsburg where the American and French armies encamped. A few days later they marched the thirteen miles to Yorktown. On October 9 the historic siege of Yorktown began.[17]

The relentless bombardment of Yorktown took its toll on the British forces who were unable to escape through the Chesapeake Bay due to the French navy. General Washington's army gained the advantage as, one-by-one, General Cornwallis's land escape routes were sealed shut and the besiegers drew closer. Two redoubts—small, enclosed earthen forts—were critical to the security of the British position. These redoubts, numbered 9 and 10, held high ground and were protected by 200 battle hardened, well entrenched soldiers. Both redoubts were fortified with abatis, felled trees with sharpened branches facing outwards towards the enemy, and surrounded by deep trenches. A frontal assault was Washington's only option to take the redoubts. Lt. Col. Alexander Hamilton asked for and was given command of three battalions, a total of 400 men, to take redoubt 10. French General Baron de Viomenil and his 400 soldiers were to take redoubt 9.[18]

Lieutenant Colonel Hamilton would personally lead the assault and asked for volunteers from his battalions to join him at the vanguard of the assault. The group called itself the Forlorn Hope as casualties were expected to be high. Capt. James Morris's company would be the company directly behind Forlorn Hope.[19]

On the evening of October 14 Washington ordered all cannons to begin firing on the redoubts to weaken them for the assault. The British

17. Ibid., 32-33.
18. www.battlefields.org/learn/articles/fix-bayonets-revolutions-climactic-assault-yorktown.
19. Morris, *Memoirs*, 33.

did not see the gathering troops in the darkness of a nearly moonless night.

The attack opened when several incandescent shells were fired into the air illuminating the ground for the attack. Noiselessly the troops advanced with "cold steel," fixed bayonets on unloaded muskets. Surprise was on their side but a stumble by a soldier over the pock-marked terrain and the accidental firing of a musket would lose their advantage. Closely behind the Forlorn Hope, Captain Morris and his company dashed across the quarter-mile of open land. Once spotted by the British, heavy musket fire ensued that landed on Morris's troops. But the men raced forward. Quickly a small section of the abatis was hacked open and Lieutenant Colonel Hamilton hopped onto the shoulders of another soldier and sprang onto the parapet. The Forlorn Hope poured through the opening. Overrun, the seventy British defenders quickly surrendered and the redoubt was taken. Stunningly the whole assault and capture took less than ten minutes.[20]

Morris wrote of the assault in his memoirs:

> On the 16th day at evening [actually the 14th] . . . the Light Infantry were ordered to take a Fort by storm . . . Accordingly as soon as twilight of the evening was gone, we began our march for that purpose. I then had the command of the first Company at the head of the column that supported the Forlorn Hope. Not a man was killed in Forlorn Hope; they were so near the Fort before they were discovered that the Enemy overshot them and the whole firing fell upon the main body. There were eight men killed near the head of the column, all within less than thirty feet of the place where I stood, and about fifty men were wounded. Yet in this dangerous situation, I by kind Providence was preserved. The Forlorn Hope, commanded by Colonel Alexander Hamilton, were successful in taking the fort.[21]

General Washington wrote of the assaults, "The bravery exhibited by the attacking Troops was emulous and praiseworthy—few cases have exhibited stronger proofs of Intripidity coolness and firmness than were shown upon this occasion."[22]

With both redoubts taken the American and French artillery were moved up and the final bombardment of the British began. On Octo-

20. Ron Chernow, *Alexander Hamilton* (New York: Penguin Books, 2004), 163-164.
21. Morris, *Memoirs*, 33-34.
22. Kim Burdick, "What They Saw and Did at Yorktown's Redoubts 9 and 10," *Journal of the American Revolution*, April 7, 2020, allthingsliberty.com/2020/04/what-they-saw-and-did-at-yorktowns-redoubts-9-and-10/.

ber 17 a red-coated drummer appeared followed by an officer waving a white handkerchief requesting a parley.[23] The next day negotiations for the British surrender were hammered out.

Of General Cornwallis's historic surrender and the subsequent American celebration, Morris wrote:

> On the 18th, a day of respite, our soldiers were directed to wash up and appear clean on the next day . . . On the 19th day our whole Army and the French Army assembled; our Army on the right and the French Army on the left, about six rods apart, and each line reached more than a mile on an extended plain. We were thus drawn up to receive the vanquished. The British Army marched between our two Armies, drums beating their own tunes, colors muffled, and after they passed in a review of our Army they piled their arms on the field of submission and returned back in the same manner into York Town . . . On the 20th day . . . General Washington ordered the Army to assemble for Devine Service and give thanks to God for the success of our arms . . . How far preferable was this to people professing to be Christians than the heathenish custom of a drunken pow-wow and exulting over the humble vanquished. Here General Washington's character shone with true lustre in giving God the Glory.[24]

After processing the captured military equipment Washington's army marched back north to the east bank of the Hudson River, arriving in November 1781. Although the war didn't end for another two years, in November 1782 Capt. James Morris was released from the army and returned back to civilian life in Litchfield, ending his Revolutionary War service.[25]

Throughout the next decades Morris was a leader in the Litchfield community, but is best remembered for his dedication to the advancement of education. In 1790 he established the Morris Academy, one of the first schools in the country to admit girls and young women after their primary education ended. He believed that, "where there was a virtuous set of young ladies there was a descent class of young men." Over the next ninety years students across the expanding United States and nine foreign countries attended the academy.[26]

23. Morris, *Memoirs*, 35.
24. Ibid., 35-37.
25. Ibid., 37-38.
26. Barbara Nolen Strong, *The Morris Academy; Pioneer in Coeducation* (Torrington, CT: Quick Print, 1976), 22, 28-34, 92-123; Morris, *Memoirs*, 53.

When the British attacked America in the War of 1812, James Morris was ceremoniously appointed First Major of Connecticut's 2nd Regiment in June 1813 but did not campaign with the army.[27]

James Morris passed away on April 20, 1820, and was buried in the Morris Burying Ground, locally known as the East Morris Cemetery.[28]

Many Revolutionary War heroes were celebrated for their service and sacrifice by having cities and towns named in their honor. George Washington has fifty-three municipalities in the United States named for him, Benjamin Franklin has fifty, and Alexander Hamilton has thirty-nine.[29] First Major James Morris from the South Farms section of Litchfield was thus honored posthumously in 1859 when South Farms separated itself from Litchfield. The new town was named Morris, Connecticut. And in 1934, the town's public school was named James Morris School.[30]

In 1891 Columbia University bought the original Morris family homestead and several adjoining farms to create a unique beloved educational summer camp named Camp Columbia, used by the university's engineering department for over a hundred years. At the beginning of the new millennium in 2000, Columbia sold the 600-acre campus to the state of Connecticut and it is now Camp Columbia State Park.[31]

Over his lifetime James Morris gathered countless stones from the field's rocky soil and used them to build the farm's traditional New England stone walls. In 1942 alumnae of Columbia's School of Engineering collected all the stones from his walls and used them to build the camp's iconic seventy-five-foot water tower a short distance from where the Morris home once stood.[32] The water tower is now all that remains of the camp and the Morris homestead and is the centerpiece of the Camp Columbia State Park. A staircase leads to a covered belvedere where visitors are treated to an unparalleled view of the surrounding New England countryside. Although not built as a monument to James Morris, it does serve as a fitting monument to his Revolutionary War service and dedication to the advancement of education in America.

27. Morris, *Memoirs*, III.
28. www.findagrave.com/memorial/66757808/james-morris.
29. en.wikipedia.org/wiki/List_of_memorials_to_George_Washington#Municipalities_ and_inhabited_areas; en.wikipedia.org/wiki/List_of_places_named_for_Benjamin_Frank lin#Municipalities; en.wikipedia.org/wiki/Hamilton.
30. Strong, *The Morris Academy,* 75-76; www.ctinsider.com/connecticut/article/Morris-Cel ebrating-Its-150th Anniversary-16872808.php.
31. portal.ct.gov/DEEP/State-Parks/Parks/Camp-Columbia-State-Park-Forest/Overview.
32. www.youtube.com/channel/UC3qbJQgVJxSVj_IANKN_ULQ.

# Danger at the Breach

❀❦ DOUG MACINTYRE ❦❀

American Patriots won a pivotal victory at Charlestown, South Carolina on June 28, 1776, six days before the Declaration of Independence. The Battle of Sullivan's Island was the Patriots' first defeat of a joint attack by the British army and navy and one of their most decisive victories of the entire war. The astonishing win changed the course of the revolution as the British suspended their long-planned Southern strategy, allowing the South to remain relatively calm under Patriot control for the next three years.

Patriots had taken over the government of South Carolina and its wealthy capital Charlestown in 1775. In early June 1776, thousands of people in America's fourth largest city witnessed a terrifying spectacle when an intimidating British force arrived offshore in more than fifty ships to begin restoring Crown rule. The expedition included a Royal Navy squadron with nine ships of war commanded by Commodore Sir Peter Parker and a British army commanded by Maj. Gen. Henry Clinton. Parker and Clinton sought a quick victory to show support for Loyalists and reestablish the Crown's presence in the South before joining the British campaign to capture New York and isolate New England. They planned to secure Sullivan's Island at the entrance to the busy harbor and leave two warships with a garrison of soldiers on the island to control the seaport until the British could return to reclaim all of Charlestown and South Carolina.[1] Commodore Parker and General Clinton developed a two-pronged strategy to capture Sullivan's Island: the navy would bombard an unfinished fort of palmetto logs and sand, and the army would assault the fort's vulnerable rear by land.

---

1. Narrative of Major General Henry Clinton in William James Morgan, ed., *Naval Documents of the American Revolution*, vol. 5, *American Theatre: May 9, 1776 - Jul. 31, 1776* (Washington, DC: U.S. Government Printing Office, 1970), 325-327; Peter Parker to Henry Clinton, June 2, 1776, in Morgan, *Naval Documents*, 351; Clinton to Lord George Germain, July 8, 1776, in Morgan, *Naval Documents*, 982.

Responding to the threat posed by the British expedition, the Continental Congress appointed America's most experienced senior military officer to command the Southern Department. Maj. Gen. Charles Lee was a brash, temperamental and demanding soldier of fortune who arrived at the same time as the British force and feverishly set about improving Charlestown's defenses. Not knowing that the enemy's objective was limited to Sullivan's Island, he and the local Patriot leaders positioned troops in and around the city, with two of the colony's most experienced officers at the points of the attack on Sullivan's Island. Col. William Moultrie of the 2nd South Carolina Regiment commanded the fort, and Lt. Col. William Thomson of the 3rd South Carolina Regiment (Rangers) commanded troops guarding the island's shoreline.

The Patriot soldiers stationed on Sullivan's Island depended upon one another. If Thomson's troops failed to stop the British army, Moultrie's fort would surely fall to the simultaneous assaults from land and sea. If the fort could not withstand the Royal Navy, the Patriots defending the island would be trapped between the powerful forces of the British army and navy. The loss of Sullivan's Island and some of the best soldiers in the Southern colonies would jeopardize the rebellion in Charlestown and South Carolina, with potentially dire consequences for the American Revolution. Fortunately for the Americans, the British attacks from land and sea were absolute failures.

Anxious eyewitnesses in the city were awestruck on June 28, 1776, as they watched Colonel Moultrie and his men heroically defend the fort on the horizon against a ferocious, day-long bombardment by the British warships. The fort's thick walls of palmetto logs and sand stood firm while the Americans returned fire slowly and deliberately to conserve their precious supply of powder and ammunition. Their well-directed cannon fire killed or wounded more than 200 British sailors and inflicted debilitating damage to the warships, with modest American losses.[2] The valiant victory at the fort was extolled throughout the colonies and became the historical focal point of the Battle of Sullivan's Island. It is commemorated today by the National Park Service at the iconic site later named Fort Moultrie.

As Patriots in the fort repelled the assault by sea, Colonel Thomson and a diverse band of Patriots repelled the British army's attempt to

2. Account of the Attack made upon Sullivan's Island by William Chambers, in Morgan, *Naval Documents,* 804; Parker to Philip Stephens, July 9, 1776, in Morgan, *Naval Documents,* 1001; William Moultrie, *Memoirs of the American Revolution,* vol.1 (New York: David Longworth, 1802), 177.

assault the fort by land. They kept the British off Sullivan's Island by blocking their crossing of an Atlantic Ocean inlet that separated Thomson's force of 780 from Clinton's army of 3,000. Thomson and his men were recognized for the victory and thanked by the Continental Congress.[3] However, their contribution was nearly lost in history like countless other remote battles of the revolution. The long and intricate battle of maneuvers and skirmishes was fought out of sight in the wilderness, witnessed by the participants only, and lacked the captivating drama of the fight at the fort. Few details were published, and the crucial victory eventually faded into obscurity. Through sources not readily available to early historians, we are learning how Colonel Thomson and his outnumbered, outgunned band maneuvered to the verge of victory *before* June 28 and thwarted the land attack on that fateful Friday.

The British target, Sullivan's Island, was a three-mile-long link in a chain of wild, sandy barrier islands separated from the mainland by marshes and creeks and separated from one another by ocean inlets.[4] The next link up the coast stretched eight miles to the northeast and was aptly named Long Island (now Isle of Palms). The inlet between Sullivan's Island and Long Island, known as "the Breach" (now Breach Inlet), was a tidal flat more than a mile wide, laced with muddy bogs and sandbars that were exposed at low tide and gradually covered by surging ocean water as the tide rose twice per day. Constantly changing, shallow streams meandered among the sandbars and tidal pools, and a channel seven feet deep ran along the northern shore of Sullivan's Island.[5]

3. Journal of the Continental Congress, July 20, 1776, in *American Archives* 1837-1853 (Washington, DC: M. St Clair Clarke and Peter Force), 1585.
4. Edward McCrady, LLD, *The History of South Carolina in the Revolution 1775–1780* (New York: The MacMillan Company, 1902), 135-36; William Faden, *A Plan of the Attack of Fort Sulivan* (London: Charing Cross, 1776); John Campbell, *Plan of the scene of action at Charlestown in the province of South Carolina the 28th June 1776* (Ann Arbor: William L. Clements Library, University of Michigan), quod.lib.umich.edu/cgi/i/image/image-idx?id=S-WCL1IC-X-864%5DWCL000958; John Campbell, *Charlestown and the British attack of June 1776* (Ann Arbor: William L. Clements Library, University of Michigan). The Faden map is the annotated map for this article; the Campbell maps were General Clinton's battle maps.
5. The inlet has changed significantly since the revolution, which can confuse those referring to maps drawn more recently. Map comparisons show that accreting sand filled much of the underwater terrain in the nineteenth century, reducing the distance between Long Island and Sullivan's Island from more than a mile in 1776 to the present one-fourth of a mile.

A unit of 210 rangers was defending the Sullivan's Island shoreline when the British expedition anchored offshore and General Clinton scouted for ways to get his army onto the island to assault the fort.[6] Clinton and Parker initially planned a sudden attack, but the general did not want to land directly on Sullivan's Island through rough surf under fire. Before verifying reports that the inlet separating Long Island from Sullivan's Island was passable on foot at low water, he chose to stage his army on unoccupied Long Island and have the troops wade across the Breach to attack Sullivan's Island on foot.[7]

BRITISH FORCE

Clinton and his two generals, Maj. Gen. Charles, Earl Cornwallis and Brig. Gen. John Vaughan, made unopposed landings in the middle of June at the northeast end of Long Island with virtually all of their regular troops, Loyalists, and support personnel.[8] The army of 3,000 included the 15th, 28th, 33rd, 37th, 46th, 54th, and 57th Regiments of Foot; grenadier and light infantry companies of the 4th and 44th Regiments; a battalion of Marines; the 2nd Battalion of the Royal Highland Emigrants; and companies of the 4th Battalion of the Royal Regiment of Artillery with cannon, howitzers, and mortars.[9] The army also had control of floating batteries, pilot boats, small armed craft, and three warships armed with at least twenty-two cannon. Schooners *Lady William* and *Saint Lawrence* were stationed in the creek flanking Long Island (now Hamlin Creek), and sloop *Ranger* was based in Spence's Inlet (now Dewees Inlet) at that island's northeast end.[10]

AMERICAN FORCE

The Patriots facing the British army across the Breach were known as the "advance guard." Their leader was a respected citizen-soldier from the South Carolina backcountry known by the sobriquet "Danger" for his bravery and daring in battle.[11] Colonel Thomson had outfitted his

---

6. Samuel Wise to Henry William Harrington, June 7, 1776, in Alexander Gregg, *History of the Old Cheraws* (Columbia, SC: The State Company, 1905), 268.

7. William B. Willcox, ed., *The American Rebellion: Sir Henry Clinton's Narrative of His Campaigns, 1775-1782*, vol. 1 (New Haven: Yale University Press, 1954), 30-31; Henry Clinton to Lord George Germain, July 8, 1776, in K. G. Davies, ed., *Documents of the American Revolution 1770-1783*, vol. XII (Dublin: Irish Academic Press, Ltd., 1976), 163.

8. Clinton Narrative, June 7 to 16, 1776, in Morgan, *Naval Documents*, 573.

9. Robert Beatson, LLD, *Naval and Military Memoirs of Great Britain from 1727 to 1783*, vol. 6 (London: Longman, Hurst, Rees, and Orme, 1804), 45; Chambers Account in Morgan, *Naval Documents*, 804.

10. Parker to Stephens, July 9, 1776, in Morgan, *Naval Documents*, 998.

11. Doug MacIntyre, "A Man Called Danger," *The Mercury Newsletter* (June 16, 2021).

3rd South Carolina Regiment with distinctive caps displaying crescents that proclaimed, "Liberty or Death,"[12] a motto befitting the Battle of Sullivan's Island. As the imposing British force was landing on Long Island, he assumed personal command of the advance guard and immediately requested reinforcements to offset his disadvantage in manpower and firepower. Patriot units were moved frantically to and from Sullivan's Island until the advance guard totaled 780 soldiers. The diverse group included Thomson's 3rd South Carolina Regiment of rangers, South Carolina state troops, North Carolina regulars, a small detachment of militia, a few artillerymen from the 4th South Carolina Regiment, and the Raccoon or Foot Rover company, which included approximately thirty warriors from the Catawba and associated Native American tribes.[13] Thomson and some of his 3rd Regiment officers and men had combat experience, but most others were raw recruits hastily assembled to defend Charlestown. Their firepower was augmented with an 18-pound cannon and one or two 6-pound cannon in palmetto log fortifications overlooking the Breach between Long Island and Sullivan's Island.[14]

After transferring his force from the ships to the northeast end of Long Island, Clinton and his officers spent nights "fording and reconnoitering those infernal bogs and creeks that lay contiguous to Sullivan's Island." He realized his false assumption about the depth of water in the Breach on June 18 and later wrote, "To our unspeakable mortification and disappointment we discovered that the passage across the channel which separates the two islands was nowhere shallower at low water than seven feet instead of eighteen inches, which was the depth reported."[15] This deep channel made wading across the inlet impossible. The general should have investigated before committing his army to Long Island, and now he was in a self-inflicted predicament.

12. Michael Scoggins, *"Here Come the Liberty Caps!" A History of the Third South Carolina Regiment* (York, SC: Culture & Heritage Museums, 2006, 2007, and 2008), 2-3; Morgan Brown, "Reminiscences of the Revolution," *Russell's Magazine*, vol. 6, October-March 1860 (Charleston, SC: Walker, Evans & Co), 62.

13. Moultrie, *Memoirs*, 142; John Drayton, LLD, *Memoirs of the American Revolution: From Its Commencement to the Year 1776, Inclusive*, vol. II (Charleston: A. E. Miller, 1821), 288-289; McCrady, *History in the Revolution*, 145. The Catawba tribe allied with the South Carolina Patriots, who often used the term "Catawba" for any indigenous warriors who fought by their side.

14. Moultrie, *Memoirs*, 142; Joseph Johnson, MD, *Traditions and Reminiscences, Chiefly of the American Revolution in the South* (Charleston, South Carolina: Walker and James, 1851), 94.

15. Willcox, *American Rebellion*, 1:30-31, 374-75.

From his camp on Long Island, Major General Clinton sent Brigadier General Vaughan to the navy anchorage to tell Commodore Parker that the army could not ford the inlet to attack the fort as initially planned.[16] The British Secretary of State for the American Colonies had directed Clinton to avoid great loss and immediately proceed to New York if the mission could accomplish nothing of consequence,[17] but no record has been found that he considered abandoning the joint attack. As overall commander of the expedition, Clinton evaluated several alternatives and settled on an amphibious assault across the Breach to support the naval attack on the fort.

AMPHIBIOUS ASSAULT TACTICS

Attacking with foot soldiers over water utilized special "flatboats" carried by the Royal Navy. These versatile boats rowed by sailors were well-suited to crossing the Breach. They were more than thirty feet long and floated in just two feet of water. Each flatboat could transport up to six tons of equipment or fifty soldiers, and they could be outfitted with sails and swivel guns (small cannon). The British expedition had fifteen functioning flatboats, enough to land several hundred men in a wave before the sailors rowed back across the inlet for another wave.[18] The soldiers packed tightly in the center of the open boats with their muskets held upright could not fire. They would disembark as fast as possible to establish a beachhead while British artillery or warships disrupted the enemy defenses with suppressing fire.[19] Thomson's troops on Sullivan's Island were more than a mile from the British artillery on Long Island, too far for effective suppressing fire. To support the amphibious crossing, Clinton needed to find high and dry ground closer to Sullivan's Island for artillery batteries or deep and wide channels inside the Breach for warships.

16. Clinton to John Vaughan, June 18, 1776, in Morgan, *Naval Documents*, 609. The British army and navy commanders were based miles apart and communicated indirectly and often ineffectually through dispatches and intermediaries, partly because Clinton was prone to seasickness and declined to stay aboard Parker's flagship.

17. Clinton Narrative, April 18 to May 31, 1776, in Morgan, *Naval Documents*, 327.

18. Capacity estimates varied from 400 to 700 per wave per sources in Morgan, *Naval Documents*, 608, 653, 782, and 783; Francis, Lord Rawdon to the Earl of Huntington, July 3, 1776, in *Hastings Family Papers* (San Marino, CA: The Huntington Library), mssHA, Box 99, HA 5116. Lord Rawdon, an officer on Clinton's staff, estimated that the flatboats would need at least one-half hour to transport each wave of troops.

19. Hugh T. Harrington, "Invading America: The Flatboats That Landed Thousands of British Troops on American Beaches," *Journal of the American Revolution* (March 16, 2015): March 5, 2023. Two months after the Battle of Sullivan's Island, General Clinton successfully employed these tactics in the Battle of Long Island, New York, where the terrain and situation were favorable and the landing was unopposed.

ADVERSE CONDITIONS

While the opposing forces searched for advantageous positions in and around the Breach, more than 4,000 British and American people on the two islands endured miserable conditions. Summer on South Carolina's sunbaked barrier islands was nearly unbearable for anyone, especially for those from cooler climates who had suffered grueling voyages, illnesses, and food shortages. A surgeon who sailed from England with the expedition wrote of the suffocating heat with "Not a breath of air stiring – thick cobwebs to push thro' everywhere, knee deep in rotten wood and dried Leaves, every hundred yards a swamp with putrid standing water in the middle, full of small Alligators . . . and no place intirely free from Rattle Snakes."[20] A young British captain told his family about living "like beasts of the field" and "lying five nights in the midst of a putrid marsh up to the ankles in filth and water."[21] A soldier encamped in the Long Island wilderness wrote to his brother,

> We have lived upon nothing but salt Pork and Pease. We sleep upon the Sea Shore, nothing to shelter us from the rains but our coats and a miserable paltry blanket. There is nothing that grows upon the island, it being a mere sand-bank, and a few bushes that harbour Millions of Musketoes, a greater plague than there can be in Hell itself . . . The oldest of our officers do not remember, of ever undergoing such hardships, as we have done since our arrival here.[22]

TEN DAYS OF MANEUVERS AND SKIRMISHES

Combat quickly made discomfort a secondary concern. An American rifleman shot a member of a British scouting party on Long Island early in the conflict. According to a Patriot, "He was dressed in red, faced with black, and had a cockade & feather in his hat and a sword by his side. By which it appears that he was an officer."[23] The action escalated when most of the British army marched to the southwest end of Long Island and set up camp directly across the inlet in view of the

20. Thompson Forster, *Diary of Thompson Forster, Staff Surgeon to His Majesty's Detached Hospital in North America, October 19th 1775 to October 23rd 1777,* June 16, 1776, unpublished typescript, 63.
21. James Murray to Bessy, July 7, 1776, in Eric Robson, *Letters from America, 1773 to 1780* (New York: Barnes & Noble, Inc., 1950), 29-30.
22. Will Falconer to Anthony Falconer, July 13, 1776, in *The South Carolina and American General Gazette,* August 2, 1776, in R. W. Gibbes, ed., *Documentary History of the American Revolution, 1776-1782* (New York: D. Appleton & Co., 1857), 19-21.
23. Richard Hutson to Isaac Hayne, June 24, 1776, in *Richard Hutson Letter Book 1765-1777* (Charleston, SC: The South Carolina Historical Society), 34/559.

Patriot advance guard. The opposing forces remained on duty day and night, as sentinels and patrols approached dangerously close to their enemies across the marshes and creeks on the west side of the Breach.[24] A British diarist noted on June 20, "One of ours was shot thro' the leg last night, and Captain Trail shot one of their Officers thro' the head this morning, I saw him fall immediately and never stired afterwards."[25]

Inexperienced Patriots incurred the wrath of General Lee by firing ineffectively from extreme distances and passing over to Long Island without orders.[26] Seeking a reward for the first prisoner captured, three Patriots paddled to a British camp at night, failed to take a prisoner, and mistakenly shot a member of their own party. The British tracked the group back to the Breach, where the advance guard opened fire, igniting hours of intense combat with casualties.[27] This action was so loud and long-lasting that Commodore Parker, anchored five miles south, thought the main battle had begun at the Breach and ordered his ships to create a diversion.[28]

On another day, Loyalist Scots Highlanders shouted in Gaelic as they attacked Patriots on a sandbar and ambushed a group of the Catawba on the Sullivan's Island beach. They shot with impressive accuracy until dislodged by grape and other shots from American artillery.[29] Thomson's cannon fired on the armed schooner *Lady William*, an armed sloop, and a pilot boat in the creek beside Long Island, hitting the ships several times before they could retreat up the creek and out of range.[30] The frequent, long-distance exchanges of artillery and small arms fire caused minimal equipment damage and casualties while revealing the abilities and limitations of both forces.[31]

---

24. Wise to Harrington, June 27, 1776, in Gregg, *Old Cheraws*, 271.
25. Forster, *Diary*, June 20, 1776, 66.
26. Charles Lee to William Thomson, June 21, 1776, in *The Lee Papers*, vol. 2, *1776-1778* (New York: Collections of the New-York Historical Society for the Year 1872), 76-77.
27. Hutson to Hayne, June 24, 1776, in Hutson, *Letter Book*. A wound likely sustained in this engagement is mentioned in a pension application transcribed by Will Graves, revwarapps.org/w8668.pdf.
28. Parker to Stephens, July 9, 1776, in Morgan, *Naval Documents*, 998.
29. Wise to Harrington, June 22 and 27, 1776, in Gregg, *Old Cheraws*, 268-273. The Royal Highland Emigrants probably included Scots from the Cross Creek (now Fayetteville) area of North Carolina who joined the expedition at Cape Fear following their defeat by the Patriots at Moore's Creek Bridge on February 27, 1776.
30. A British Journal of the Expedition to Charleston, South Carolina, June 25, 1776, in Morgan, *Naval Documents*, 747. The creek is known today as Hamlin Creek. Gazette, August 2, 1776, in Gibbes, *Documentary History 1776-1782*, 15.
31. Wise to Harrington, June 27, 1776, in Gregg, *Old Cheraws*, 271-272; Hutson to Hayne, June 24, 1776, in Hutson, *Letter Book*; Forster, *Diary*, June 21-22, 1776, 67 68; Brown, "Reminiscences," 64-65. British surgeon Forster and American sergeant Brown estimated

After ten days of combat at the Breach,[32] General Lee ordered 100 more troops to ease the burden on Thomson[33] and sent thanks to his regiment for the "cheerfulness and alacrity for which they have done very hard duty."[34]

## BRITISH ADVANTAGE

A successful amphibious attack became plausible when the British army on Long Island discovered and occupied high ground on marsh islands significantly closer to Sullivan's Island. Portions of Green Island (1 on the map, page 146) could support infantry and long-range artillery approximately one mile from Sullivan's Island.[35] High oyster banks on a small island at the west end of the Breach could serve as natural breastworks (2) within a half-mile of Thomson's shoreline defenses (3).[36] The British gained a tactical advantage by emplacing two howitzers, two Royal mortars, and two 6-pound cannon behind an oyster bank breastwork and firing exploding shells into the advance guard's positions. The gunfire disabled an American 6-pound cannon and caused casualties, proving that the artillery was close enough to suppress the American defenses during an amphibious crossing of the Breach.[37] A Patriot major was sure the British artillery would "cover their landing in spite of all we can do," and said every officer in the advance guard considered the situation desperate and expected to be sacrificed, although they would "not quit the island were they certain of death."[38] Encouraged,

large numbers of enemy killed and wounded. Their estimates appear exaggerated and are not corroborated by other sources.

32. Wise to Harrington, June 27, 1776, in Gregg, *Old Cheraws,* 271-272.

33. Moultrie, *Memoirs,* 165.

34. Charles Lee to John Armstrong, June 27, 1776, in Lee, *Papers,* 89.

35. Green Island, also called Willow or South Island, remains uninhabited and is now known as Little Goat Island.

36. Faden, *Plan of Attack;* Campbell, *Plan of the scene;* Campbell, *Charlestown and the British attack.* Two symbols for batteries behind the breastworks appear on the Faden companion map and General Clinton's battle maps by John Campbell. Notes on the Campbell maps indicate that the artillery retired to the northern oyster bank when the southern bank overflowed. This hummock, now known as Clubhouse Point, lies between Inlet Creek and Swinton Creek, 350 yards north of the modern bridge connecting Sullivan's Island and Isle of Palms.

37. Forster, *Diary,* June 22, 1776, 68. The advance guard positions 700-1,000 yards away were within the maximum range of these British artillery pieces. Cannon of the era could fire iron balls more than 1,000 yards, Royal mortars fired exploding shells up to 1,000 yards, and howitzers fired balls or shells up to 700 yards. The most effective fire was from less than half these ranges, depending upon powder quality, winds, humidity, crew skills, incoming fire, and other factors.

38. Wise to Harrington, June 22, 1776, in Gregg, *Old Cheraws,* 269.

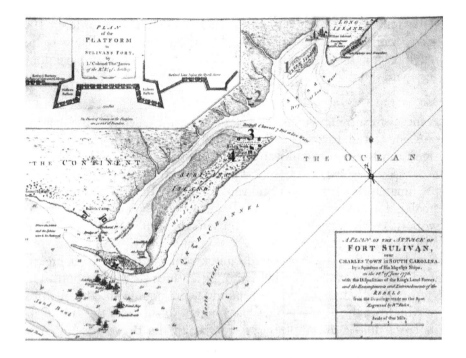

General Clinton and Commodore Parker arranged to launch simultaneous attacks the next day if the winds were favorable for the naval attack on the fort. Parker closed a dispatch to Clinton with confidence: "I trust, that I shall to Morrow Evening have the Honor of taking You by the Hand on Sullivan's Island, and congratulating You on the Success of His Majesty's Arms by Land and Sea."[39]

MOMENTUM SHIFT

Commanding from the mainland, Maj. Gen. Charles Lee gave Moultrie and Thomson scathing critiques about maintaining discipline and firing only within prescribed ranges. He added this postscript to a dispatch: "PS: Those two field pieces at the very end of the point [3], are so exposed that I desire you will draw them off to a more secure distance from the enemy; in their present situation, it appears to me, they may be carried off whenever the enemy think proper."[40] Danger Thom-

39. Parker to Clinton, June 22, 1776, in Morgan, *Naval Documents,* 689. The winds were not favorable for an attack on June 23.

40. Lee to William Moultrie, June 21, 1776, in Lee, *Papers,* 79; Moultrie, *Memoirs,* 158-162. Messages from the mainland to Thomson frequently were sent through Moultrie, who was stationed at the fort between the mainland and the Breach with overall responsibility for the defense of Sullivan's Island.

son immediately established new positions that not only diminished the British artillery threat, but also gave the Americans a critical advantage. He moved his soldiers and cannon away from the Breach to a new location (4),[41] further outside the effective range of British heavy artillery on Green Island and barely inside the range of British light artillery behind the high oyster banks. From this less vulnerable position, Thomson's cannon remained close enough to fire on unprotected British troops in flatboats before they could land on the Sullivan's Island beach. General Clinton described the momentum shift:

> The Rebels had time to perfect another Battery and Intrenchment that was begun on the 22d. This being 500 yards back from their first Position on the Point, in very strong Ground with a much more extended front, having a Battery on the right and a Morass on the left, & abattis in front, obligd us to make an entire Change in the Plan of operations on our Side. For it was apparent, that the few men I had Boats for, advancing singly through a narrow channel uncovered & unprotected, could not now attempt a landing without a manifest Sacrifice.[42]

Prompted by Lee's postscript, Danger Thomson and his men had outmaneuvered the British army. General Clinton was dejected after the Americans' rapid change to the new position, which he described as "defended and sustained by 3 to 4000 men [with] a formidable appearance."[43] Actually, the advance guard was only one-fourth that size.

BLOCKED AT THE BREACH

Clinton had few options for his army following Thomson's move, and he may have lost resolve after ten days of planning, skirmishing, and maneuvering. Realizing the hazards of attacking across the well-defended Breach, he offered troops to assist the navy at the fort, which Sir Peter Parker did not accept. He also considered attacking Haddrell's Point at Mount Pleasant on the mainland (Hetheral Pt on the map). This impractical and dangerous alternative diverged from the mission of occupying Sullivan's Island, and it entailed more problems than at-

---

41. Faden, *Plan of Attack*; Campbell, *Plan of the scene*; Campbell, *Charlestown and the British attack*. The Patriots' first and second lines of defense appear on all three maps. The second line extended across Sullivan's Island near modern-day Stations 29 and 30.

42. Willcox, *American Rebellion*, 1:32; Clinton to Germain from camp on Long Island, July 8, 1776, in Morgan, *Naval Documents*, 983-984. Germain was the British secretary responsible for the American colonies.

43. Clinton to Germain, July 8, 1776, in Morgan, *Naval Documents*, 984. Thomson's defenses may have deceived the general, or Clinton may have overstated enemy strength to excuse his failure to capture Sullivan's Island.

tacking across the Breach. The British explored the creeks and two-mile wide marsh between Long Island and the mainland, and Clinton asked Parker to provide naval support for an attack or diversion toward Mount Pleasant. Parker planned to enfilade the fort with three ships, which he suggested might be useful if the army attacked the mainland.[44] In his final dispatch before the main battle began, the beleaguered general told his naval counterpart that his situation was "rendered more difficult every hour, from the preparations the Rebels are making to defend themselves . . . every where intrenching themselves in the strongest manner." With no firm plan for attacking the strengthened American defense, he told Parker, "It is impossible for me at this time and under my Particular Situation to enter upon a detail of the operations of the Troops on the day of your attack, they will in all probability depend upon different circumstances, subject to a variety of changes as occasion may arise." He reiterated his ambiguous promise that "the Troops under my command will cooperate with you to the utmost for the good of His Majestys Service as soon as Wind and Weather shall favor the attack of the Fleet."[45] The outnumbered and outgunned Americans had neutralized the British army, and they were on the verge of victory when conditions favored the British naval attack.

JUNE 28, 1776

Col. William Moultrie and Lt. Col. William Thomson were together at the Breach on Friday morning, June 28, when they saw the British flatboats and warships spring into action. Moultrie galloped back to the fort and led his men to a resounding victory over the Royal Navy in a vicious battle.[46] Contemporary descriptions of the long day's action at the Breach varied from an innocuous demonstration reported by Clinton to deadly fire reported by others. Some accounts may have been exaggerated, but all agreed that the strong American defense thwarted the land attack and made possible the astounding victory on Sullivan's Island.

The battle began mid-morning when the Royal Navy opened fire on the fort and the British army opened fire on the advance guard. One of Lord Cornwallis's brigades crossed a creek in flatboats and moved to the marsh island where the British light artillery battery fired from behind a high oyster bank breastwork (2). From a flatboat, Cornwallis'

---

44. Parker to Clinton, June 25, 1776, in Morgan, *Naval Documents*, 745. These ships ran aground on June 28 and Clinton did not attack the mainland.
45. Clinton to Parker, June 26, 1776, in Morgan, *Naval Documents*, 760-61.
46. Moultrie, *Memoirs*, 174.

surgeon saw a large British Coehorn mortar initiate the attack by throwing nine-inch shells into the Patriot trenches and artillery positions. He watched the howitzers, mortars, and cannon raining fire on the American defenses from the oyster bank, and he saw the Americans returning fire with musket balls and grapeshot from the 18-pounder "supplied entirely by slaves."[47]

ATTEMPTED AMPHIBIOUS CROSSINGS

Tides governed actions in the battle at the Breach. After firing artillery to disrupt the American defenders, the British launched the amphibious operation as the predictable tide was rising several feet from its low point at about 10:30 a.m. to its high point at about 5:00 p.m.[48] Charles Stedman, a respected British officer and historian who served with Clinton and Cornwallis, summarized the first crossing attempt: "At twelve o'clock the light-infantry, grenadiers, and the fifteenth regiment, embarked in boats, the floating batteries and armed craft getting under way at the same time to cover their landing on Sullivan's Island."[49] Shallow water and Patriot artillery foiled support from the British warships. Clinton reported, "While the sands were uncovered [i.e., when the tide was still low], I ordered small armed vessels to proceed towards the point of Sulivan's Island but they all got aground."[50] One of his senior aides observed, "The foremost of the Vessels suffered considerably" from Thomson's 18-pounder,[51] and a Loyalist aboard the British armed schooner *Lady William* reportedly said that it was impossible to withstand the destructive fire the Americans poured in.[52] The flatboat flotilla abandoned the crossing under fire. Stedman wrote, "Scarcely, however, had the detachment proceeded from Long Island, before they

47. Forster, *Diary,* June 28, 1776, 69-70. Forster's meaning is unclear because the term "slaves" was used for common soldiers as well as enslaved people. African Americans in the advance guard included a drummer mentioned in Wise to Harrington, June 27, 1776, in Gregg, *Old Cheraws,* 272-273, and a soldier granted a federal pension for the service described in his pension application transcribed by Leon Harris, revwarapps.org/w11223.pdf.
48. C. Leon Harris, *An Estimate of Tides During the Battle of Sullivan's Island SC, 28 June 1776,* 2010, thomsonpark.org. Other sources predict tides within minutes of Harris's timeframe.
49. Charles Stedman, *The History of the Origin, Progress, and Termination of the American War,* vol. 1 (London: J. Murray, J. Debrett, J. Kerby, 1794), 186.
50. Clinton to Germain, July 8, 1776, in Davies, *American Revolution,* 164; Moultrie, *Memoirs,* 174. The incoming tide would have deepened the inlet channels in favor of the British vessels, although the strongest currents would have made rowing and sailing most challenging during the middle of the tide cycle in the afternoon.
51. Rawdon to Huntington, July 3, 1776, in *Hastings Family Papers.*
52. Johnson, *Traditions,* 95.

were ordered to disembark and return to their encampment: And it must be confessed that, if they had landed, they would have had to struggle with difficulties almost insurmountable."[53] An American stated, "One Brigade had either embarked in their flat bottom boats or were about it, when they Received such a fire from our troops as made them think it would be out of their power to get Thomson's consent to land, without which their Army would have pretty well melted down, by the time they would have got to the Fort."[54] A Patriot leader wrote that the British "Land Forces on Long Island in the meantime strained every Nerve to effect a Landing on the Back [of Sullivan's Island], but the Eighteen Pounder with Grape shot spread Havock, Devastation, and Death, and always made them retire faster than they advanced."[55] Awed by the American cannon loaded with grapeshot, a British soldier wrote to his family, "They would have killed half of us before we could make our landing good."[56]

Further amphibious crossing attempts would have been futile. After low tide and Patriot cannon fire turned back the warships and flatboats, the rising tide forced the British to evacuate their indispensable artillery battery at the high oyster banks. Notes in Clinton's papers say, "As the Tide rose very fast it was reported to the General that the Artillery could stay no longer with safety . . . as therefore there was no one single thing that could go down to cover our landing, till such protection could be obtained, it was thought by all rash to attempt it."[57] With the enemy's warships and most effective artillery out of action, Thomson could more safely move soldiers and cannon from his second line of defense (4) back to his initial positions at the shore (3) and fire directly at British troops attempting to cross the Breach. Unprotected soldiers and sailors in slow-moving flatboats had little chance of establishing a beachhead through a point-blank barrage of bullets, balls, or grapeshot.

Major General Lee reinforced the advance guard with hundreds of fresh troops from Virginia and South Carolina after 5:00 p.m.[58] The

53. Stedman, *History*, 186.

54. William Bull to John Pringle, 13 August 1776, in Anne King Gregorie, ed., *The South Carolina Historical and Genealogical Magazine*, vol. L, 1949 (Charleston, SC: The South Carolina Historical Society), 148.

55. Richard Hutson to Thomas Hutson, June 30, 1776, in Hutson, *Letter Book*.

56. Will Falconer to Anthony Falconer, July 13, 1776, in Gibbes, *Documentary History 1776-1782*, 20.

57. Particulars Relative to the Attack [on Sullivan's Island], June 29, 1776, in Morgan, *Naval Documents*, 827-828.

58. Lee to Moultrie, June 28, 1776, in Lee, *Papers*, 91-92; Drayton, *Memoirs*, 296. Col. Peter Muhlenburg and his 8th Virginia Regiment had marched to Charlestown with General Lee and were stationed at Haddrell's Point.

well-armed British continued firing long-distance artillery across the inlet until nightfall, and the Americans nearly exhausted their supply of ammunition and gunpowder. When firing stopped, they reserved enough powder for only two shots from each cannon.[59] Frustrated and unaware of the severe beating sustained by the Royal Navy at the fort, General Clinton met with his officers that night and decided to make another crossing attempt the following morning despite the risk.[60] After eighteen hours under arms in the marsh, Lord Cornwallis' troops were reloaded into the flatboats and started across the Breach at daybreak on June 29. When Clinton learned that the naval assault had failed and the battle was lost, the attack orders were countermanded and the British regulars in the flatboats returned to shore.[61] For the first time, the revolutionary Americans had defeated a joint attack by the British army and Royal Navy.

INTERNATIONAL NEWS

The victory on Sullivan's Island brought hope to the American cause. The stunning news appeared in dispatches, letters, and the same American and European publications as the Declaration of Independence and the massive campaign for New York. King George III, who had personally approved the expedition eight months prior, expressed his dismay with classic British understatement: "Though the attack upon Charles Town has not been crowned with success, it has by no means proved dishonorable; perhaps I should have been as well pleased if it had not been attempted."[62] Clinton and Parker argued after the battle and alluded to each other's deficiencies in their carefully crafted accounts.[63] Clinton depicted his army's fire and movement as a demon-

59. Manuscript of William Henry Drayton, June 28, 1776, in Gibbes, *Documentary History 1776-1782*, 10.

60. Willcox, *American Rebellion*, 1:35; Particulars, June 29, 1776, in Morgan, *Naval Documents*, 827–28. The high tide that coincided with sunrise on June 29 provided deeper water for warships and flatboats, while precluding artillery support from the oyster banks.

61. Forster, *Diary*, June 29, 1776, 72-73; Particulars, June 29, 1776, in Morgan, *Naval Documents*, 827–28; Lee to George Washington, July 1, 1776, in Lee, *Papers*, 102. The action on June 29 accounts for the second crossing attempt mentioned in several reports of the action at the Breach. Reports of three or more attempts are not well-documented.

62. King George III to John Montagu, August 21, 1776, in B.R. Barnes and J.H. Owen, eds., *The Private Papers of John, Earl of Sandwich, First Lord of the Admiralty, 1771-1782*, vol. 4 (London: Navy Records Society, 1932-1938), 44.

63. Washington to John Hancock, August 7, 1776, in *Founders Online*, National Archives, founders.archives.gov/documents/Washington/03-05-02-0453. Deserters from the British warship *Solebay* told General Washington in New York, "That the Admiral turn'd Genl Clinton out of his Ship after the Engagement with a great deal of abuse – Great Differences between the principal naval and military Gentlemen."

stration or diversion and did not comment on the skirmishes, casualties, or attempted crossings.[64] He was highly offended by Parker's official report to the British Admiralty in London, which stated, "Their Lordships will plainly see by this Account, that if the Troops cou'd have co-operated on this Attack, that His Majesty wou'd have been in possession of Sulivan's Island."[65] According to *The Annual Register*, a contemporary summary of 1776 British history, "During this long, hot, and obstinate conflict, the seamen looked frequently and impatiently to the eastward, still expecting to see the land forces advance from Long Island, drive the rebels from their intrenchment, and march up to second the attack on the fort. In these hopes they were grievously disappointed."[66] The epic failure in his first major command would haunt Henry Clinton for the rest of his life, leading the editor of his memoirs to wryly observe, "Britain had worse defeats in the course of the war, but no more egregious fiasco."[67]

UNSUNG HEROES

Lt. Col. William Thomson's advance guard won the battle at the Breach and assisted in the grand victory on Sullivan's Island with brave conduct by people from all echelons of society – Black men and Native Americans as well as White farmers and workers from the backcountry of South Carolina, North Carolina, and Virginia. Like countless others in forgotten fights, the hastily assembled soldiers were not schooled in the art of warfare, and they made mistakes, yet they overcame adversity to prevail against enormous odds. The Americans strengthened their positions during British delays, adapted smartly to enemy maneuvers, seized the initiative by relocating their defenses, gained valuable skills and confidence over ten days of combat, and took advantage of the terrain and tides on June 28. Danger Thomson and his diverse band of unsung heroes were instrumental in winning one of the earliest, most complete, and most shocking victories of the American Revolution.

64. Clinton to Germain, July 8, 1776, in Morgan, *Naval Documents*, 984. Clinton reported that his troops were positioned to attempt a landing on either Sullivan's Island or the mainland. He knew that three Royal Navy frigates ran aground while attempting to enfilade the fort, and he did not send troops toward the mainland.
65. Parker to Stephens, July 9, 1776, in Morgan, *Naval Documents*, 999-1001.
66. *The Annual Register or a View of the History, Politics, and Literature For the Year 1776*, (London: J. Dodsley, 1779), 160-163. This reference work was widely read on both sides of the Atlantic.
67. Willcox, *American Rebellion*, xxi. General Clinton learned from the experience. He returned and captured Charlestown with a highly successful siege in 1780.

# Engaging the *Glasgow*

**❄️ ERIC STERNER ❄️**

On April 18, 1776 Captain Tyringham Howe of His Majesty's Ship *Glasgow* arrived in Halifax, Nova Scotia. Two weeks prior, the twenty-gun sloop had engaged a task force from the Continental Navy and given better than she received. Vice Admiral Molyneux Shuldham, who briefly commanded Royal Navy in American waters, expected *Glasgow* to be carrying dispatches from himself and Gen. William Howe to New York and then southward.[1] Thus, her appearance came as a surprise.

On March 17, *Glasgow* cruised off Newport, Rhode Island, where Captain Howe observed the American rebels breaking ground on new fortifications.[2] He passed up Narragansett Bay and anchored off the eastern side of Prudence Island, where *Glasgow* joined with *Rose*, *Swan*, *Bolton*, three armed tenders, and a large transport to constitute a small squadron.[3] The Royal Navy ship *Nautilus* arrived on March 30 with orders for *Glasgow* to carry dispatches south.[4]

Far to the south, the Continental Navy's first fleet plodded northward from the Bahamas after a successful raid on Nassau. Created in part do clear the coasts of British ships like the *Glasgow*, the American commander, Commodore Esek Hopkins, had instead raided New

---

1. "Vice Admiral Molyneux Shuldham to Philip Stephens, 8th March 1776," William Bell Clark, ed., *Naval Documents of the American Revolution, American Theatre* (Washington: U.S. Naval History Division, 1962 - ), 4:230 (NDAR).
2. "Journal of H.M.S. Glasgow, Captain Tyringham Howe, March 17, 1776," NDAR, 4:384.
3. "Disposition of His Majesty's Ships and Vessels in North America under the Command of Rear [Vice] Admiral Shuldham," NDAR, 4:448; "Newport Mercury, March 25, 1776," NDAR, 4:504.
4. "Journal of H.M. Sloop Nautilus, Captain John Collins, March 28, 29, 30, 31, 1776," NDAR, 4:594; "Journal of H.M.S Glasgow, Captain Tyringham Howe, March 29, 30, 31, 1776," NDAR, 4:595.

Providence. After successfully seizing the port and its two defending forts, Hopkins and his fleet spent two weeks removing guns, firearms, gunpowder, shot and other supplies from public buildings and vessels captured in port.[5] On March 17, while Captain Howe was observing the immature American earthworks outside Newport, Commodore Hopkins and his squadron left Nassau bound for Block Island Channel.[6]

By April 4, Hopkins reached the waters around Block Island and began capturing ships belonging to the Royal Navy operating out of Narragansett Bay. These included the schooner *Hawke*, the first warship of the Royal Navy captured by the Continental Navy, and the twelve-gun brig *Bolton.*[7] On April 5, Capt. James Wallace, aboard *Rose*, attempted to lead the "Newport Squadron," including *Glasgow*, out of Narragansett Bay. Wind and weather, however, foiled some of the smaller vessels and Wallace returned to port. Aboard *Glasgow*, Howe pressed on, which brought him southeast of Block Island on the night of April 5-6.[8]

The night was calm, with a light breeze and smooth water. Some-time between 1 and 2 am, Capt. Nicholas Biddle of the Continental brig *Andrew Doria* reported seeing two sail to the east-southeast while Howe detected the American squadron to his northwest, about eight leagues (perhaps twenty-four nautical miles) distant. Howe tacked to the northwest to investigate, while Biddle signaled to Commodore Hopkins and the rest of the American squadron to bear down on the unknown ship.[9] By any measure, it would be an unfair fight when the two sides met.

---

5. Jeff Dacus, "Gunpowder, the Bahamas, and the First Marine Killed in Action," *Journal of the American Revolution*, May 2, 2019, allthingsliberty.com/2019/05/gunpowder-the-bahamas-and-the-first-marine-killed-in-action/.

6. Gardner W. Allen, *A Naval History of the American Revolution*, Vol. I (Boston: Houghton Mifflin Company, 1913), 100.

7. Nathan Miller, *Sea of Glory: A Naval History of the American Revolution* (Annapolis, MD: Naval Institute Press, 1992), 112-113; Joseph Allen, *Battles of the British Navy*, New Edition, Revised and Enlarged, Vol. I (London: Henry G. Bohn, 1852), 229.

8. "Captain Wallace to Vice Admiral Shuldham, 10th April 1776," Robert Wilden Neeser, ed., *The Despatches of Molyneux Shuldham, Vice-Admiral of the Blue and Commander-on-Chief of His Britannic Majesty's Ships on North America, January-July, 1776* (New York: The DeVinne Press for The Naval History Society, 1913), 178-179.

9. "Journal of Continental Brig Andrew Doria, Captain Nicholas Biddle, 6th April 1776," NDAR, 4:679; "Remarks on board his Majesty's Ship Glasgow, 6th April 1776," Neeser, ed., *The Despatches of Molyneux Shuldham*, 180. The "Remarks" were recorded by Captain Howe and reported to Admiral Shuldham.

Five ships comprised the American squadron. *Alfred* carried twenty 9-pounders and ten 6-pounders. *Columbus* sported eighteen 9-pounders and ten 6-pounders. *Andrew Doria* boasted fourteen 4-pounders.[10] *Cabot* carried fourteen 6-pounders and twelve swivels while *Providence*, the fastest American ship, held another twelve 4-pounders and ten swivels.[11] For her part, *Glasgow* boasted twenty 9-pounders.[12] She had some advantages, however. Royal Navy sailors and officers were better trained to their tasks. Moreover, the American vessels were arriving from the Caribbean, which had a tendency to foul hulls and slow sailing speeds.

Both sides beat to quarters as they closed, preparing for a potential battle, although neither knew the identity of the approaching ship or ships. About 2:30 am, *Cabot* came within hailing distance of *Glasgow*, but refused to identify herself initially, preferring to close the distance, a necessity if her captain, John Hopkins, the commodore's son, hoped to do any damage with *Cabot's* tiny 6-pounders. Receiving no replies to his requests for identification, Captain Howe changed tactics and asked what ships were accompanying the vessel. The cry "the Columbus and Alfred, a two and twenty Gun frigate" rang across the gap between the two vessels, which by then were sailing quite close together.[13]

*Alfred*, at that point, was just 100 yards behind *Cabot*.[14] Whether due to nervousness, eagerness, or command, someone in *Cabot's* tops dropped a grenade onto *Glasgow's* deck, immediately after which *Cabot* fired a full broadside. Howe, no stranger to meeting unidentified ships in hostile waters, promptly replied with two broadsides before the *Cabot's* crew could reload, reflecting the superior training and practice

10. "Andrew Doria I (Brigantine)," *Naval History and Heritage Command Dictionary of American Naval Fighting Ships*, www.history.navy.mil/research/histories/ship-histories/danfs/a/andrew-doria-i.html.

11. "Enclosure C" Neeser, ed., *The Despatches of Molyneux Shuldham*, 182-183. The British estimate was remarkably accurate, only crediting *Andrew Doria* and *Providence* with a greater weight of broadside. "Providence I (slp)," *Naval History and Heritage Command Dictionary of American Naval Fighting Ships*, www.history.navy.mil/research/histories/ship-histories/danfs/p/providence-i.html.

12. Tim McGrath, *Give Me a Fast Ship: The Continental Navy and America's Revolution at Sea*, Kindle ed. (New York: NAL Caliber, 2014), 60 of 544.

13. "Remarks on board His Majesty's Ship Glasgow, 6th April 1776," Neeser, ed., *The Despatches of Molyneux Shuldham*, 180.

14. Gardner W. Allen, *A Naval History of the American Revolution*, 102. Allen relies on the first hand report of Captain Samuel Nicholas of the Continental Marines, commanding the marine detachment aboard Alfred.

of Royal Navy crew.[15] Vastly outgunned and now damaged, *Cabot* sheered away, opening up a spot for *Alfred*, but in the process fouling the *Andrew Doria*'s wind and causing her to tack away as well.[16]

On paper, *Alfred* under Capt. Dudley Saltonstall and Captain Howe's *Glasgow* were relatively well matched. *Alfred* threw a greater weight of metal and *Glasgow* had already received one broadside, but the British ship was a functional warship and the American was a converted merchantman. Moreover, as John Paul Jones, then an officer in charge of *Alfred*'s first battery noted, piercings for *Alfred*'s larger guns were too close to the waterline, limiting their field of fire. He called them "fit for nothing except in a harbour or a very smooth sea."[17]

Howe reported smaller ships moving into position fore and aft to rake *Glasgow*, that is, fire stem to stern and vice versa, while she exchanged broadsides with *Alfred* for roughly thirty minutes. These were probably *Andrew Doria* and *Columbus* trying to get into the battle, albeit with little success. Chance, however, plays a role in many fights and after thirty minutes of fire, a lucky shot carried away *Alfred*'s wheel ropes and blocks, severely impacting her maneuverability.[18] Howe was quick to seize the opportunity and move ahead of *Alfred*, from where he turned to rake her stem to stern. Captain Biddle, aboard *Andrew Doria*, used the opportunity to move behind *Glasgow* and fire into her stern. It was an opportunity for Howe to attempt an escape and he turned his vessel to the northeast, in the general direction of the British squadron at Narragansett Bay. Meanwhile, *Alfred*'s crew had repaired their steering well enough to return to the fight and Captain Saltonstall moved up on *Glasgow*'s port while *Andrew Doria* sailed to her starboard and Captain Whipple's *Columbus* finally got into the fight behind *Glasgow*.[19] Fearing things were not going well, the *Glasgow*'s clerk loaded Admiral Shuldham's and General Howe's dispatches into a canvas bag, weighted it with a shot, and dumped it overboard to prevent their capture.[20]

Lady luck intervened again as the wind shifted and gave Howe an opportunity to pour on speed for the northeast. *Alfred*, leaking, with

---

15. "Journal of Continental Brig Andrew Doria, Captain Nicholas Biddle, 6th April 1776," NDAR, 4:679.

16. Ibid.

17. "Journal of John Paul Jones," NDAR, 4:679-680.

18. Allen, *A Naval History of the American Revolution*, 102; McGrath, *Give Me a Fast Ship*, 62.

19. McGrath, *Give Me a Fast Ship*, 63.

20. "Remarks on board His Majesty's Ship Glasgow, 6th April 1776," Neeser, ed., *The Despatches of Molyneux Shuldham*, 180.

her sails and rigging shot full of holes, could not keep up. She and *Andrew Doria* fell away. Captain Whipple pursued with *Columbus*, but did little more than exchange chaser fire until Hopkins signaled to break off. At 6:30, roughly five hours after the two sides sighted one another, Hopkins turned his little squadron to the south-southwest, bringing a final close to the engagement.

Firing signal guns to alert the British squadron left behind at Newport, Howe's *Glasgow* finally returned to the bay about 9:30. Captain Wallace, commanding *Rose*, took his little squadron back to sea as quickly as possible, perhaps to renew the fight or recover the prizes, but found the waters around Block Island empty. *Glasgow*, meanwhile, was so shot up that he later ordered her to sail north for repairs at Halifax, where she arrived on April 18.

Commodore Hopkins' fleet sailed for New London, Connecticut, arriving at the anchorage on April 7. Hopkins' decision to raid Nassau rather than clearing the American coast of British blockaders proved controversial. The dissatisfying engagement with *Glasgow* only worsened his reputation. Both the commodore and Captain Saltonsall were hauled before the Congressional Maritime Committee to answer for *Alfred*'s performance. While the committee accepted the "lucky shot" that disabled *Alfred*'s steering, Hopkins' reputation never fully recovered. Captain Whipple of *Columbus* was court-martialed for cowardice, but acquitted on the grounds of poor judgment rather than cowardice. Capt. John Hazard of *Providence*—which never truly engaged in the fight—was court-martialed on several grounds and convicted, losing his command.[21] Only Captain Biddle of *Andrew Doria*, who was saddled with many of the squadron's sick, escaped major censure.

21. Louis Arthur Norton, *Captains Contentious: The Dysfunctional Sons of the Brine* (Columbia, SC: The University of South Carolina Press, 2009), 68-69; William M. Fowler, Jr., "Esek Hopkins: Commander-in-Chief of the Continental Navy," James C. Bradford, ed., *Command Under Sail: Makers of the American Naval Tradition* (Annapolis, MD: Naval Institute Press, 1988), 12-13.

# George Washington's Information War

## ❧ BENJAMIN M. GEORGE ❧

Information has been as powerful a weapon as any in the history of warfare. Modern militaries continue to grapple with the power of information by developing and incorporating specific information strategies into their warfighting arsenals. In 2017, the U.S. military established information as a warfighting function to define and harness "the military role of information at the strategic, operational and tactical levels within today's complex operating environment."[1] While such a step signifies the deliberate effort to integrate more intensively the informational aspects of modern technologies into traditional combat operations, leveraging information for a military advantage is hardly a new phenomenon. Though exquisite technologies and capabilities have altered the applications of information warfare, the underlying principles remain unchanged and can be found in the day-to-day operations of the Continental army during the American Revolution.

At its most basic level, information warfare is the use or manipulation of information to pursue a competitive advantage by influencing targets to make decisions in the interest of those conducting the operation. Military deception, psychological operations, and propaganda are but a few information-related activities that constitute the larger information warfare concept. The term *information warfare* is an anachronism for Colonial America, but its tenets are evident in Gen. George Washington's war correspondence as it pertains to specific information threats and vulnerabilities. Washington demonstrated a keen awareness of the power of information and its capacity to influence

---

1. James N. Mattis, "Information as a Joint Function." *Memorandum*, Secretary of Defense, September 15, 2017, www.rmda.army.mil/records-management/docs/SECDEF-Endorsement_Information_Joint%20Function_Clean.pdf.

combat operations and public perceptions, and sources indicate he deliberately pursued advantages at both the strategic and tactical levels of warfare through his use of information.

The role and impacts of propaganda during the American Revolutionary War have been thoroughly studied. Historian Philip Davidson argues that "propaganda was . . . indispensable to those who first promoted resistance to specific British acts and ultimately urged revolution," and states further that "the evidences of a conscious, systematic effort on the part of certain colonial leaders to gain public support for their ideas are unmistakable."[2] Carl Berger writes that the conflict "was a war of words as well as gunpowder," during which "the atrocity story, kidnappings, false rumors, and bribery stirred the people" in attempts by both Americans and the British to gain influence with specific groups.[3] These scholars reveal propaganda as a significant component of the American war effort, including building anti-British sentiment, lobbying France for direct support, and reinforcing the French alliance domestically.

Davidson and Berger use *propaganda* as a catch-all term for different types of information-related actions, but do not account for the variety of ways that military leaders managed information threats and created and leveraged information advantages for specific purposes in a warfighting context. Berger states he is "much less concerned with the important military operations of the war than with what was said and done in support of them."[4] The information war should be understood as more than propaganda alone, especially because the military leaders that engaged in physical combat on the battlefield also fought information battles away from it, seeking influence equal to any pamphleteer or newspaperman. General Washington is a prime example. Washington faced a variety of information threats and challenges during the war, some tactical in nature while others were more strategic, but all of which required tailored and deliberate responses to prevent potential vulnerabilities from becoming major setbacks.

Away from the battlefield, British disinformation proved enough of a threat at the tactical level that General Washington felt compelled to address it directly. In the summer of 1776, Daniel Roberdeau, a brigadier general of the Pennsylvania militia serving in New Jersey, corresponded

---

2. Philip Davidson, *Propaganda and the American Revolution, 1763-1783* (Chapel Hill: The University of North Carolina Press, 1941), xiv.
3. Carl Berger, *Broadsides and Bayonets: The Propaganda War of the American Revolution* (San Francisco: Papamoa Press, 2017), 10.
4. Ibid.

directly with Washington, who was then headquartered in New York City. In a series of letters between them, Roberdeau provided Washington with useful intelligence delivered to him by two prisoners who escaped detention by the British fleet. In a letter dated August 15, 1776, Roberdeau notified Washington of receiving the two escapees, captains Alexander Hunter and Isaac Farrier, and enclosed with the letter their accounts of British force dispositions. Both accounts informed Washington of British forces receiving reinforcements of Hessian troops; Hunter added "That it is expected an Attack will be made [against Washington in New York] in Eight or Ten days and not before."[5] Roberdeau followed with another urgent letter to Washington on August 19, writing,

> Sir, The Post rider just past through here with a very incredible story which he told with great Confidence vizt that you had received a Flag from Lord Howe 'proposing to retire with the Fleet and Army and that he was willing to scttle the present dispute on any terms you should ask' for which he quoted the Authority of an Officer in your Army who told him that he might spred the News without the least reserve for that the Officer offered to sware to the truth for that he had it from you.[6]

The urgency with which Roberdeau relayed this information is readily apparent in the conclusion of the letter: "As this Intelligence might have a tendancy to lull the Inhabitants I thought it duty to make it the subject of an Express without consulting Genl Mercer who is gone forwards towards Amboy," Roberdeau continued, then closed the letter with a postscript that stated, "The Intelligencer further informed that the Reason of this hasty move from Ld Howe was news from England of a Rumpus wt. France."[7]

Understanding the deleterious effect that such disinformation could have on his troops' readiness and willingness to fight, Washington wasted no time in working to dispel the rumor. In a return letter dated the same day, Washington wrote,

> The Report propagated by the post Rider, is totally destitute of truth in every instance, & as It may have the fatal tendency you seem but too Justly to apprehend, I beg Sir, that you will take Such Steps to contradict & Suppress It, as you shall think most likely to effect It.[8]

5. Daniel Roberdeau to George Washington, August 15, 1776, founders.archives.gov/documents/Washington/03-06-02-0028.
6. Roberdeau to Washington, August 19, 1776, founders.archives.gov/documents/Washington/03-06-02-0075.
7. Ibid.
8. Washington to Roberdeau, August 19, 1776, founders.archives.gov/documents/Washington/03-06-02-0076.

Washington thought the information threat severe enough to rein-force his directive to Roberdeau by directly addressing the disinforma-tion in the general orders he issued the following day, which stated:

> The General being informed, to his great surprize, that a report pre-vails and is industriously spread far and wide that Lord Howe has made propositions of peace, calculated by designing persons more probably to lull us into a fatal security; his duty obliges him to declare that no such offer has been made by Lord Howe, but on the contrary, from the best intelligence he can procure—the Army may expect an attack as soon as the wind and tide shall prove favourable: He hopes therefore, every man's mind and arms, will be prepared for action, and when called to it, shew our enemies, and the whole world, that Freemen contending on their own land, are superior to any mercenaries on earth.[9]

Through this series of correspondence, it is clear Washington understood the importance of the information war, and responded swiftly and thoroughly to counter a very real information threat by informing his troops and ensuring their preparedness for a potential enemy attack.

Not all information threats are propagated by the enemy. One of the most significant information threats to organizational cohesion and effectiveness is the spread of distrust and disaffection from within the group itself, with any spillover potentially causing a loss of public faith in the organization. This reality was no different in colonial America, where the Continental army fought on behalf of a people whose support it hoped to win through trust and vigilance. *A People Numerous and Armed* is a work notable for marrying the military history of the war with the politics and social issues of the Revolutionary period. In it, John Shy stresses "the importance of perception to decision and action" for the colonial population, who stood to influence the military conflict one way or the other.[10] Shy argues, "the widely ramifying effects of a legally armed population" could either help or hinder the revolutionary cause, hence the book's title.[11] Those who were neither avowed Loyalists nor anti-Loyalists stood as potential sympathizers to each cause, lacking only an effective influence to push them to action. Therefore, the information battle within the greater war was critical to the fight for independence, both on a broad strategic scale and at the tac-

---

9. General orders, August 20, 1776, founders.archives.gov/documents/Washington/03-06-02-0079.
10. John Shy, *A People Numerous and Armed: Reflections on the Military Struggle for American Independence* (N32 York: Oxford University Press, 1976), 3.
11. Ibid., 4.

tical level within villages and towns throughout the colonies. Once advocates were recruited to the revolutionary cause, their support needed to be won every day, lest disaffection spread and staunch the fight for independence from within.

George Washington's response to information threats indicate that he believed no such threat was insignificant, as evidenced by his response to the disinformation regarding a rumored truce with General Howe. Enter Dr. Penuel Cheney, whose potentially toxic influence Washington took quick measure to mitigate before it could lead to serious consequences. Penuel Cheney was a surgeon's mate in the 3rd Connecticut Regiment who was accused of making "fraudulent Draughts upon the Commissary's Store and other malpractices" and was set to face a military court of inquiry, as directed in Washington's general orders from July 22, 1775.[12] In a letter dated September 4, 1775, Cheney wrote to Washington, requesting that "but for the Benefit of the Regiment the good of my Cuntry and the noble Cause in which this Army & Continent are now ingaged I would therefore humbly beseech your Excellency to discharge me from any future Attendence on said Regiment."[13] Cheney's request was approved and he was discharged from further service, but was later appointed as the surgeon for the same unit on October 4.

Not one to accept willingly the service of officers with questionable conduct records, Washington wrote to Jonathan Trumbull, Sr., on October 29, to inquire about the details of Cheney's appointment:

> I was somewhat surprised to find, that in one of the Regiments lately from Connecticut Dr Cheney had been commissioned as a Surgeon— As I am persuaded he must have obtained this Appointment by some misrepresentation I think it proper to apprize you of his conduct and behaviour last Summer.[14]

He then recounted the nature of Cheney's charges from May and explained that Cheney evaded his trial "by requesting a desmission, which was granted him." Washington continued,

> I am very credibly informed, he returned to his Colony where he has propagated the most infamous reports of some of the General Offi-

12. General orders, July 22, 1775, founders.archives.gov/documents/Washington/03-01-02-0091.
13. Penuel Cheney to Washington, September 4, 1775, founders.archives.gov/documents/Washington/03-01-02-0304.
14. Washington to Jonathan Trumbull, Sr., October 29, 1775, founders.archives.gov/documents/Washington/03-02-02-0235.

cers—Reports tending to impress the minds of the Soldiery and Country with prejudices which would dissolve that confidence which ought to subsist between Troops and their Officers. Since he has returned to Camp he has renewed his draughts upon the Stores but being immediately detected I have ordered him under an arrest, and hope sufficient evidence may be had to convict him, so as to rid the Army of him entirely.[15]

Not only did Washington take exception to Cheney's previous misconduct and express concern over his return to military service, but was sure to note that Cheney's efforts to bring disrepute to the officers of the Continental army were equally troubling.

Further correspondence between Washington and Trumbull discussed the nature of Cheney's re-appointment as surgeon, Washington's assurance that Cheney would receive an impartial trial, and Washington's subtle request that Trumbull—and all others of equal position and influence—take great "Strength, Care, Firmness and Union" in such efforts as appointing officers to military service to support the fight for independence.[16] According to the general orders issued on November 21 and 22, 1775, the Cheney affair ended with a court martial that found Cheney "guilty of speaking words tending to the dishonour of the Character of Major Genl Putnam, and therefore adjudge him to be cashiered," a sentence that Washington approved and ordered to take place immediately.[17] The Cheney incident shows how seriously Washington took the issue of slander and its potential impact on the good order and discipline of his army, and the likely second- and third-order negative effects it could have on support for the American war effort.

A consequential information campaign for both American and British leaders during the war was the fight for influence with Native Americans to gain their military support. The battle between Americans and the British to garner Native allies was not only about gaining a military advantage during the war, but also would have longstanding impacts on the relationship between Native peoples and the winners of the war. The contest to win Native American support was rife with potential pitfalls, and inaction could be particularly risky. If a side de-

15. Ibid.

16. Washington to Trumbull, November 15, 1775, founders.archives.gov/documents/ Washington/03-02-02-0348.

17. General orders, November 21, 1775, founders.archives.gov/documents/ Washington/ 03-02-02-0378; General orders, November 22, 1775, founders.archives.gov/ documents/ Washington/03-02-02-0381.

cided not to pursue Indian allies, or at least promote Indian neutrality in the conflict, they might cede the advantage to their enemy. Conversely, to engage with and attract Indian allies could risk losing the support of various colonial populations who either feared Indians or were already competing with them for land and resources. Thus, the war for influence with Indian allies was extremely nuanced and cautious. As historian Colin Calloway writes,

> both sides courted Indian allies, and both sides hesitated to employ them. Messengers and scouting parties crisscrossed the northern borderlands, and reports and rumors of enemy agents in Indian country created a tense environment. Indian communities tried to figure out what was going on and what it would mean for them . . . Like the Americans, the British worried that if they did not employ Indian allies, the enemy would.[18]

George Washington's wartime correspondence offers further evidence of the evolving approach to persuading Indian allies to the American cause.

The Continental Congress created three departments for managing Indian affairs: the northern department focusing on the Six Nations of the Iroquois confederation, the middle department concentrating on the Kentucky-Ohio territory and the loose western confederation of the Shawnee, Delaware, Miami, and other tribes, and the southern department covering the Virginia-Georgia-Carolina backcountry where the Cherokee, Creek, and Chickasaw tribes were the most influential.[19] Establishing these departments was a strategic necessity to account for the regional inter-tribal dynamics and relationships that were essential to maintaining influence with the different Native groups.

In the war's early years, Washington seemed to value Indians more as agents of the information war rather than as allied combatants. Washington detailed an interaction he had with several Mohawk warriors in a letter to Maj. Gen. Philip Schuyler on May 3, 1776. Washington writes that at least one of the warriors wanted "a Commission to raise Men & fight against the Regulars." However, Washington believed the Indians did "not appear to be Persons of any Sort of Consequence," and instead commented that

> As they have been at Boston & Eye Witnesses of the Departure of the Kings Troops, & the many things left by them, whether would It

---

18. Colin G. Calloway, *The Indian World of George Washington: The First President, the First Americans, and the Birth of the Nation* (Oxford: Oxford University Press, 2018), 218.
19. Berger, *Broadsides and Bayonets*, 38-39.

not be Good Policy to hasten them home as fast as possible, that they may Communicate the Intelligence, their Tale will Carry more Conviction than the Report of twenty white men.[20]

Washington wrote to Schuyler again on October 10, 1776, sharing similar sentiments. Washington wrote that two Sachems of the Cayugas had spent several days with him, wherein he

> shewed them every Civility in My Power & presented them with such Necessaries as our Barren stores afforded and they were pleased to take; I also had them shewn all our Works upon this Island, which I had manned, to give them an Idea of our Force & to do away the false Notions they might have imbibed from the Tales which had been propagated among 'em.[21]

He concluded his account of the interaction by stating "They took their Departure Yesterday morning & I hope with No Unfavorable Impressions."[22] Still later in 1776, Washington corresponded directly with chiefs of the Passamaquoddy Indians, writing,

> Our Enemy the King of Great Britain endeavoured to Stir up all the Indians from Canada to South Carolina Against Us, But our Bretheren of the Six Nations and their Allies the Shawanese and Delewares would not hearken to the Advice of the Messengers sent among them but kept fast hold of our Ancient Covenant Chain; The Cherokees and the Southern Tribes were foolish enough to listen to them, and to take up the Hatchet Against us.[23]

Then, attempting to retain Passamaquoddy support, Washington stated, "Now Brothers never lett the Kings Wicked Councellors turn your Hearts Against Me and your Bretheren of this Country."[24]

In March 1777, Washington wrote to John Hancock, then president of the Continental Congress, to recount his interaction with an Oneida chief and several warriors. Washington wrote that the Oneidas came "to enquire into the true state of matters, that they might report them to a Grand Council to be shortly held. they said, things were so falsely and variously represented by our Enemies through their Agents, that

---

20. Washington to Philip Schuyler, May 3, 1776, founders.archives.gov/documents/Washington/03-04-02-0159.
21. Washington to Schuyler, October 10, 1776, founders.archives.gov/documents/Washington/03-06-02-0403.
22. Ibid.
23. Washington to the Chiefs of the Passamaquoddy Indians, December 24, 1776, founders.archives.gov/documents/Washington/03-07-02-0340.
24. Ibid.

they did not know what to depend on." Washington continued, writing that "they were well satisfied with what they had seen, and that they were authorized to tell their Nation, All they had heard from the Enemy was false. being told that France was assisting us & about to join in the War, they seemed highly pleased." He added that Rev. Samuel Kirkland, a Protestant missionary who lived among the Oneidas, "was persuaded it would have a considerable effect on the minds of several of the Nations and secure to us their neutrality if not a declaration & commencement of Hostilities in our favor."[25]

These few examples of Washington's correspondence discussing Native American neutrality, along with the other information-centric operations discussed herein, are but a small sample of the information war within the American Revolution. Information was as crucial a weapon to military orders and movements as it was to broadsides, pamphlets, and newspapers on both sides of the Atlantic. As these examples show, the information war was more than propaganda spread across colonial and British populations. Success in information warfare, not unlike in traditional war, requires advantages at the tactical and strategic levels to provide the greatest likelihood of victory.

Historian Woody Holton writes that manipulating morale was a central strategic imperative during the war. As both sides constantly sought to rally and maintain support from their own populations, "the most important target of commanders' morale influence operations was always their own side," both civilians and soldiers.[26] Propaganda, disinformation, morale, and influence were all pieces of the larger information war, and military leaders were in the very thick of that information fight. The examples herein provide insight into just how nuanced and layered the information battle was for the Continental army, from tactical to strategic considerations. While much scholarship on information during the American Revolution has focused largely on the nature, methods, and practitioners of propaganda, by promoting a more nuanced understanding of the military's role to leverage the power of information, it becomes clear that the elements of information warfare are as relevant today as they were during the fight for American independence.

25. Washington to John Hancock, March 29, 1777, founders.archives.gov/documents/Washington/03-09-02-0013.
26. Woody Holton, "Morale Manipulation as the Central Strategic Imperative in the American Revolutionary War," *Journal of the American Revolution* August 3, 2021, allthingsliberty.com/2021/08/morale-manipulation-as-the-central-strategic-imperative-in-the-american-revolutionary-war/.

# John Adams and Nathanael Greene Debate the Role of the Military

## CURTIS F. MORGAN

Nathanael Greene is rightly remembered as one of the great combat leaders of the American Revolution. But he was also a deep political thinker, a Rhode Island politician before the war who did not hesitate to discuss the broader ramifications of the American Revolution with a wide range of Patriot notables, some of whom never picked up a sword.

These literary exchanges are revealing when it is remembered that the American "system" was not created at Philadelphia in 1787 (or even 1781), but to a great extent in the camps of the Continental Army, where the struggle was not just against the imperial foe, but also over what exactly the rebels hoped to achieve beyond "mere" independence. Few issues were more vital than the nature of the army itself: to what extent should the force fighting for American "Liberty" reflect the deepest ideals of that concept? Put another way, should the Continental Army be composed of volunteer militia who were fighting for the "Glorious Cause" above all? Or should it confront the greatest professional army in the world with a disciplined professional army of its own? Greene (together with his mentor, George Washington) insisted on the latter.

Greene had a brief exchange on the subject in 1776-77 with John Adams, another New England "pol" who had very different ideas about the army and its role in the struggle for American liberty. Some of the ideas they debated are still current in American life today: What should be the role of the military in a democracy? Is a professional force a standing threat to civil liberties? Would a "national guard" be too unruly and undisciplined to be relied on when the survival of the republic is at stake? When do the ends justify the means?

# I

In the beginning, the American Revolution was a rebellion of colonists accustomed to governing themselves against an Empire enforcing its rule through a professional military. But could "Minutemen" resist and even defeat "Redcoats"? Officers like Washington and Greene looked upon militia with disdain. Americans faced a professional military; but the militia "was a most unmilitary outfit by European standards."[1] No uniforms; no uniformity of arms; elected officers; lax or non-existent discipline. Such informality weakened the militia in combat; additionally, the militias were state-raised and -run, and served under short-term enlistments that played havoc with long-term planning. Despite these drawbacks, some political leaders saw militiamen as preferable to professional soldiers. John Adams declared:

> Although it may cost us more, and we put now and then a battle to hazard by the method we are in, yet we shall be less in danger of corruption and violence from a standing army, and our militia will acquire courage, experience, discipline, and hardiness in actual combat.[2]

Greene disagreed. He wrote to his state governor in July 1775 that "the task is difficult and trouble great to form people into any regular Government that comes out with minds possest of notions of Liberty that is nothing short of Licentiousness."[3] He would later complain that his militiamen were "the worst in the world" and "of no more use than if they were in the moon." Discipline and order required submission, but "With the militia everybody is a general, and the powers of government are so feeble, that it is with the utmost difficulty you can restrain them from plundering one another."[4] To expect such men to stand up in combat was ludicrous, and far too much to expect of

> militia men who come and go every month . . . People coming from home with all the tender feelings of domestic life are not sufficiently fortified with natural courage to stand the shocking scenes of war. To march over dead men, to hear without concern the groans of the

---

1. Daniel J. Boorstin, "A Nation of Minutemen," in *The Americans: The Colonial Experience* (New York: Vintage, 1958), 335.

2. John Adams, quoted in ibid., 368. See also Charles Royster, *A Revolutionary People at War: The Continental Army and American Character, 1775-1783* (Chapel Hill: University of North Carolina Press, 1979), 36-39.

3. Nathanael Greene to RI Gov. Nicholas Cooke, July 4, 1775, *The Papers of General Nathanael Greene, Volume 1 December 1766-December 1776*, ed. Richard K. Showman and Dennis Conrad (Chapel Hill: University of North Carolina Press, 1976), 1:95 (*NG*).

4. Greene to Jacob Greene(?), September 28, 1776, ibid., 1:303-304.

wounded, I say few men can stand such scenes unless steeled by habit or fortified by military pride.

In one of his first general orders, Greene urged officers to treat "Troops that behave well with all gentleness" but to "Punish the Refractory and Seditious with Exemplary Punishment," calling for particular attention to "Debauchery and Vulgar Language Inconsistent with the Character of Soldiers."[5] His work was cut out for him.

## II

After more than a year in command, Greene reached out to the political leadership in the Continental Congress to air some concerns he had about the conduct of the war. Although Greene asserted that "Modesty will forever forbid me to apply to [Congress] for any favors," in the summer of 1776 he began a fascinating exchange of letters with one of the most powerful men in Congress, John Adams. Why the exchange began is unknown (the first letters of both men are lost), but it is clear that for his part Greene was doing a lot of thinking about political and administrative matters and wanted someone in Congress to know it. He had recently lost his foremost ally and mentor, Samuel Ward, Sr., who died of smallpox while attending Congress in Philadelphia in March. Greene needed a new patron; Adams was a fellow New Englander who would understand him; he was also a member whose opinion carried much weight. In the first letter we have, of June 2, Greene pressed for a pension system for wounded soldiers (regulars and militia), decried the lack of shelter for the troops, complained of the inadequate pay officers received, warned that Congress's "Emision of such large sums of [Continental] money" would aggravate inflation and depreciation (further eroding military pay), and urged (without naming his personal interest) that officer promotions be based on seniority, not merit. (He feared, as the lowest-ranked brigadier general, being passed over for promotion to major general by a more-recently appointed brigadier). "For my own part," he warned, "I would never give any Legislative body an opportunity to humiliate me but once." His candor is striking, blunt while avoiding open disrespect. It indicates both a zeal for "the Cause" and a familiarity with Adams that gave Greene the confidence to speak his mind.

> I flatter my self I know the History, Strength, and state of the army almost as well as any in it . . . You think the present army assisted by the militia is sufficient to oppose the force of Great Britain, formidable

5. General orders, June 4, 1775, ibid, 1:84.

as it appears on paper. I can assure you its necessary to make great allowances in the calculation of our strength from the Establishment or else you'l be greatly deceivd. I am confident the force of America if properly exerted will prove superior to all her Enemies, but I would risque nothing to chance. It is easy to disband when it is impossible to raise Troops.[6]

Adams waited two and a half weeks to reply; understandable in light of the fact that on June 7 Richard Henry Lee of Virginia had moved a resolution on independence and on the 11th Congress had named Adams, Thomas Jefferson, Benjamin Franklin, Roger Sherman and Robert Livingston to a committee to draft a declaration of independence. (Greene was ignorant of this; growing impatient, he fumed to his brother Christopher: "That dam'd Idea of Reconciliation is continually damping and dividing the Assembly.") Adams answered Greene's letter point by point. "Your Reasoning" regarding pensions for wounded soldiers "is extremely just, and cannot bee answered," he wrote. The problem lay in how large a pension, how to pay for it, etc. A plan was needed. As for raising officers' pay, Adams was dubious. "Officers present themselves in supernumerary abundance," he complained. "As to pay there is no end to the Desire and Demand of it. Is there not too much Extravagance and too little Economy among the officers?" This irked Greene; but Adams' (and many others') perception of the pomp and airs of the officer corps had more than a grain of truth to it. One study found that 84 percent of New Jersey officers came from the wealthiest one-third of society. They were respected in their communities and expected to receive both honor and pay commensurate with their status. One could almost hear Adams' Puritan forebears clucking in disapproval of this ostentatious display. Greene's Quaker ancestors would no doubt have agreed, but Greene in many respects had already declared his own independence from his family's ethos.

Adams continued: "That the Promotion of extraordinary Merit may give disgust to those officers is true, over whom the advancement is made, but I think it ought not. That this Power may be abused, or misapplied, is also true ... But where will you lodge this Power? To place it in the General [Washington] would be more dangerous to the public liberty," he argued. "Will it do," he asked, "to lay it down as an invariable Rule, that all officers in all cases shall rise in succession?" (Ironically,

---

6. For Ward's death, see note at *NG* 1:233. Greene's first letter to Adams was dated May 24; Adams's reply May 26; both letters are lost. Greene to Adams, June 2, 1776, *NG* 1:222-227, and accompanying notes.

Congress, riven by local jealousies, would in effect decide that it *would* "do," and as a result drive several ambitious officers into bitter resignation, and one talented and vigorous general, Benedict Arnold, into treason.) Adams concluded by forwarding to Greene a copy of a resolution establishing a Board of War and Ordinance to delve into these issues, and humbly asked Greene for his opinions on it, admitting his ignorance of military matters. "I am called to the Discharge of Trust to which I feel myself so unequal, and in the Execution of which I can derive no assistance from my Education or former Course of Life," he lamented.[7]

Greene heartily agreed. "You cannot more sincerely lament the want of knowledge to execute the business that falls in your department than I do that which falls in mine," he replied on July 14, "and was I not kept in countenance by some of my superior officers I should be sincerely disposed to quit the command I hold in the Army." But he intended to make up for his ignorance through "Watchfulness and Industry." He went on to explain his opinion about officers' pay and promotions:

> You query whether there is not a want of Oeconomy in the Army amongst the officers. I can Assure you there is not among those of my Acquaintance. The expences of the Officers runs very high, unless they dress and live below the Gentleman. Few that have ever lived in Character will be willing to descend to that. As long as they continue in service they will support their Rank, and if their pay is not sufficient they will draw on their private fortunes at Home.[8]

It was no secret that Washington was doing so, foregoing any salary at all, and only billing Congress for his expenses. Greene was not alone in his irritation that men in Congress and other prominent civilians who faced no mortal danger on the battlefield themselves seemed to view military officers as "grasping mercenaries, instead of dedicated, virtuous citizens of the aspiring republic" in the words of two historians.[9]

This goes far to explain the touchiness of Greene and his fellow officers in matters of pay and promotion. One's status as a gentleman,

7. Mark M. Boatner, ed., *Encyclopedia of the American Revolution* (New York: Stackpole, 1976), 539-540; Greene to Christopher Greene, June 7, 1776, *NG* 1:232; Adams to Greene, June 22, 1776, ibid, 238-240; James Kirby Martin and Mark Edward Lender, *A Respectable Army: The Military Origins of the Republic, 1763-1789*. 3d ed. (Maldon, MA: Wiley Blackwell, 2015), 109.
8. Greene to Adams, July 14, 1776, *NG* 1:253-256.
9. Martin and Lender, *A Respectable Army*, 109-110.

the defense of one's honor, was at least partially reflected in the pay and rank one received (and hence deserved, indeed had *earned* defending the Cause). Greene and others would threaten resignation repeatedly over these issues in the coming years, insisting that it was the members of Congress who were being petty and grasping, by withholding or "economizing" what was their due as officers in any army.

Regarding promotion (which he still hoped for at this time), Greene explained: "I am not against rewarding merit or encourageing Activity, neither would I have promotions confind to a regular line of succession ... but I should think the Generals [i.e. Washington's] recommendation is the best testimonial of a Persons deserving a reward that the Congress can have." Greene must have been pleased with Adams' reply of August 4, in which he declared Greene's views on promotion "so nearly agreeable to mine," and with Adams' implied inclusion of Greene with other officers he characterized: "A General officer ought to be a Gentleman of Letters and General Knowledge, a Man of Address and Knowledge of the World." If any of Greene's feathers remained ruffled, this comment should have smoothed them. Confirmation came five days later, with Greene's elevation to major general by vote of Congress.[10] This exchange of letters was the first official contact Greene had with Congress. Although it began cordially enough, it would not remain so. Greene would gradually lose patience with Congress, and his outspokenness would lose him much support among its members, including John Adams.

## III

Early in 1777, Washington sent Greene to Philadelphia to meet with Congress. Greene was on good terms with John Adams, with whom he resumed the correspondence begun some time before. "It is a long time since I wrote to you or you to me," Greene wrote on March 3, "therefore I shall begin anew."[11]

"I am sensible you have not the most exalted opinion of your *Generals*," he began. The Continental army had operated under "inconcievable" difficulties during the previous campaign, hastily assembled, inexperienced, facing a well-equipped, veteran force led by an aggressive commander. "General Washington as every defender ought has fol-

---

10. Adams to Greene, August 4, 1776, *NG* 1:273-274 and 275n5. For more on Greene-Adams correspondence, see William P. Leeman, "Rhode Island's Controversial General: Nathanael Greene and the Continental Congress, 1776-1780," *Rhode Island History* 59:3 (2001): 85-86.
11. Greene to Adams, March 3, 1777, *NG* 2:28.

lowed directly the contrary conduct, by indeavoring to skirmish with the Enemy at all times, and avoid a general engagement." Greene was confident of eventual success. "America abounds with Materials to form as good an army as the World can produce, but it requires time" and, assuming the recruiting effort was successful, the army "will display . . . as much heroism and bravery as Europe can boast off [*sic*]."[12]

Adams replied a few days later that "Some busy Body" had been putting words in his mouth about his opinion of the generals. He deleted a following sentence that stated "Untill then I believe my Opinion of our Generals will continue not very exalted," and instead continued, "Notwithstanding this I have a sincere Esteem of our General Officers taken together as a Body." He then turned to the subject of recent promotions, and some of the officers' reactions to them:

> This delicate Point of Honour, which is really one of the most putrid
> Corruptions of absolute Monarchy, I mean the Honour of maintaining
> a Rank Superior to abler Men, I mean the Honour of preferring a single
> Step of Promotion to the Service of the Public, must be bridled. It is
> incompatible with republican Principles.[13]

He believed that Congress should annually elect all the generals! Greene must have choked on his tea when he read that, but Adams was serious, and merely expressing a deeply ingrained political culture that had long revered local control and saw a standing army as a threat to liberty. Greene and his compatriots shared Adams's world view but saw the other side of the coin as well: that the success of the American Revolution demanded both unity of purpose in Congress (the sublimation of local interests to "continental" ones) and the resort to a standing army to win independence. Adams was not yet ready to accept the dilemma that the ends for which Americans were fighting conflicted with the means necessary to achieve them.[14]

## IV

Greene's first encounter with the civilian leadership had not been encouraging. He had discovered that responsibility for supplying the Continental Army was divided among several Congressional committees, state authorities, military officers, and civilians. In a word, it was a mess. Greene was also hampered by the fact that only five members of Congress had any army administrative experience at all. Congress

12. Ibid., 2:28-29. Emphasis in original.
13. Ibid.
14. Adams to Greene, March 9, 1777, *NG* 2:37, 39-40.

was blissfully ignorant of how an army was run or what it needed. When its visceral anti-militarist attitude is added to the mix, it is easy to see the difficulties Washington and Greene faced.[15]

The distrust between Congress and the officer corps further increased that summer, and Greene was in the thick of it. The generals' distrust of Congress was coupled with distress at their own inability to determine the British army's intentions. Within days of returning to camp at Morristown, Greene resumed his correspondence with Adams on a variety of matters facing the army and the Cause. Greene wrote to Adams more than vice versa, and clearly felt comfortable addressing him familiarly. This may be what led to trouble.[16]

Since the summer of 1775, Greene had increasingly viewed Washington as the living embodiment of the Revolution and was sensitive to any perceived slight to his mentor. It is therefore ironic that it was Adams, the man who had moved Washington's appointment as Commander in Chief, who provoked a testy exchange with Greene over His Excellency's merits. Perhaps Adams was disturbed, when he met Greene in Philadelphia, by what he perceived as hero-worship on Greene's part and wished to deflate it somewhat; whatever his motives, in a letter of April 27 (now lost), Adams drew Greene's ire by stating that "there is no one man either in the Civil or military line that is of such mighty consequence that the liberties of America are dependant upon his will or existence" and that "a certain General" (Washington?) "might be of more importance to the Continent if he thought himself of less."[17] Greene countered that "there are several" (including himself?) "that America might sensibly feel the loss off [sic] at this time" and that Adams' opinion of Washington "is very different (if I remember right) from what it was last Summer upon a similar occasion." Speaking more generally, Greene wrote that although he acknowledged that Congress was entitled to "dignity in every instance, yet I hope they will carefully avoid sporting with the finer feelings of the Gentlem[e]n of the Army." In this connection, he brought up a sore point. "I have no wish to see such a large propo[r]tion of important offices in the Military depart-

---

15. E. Wayne Carp, *To Starve the Army at Pleasure: Continental Army Administration and American Political Culture, 1775-1783* (Chapel Hill: University of North Carolina Press, 1984), 19, 20; for more on Mifflin and Trumbull, see Boatner, *Encyclopedia*, 704-705, 1122-1123.

16. Greene to Adams, April 5, April 13, May 2, 1777, *NG* 2:51-52, 55-56, 64-65; Adams to Greene, May 9, 1777, ibid, 74-75. Not all of Adams's letters are extant; we know of some only because of Greene's references to them in his own letters.

17. Adams's arguments in his April 27 letter are paraphrased in Nathanael Greene's reply, May 7, 1777, *NG* 2:69-70.

ment in the hands of foreigners. I cannot help considering them as so many Spies in our Camp," pursuing personal interest at the expense of the Cause; native officers had more binding ties to the nation, namely "Interest and family connexion."[18]

What Greene was hinting at was the recent arrival of an entire shipload of eighteen French officers, ten sergeants, and assorted munitions arranged by America's agent in Paris, Silas Deane. Desperate to wheedle French assistance, Deane had exceeded his authority by promising a major general's commission and appointment as "General of Artillery and Ordinance" to one Philippe Charles Jean Baptiste Tronson de Coudray, a *chef de brigade* (brigadier general) with a background in artillery and ties (through his brother Alexandre) to Queen Marie Antoinette. Congress had not yet decided what to do with this and other proposed foreign appointments; but such was the mutual distrust of officers and officials that Greene assumed that the appointment, which would in effect replace Gen. Henry Knox with de Coudray, was a "done deal." After all, he had just been to Philadelphia, and knew how those conniving pols operated. He also knew well that there was little love lost in the capital for the officer corps. Replacing a tried-and-true Patriot Gentleman like Henry Knox with a well-born, fawning Frenchman with pretensions of grandeur was *just* the kind of thing they would do. It is instructive that Greene was inclined to believe another rumor ("hinted to me") that Gen. Philip Schuyler was to replace Hancock as President of Congress! "I take this opportunaty of expressing my abhorrence of such a measure. No free people ought to admit a junction of the Civil and Military," he wrote, as if Adams, of all people, needed convincing of this. Greene's ignorance of Congressional sentiment in this regard is astonishing. In fact, Schuyler was one of the officers most in foul odor with the politicians; he had just lost his northern command to Horatio Gates, but Greene assumed Schuyler (a patrician of Dutch ancestry) was a man of influence.[19]

18. Ibid, 2:70-71. Adams wrote a reply that may not have been sent. On the dignity of officers, he was suspicious, to say the least. "I am much mistaken and much misinformed, if the nice Feelings[,] the Pride, the Vanity, the Foppery, the Knavery and Gambling among too many of the Officers do not end in direct Endeavours to set up a Tyrant sooner or later, unless early Endeavours are used to controul them." It is telling that Greene made no mention of this provocative statement in his replies. Adams to Greene, May 10, 1777, ibid, 2:76-77 and accompanying note.

19. For more on Schuyler, see Boatner, *Encyclopedia*, 991-993, and John H.G. Pell, "Philip Schuyler: The General as Aristocrat," in George A. Billias, ed. *George Washington's Generals and Opponents: Their Exploits and Leadership* (New York: Da Capo Press, 1994), 1:54-78.

Greene pressed Adams on the de Coudray rumor, and went into the lists on behalf of his good friend and favorite bookseller Knox. "I must again repeat the impropriety of creating so many foreign Officers," he wrote.

> I am told . . . that one De Cudre is engaged by Mr Dean as Major General of the [Artillery] Train. The impropriety of putting a foraigner at the head of such a Department must be obvious to every body. Besides the Impropriety, you will deprive the Army of a most valuable Officer, universally acknowledged as such . . . a man who has serv'd you with Fidelity and Reputation.[20]

Adams replied on June 2. After dismissing the Schuyler report as "a Mistake," he agreed with Greene that no one should hold both a seat in Congress and a general's commission. He then tried to put the de Coudray matter to rest. "I agree entirely in your sentiments concerning the Danger of entrusting so many important Commands to foreigners. Mr Deane I fear has exceeded his Powers. Mr Du Coudray shall never have my Consent to be at the Head of the Artillery, and I believe he will have few advocates for placing him there. I hope, none." Then, in what would prove an ominous afterthought, Adams wrote, "Pray what is your opinion of General Conway. He acquired a good Reputation here." Perhaps Adams put Greene's fears to rest; nothing more was written about de Coudray for almost a month.

Then, at the beginning of July, at the first anniversary of the Declaration of Independence, the controversy resurfaced. President John Hancock received the following letter from Greene:

> A report is circulating here at Camp that Monsieur de Coudray a French Gentleman is appointed a Major General in the service of the United States, his rank to commence from the first of last August. If the report be true it will lay me under the necessity of resigning my Commision as his appointment supercedes me in command. I beg youl acquaint me with respect to the truth of the report, and if true inclose me a permit to retire.[21]

Hancock received similar letters from John Sullivan and Henry Knox (the immediately aggrieved party). They all referred to anonymous "reports" that the appointment was an accomplished fact. Actually, Congress had just received the report on the appointment from its

---

20. Greene heard the rumor from another French officer in the American army, "Capt Moduit" (Thomas-Antoine, Chevalier Mauduit de Plessis). Greene to Adams, May 28, 1777, *NG* 2:98-99.
21. Greene to John Hancock, July 1, 1777, *NG* 2:109.

Committee on Foreign Applications, and had resolved to take it up the following week.[22] The rumor mill was working its usual havoc, and although Congress perceived ulterior motives and doubted that the generals believed that de Coudray had already been appointed, the fact is that the generals imperfectly understood the operations of Congress; assumed Deane had more influence than he had; and were inclined to believe the worst about the political leadership. Unfortunately, the distrust was mutual.

Greene, Sullivan, and Knox were all headstrong, proud men, sensitive to perceived slights, and this was a big one. According to the rumor, not only would de Coudray replace Knox as head of artillery, but his commission as major general would be back-dated to 1776, so that he would outrank (by seniority) Sullivan and Greene. On July 2 the Foreign Appointments Committee presented its report and recommended that the matter be "referred to the committee of the whole Congress," whereupon it was decided to postpone consideration of the various papers involved, including "letters" from Washington and others until "Saturday next" (July 5). On that day, the letters from Greene and Knox were brought up, and discussion postponed again. On July 7, Congress resolved to call the generals' bluff.

> Congress resumed the consideration of the letters from Generals Sullivan, Greene, and Knox, all dated the 1 July; Whereupon, Congress came to the following unanimous resolution:
>
> That the president transmit to General Washington copies of the letters from Generals Sullivan, Greene, and Knox, to Congress, with directions to him to let those officers know that Congress consider the said letters as an attempt to influence their decisions, and an invasion of the liberties of the people, and indicating a want of confidence in the justice of Congress; that it is expected by Congress the said officers will make proper acknowledgments for an interference of so dangerous a tendency; but, if any of those officers are unwilling to serve their country under the authority of Congress, they shall be at liberty to resign their commissions and retire.[23]

Hancock sent a cover letter to Washington that stated:

> I have the Honour to transmit at this Time copies of three Letters from Generals Sullivan, Green, and Knox to Congress, the Receipt of

---

22. Ibid., and note, 109-110; Leeman, "Rhode Island's Controversial General," 88-89; *Journals of the Continental Congress* 8:507 (*JCC*). For accounts involving the other generals, see Charles P. Whittemore, "John Sullivan: Luckless Irishman," and North Callahan, "Henry Knox: American Artillerist," in Billias, *George Washington's Generals*, 1:147, 248-249.
23. *JCC* 8:525-526, 535, 537.

which, as the Contents were highly derogatory to the Honour and Justice of Congress, could not fail to be extremely displeasing. They have therefore come to the enclosed Resolve on the Subject, to which, as it clearly expresses their Sense of the Impropriety of the Conduct of those Officers, I beg Leave to refer to your Attention, and to request you will make them acquainted therewith.[24]

John Adams went to greater lengths to express his anger to Greene. "I never before took hold of a Pen to write to my Friend General Green[e] without Pleasure, but I think myself obliged to do it now upon a Subject that gives me a great deal of Pain," he began. The letters from Greene, Knox and Sullivan had "interrupted the Deliberations of Congress" and had caused "much Uneasiness." Greene and his colleagues were off base, Adams contended. "The Contract between Mr Deane and Monsr. Du Coudray is not yet decided upon." How then was Congress to react to three letters from generals, "threatening that if We fulfill the Contract, Three Officers, on whom we have depended, will resign in the midst of the Campaign when the Attention of every officer ought to be wholly taken up in penetrating the Designs of the Enemy, and in Efforts to defeat them"? Adams scolded Greene (as well as Knox and Sullivan) for disregarding "the necessity of preserving the Authority of the Civil Powers above the military," and referred to the Congressional resolution, which "expresses an Expectation that some Acknowledgment or Apology will be made." Adams closed by urging that Greene present "a Declaration that you had no Intention to influence Congress," calling this "the least that you can do."[25]

How Greene reacted to this is not clear, except that this appears to be the last letter to pass between to the two men for at least three years. The immediate fallout was minimal; Washington studiously avoided involvement in the affair, except to pass along the resolution to the generals. He clearly sympathized with them; he declined to reprimand the three, even though they had broken the chain of command by writing directly to Congress (perhaps they had done so to avoid enmeshing him in the matter; he was doubtless grateful for this). Although the resolution in effect called for their resignations, none were offered, and Congress did not pursue the matter further.

Only Greene responded to the resolution directly. In a July 19 letter to Hancock, he carefully explained his intentions while avoiding a di-

24. Hancock to Washington, July 8, 1777, *The Papers of George Washington: Revolutionary War Series*, ed. W.W. Abbot et al. (Charlottesville: University Press of Virginia, 1985-2009), 10:227; Washington's non-committal reply to Hancock July 12 is found at ibid, 254.
25. Adams to Greene, July 7, 1777, *NG* 2:111-113 and accompanying notes.

rect apology. He expressed surprise that Congress had reacted as it did, and even convinced himself (so he says) that upon "a dispassionate review of the matter" it would "recall a censure equally severe, unmerited, and injurious." He insisted that he had no intent to influence Congress, but merely to express a desire "to be permitted to retire." How could it be perceived otherwise? At the heart of the matter was the affront to his dignity provoked by Congress's plan to promote a foreigner over himself ("what I thought had happened"). He ended his diatribe with a non-resignation resignation: "In my military capacity I have and will serve my Country to the utmost of my ability while I hold it, but I am determined to hold it not a moment longer than I can do it unsullied and unviolated." There the matter ended, more or less; de Coudray was commissioned a major general "of the staff," that is, he had no seniority over generals "of the line," and was appointed to the largely honorific position of "Inspector General of Ordinance and Military Manufactories." Then (to everyone's relief), that September the Frenchman fell off a Schuylkill River ferry boat and drowned.[26]

This lengthy account of a non-event (the resignation or dismissal of Greene from the Continental service) demands an explanation. Its importance is seen on several levels: First, the episode unfolded against a background of mutual distrust between the Congress and the Continental officer corps that, as we have seen, had deep roots: the colonial militia tradition and its hostility to a standing army; the disparagement of militia by Washington and his generals (Charles Lee excepted), and their repeated pleas for a long-enlistment standing force capable of matching the British Army; the egalitarian ideals of the Revolution, clashing with the officers' fervent belief in a meritocracy ("Gentlemen" who had earned the right to be called such, and to be regarded as better than "the meaner sort" of men serving in the ranks); Congress's insistence on civilian control of the military, colliding with the growing disdain by the officer corps for a legislature nearly bereft of men who had served in the military or understood its values and, most shockingly, its most basic needs: food, tents, blankets, money, *respect.*

Patriotic legend (perhaps also the fact that Washington himself was sequentially congressman, general and President of the United States) has obscured a seething "cold war" between the politicians and the soldiers that, on several occasions, threatened to derail the Revolutionary War effort. In this, at times Congress seems to have dreaded victory as much as defeat. The "Solons" also resented the officers' relentless de-

---

26. Greene to Hancock, July 19, 1777, ibid, 123-125. For De Coudray's demise, see Boatner, *Encyclopedia*, 1117-1118.

mands for higher pay and pensions, their desire for heightened status, and their barely-disguised political ambitions (perhaps this partially explains the predilection for foreign officers; most of them did not aspire to be, but were *already* noblemen, and they could be expected to return to Europe when the war was over!). Relations between the civilian and military leadership were abysmal, and Greene would harbor deep distrust of Congress throughout his career; he would be scrutinized throughout his tenure as quartermaster general and only emerge into the sunlight of Congressional approval in the wake of his successful campaigns in the Carolinas in 1781-82.[27] These tensions are in stark relief in the exchange of letters between Nathanael Greene and John Adams in the first years of the Revolutionary War.

27. For officer attitudes, the reader is directed again to the magisterial work of Royster, *A Revolutionary People at War*, especially 79-96.

# The Delcastle Cannonball

✸ WALTER A. CHIQUOINE ✸

Several years ago, I set out to understand the movements of the British army through Delaware and into Pennsylvania in early September 1777. It was a small piece of the Philadelphia campaign of Gen, Sir William Howe, who led a combined army of about 16,000 that landed on Elk Neck on August 25 and captured Philadelphia by mid-October. The campaign is probably best known for the engagements at Brandywine Creek and at Germantown.

I was most interested in September 8 through 10, when the British and Hessian troops moved from Pencader, Delaware to Kennett Square in Pennsylvania, a movement that took them within a mile or so from my former home. There are quite a few records of this period, mostly among British and Hessian sources, but no one in recent times had done an accurate job of actually drawing it on today's map. I was able to find the headquarters of General Howe on September 8 and 9 and used a sketch made by Capt. John André to locate the encampment along the Limestone Road, and thus could map the British movements.[1] Once properly oriented, the narratives all made sense. It dovetailed with work being done by researchers in Chester County, Pennsylvania and for the Brandywine Battlefield, kudos to them.

What this research confirmed was an event on September 8 that should be recognized as a meaningful part of Delaware's Revolutionary War history. It's easy to believe that September 8 was simply a day of maneuver, and for the most part it was. Howe did not attack the Continentals entrenched behind Red Clay Creek, instead headed north to flank them in an extraordinary march that moved his entire army four-

---

1. Walter Chiquoine, Finding the Daniel Nichols House: a New Interpretation of the British March Through Mill Creek Hundred, www.academia.edu/26580954/FINDING_THE_DANIEL_NICHOLS_HOUSE_A_NEW_INTERPRETATION_OF_T HE_BRITISH_MARCH_THROUGH_MILL_CREEK_HUNDRED.

teen miles northward in about twenty-four hours. The armies met later at Brandywine Creek on September 11.

The British and Hessian maneuvers kept the Continentals in their fortified lines for the entire day, with one exception—one Continental brigade marched forward to near Mill Creek. The British occupied the hillside to the west of Mill Creek, in a line that extended up the Limestone Road almost five miles from near Milltown to New Garden, Pennsylvania. The Continental brigade of Gen. George Weedon made contact with the Hessian Jäger Corps across a steep valley on Mill Creek, near today's Delcastle Recreation Area. This foray is reported by sources on both sides, and the location is clear.

During this contact, the Jägers got off several shots with their amusettes, light field cannon also known as 1-pounders. And this story is about a one pound cannonball found in 1992 in a small creek in the Hyde Park neighborhood[2], well behind the Continental brigade but in a direct line of fire from the Jäger amusettes through the Continental position at Delcastle. It's too far away to be a direct shot. You can believe it or not, but the distance was likely due to at least one incredible bounce.

THE CONTACT

The British troops, coming from Newark and Christina Bridge, reached the Limestone Road before noon. Captain Friedrich von Muenchhausen, an aide to General Howe, wrote,

> We saw two regiments coming from Newport on two different roads ... I was ordered by the General ... to lead the Hessian Jaegers diagonally through the woods to cut off these troops ... but the rebels ... retreated quickly. Notwithstanding this, the jaegers got close enough to send a few amusette balls at them.[3]

Based on a diagram of the British camp on September 8 sketched by Captain André[4], the Jägers (called Chasseurs on his map[5]) were probably on the hillside above Henry Brackin's house (now Limestone

---

2. *The News Journal*, July 15, 1993.

3. Ernst Kipping, *At General Howe's Side 1776-1778, a translation of the diary of Captain Friedrich von Muenchhausen* (Monmouth Beach, NJ: Philip Freneau Press, 1974), 30.

4. Major John André, "Position of the Army at New Garden the 8th Sept. 1777 [Map]", *Major André's Journal: Operations of the British Army under the Lieutenant Generals Sir William Howe and Sir Henry Clinton, June 1777 to November 1778* (Boston: Bibliophile Society, 1903).

5. Jägers, also written Jaegers or Yagers, also called Chasseurs by the French, were skilled woodsmen and marksmen, armed with rifle and small sword, self-reliant and capable of working in small units.

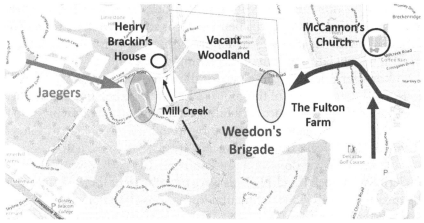

Figure 1. The Jäger and Continental positions on the afternoon of September 8. Map data from OpenStreetMap.

Hills), and were pushed forward to the hilltop that is now the North-pointe development just south of Stoney Batter Road.

On the opposite hillside, across Mill Creek and on the farm of the Samuel Fulton family, there arrived a brigade of Continentals under Gen. George Weedon. Lieutenant James McMichael of the Pennsylvania Line, in his diary, described how the Continentals were drawn up in line of battle behind Red Clay Creek on the morning of September 8. Then,

> Here we remained for some time, when Gen. Weedon's brigade (of which my regiment was a part) was detached to the front to bring on the attack. We crossed the creek and marched about a league to an eminence near Mr. McCannon's meeting house [now Red Clay Creek Presbyterian Church], and there awaited the approach of the enemy, who were within half a mile of us. They however, encamped, which occasioned us to remain under arms all night, the sentries keeping up a constant fire.[6]

The second Continental regiment under Weedon was probably the 3rd Virginia, a unit that Weedon previously commanded, and the "constant fire" was signal fire from the pickets that communicated an all-clear on a dark night.

What neither of these accounts describes is how the Mill Creek valley separating the forces was probably wooded and dropped down

---

6. "Diary of Lieutenant James McMichael of the Pennsylvania Line, 1776-1778," *Pennsylvania Archives* Vol. 15, Series 2 (Harrisburg, PA: E. K. Myers, 1890), 210.

steeply about one hundred feet on both sides; an assault from either side was simply not possible. Their positions that afternoon are shown in figure 1, with the Jägers firing left to right over Henry Brackin's mill on Mill Creek, later the site of the Spring Grove mill.

Fulton's farm later became part of the New Castle County Workhouse, and is now a part of the county's Delcastle Recreation Area. The Continentals could advance on a hilltop trail along the Fulton property line until the trail bent away to the right and followed a small valley down to Mill Creek, through a vacant tract. (A New Castle County road petition survey done in 1784 confirms this path, essentially the modern Mill Creek Road.) Patrols were probably sent forward through the trees and brush while regimental formations stayed on cleared land near the highest hilltop.

## THE JÄGER AMUSETTES

The mid 1700s saw a lot of conflict in Europe. Round ball ordnance of the American Revolution was generally derived from early cannon of that century, as well as changes and upgrades developed by all sides during the Seven Years War (including the French and Indian War of 1754 to 1763). This war also sowed the seeds for increased British taxation of its American colonies, and perhaps the Revolution itself.

Artillery was a practical rather than political art, and technology spread amongst allies. In a general way, technology and practitioners moved between Britain and its ally Prussia, while French technologists moved west into Denmark, Austria, and many small German states, even to Spain. This led to some standardization, as it was easier to copy technology rather than invent it. Cold hard experience helped drive the design of brass cannon into basic formulas for ball size (caliber), bore, length, and weight, and the ratios among these parameters were similar from 1-pound to 12-pound cannon. Not much was written down at the time; a book by John Muller printed in 1768 laments the lack of meaningful data available on the subject.[7] Later studies, written in the late eighteenth and early nineteenth centuries, are much more thorough and comprehensive—yet they are basically reporting on the same cannon types used during the American Revolution.

A cannon was always defined by its purpose; the amusette was a field gun. The artillerists dependent on field guns were focused on heavy 6-pound and 12-pound guns, and they tend to be what were described and reported on. Even the 3-pounders that might travel with a light infantry battalion required teams of horses for the piece and its

---

7. John Muller, *A Treatise of Artillery* (2nd Ed.) (London: John Millan, 1768), viii.

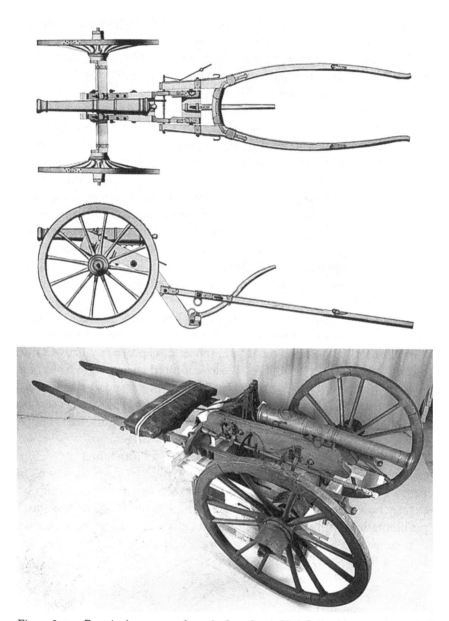

Figure 2, top. Rostaing's amusette, from the Jean-Louis Vial Collection, www.kronoskaf. com. Figure 3, middle. Rostaing's amusette, from the Jean-Louis Vial Collection, www.kro-noskaf.com. Figure 4, bottom. Danish amusette cast in 1768, courtesy of the Swedish Ar-mémuseum.

caisson, but a 1-pound gun? It was simply a novelty or distraction to most artillerists, and thus was christened "amusette."

The first amusette was mentioned in about 1741 in France, a one-inch bore wall gun mounted on a carriage. These were pulled from service a few years later. But by the 1750s the French artillerist Philippe Joseph, comte von Rostaing, while deployed to India, developed a 1-pound brass cannon that used a limonier for a carriage—a light two-pole harness (figures 2 and 3) that could be pulled by one horse or several men.[8] The 1-pounder had a bore of slightly over two inches.

Rostaing's amusette was a contemporary of light 4-pounders in the French arsenal referred to as *à la suédoise*, or of Swedish design. It is believed the 1-pounder had low recoil and a range comparable to the 4-pounder, and Rostaing even proposed to replace the 4-pounders with his amusette.[9] This 1-pounder amusette, officially introduced in 1757, had a bore of approximately 53 mm and a bore length of 20.6 calibers or about 110 cm. This ratio of bore to tube length was typical of early field artillery.

It is believed that forges in Austria, Denmark, and many German provinces, all allies of France, embraced the brass amusette at least on a small scale.[10] There is a record of amusettes captured by Prussia from Saxony in 1756.[11] In 1808, the Swedes captured an amusette from Norwegian Jägers, and that cannon (figure 4) is preserved at the Swedish Armémuseum.[12] It was forged in Denmark about 1768 (forty years before its capture), and it should be typical of the amusettes held by Hesse-Cassel that were shooting at Weedon's Brigade.

The amusette at the museum has a bore of 55 mm and a bore length of about 21 calibers or 115 cm, again the typical barrel proportions for field cannon of that era. It allowed for several degrees of elevation but exactly how far is uncertain. And determining the range of this gun is problematic, simply due to the limited data. Clearly, the amusette was a "man-portable" cannon with a 2-inch ball, something that gave the Jägers a little extra "pop" when needed.

8. Stephen Summerfield, "M1732 Vallière System (1732-1765)," *Smoothbore Ordnance Journal* issue 4 (June 2012), www.napoleon-series.org/military-info/OrdnanceJournal/Issue4/SOJ_4-2b-Valliere.pdf, 44.

9. Jean-Louis Vial (2012), "French Artillery à la Rostaing," www.kronoskaf.com/syw/index.php?title=French_Artillery_%C3%A0_la_Rostaing.

10. Ibid.

11. Hans Bleckwenn, "Prussian Field Gun Models 1756-1762 in Relation to General Tactics," translated by Digby Smith, *Smoothbore Ordnance Journal* issue 6 (March 2013), www.napoleon-series.org/military-info/OrdnanceJournal/Issue6/SOJ-6-1_Bleckwenn.pdf.

12. Swedish Armémuseum, digitaltmuseum.se/011024265642/1-pundig-kanon.

As for the presence of the amusettes, it was established in the "treaties" between Britain and Hesse-Cassel that two Jäger companies traveling to America each had two light artillery pieces.[13] One of those companies, under Capt. Johann Ewald, was with General Howe on September 8, and in the right place according to André's diagram.

Figure 5. The 1 lb, 7.7 oz iron ball (672 gm and 54 mm in diameter).

There is confirmation in an account signed by Gen. Leopold Philip von Heister, overall commander of the Hessian troops in America, to his superiors back in Germany. Written by a staff member and translated in the early twentieth century, it describes aspects of the engagement on September 3 between Jägers and General Maxwell's Continentals near Iron Hill. The account states, "The Jaegers loss in this attack was one death, and eight severely and ten slightly wounded. Among these were two Artillery men and two Grenadiers (which had been detached to the Amusettes) as also one Corporal and one Jaeger of the Anspachers Company who were with them."[14] There is no clear indication that the amusettes were actually deployed near Iron Hill, but they were an obvious target for Maxwell's light troops that day.

The cannonball of this story was found in a stream by a three or four year old boy near Delcastle in 1992. It is about 2 1/8 inches or 54 mm in diameter and weighs 1 pound 7.7 ounces (1.48 pounds), indicating it was wrought iron (hammered) and not the lighter cast iron. Its size is consistent with a cannon such as the one above—a 54 mm ball in a 55 mm gun gives a gap or windage of 1 mm, within the 2 mm specification of that time.[15] It certainly fits the description of an amusette ball. But if this cannonball came from a Jäger amusette, it's a heck of a long shot. The ball was found about 8,500 feet or 1.6 miles from the Jäger position, fired through or over the Continentals.

---

13. Bernhard A. Uhlendorf, trans., *Revolution in America: Confidential Letters and Journals 1776-1784 of Adjutant General Major Baurmeister of the Hessian Forces* (New Brunswick, NJ: Rutgers University Press, 1957), 17.

14. "Account of the North American War", Letter AA Part 2, p. 70, Lidgerwood Collection of Hessian Transcripts, Morristown National Historic Park, Morristown, NJ.

15. For example, see Stephen Summerfield, "Gribeauval Cannon 1765-1789," *Smoothbore Ordnance Journal* issue 4 (June 2012), www.napoleon-series.org/military-info/Ordnance-Journal/Issue4/SOJ_4-2c-Gribeauval.pdf, 50.

ARTILLERY DATA

Some readers like hard data, others less so, but to understand this cannonball we have to dig in to the "numbers" that we can find. Ballistics equations from physics class are only so helpful, as air resistance or drag had a very significant effect. Drag was not something the early gunners could calculate, it had to be learned. Of course, the bounce mattered as well.

There is some early data on cannon range, but as Muller advised, it doesn't give ball weight, charge, or elevation, and these are all elements that affect the shot. There is little data for a 1-pounder; we're left assuming that 3-pounder, 4-pounder, and 6-pounder data will have to do. But most importantly, field artillery against infantry or cavalry was all about bouncing or skipping the shot along the ground to mow down the adversary, called the ricochet shot. High angle shots that just buried themselves three feet into the ground served little purpose.

Muller referred to very early writings of St. Remy, "said to be the oldest upon record. It is easily perceived, that no dependence can be had on these experiments." But despite his skepticism, he provided the data anyway, noting a "Point Blank" range of 150 paces and an "At Random" range of 1,500 paces for a 4-pound gun.[16] "Point Blank" referred to a gun at zero elevation; "At Random" could be any elevation above that. Using a 4-pound gun as representative of an amusette, the 1,500 paces is at least 3,750 feet, almost three-quarters of a mile.

A second source is a 1957 work by Hans Bleckwenn based on work of German historians from 1842 and 1844.[17] Bleckwenn's focus was Prussian artillery in the Seven Years War, and he mentions the 1-pounder amusettes in Prussian service in that era. Bleckwenn borrows from Curt Jany, another German historian writing in 1928, that a 3-pounder of 1747 vintage was tested at 300 paces fired horizontally, and at 1,500 paces fired at 45 degrees elevation. In this case, the Prussian "pace" was about 2.4 feet, so these reported ranges may be close to 725 and 3,600 feet.[18]

The third source is a history of the Wurtemberg artillery written in 1882. On ranges for round shot in the 1790s, it says that the maximum range of a 3-pounder was 1,200 paces (3,000 feet). It further reports on test shoots from 1803 where a 6-pounder ranged to 1,300 paces (3,250 feet) first strike, and the shot rolled on (ricocheted) to 2,200

16. Muller, *A Treatise of Artillery*, p. viii.
17. Bleckwenn, "Prussian Field Gun Models."
18. Ibid.

paces (5,500 feet). No other description of elevation or powder charge is given.[19]

Rigorous data on round ball cannon range appeared in the early nineteenth century, and was variously captured by several sources: "Handbuch der Artillerie" by Scharnhorst (1793), Adye's "Pocket Gunner" (1804—1830's), and "The Elements of the Science of War, Vol. III" by William Müller (1811). Scharnhorst was referenced by Adye and Müller; Adye and Müller also referenced one another. So while the primary source is fuzzy, it is Müller who gave the first credible and quantified description of the ricochet shots of field artillery. All generally gave an average distance of about 3,750 feet to "first graze" for the smaller caliber cannon.

There is remarkable research recorded by the Prussian military historian Karl von Decker in 1823. He wrote in detail of very rigorous testing of a British 6-pound gun performed in 1822. Over eighty rounds were fired and measured; he gave an average "first graze" at about 3,150 feet for 3.25 deg elevation, and about 3,520 feet for 4 degree elevation. The longest shot at 4 degree elevation traveled 4,100 feet first graze.[20]

During these tests, the distances between grazes were also measured. Von Decker reported:

At 4 degree elevation, the second graze averaged almost 700 feet, while one bounced almost 900 feet.

Some shots went for seven or more grazes, some traveled beyond the one mile test range.

While conventional wisdom said that the distance between grazes should decrease, the data showed more shots actually had grazes that became longer rather than shorter.

The notion that higher gun elevation should on average result in shorter and fewer grazes was also refuted.

Von Decker's results overturned some conventional wisdom, and in a general sense it demonstrated that any specific shot could dissipate its kinetic energy in very unpredictable ways.

---

19. "Weissenbach s History of the Royal Württemberg Artillery—Organisation and Equipment 1734-1815," *Smoothbore Ordnance Journal* issue 2 (December 2010), www.napoleon-series.org/military-info/OrdnanceJournal/Issue2/SOJ-0207.pdf, 75-82.
20. "Prussian Tests of the British 6-pdr," "Firing Roundshot from a British 6-pdr," and "Ricochet Shots ('Rollschüsse') of British 6-pdr," *Smoothbore Ordnance Journal* issue 7 (October 2013), www.napoleon-series.org/military-info/OrdnanceJournal/Issue7/SOJ-07_Part2_British_6-pdr.pdf, 41-61.

TOPOGRAPHY AND "THE SHOT"

To understand the shot that landed our cannonball so far away from its source, one has to next understand the topography. The evidence suggests at least one Jäger amusette reached the firing position shown in Figure 6, at left. A nearly straight trajectory is offered here, extending about 8,500 feet to where the ball was found. At the far end is a possible landing zone, whereby the ball may have bounced, rolled, or slowly washed down a long hillside to its final resting place. The shot could have veered left or right.

Following the ground elevations, the ball had to reach the 280-foot hilltop at about 3,500 feet distant, which was reasonably in range for the amusette assuming the gunner knew how best to use his charge, his gun elevation, and the heavier ball. As the first hilltop was at a higher elevation than the gun, the ball may have struck the hilltop at a shallower angle and therefore ricocheted further.

Beyond 3,500 feet is another small valley dropping to about 210 feet; any ball on first strike or bounce that landed there (3,500 to about 5,000 feet) would not have bounced out. For any ball to continue its trajectory, it would need to clear the next high point on the current McKennan's Church Road, a 250-foot elevation about 6,000 feet distant. This requires a first bounce of at least 1,500 feet—it's a long way, but to a lower elevation—and then another bounce of 1,000 feet, or maybe several more skips. It's all downhill from McKennan's Church Road down to the creek where the ball was found. That last travel could have taken two centuries for all we know.

So the shot is possible if not probable to our senses. Much of our take on history is conjecture, hopefully supported by sound theory and research. I can't prove the Delcastle cannonball came from a Hessian amusette, but I believe the story is credible. Locations, armaments, the ball, and the narratives are consistent. Prior research independently puts the Jägers and Weedon on these two hilltops and we know that the amusettes were used.

I have looked for another explanation for the ball and I can't find one. The Continentals had no reason to be carrying 2-inch cannonballs at that location and in that era. There is no evidence to believe it is a Civil War relic. We know almost exactly where the ball was found, by a young child who can't be accused of any guile or intrigue regarding its location. Any alternative theories must pass the test of Occam's razor—what is the simplest explanation?

Somehow the shot made it. I believe this cannonball is genuine evidence of the British presence in Delaware in September 1777. And it's been reasonably pointed out to me that Weedon's position was the

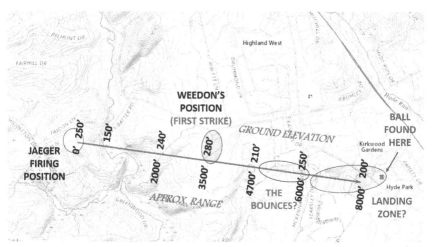

Figure 6. The approximate trajectory of the amusette ball showing both distance traveled (range) and ground elevation at that point. Map courtesy of Topozone.

closest eyes and ears that General Washington had on the British movements that afternoon and evening. There are stories that Washington himself visited nearby Milltown and possibly a "Council Oak" near Brandywine Springs the evening of September 8, perhaps to meet with Weedon or his aides.

The knowledge that the British units "encamped" was critical intelligence that sent the entire Continental army marching to John Chad's ford on the Brandywine just a few hours later, about 2am on September 9. If Howe had crossed the Brandywine Creek uncontested, the Continentals could have been trapped with their backs against the Delaware River, already controlled by the British fleet. From a strategic standpoint, Weedon's foray with its Delcastle cannonball was a very significant military event in Delaware.

# Smallpox Threatens an American Privateer at Sea

## ☗ CHRISTIAN MCBURNEY ☗

Two important books in the twenty-first century have focused on the impact of terrifying smallpox contagions on the American Revolutionary War.[1] Understandably, most of their stories are about smallpox infecting soldiers on land. As the two books relate, smallpox wrought havoc on Benedict Arnold's small army outside Quebec in 1775 and 1776, and likely killed thousands of Continental Army troops, many of them prisoners of war. The smallpox scourge impacted the miliary strategy of both side's armies.

Smallpox posed a unique danger to warships at sea because of the relatively small size of sailing vessels and the often-crowded quarters. Indeed, the disease could threaten to kill so many of a crew that the ship's mission might have to terminate, and the ship might be forced to return to a safe harbor. The Rhode Island privateer *Marlborough* faced such a risk in January 1778.

On January 2, the *Marlborough* departed Edgartown in Martha's Vineyard, commencing one of the most extraordinary voyages ever undertaken by an American privateer during the war. Its mission was to attack and plunder British slave forts and capture British slave ships operating on the West Coast of Africa.

1. See Elizabeth A. Fenn, *Pox Americana: The Great Smallpox Epidemic of 1775–1782* (New York: Hill and Wang, 2001) and Ann M. Becker, *Smallpox in Washington's Army: Disease, War and Society During the Revolutionary War* (New York: Lexington Books, 2022). Fenn estimates that the American Army lost more than 1,200 soldiers to smallpox alone during the siege of Quebec and the American retreat from Canada in 1775 and 1776. See Fenn, *Pox Americana*, 265-66 and 274. Fenn also mentions an outbreak of smallpox at sea in February 1776 in four Continental Navy ships, in a flotilla commanded by Rhode Island's Esek Hopkins. Ibid., 85-86. Becker did not include in her book an estimate of the losses from smallpox in the American Army.

The story started in Providence, Rhode Island, with John Brown, the main investor and mastermind behind the voyage. He belonged to the Brown family of Providence, among the most successful merchants in the state. In 1772, he organized and led the burning of the British revenue cutter *Gaspee*, an important early violent act of resistance against Great Britain leading to the Revolutionary War.

In 1776 and 1777, Brown got rich investing in privateers. America's most effective weapon at sea by far was privateering—the operation of privately owned commerce raiders. From British ships, Americans captured gunpowder, weapons, food and other supplies they desperately needed. Privateers were not pirates. Privateers were commissioned by the Continental Congress to attack only enemy shipping.

The net proceeds from a privateering voyage would be divided, typically 50 percent to the privateer's investors and the rest among the privateer's officers and crew pursuant to a formula agreed to before the voyage.

In the early years of the war, American privateers easily seized hundreds of poorly defended merchant ships sailing between Britain and both the Caribbean and Canada. Brown grew rich. But the days of easy conquests eventually ended. Powerful Royal Navy warships began protecting commercial vessels in convoys and seizing privateers. Most crews of captured privateers went to horrible British prisons in New York or back in Britain. Many prisoners died of malnutrition and disease (including smallpox).

Brown decided in the second half of 1777 that, with his new wartime profits, he could afford to construct a large privateer that carried at least twenty cannons. Such a privateer could avoid capture by a British sloop-of-war and defeat armed merchantmen. But it could still be captured by a thirty-two-gun Royal Navy frigate, many of which were hunting for privateers in the Caribbean and on the Canadian coast. What to do? Brown had the brilliant idea of sending his new privateer to the coast of West Africa.

Brown figured, correctly, that the Royal Navy was overstretched. It had few ships remaining to patrol the far-away African coast and British interests there. At the time, Britain's merchants were the world leaders in the transatlantic African slave trade. Brown also had personal experience investing in two slave trading voyages, so he knew about the West Africa Coast.

In late 1777 in Providence, Brown completed construction of his new twenty-gun, three-masted brig. He named it the *Marlborough*. After breaking through a blockade of British warships in Narragansett Bay (a narrow escape), the privateer sailed to Martha's Vineyard where it enlisted twenty-four more sailors, to round out its crew of "men & boys" to ninety-six.

The choice of the captain of a privateer could make or break a voyage. Brown chose George W. Babcock of the small port of Updike's Newtown (now Wickford) in North Kingstown, Rhode Island. It was somewhat of a risky choice, for Babcock may not have previously commanded a privateer. However, he had served as a lieutenant on one of Brown's privateers, so Brown must have known and trusted him. Whether Brown made a suitable selection would soon be put to a major test.[2]

What we know about the *Marlborough*'s voyage mostly comes from a journal kept by John Linscom Boss, the clerk to Captain Babcock. Boss recorded the key events of each day.[3]

On January 13, Babcock's first crisis began to take shape. Samuel Babcock, the ship commander's younger brother, became ill. That evening Captain Babcock, the ship's doctor, and the rest of the officers diagnosed Samuel as suffering from smallpox. Some of the sailors, prior to the voyage, had already had the dreaded disease or had been inoculated for it and were therefore immune from catching it again. But more than half of the sailors had not had the disease or been inoculated. If the smallpox virus spread to the unprotected crew the natural way, by human contact, it could kill dozens of sailors and cut the voyage short.

A key reality was that the *Marlborough*, while large for an American privateer, had a confined space. Its hull was about 100 feet long; the beam was about 26 feet wide; and the depth in the single hold below the main deck was 13 feet.

The ship was also crowded with crew members and marines. A merchant ship the size of the *Marlborough* could be sailed by a crew of around twenty-nine. But during war, a privateer needed a larger crew, with extra men needed to man the cannon, be ready to storm the decks of an enemy ship or defend against an attack. Marines on board also helped the ship's officers maintain control over the crew. Thus, the *Marlborough* carried a relatively large crew of ninety-six. The officers and crew worked in a small and crowded space and could easily infect

---

2. The summary of how the idea for the *Marlborough*'s voyage to West Africa was decided upon and the initial stage of the voyage is from Christian McBurney, *Dark Voyage: An American Privateer's War on Britain's African Slave Trade* (Yardley, PA: Westholme Publishing, 2023), 1-85.

3. See John Linscom Boss, Journal of a Voyage in the Good Ship Marlborough George Wt. Babcock Commander Bound on a Five Month Cruise Against the Enemies of the United States of America from Rhode Island, Dec. 23, 1777–June 12, 1778, microfilm, Morristown National Historical Park, Morristown, NJ (Journal of the *Marlborough*)

each other. It would be difficult to contain the contagion unless extraordinary measures were taken.

On land, a traditional approach was to isolate smallpox victims in a so-called pest house to avoid contagion. Captain Babcock decided to isolate the stricken Samuel from the rest of the crew. "For the preservation of those that never had it," the ship's commander ordered Samuel to be placed by himself halfway up the foremast on a small flat platform called the foretop. It must have been a wrenching decision for Babcock to take this harsh step, but he decided to risk sacrificing one sailor in order to spare others, even if that one sailor was his own brother.

After Samuel Babcock spent a night at the foretop alone and seeing him suffer in front of the entire crew, the captain reconsidered his prior order. He directed a sailor, identified only as Mr. Smith, to care for Samuel at the foretop but "to be careful not to spread the smallpox in the ship." The next day, Boss wrote in his journal, crewmen "Thomas Carpenter & Thomas Brown stationed in the foretop to watch and take care of S. Babcock there to stay night & day & Smith to go up and down."[4] Presumably, Smith climbed up and down the rigging of the mainmast bringing water and food as needed. The three men must have previously had smallpox, leaving them immune from contagion.

The patient's illness lingered for twelve days. Spending all that time in the foretop, exposed to the weather, must also have weakened him. In the early morning of January 24, Boss wrote in his journal, "Samuel Babcock departed this transitory life in hopes for a better." His lifeless body was "decently sewed up in Captain Babcock's hammock," a high honor. At 8:00 a.m., in a driving rain, Boss "read prayers over his body" and "it was committed to the watery deep."[5]

Captain Babcock's precautions did not entirely contain the smallpox outbreak. In the afternoon of January 20, crewman David Wilcox displayed symptoms of the disease. The next day, John Larkin did too. They contracted it "the natural way," by exposure to a crewman who had the disease, the deadliest way to catch the virus. Wilcox died nine days later, but Larkin survived.

Babcock then considered an alternative measure, inoculation. If adopted, it would mean that each crew member who had never had smallpox would have live *Variola* virus deliberately implanted into an incision on his hand or arm. The disease from inoculation was generally mild and the death rate from the procedure was much lower than for

---

4. Journal of the *Marlborough*, January 13–14, 1778.
5. Journal of the *Marlborough*, January 23, 1778. The ship's log was kept from noon one day to noon the next day; Samuel Babcock died after midnight on January 24.

those contracting the illness naturally. Still, on occasion someone who contracted the illness through inoculation died of it. More importantly, those who fell ill could spread the disease to others in the more deadly natural way.[6]

Seeing how the disease had decimated his army's ranks, and in contradiction of a 1776 proclamation by the Continental Congress prohibiting inoculations, in February 1777 George Washington ordered his Continental troops inoculated.[7] Babcock, of course, was not under Washington's orders.

While a North Kingstown resident in April 1777, Babcock had been inoculated in a pest house in neighboring Exeter, where he was raised. But because he did it without permission from the Exeter Town Council and was not then an Exeter resident, the council fined him six dollars. Babcock must have regretted not bringing Samuel with him, even if that might have doubled his fine.

Babcock made his decision: "for the benefit of the cruise," all sailors who had never had smallpox were ordered to be inoculated.[8] This meant about forty-five men and boys went through the procedure.

On January 27 and 28, inoculated crew members broke out with smallpox. Most of them had mild cases of the disease. They were likely quarantined to the extent possible, so as to prevent others from catching the illness. Still, a few others who had not been inoculated complained of having smallpox symptoms.[9]

---

6. Fenn, *Pox Americana*, 32–33. Ann Becker wrote, "The fatality rate from smallpox induced through artificial means [i.e., from inoculation] was considerably lower at 2 percent as compared to the 14 percent rate seen in Boston during the 1721 epidemic among those infected naturally." Becker, *Smallpox in Washington's Army*, 28.

7. George Washington to Dr. William Shippen, February 6, 1777, founders.archives.gov/documents/Washington/03-08-02-0281. The commander in chief wrote, "Finding the smallpox to be spreading much and fearing that no precaution can prevent it from running through the whole of our Army, I have determined that the troops shall be inoculated. This expedient may be attended with some inconvenience and some disadvantages but yet I trust its consequences will have the most happy effects. Necessity not only authorizes but seems to require the measure, for should the disorder infect the Army in the natural way and rage with its usual virulence, we should have more to dread from it than from the sword of the enemy."

8. Town Council minutes, December 10, 1777, Town Council and Probate Records, vol. 4, 1756–1786, 38, Exeter Town Clerk's Office, Exeter, RI.

9. Journal of the *Marlborough*, January 20 and 29, 1778. Wilcox died on January 29. The American privateer *Defence*, shortly after sailing out of New London, Connecticut, in early 1778, had five sailors break out with smallpox, at least one of whom died of the disease. Journal entries, April 7 and 9, 1778, in Timothy Boardman, *Remarks of Our Gunner on Charlestown, in S.C., in Timothy Boardman, Log-Book of Timothy Boardman; Kept on Board*

Two crewmen who underwent the procedure died on February 1 and 2: sailor Jedidiah Collins and "gunners boy" Stephen Congdon. The last victim was John Davis, who claimed he had contracted small-pox as a young boy in the west of England. As a result, he was not in-oculated. Davis must have been mistaken. He died on February 12.[10]

Fortunately for the surviving crewmen, no other sailors died of the disease, and the crisis ended. The inoculations finally contained the outbreak, even if there had been a steep cost. Captain Babcock had passed his first command test. But with the five deaths, his crew was reduced to ninety-one "men & boys."[11]

For the surviving officers and crew, while the first crisis was behind them, many more adventures, dangers and challenges, as well as scenes of wonder and cruelty, lay ahead of them.[12]

the Privateer *Oliver Cromwell, During a Cruise from New London CT., to Charleston, S.C., and Return in 1778; also a Biographical Sketch of the Author by the Rev. Samuel W. Boardman, D.D.* (Albany, NY: Joel Munsell's Sons, 1885), 51. See also Kylie A. Hulbert, *The Untold War at Sea: America's Revolutionary Privateers* (Athens: University of Georgia Press, 2022), 56-58.

10. Journal of the *Marlborough*, January 26–27, 1778.

11. Journal of the *Marlborough*, February 1, 5, and 11, 1778. Collins died on February 1 and Congdon on February 2.

12. For a full account of the voyage, see McBurney, *Dark Voyage, An American Privateer's War on Britain's African Slave Trade.*

# The Highs and Lows of Ethan Allen's Reputation as Reported by Revolutionary Era Newspapers

**GENE PROCKNOW**

Ethan Allen's prevailing reputation among the general population remains that of a daring hero but has suffered in the eyes of recent historians. Casual readers, aided by the embellishments of nineteenth-century biographers, remember Vermont's Allen as the leader of the rebellious but honorable Green Mountain Boys and the conqueror of British-held Fort Ticonderoga. As a result of his widely-touted Revolutionary Era exploits, people commemorated Allen's contributions to Vermont's founding by erecting statues in the United States Capitol and the Vermont statehouse and naming national guard units, ships, highways, trains, and mountains after him. On the other hand, twenty-first-century historians are increasingly uncovering a darker side to Allen's legacy. Recent monographs depict a thuggish brigand whose extra-legal actions thwarted legitimate New York control over the Vermont territory.[1] Further, several historians allege that Allen committed treason by negotiating the return of Vermont to the British Empire during the dark stages of the Revolutionary War.[2]

So, what is Allen's legacy, and what should be his reputation? Returning to public voices expressed contemporaneously can help answer these questions. Ethan Allen's activities were highly newsworthy, with

---

1. For example, see John J. Duffy, H. Nicholas Muller, and Gary G. Shattuck, *The Rebel and the Tory: Ethan Allen, Philip Skene, and the Dawn of Vermont* (Barre, VT: Vermont Historical Society, 2020).
2. David Bennett, *A Few Lawless Vagabonds: Ethan Allen, the Republic of Vermont, and the American Revolution* (Havertown, PA: Casemate Publishers, 2014), 217.

hundreds of articles and citations in Revolutionary Era newspapers. Allen first generated a public reputation as the leader of the Green Mountains Boys, opposing New York authority before the Revolution. After hostilities commenced, Allen became famous for seizing Fort Ticonderoga from the British and being captured outside Montreal. After reportedly cruel internment, Allen returned to aggressively advocate formal recognition of Vermont by the Americans or the British. After American independence, he continued to be involved in high-profile populist causes, including the Shays' Rebellion and the Pennsylvania/Susquehanna Company dispute. In later years, Allen professed radical deist beliefs in defiance of prevailing religious orthodoxy. During his life, Allen's reputation oscillated between heroic and reckless, patriotic and traitorous, a populist politician and member of a lawless mob, and a celebrated and graceless public figure.

Ethan Allen's first newspaper appearance in 1772 depicted his active participation in a land title clash between the New Hampshire land grant settlers and the state of New York. On behalf of Seth Warner, Remember Baker, and Robert Cochran, Allen asked the *Connecticut Courant's* publisher to insert a letter from New York Gov. William Tryon and a response from those disputing New Hampshire grant holders.[3] As the dispute deepened and turned violent, New York and Connecticut newspapers unflatteringly identified Allen and others as wanted criminals. As might be expected by a 1774 New York paper, Allen was named a "member of the Bennington mob" disputing New York's land titles. However, the article did not label the mob as the Green Mountain Boys or cite Allen as its leader.[4] Several months later, papers elevated Allen's role by publicizing a fifty-pound reward for his capture.[5]

Within a year, newspapers transformed Allen's reputation from outlaw to hero. The same *Connecticut Courant* propagating the fifty-pound reward cited "the intrepid Col. Ethan Allen" and the "valiant Green Mountain Boys" after the capture of Fort Ticonderoga's British garrison. The initial report of the Ticonderoga seizure named Ethan Allen as the assault force commander and highlighted the participation of colonels James Easton and John Brown and two local captains, Edward Mott and Noah Phelps. There was no mention of Benedict Arnold,

---

3. "Legislative Acts/Legal Proceedings," *Connecticut Courant,* June 28, 1774, Supplement edition, 1–2.
4. "New York, February 10," *The New-York Journal or, The General Advertiser,* n.d., sec. February 10, 1774, 3.
5. "To the Publisher of the Connecticut Courant," *The Connecticut Courant,* June 21, 1774, 1.

whom later historians credit as co-commander of the hastily-formed militia forces.[6]

A few days later, the New Hampshire *Gazette* published a second account of the Ticonderoga capture written by Colonel Easton, professing joint command with Ethan Allen. Easton claimed to have "clapped the [fort's] commanding officer's shoulder and demanded, in the name of America, an instant surrender of the fort." Easton's letter noted that Allen remained in the fort as the senior officer, again with no mention of Benedict Arnold.[7] Historians discount Easton's account as inaccurate and self-serving.[8]

It would take several months for Arnold's story to emerge. Then, finally, an article published under the pseudonym Veritas appeared in the New York *Journal*, which named Allen and Arnold as co-commanders and diminished Easton's role in the Ticonderoga capture. Written by Arnold or one of his supporters, the article ended by describing a testy conflict between Arnold and Easton, concluding that Easton acted as a "doughy hero."[9]

Within a few days, Allen's reputation took a nose dive. First, Allen proceeded down Lake Champlain to Quebec against Arnold's advice. Then, recklessly endangering his command, "he was attacked by two hundred regulars and obliged to decamp and retreat" with the loss of three men.[10] A few weeks later, Allen again ventured into Quebec and attempted an ill-fated attack on Montreal in which a cobbled-together British force captured him and most of his command. A newspaper report indicated that Allen proceeded "without orders from the general and from whom (as well as others) he received much censure." The article described Allen as a "high flying genius" who "pursues every scheme on its first impression without consideration, but less judgment."[11]

Over the next three years, harsh British treatment resurrected Allen's reputation, as described in the newspapers. A succession of new articles labeled Allen as "intrepid and deservedly famous"[12] who "suffered much

---

6. "Extract of Another Letter from the Same Gentleman, Dated May 18th," *The Connecticut Courant*, May 22, 1775, 3.

7. James Easton, "Yesterday, Col. Easton Arrived Here from Ticonderoga," *New-Hampshire Gazette*, May 26, 1775, 3.

8. Allen French, *The Taking of Ticonderoga in 1775: The British Story* (Cambridge, MA: Harvard University Press, 1928), 32.

9. Veritas, "Mr. Holt," *New-York Journal*, August 3, 1775, 3–4.

10. "New-York, May 29," *Pennsylvania Evening Post*, May 30, 1775, 221.

11. "Philadelphia, October 21, Extract of a Letter from Ticonderoga, October 5," *Maryland Journal*, October 25, 1775, 3.

12. "Hartford, July 7, 1777," *Pennsylvania Evening Post*, July 15, 1777, 374.

in the cause of his county"[13] with the hope that "he may again return to the bosom of his grateful country."[14] Newspapers throughout the continent prominently reported Allen's May 6, 1778, release from British captivity. Several editors included Allen's exchange with the coverage of the sensational exchange of Maj. Gen. Charles Lee, while the *New-Jersey Gazette* praised "the much-abused Colonel Ethan Allen" for enduring harsh treatment.[15]

In the spring of 1779, Allen published an account of his travails while a British prisoner, *A Narrative of Colonel Ethan Allen's Captivity*, the first prisoner of war account by an American.[16] Allen's *Narrative* became an instant hit, reprinted eight times within a year.[17] Historians estimate that readers purchased over twenty thousand copies.[18] If true, only Thomas Paine's *Common Sense* sold more copies during the Revolutionary War years. Overall, Allen's *Narrative* created the image of a notable patriot throughout the rebelling colonies.

Allen's reputation soared after his release, and he became a feted celebrity. In particular, the Boston papers most favorably reported on a fall 1779 visit to the city. The *Boston Gazette* characterized Allen as "a gallant and meritorious Officer, and distinguished for his sufferings and exemplary resignation and spirit while in Captivity."[19] Later, papers as far as Virginia reprinted the Boston articles describing the Vermont rebel leader as "an officer of exemplary fortitude and distinguished merit."[20]

While the Rebel press gushed praise for Allen, the Loyalist newspapers raised the specter of an armed conflict between Vermont and New York. Coincident with the favorable Boston reporting, the *Royal Gazette* in New York alleged that Allen raised fifteen hundred soldiers to repel a New York attack led by Gov. George Clinton.[21] As opposed to fighting the New Yorkers, The *Providence Gazette* reported that Allen attacked a combined force of British regulars, Loyalist fighters,

13. "In Congress, July 22, 1776," *Norwich Packet*, August 19, 1776, 3.

14. "Hartford, November 25," *Connecticut Courant*, November 28, 1776, 3.

15. "Worchester, April 16," *New-Jersey Gazette*, May 13, 1778, 2.

16. Greg Sieminski, "The Puritan Captivity Narrative and the Politics of the American Revolution," *American Quarterly* 42, no. 1 (1990): 36.

17. Ethan Allen, *A Narrative of Colonel Ethan Allen's Captivity*, ed. Stephen Carl Arch (Acton, MA: Copley Publishing Group, 2000), x.

18. Sieminski, "The Puritan Captivity Narrative and the Politics of the American Revolution," 47.

19. "Boston, Last Thursday," *Boston Gazette*, October 29, 1779, 3.

20. "Boston, December 25," *Virginia Gazette* (Dixon and Nicolson), January 29, 1780, 2.

21. "Letter to Mr. Rivington," *Royal Gazette* (New York), November 3, 1779, 3.

and Native Americans in late 1780. "General Ethan Allen, with thirteen hundred brave Green Mountain Boys under his command, having pursued fourteen-hundred of the enemy . . . and that Gen. Allen had killed and taken six hundred of them."[22] This wild claim proved false but demonstrated the increasingly uncertain political environment in the Champlain Valley.

In late 1780 and January 1781, rather than fighting the New Yorkers or the British, Loyalist newspapers reported that Ethan Allen had deserted the Rebel cause and now militarily supported the British. Historians now know there was some truth to the idea that Allen and other Vermont leaders flirted with the British governor of Quebec, Frederick Haldimand, about re-joining the British empire. The *Royal Georgia Gazette* reported that Ethan Allen and Seth Warner "revolted from the Rebel cause."[23] A Loyalist New York newspaper related that Allen gathered five to six hundred men to work in concert with the British garrison at Fort Ticonderoga.[24] Countering the Royal press, a Rebel newspaper scorned the reports of Allen's "duplicity and treacherous intentions" by characterizing the source as "the lying Royal Gazette" published by James Rivington.[25] Another Rebel paper disputed Rivington's assertion that Allen deserted to the British, decrying "Jemmy's arrogance."[26] A French-language newspaper published in Newport, Rhode Island, further stated that the British feared "this brave soldier every day."[27]

While rumors of Allen's treasonous behaviors may have negatively impacted his reputation in some quarters, his name largely disappeared from newspapers, especially those outside Vermont. The situation dramatically changed after Allen published his second book, *Reason, the Only Oracle of Man; or a Compendious System of Natural Religion*, in 1785. Allen's deist monograph challenging Christian orthodoxy generated a flurry of negative press, greatly diminishing his reputation far more than the Haldimand negotiations. A Connecticut writer described the Vermonter as "prayerless and graceless."[28] Another paper referred to Allen as "incendiary" and "his atheistical highness."[29] Dr.

---

22. "New London, November 7, 1780," *Providence Gazette*, November 15, 1780, 3.

23. "New York, January 10," *Royal Georgia Gazette*, March 15, 1781, 3.

24. "New York, January 3," *Royal Gazette* (New York), January 3, 1781, 3.

25. "New York City, November 29," *Thomas's Massachusetts Spy Or, American Oracle of Liberty*, December 28, 1780, 2.

26. A Soldier, *Newport Mercury*, January 15, 1781, 3.

27. "Newport," *Gazette Francoise*, January 2, 1781, Supplement edition, 2.

28. "Litchfield, February 28," *Litchfield Monitor*, February 28, 1786, 3.

29. "Philadelphia, June 28," *Columbian Herald* (Charleston, SC), July 31, 1786, 3.

Lemuel Hopkins, one of the notable Hartford Wits, penned a derogatory poem reprinted in papers throughout the new nation. Hopkins concluded the twenty-four-line sarcastic poem with

> And brays tremendous like as ass;
> One hand is clench'd to batter noses,
> While tother scrawls 'gainst Paul and Moses.[30]

The mocking newspaper articles accelerated with the publication of a purported letter from Lord George Gordon declining to have *Reason* dedicated to him. Most known for inciting the deadly 1780 anti-Catholic riots in London, Gordon later converted to the Jewish faith and ran afoul of British laws. Allegedly, Allen sent four copies of his deist philosophy to Lord Gordon, who replied in the published letter that he forwarded a copy to the Grand Vizier in Constantinople. Newspapers throughout the country reprinted these outrageous and sardonic reports of the impact of Allen's *Reason* monograph. The *Columbian Herald* in Charleston, South Carolina, conveyed that Allen had "undergone a certain Jewish and Mahometan ceremony in order to qualify him for the office to which he has been lately appointed by the venerable Mufti."[31] Lastly, a report referred to "St. Ethan" who received a gift from the Grand Signior of four concubines for changing Constantinople's religion from Mahometanism to ALLENISM."[32] A reader likely inserted this item to make clear that Lord Gordon's letter was a fraud. Only the most gullible readers would believe these Lord Gordon articles, but many enjoyed the ridicule and disrespect for Allen's philosophy.

While controversy swirled around the *Reason* monograph, Allen's participation in the Wyoming Valley dispute in northeastern Pennsylvania tarnished his reputation further. Like the New Hampshire Grants/New York land title disputes, the Pennsylvania authorities disputed the land titles of Susquehanna Company settlers, which Connecticut issued. The Allen family had a history of owning rights granted by the Susquehanna Company.[33] Additionally, the company directors enticed Allen with twelve land shares to visit the valley to help prosecute their land claims.

---

30. Lemuel Hopkins, "From the American Mercury," *Pennsylvania Evening Herald*, August 2, 1786, 12.
31. "Extract from a French Journal of Literature, Paris, April 30, 1786," *Columbian Herald* (Charleston, SC), September 11, 1786, 2.
32. "From the Vermont Gazette," *American Mercury*, July 10, 1786, 3.
33. Levi Allen, "Levi Allen," *Connecticut Courant*, December 19, 1774, 1.

Dripping with sarcasm, a New York newspaper article related that "Ethan Allen, seized with the *devine* flame of propagating his *gospel*, has lately paid a visit to the Wioming settlers, to whom he preached some of his *pious lectures*, to their wonderful edification. The *disinterestedness* of this *holy man*, cannot be too highly celebrated as, for the *very trifling* recompence of *two townships*."[34] Pennsylvania papers derided Allen as an "atheistical highness" and "Vermont apostle" who instilled in the mind of the Wyoming residents a "wild and fanciful scheme of Independence."[35] Allen's participation became moot as the Pennsylvania government, with the assistance of Timothy Pickering, settled the dispute amicably. However, the scathing attacks from the anti-Allen New York and Pennsylvania press further blemished Allen's reputation.

Over the next two years, Allen's *Reason* remained in the news. Papers advertised Josiah Sherman's monograph refuting Allen's *Reason*,[36] printed allegations that Allen plagiarized Charles Blount's 1693 *Oracles of Reason*,[37] and widely reported the prospect of Allen publishing an Appendix.[38] However, the polemic intensity in the nation's newspapers decreased.

Ethan Allen died before the *Reason* appendix could be published. A widely republished Vermont obituary touted the patriotism of a "great man," noted his "exalted character," and lamented the "loss of a man who has rendered them great service, both in council and in arms; and his family, an indulgent friend, and tender parent."[38] Other death notices recalled Allen as honorable, respectable,[39] and "celebrated and truly eccentric."[40] Most obituaries noted Allen's military services and called his philosophy volume "Allen's Bible."[41] Eulogists omitted Allen's leadership of the "Bennington Mob," his 1780-1 flirtations with rejoining the British, and the bitterness surrounding his deist views from the death notices. Presaging Allen's nineteenth-century transformation into a folklore hero, several papers printed an apocryphal story of Allen's passing:

34. "New York, June 15, 1786," *New-York Journal, Or the Weekly Register*, June 15, 1786, 2.
35. *Pennsylvania Gazette*, July 5, 1786, 3.
36. *Middlesex Gazette* (Middletown, CT), December 24, 1787, 4.
37. G Woolston, "The Following Is Said to Be a Genuine Copy of a Letter from Mr. Woolson of London, to General Ethan Allen," *Vermont Gazette*, May 5, 1788, 2.
38. *Litchfield Monitor*, March 2, 1789, 3.
39. "March 16, 1789," *Vermont Gazette*, March 16, 1789, 2.
40. "March 5, 1789," *Cumberland Gazette* (Falmouth, MA), March 5, 1789, 3.
41. "March 5, 1789," *Thomas's Massachusetts Spy Or, American Oracle of Liberty*, March 5, 1789, 3.

The manner of death of Ethan Allen, Esq. was nearly as he had frequently wished it to be.—He was in his barnyard and feeling his dissolution rapidly approaching, said to a boy with him, "Take good care of the Creatures," and fell dead on the ground.[42]

At his death, newspapers remembered Allen as a celebrated hero, not for his military failures, potentially treasonous activities, and rougher edges.[43]

Over Allen's fifty-one years, he garnered well over five hundred positive and negative newspaper mentions. While modern-day readers recall Allen as the Green Mountain Boys leader, Fort Ticonderoga's conqueror, and the Vermont politician who toyed with the British, his contemporaries remember him for his *Narrative* and *Reason* monographs. These two publications created blockbuster news, which the period press reported widely. While other primary sources besides newspapers are required to fully understand a person's reputation, newspaper accounts are vital in assessing Allen's public persona and augmenting the historical record. Additionally, the public reception of his two books significantly contributes to understanding Allen's reputation among his contemporaries.

---

42. "March 9, 1789," *Boston Gazette*, March 9, 1789, 3.
43. For a mixed account of Allen's immediate legacy, see John J. Duffy and H. Nicholas Muller, *Inventing Ethan Allen* (Hanover, New Hampshire: University Press of New England, 2014), 16–18.

# Two Encounters: Prince Pitkin, a "Negro Man" and Captain Abraham Van Dyck

## ❦ BENJAMIN L. CARP ❦

Captain Abraham Van Dyck of New York faced military justice twice during the Revolutionary War: first by the British for burning his hometown, and then by his fellow Continental Army officers for killing a Black soldier in camp. In each case, imperfect evidence presents historians with a puzzle. Notably, African-American men were central to each incident.

I came across the stories of Van Dyck and his encounters with two Black men while researching the Great Fire of New York City in 1776. Although pieces of Van Dyck's life survive in archives, it was difficult to recover much about the inner thoughts and motivations of the two Black men. Still, Van Dyck's story offers a telling account of race and justice during the Revolutionary War.

Abraham Van Dyck was fifty-seven years old in 1776. A former felt-maker, he kept an inn with an enclosed tennis court at the corner of Broadway and John Street in New York City, and he treated his customers to spectacles like an eleven-foot cow and a chained leopard. He had apparently served as a marine lieutenant during the Seven Years War. Then, as captain of the New York Grenadiers, an independent company of volunteer militiamen, he hosted drill exercises and weekly meetings of local militia officers. An elite company formerly commanded by Lord Stirling, the Grenadiers wore blue coats with red facings over white waistcoats, breeches, and stockings.[1]

---

1. Warren B. Stout, "Ancestral Line of the Somerset Van Dykes," *Somerset County Historical Quarterly* 4, 4 (Oct. 1915): 264; William B. Aitken, *Distinguished Families in America Descended*

When the war broke out and British troops evacuated their Manhattan barracks on June 6, 1775, Marinus Willett and a crowd of active rebels stopped the soldiers and confiscated the spare weapons they were carting out of town. To hide the weapons, Willett chose the tennis court of Van Dyck, "a good Whig." Willett and other captains in the 1st New York Regiment were soon using the tavern as a recruiting center and distributed some of the British soldiers' arms to their men. On October 19, the "Captain of Grenadiers" helped lead a funeral procession for Michael Cresap, a Maryland rifleman (and notorious murderer of Native Americans) who had died in town.[2] The Continental Army and New York Committee of Safety soon began fortifying Manhattan in anticipation of the British military's return. Van Dyck's grenadiers volunteered to build a circular battery on the Hudson River, just outside the city, "on the first Alarm of danger from the Enemy." Upon completion, they received special commendation from General Stirling and Gen. George Washington, who had recently arrived in town on April 13, 1776.[3]

*from Wilhelmus Beekman and Jan Thomasse Van Dyke* (New York: G. P. Putnam's Sons, 1912), 226; "The Burghers of New Amsterdam and the Freemen of New York, 1675–1866," *Collections of the New-York Historical Society* 18 (1885), 183; General Orders, August 21, 1776, in Philander D. Chase and Frank E. Grizzard Jr., eds., *The Papers of George Washington, Revolutionary War Series* (Charlottesville: University Press of Virginia, 1994), 6:96, 97 n4 (*PGW:RS*); William Dunlap, *History of the New Netherlands, Province of New York, and State of New York, to the Adoption of the Federal Constitution* (New York, 1840), 2:CLXXXVI; *New York Packet*, February 20, 1787; Alexander McDougall to George Washington, February 17, 1778, *PGW:RS* (2003), 13:572; Alan C. Aimone and Eric I. Manders, "A Note on New York City's Independent Companies, 1775–1776," *New York History* 63, 1 (January 1982): 59–73; *New-York Gazette and Weekly Mercury*, August 1, November 7, 1768.

2. "Colonel Marinus Willett's Narrative," in *New York City during the American Revolution . . . from the Manuscripts in the Possession of the Mercantile Library Association of New York City* (New York, 1861), 53–65 (quote 65); William M. Willett, *A Narrative of the Military Actions of Colonel Marinus Willet, Taken Chiefly from His Own Manuscript* (New York, 1831), 29–32; Joseph S. Tiedemann, *Reluctant Revolutionaries: New York City and the Road to Independence, 1763–1776* (Ithaca, NY: Cornell University Press, 1997), 231–32; *New-York Journal*, July 20, 1775; T. W. Egly, Jr., *History of the First New York Regiment, 1775–1783* (Hampton, NH: Peter E. Randall, 1981), 1–5; Robert G. Parkinson, "From Indian Killer to Worthy Citizen: The Revolutionary Transformation of Michael Cresap," *William and Mary Quarterly* 63, 1 (2006): 97–122.

3. General Orders, April 29, 1776, *PGW:RS* (1991), 4:163 ("Alarm"), 163–64 n2; *New-York Gazette and Weekly Mercury*, May 6, 1776; Peter Force, ed., *American Archives* [...], 4th ser. (Washington, D.C., 1844), 5:218–20; John Varick, Jr., to Captain Richard Varick, May 14, 1776, *New York City during the American Revolution*, 92.

Then things took a darker turn. Later that spring, the Grenadiers led a hostile crowd that harassed one of Van Dyck's neighbors. After two days of threats and thrown stones, the Loyalist Christopher Benson heard "that the Grenadiers were just coming" to murder him. He escaped, but the crowd moved on to ride four other Loyalists on rails. The grenadiers understood that "the army would not interfere ... let what would be done among the Inhabitants." In other words, if the grenadiers wanted to assault the town's remaining Loyalists, Washington was willing to look the other way. Even so, Van Dyck's grenadier company was quickly incorporated into Col. John Lasher's regiment of New York levies.[4]

Van Dyck and his comrades failed to defend New York City from the British. When the redcoats landed at Kip's Bay on September 15, most of his men fled with the rest of the Continental Army to northern Manhattan. But Van Dyck himself was left behind. "He being a heavy fat man," wrote Gen. Alexander McDougall, "became so fatigued in the retreat from the City of New York, that he could not retire with that corps, and secreted himself in the Cedars between the City and Harlem." British troops marched westward across the island and cut off his retreat. "Finding no prospect of escape," he trudged back southward and "concealed himself in the City." He later insisted that he was in the process of trying to surrender when the British found him.[5]

How and when the British found him became a matter of dispute. The records indicate that Van Dyck was arrested and imprisoned on September 16. Yet somehow, five days later, Van Dyck was still at large. On the morning of September 21, the Great Fire of New York burned a fifth of the city. British soldiers believed the fire was deliberate, and they caught perpetrators in the act. They killed several of them and imprisoned dozens more. Witnesses vividly remembered that Van Dyck was apprehended on the 21st. How could Van Dyck have suddenly emerged from his prison? Although the Americans insisted that Van

4. Deposition of Christopher Benson, June 16, 1776, Frederick Mackenzie Papers, Box 1, folder 2, William L. Clements Library; *Gaine's Universal Register, or American and British Kalendar, for the Year 1776* (New-York, 1776), 160–61; *Calendar of Historical Manuscripts Relating to the War of the Revolution...* (Albany, N.Y., 1868), 223–24, 260, 288, 340, 370–72; *PGW:RS*, 6:97 n4; Force, *American Archives*, 4th ser. (1840, 1846), 3:149–50, 1627–29, 6:1152, 1173–74, 1179, 1366; Aimone and Manders, "Independent Companies," 71.

5. McDougall to Washington, *PGW:RS*, 13:572 (quotes); David L. Sterling, ed., "American Prisoners of War in New York: A Report by Elias Boudinot," *William and Mary Quarterly* 13, 3 (July 1956): 388; see also Minutes of a Commission to Investigate the Causes of the Fire in New York City, New-York Historical Society [hereafter CCM], 68.

Dyck was put in close confinement after he was captured, perhaps the British paroled him and allowed him to wander the streets of the city?[6]

SEPTEMBER 1776: THE "NEGRO MAN"

Van Dyck had chosen the Leary family's livery stables on Cortlandt Street for his hiding place. He was just across Broadway from his own inn, and he probably knew the Learys, who were fellow officers in his regiment. Rather than scrounge for food himself—perhaps because he feared being recognized—he dispatched a Black man to bring him sustenance. Perhaps this man was enslaved by the Learys, or by Van Dyck himself. Regardless, Van Dyck's choice turned out to be a mistake.[7]

Lt. John Innes of the Royal Artillery remembered that on September 21, as the fire raged, a "Negro man ... accosted" him "in the Street" and offered to "show him a Man that set fire to the City." Innes followed the informant to Leary's house and found Van Dyck, "secreted in a Closet of one of the Bed-Chambers, which a young Lady endeavored to prevent his going into." Innes's encounter comes from the 1783 testimony of Maj. Stephen Payne Adye, another artillerist as well as deputy judge advocate general in the British army. As he listened to Adye's testimony, Brig. Gen. William Martin (one of the investigating officers) piped up, recalling that he remembered Innes—one of his subordinates—telling the same story; he also recalled that he "saw this Man Vandyke soon after going by to the Provost under Guard." The firefighter John Burns also pinpointed the timing of Van Dyck's arrest to September 21:

> I particularly remember that one Ab. Vandyke a Captain of Grenadiers in the American service was found on the morning of the fire hid in the Leary's stables ... I saw him taken out of these Stables

6. Sterling, "American Prisoners," 388; Joshua Loring, "Return of Prisoners taken on the Island of New-York 15th and 16 of Septr. 1776," enclosed in George Washington to John Hancock, September 25, 1776, Letters from George Washington, vol. 2, transcripts 1776, 260, Papers of the Continental Congress, National Archives and Records Administration [hereafter NARA]; New York Committee of Safety to George Washington, Feb. 13, 1777, in Frank E. Grizzard, Jr., ed., *PGW:RS* (1998), 8:326–27; see also J. J. Boudinot, ed., *The Life, Public Services, Addresses and Letters of Elias Boudinot* [...] (Boston and New York, 1896), 1:94; Helen Jordan, ed., "Colonel Elias Boudinot in New York City, February, 1778," *Pennsylvania Magazine of History and Biography*, 24, 4 (1900): 456, 461–62; Benjamin L. Carp, *The Great New York Fire of 1776: A Lost Story of the American Revolution* (New Haven, Conn.: Yale University Press, 2023).
7. CCM, 15 ("Negro man"), 16, 59; *Gaine's Universal Register*, 161; Michael J. O'Brien, "The Story of Old Leary Street, or Cortland Street: The Leary Family in Early New York History," *Journal of the American Irish Historical Society* 15, 1 (April 1916): 112–17.

when I was assisting in pulling them down to stop the progress of the fire.[8]

The British claimed that they had either first laid hold of Van Dyck on the 21st or recaptured him during the fire, and they believed he was responsible for "setting the City on Fire."[9] Adye recalled examining Van Dyck, "whose Person he had before known," in the Provost afterwards.[10] The British officers asked around, and they discovered that Van Dyck had threatened to burn New York "the Summer before the Town was taken," though Van Dyck denied this.[11]

Americans disputed the date of Van Dyck's capture—they insisted that he had been closely confined from the 16th onward—but they agreed that his Black emissary was important to the story. McDougall wrote that "the Negro, who brought him victuals betrayed him." What motivated this man to turn Van Dyck in? Perhaps he was trying to gain favor with the British army. Perhaps he resented Van Dyck specifically, particularly if Van Dyck was his enslaver—many Black people at this time were running away, tying up the local militia, engaging in espionage, and enlisting with the British against their former enslavers. Or perhaps he saw it as a collective act of Black solidarity against a white officer. And what exactly did McDougall mean by "betrayed"? Had the "Negro Man" merely betrayed Van Dyck's hiding place, or whites' expectation that Blacks ought to serve faithfully? Van Dyck may have believed that this man owed him obedience, or at least secrecy. This anonymous Black New Yorker apparently disagreed.[12]

Van Dyck languished in the Provost for almost twenty months, because his political career as a terrorizing militia captain had made him "peculiarly Obnoxious to the Enemy." The British were "much exasperated against him, because the Granadier Company and other Corps, used to exercise in his Tenis Court, and inclosures." Reports surfaced that he and his fellow prisoners were victims of "the greatest Cruelty." All the while, Van Dyck seems to have been seething over the Black man who ostensibly betrayed him.[13]

8. CCM, 15 ("secreted"), 16 ("saw"), 59 ("particularly").

9. McDougall to Washington, *PGW:RS*, 13:572; Edwin G. Burrows, *Forgotten Patriots: The Untold Story of American Prisoners during the Revolutionary War* (New York: Basic, 2008), 21–23, 269 n2.

10. CCM, 16, 51.

11. Sterling, "American Prisoners," 388.

12. McDougall to Washington, *PGW:RS*, 13:572 ("betrayed"); CCM, 15–16; Leslie M. Harris, *In the Shadow of Slavery: African Americans in New York City, 1626–1863* (Chicago: University of Chicago Press, 2003), chaps. 1–2.

13. New York Committee of Safety to Washington, Feb. 13, 1777, in *PGW:RS*, 8:326–27

JANUARY 14, 1780: PRINCE PITKIN AND ABRAHAM VAN DYCK

The winter of 1779–80 found Van Dyck bivouacked with the Continental Army encampment in Morristown, New Jersey. It was a bitter season, one that "proved the most intense of any winter for the last half century," according to Capt. Samuel Richards. At one point, provisions were suspended for three days, and Richards considered killing his dog, Hector, for food. The officers huddled in worn-out clothes and their increasingly worthless pay was withheld for months. Yet the officers fared better than their men, and at least Richards had the good grace to be abashed: "our soldiers looked up to us urging a fulfillment of promises."[14]

Prince Pitkin of Hartford, Connecticut, was among these suffering soldiers. His first name hints at his enslaved status at birth, while his last name was bestowed by one of Connecticut's first families. William Pitkin III, who preceded Jonathan Trumbull as governor, died in 1769. His sons included the minister of Farmington, a superior court clerk, and a state legislator. The eldest, William Pitkin IV, manufactured gunpowder at the mill he inherited from his father and served on the state's Council and Council of Safety; later he sat on the Superior Court and in the Continental Congress. Prince Pitkin used the family's august surname without quite sharing in the benefits that the white Pitkins claimed as their birthright.[15]

Prince Pitkin enlisted in Capt. John Barnard's company in Col. Samuel Wylly's 3rd Connecticut regiment as a private soldier on May 14, 1777, for the duration of the war. Pitkin was part of a new wave of Black enlistment in the Connecticut Line, a way of filling the state's quotas while keeping wealthier white men out of the service. He be-

---

("Obnoxious"); Elias Boudinot to Washington, June 26, 1777, *PGW:RS*, ed. Frank E. Grizzard, Jr. (2000), 10:128, 129 ("Cruelty"); McDougall to Washington, *PGW:RS*, 13:572 ("exasperated"). For Van Dyck's exchange on May 8, 1778, see "A List of Prisoners of War, and State Prisoners Confin'd in the Provost Goal, New York, 5th. November 1777," [John Fell], Memorandom in the Provost Goal, New York, New York Society Library.

14. *Diary of Samuel Richards: Captain of Connecticut Line, War of the Revolution, 1775–1781* (Philadelphia: Leeds and Biddle, 1909), 64 ("intense"), 65, 66 ("soldiers").

15. "Revolutionary War Rolls, comp. 1894–1913, documenting the period 1775–1783," NARA M246, RG 93, roll 8, Connecticut, 3d Regiment, 1777–80, folder 43, 386; Prince-Pitkin Papers, 1780–82, Connecticut Historical Society; A. P. Pitkin, *Pitkin Family of America: A Genealogy of the Descendants of William Pitkin* [...] (Hartford, Conn, 1887); Joseph O. Goodwin, *East Hartford: Its History and Traditions* (Hartford, Conn, 1879), chap. 21; John Wood Sweet, *Bodies Politic: Negotiating Race in the American North, 1730–1830* (Baltimore: Johns Hopkins University Press, 2003), 69–70; Judith L. Van Buskirk, *Standing in Their Own Light: African American Patriots in the American Revolution* (Norman: University of Oklahoma Press, 2017), 11–12, 110.

came one of dozens of Black soldiers in his regiment—one of thousands to fight for Independence. For many enslaved Black people, the burdens of Continental Army service were worth the bounty: Councilor William Pitkin apparently offered Prince and the other enslaved men on his estate their freedom in exchange for enlistment. Prince helped fill Hartford's quota; he drew the same pay and clothing allowance as white privates. He spent many months of his service too ill to fight, which was hardly uncommon. His commanders occasionally gave him assignments away from camp. In March 1779, Col. Thomas Grosvenor granted him a furlough. Surviving muster and pay rolls give a monthly account of him until the night of January 14, 1780, when Van Dyck apparently took Prince Pitkin's life.[16]

The men had been "starving and freezing" in a six-foot stratum of snow. As Dr. James Thacher recalled, "the sufferings of the poor soldiers can scarcely be described"—many lacked shoes, and the men slept with just a single blanket around them. "The soldiers are so enfeebled from hunger and cold, as to be almost unable to perform their military duty, or labor in constructing their huts." In response, soldiers took up "the practice of pilfering and plundering" livestock from local farms. Did Pitkin, desperately cold and hungry, resort to stealing food or a blanket? Did he raise a hand against his officers? The evidence does not say, but Thacher noted that some men received "exemplary punishments" after a "fair trial, and conviction by a court martial" (Washington did sentence two Pennsylvanians to death for robbery in February). But perhaps when the offender was Black, an officer like Van Dyck might decide to skip the formalities and enact a more brutal justice. Or perhaps Pitkin had done nothing wrong at all.[17]

16. Henry P. Johnston, ed., "The Record of Connecticut Men in the Military and Naval Service during the War of the Revolution, 1775–1783," in *Record of Service of Connecticut Men in the I. War of the Revolution* [...] (Hartford, Conn., 1889), 177; "Revolutionary War Rolls," NARA M246, RG 93, rolls 8–9, folder 43: 386, 398, 402, 416, 427, 449, 472, folder 46: 1–62, 95–129; Connecticut Archives, Revolutionary War, ser. 1, 30:3e; ser. 2, 56:6–15, Connecticut State Library; Receipt for balance due the soldiers of 3rd Regiment due to Depreciation of Currency, January 1, 1780, in Continental Army 1777–81, 3rd Conn. Reg.'t, Extracts from an Orderly Book 1778–79 and Papers Connected with Adjustment of Pay of Soldiers of Col. Wyllys' Reg.'t, 1778–81, Connecticut State Library; Prince-Pitkin Papers (including informal notation), 1780–82, Connecticut Historical Society ("Free Negro"); see also Benjamin Quarles, *The Negro in the American Revolution* (1961; Chapel Hill: University of North Carolina Press, 1996), 54, 58, chap. 5; David O. White, *Connecticut's Black Soldiers, 1775–1783* (Chester, Conn.: Pequot Press, 1973), 18–21.
17. [Joseph Plumb Martin], *Narrative of Some of the Adventures, Dangers and Sufferings of a Revolutionary Soldier* [...] (Hallowell, Maine, 1830), 125 ("starving and freezing"); James

One way or another, Van Dyck appears to have slain Pitkin, a "Negro man" and "Negro soldier" who was "killed on the night of the 14th. day of January." On March 7, Van Dyck requested a court martial to clear the matter up. Washington's staff ordered the Maryland and Pennsylvania brigades to furnish captains to serve as jurors. With Col. Oliver Spencer of New Jersey presiding, these officers "made strict examination" into Van Dyck's conduct and found it "highly justifiable." The killing of Prince Pitkin was something Van Dyck had done "in the line of his duty" or "in the Execution of his Duty." Washington approved the judgment.[18]

Pitkin's Connecticut regiment treated him equally—at least on paper—but the officers of the mid-Atlantic treated him as disposable. They called his killing "highly justifiable." This may have been true—at least in their eyes—on the basis of the evidence. Still, the war had already motivated thousands of enslaved people to flee their enslavers, including Washington and Spencer themselves. As aggrieved slaveholders, these army officers had little reason to doubt that the taking of a Black man's life was "justifiable" on the basis of custom, property rights, and a belief in white superiority. The Revolution inspired not just a radical "black revolt" against slavery, but also a white reaction to that radical revolt.[19]

Thacher, *A Military Journal during the American Revolutionary War, from 1775 to 1783* (Boston, 1823), 221 ("sufferings," "enfeebled"), 222 ("pilfering," "exemplary," "fair trial"); see also S. Sydney Bradford, "Discipline in the Morristown Winter Encampments," *Proceedings of the New Jersey Historical Society* 80, 1 (January 1962): 15–17; Almon W. Lauber, ed., *Orderly Books of the Fourth New York Regiment, 1778–1780, The Second New York Regiment, 1780–1783* [...] (Albany: University of the State of New York, 1932), 266–67, 269, 272.

18. For this and the following paragraph, see General Orders, March 7, 1780, in Benjamin L. Huggins, ed., *PGW:RS* (2016), 24:646 ("Negro man," "killed on the night"); General Orders of March 7, 12, 1780, *The Writings of Washington from the Original Manuscript Sources, 1745–1799*, ed. John C. Fitzpatrick (Washington, D.C.: U.S. Government Printing Office, 1937), 18:81, 108 ("examination," "Negro soldier"), 109 ("line," "highly justifiable"); Orderly Book, February 21 to May 15, 1780, Numbered Record Books Concerning Military Operations and Service, Pay and Settlement of Accounts, and Supplies in the War Department Collection of Revolutionary War Records, Record Group 93, NARA Microfilm Publications M853, ser. 6, 35:29–30, 39, 40 ("Execution"). Fritz Hirschfeld, *George Washington and Slavery: A Documentary Portrayal* (Columbia: University of Missouri Press, 1997), chap. 15, argues that Washington treated black soldiers with equity in accordance with military protocol, but also upheld the slave system.

19. For "black revolt," see Graham Russell Hodges, "Black Revolt in New York City and the Neutral Zone, 1775–1783," in *Slavery, Freedom and Culture among Early American Workers* (1998; New York, Routledge, 2015), 65–86. In the "Book of Negroes," Luke Spencer was "[Formerly slave] to Oliver Spencer" and had emancipated himself in 1777;

Pitkin himself, though, did not die a slave. "Prince a Free Negro" had £44.11.7 to his name—almost two years' pay—when a probate judge back in Hartford settled his affairs. William Pitkin IV, his erstwhile master, agreed to administer Prince's humble, hard-earned estate. It was the legacy of Prince's short life as a soldier and a free man.[20]

After winter's end, Washington and Gen. Philip Schuyler took a personal interest in Van Dyck's service. In May 1780, Washington recommended him to Congress's Board of Admiralty to be appointed a marine captain: he noted that Van Dyck "was particularly obnoxious" to New York City Loyalists "on account of his fixed opposition to their measures," and those Loyalists' "influence" had led to harsh treatment of "uncommon rigor" during his "long captivity." Washington was convinced, "from a knowledge of his character and his circumstances," that "no man, considering his abilities, has made greater sacrifice for the cause." It was quite an endorsement for a man imprisoned for incendiarism—though Washington and his men, of course, denied that anyone in the Continental Army had acted as incendiaries.[21] Schuyler concurred: "everybody about headquarters speaks well, very well of him;" he was grateful that Van Dyck had "maintained his principles" even "under the severest tryals." Congress assigned Van Dyck to service as a marine lieutenant aboard the frigate *Saratoga*, but before the year was out, he had resigned his commission. By the end of the war, he was dead.[22]

### RACE, JUSTICE, AND THE REVOLUTION

Van Dyck remained angry at the "Negro man" who had "betrayed" him in 1776; maybe the big grenadier captain recalled this betrayal during the snowy winter of 1780 when he killed Prince Pitkin at the Morristown encampment. We can only speculate. What seems clearer is this:

Graham Russell Hodges, ed., *The Black Loyalist Directory: African Americans in Exile after the American Revolution* (New York: Garland, 1996), 16, 35–36 (quote), 111–12; see also David Waldstreicher, "The Hidden Stakes of the 1619 Controversy," *Boston Review* (Jan. 24, 2020), http://bostonreview.net/race-politics/david-waldstreicher-hidden-stakes-1619-controversy.

20. Prince-Pitkin Papers, 1780–82, Connecticut Historical Society.

21. George Washington to Board of Admiralty, May 29, 1780, *Writings of Washington*, 18:443–44 (quotes), 444 n82.

22. Philip Schuyler to James Duane, June 5, 1780, "The Duane Letters (Continued)," *Publications of the Southern History Association* 8, 5 (Sept. 1904): 383; Gaillard Hunt, ed., *Journals of the Continental Congress, 1774–1789* (Washington, D.C.: Government Printing Office, 1910), 17:650–51, 661; *PGW:RS*, 6:97 n4; *At a general meeting of the Committee of Mechanicks, at Mrs. Van Dyke's, the 27th December, 1783* (New York, 1783); *New-York Packet*, May 5, 1785, February 20, 1787; *Daily Advertiser* (New York), October 26, 1786.

Van Dyck was a freeman, a property-owner, and an officer who probably expected obedience from Black men. The "Negro man" of Manhattan and Prince Pitkin, by contrast, were waging their own fights for respect, security, and freedom despite the heavy obstacles that stood in their way.[23]

During the Great Fire of New York, a "Negro man" may have exacted a bit of revenge against the injustices of the slave system: he exposed Van Dyck as a guilty man—or framed an innocent one. We do not know what happened to this Black New Yorker. Perhaps he enlisted with a Loyalist unit and fought for the Crown. If he survived the war, he may have joined the exodus of Black Loyalists who settled in Canada, England, Sierra Leone, and elsewhere. If he stayed put, he may have remained enslaved (there were slaveowners named Van Dyck and Leary in the 1790 census) or walked free, as a third of the city's Black population soon did.[24]

Van Dyck himself endured almost twenty months imprisoned in the Provost, no doubt at great cost to his health. A year and a half after his release, he killed Pitkin, a free "Negro soldier." Pitkin, too, fought for American freedom, until a harsh winter and a looming officer snuffed out his dreams. We probably ought to conclude that Pitkin was the one betrayed. This time, Van Dyck went unpunished.

23. White, *Connecticut's Black Soldiers*, 29–35, 39–43; Gwendolyn Evans Logan, "The Slave in Connecticut during the American Revolution," *Bulletin of the Connecticut Historical Society* 30, 3 (January 1965): 73–80; Van Buskirk, *Standing*, chaps. 2–3.

24. Ned Benton and Judy-Lynne Peters, eds., *New York Slavery Records Index: Records of Enslaved Persons and Slave Holders in New York from 1525 though the Civil War* (New York: John Jay College of Criminal Justice, 2017), https://nyslavery.commons.gc.cuny.edu/ (accessed July 30, 2018); Harris, *Shadow of Slavery*, 55–56.

# Mercy Otis Warren, Revolutionary Propagandist

## ❦ JONATHAN HOUSE ❦

On March 26, 1772, *The Massachusetts Spy* ran an unusual item on page 3 of that day's newspaper: an advertisement for a dramatic performance of *The Adulateur* at the Grand Parade in Upper Servia. Filling nearly half the page, the notice contained a list of dramatis personae and a couple of scenes from the play. In the opening soliloquy, Rapatio, the bashaw of Servia, exults in the success of his schemes "To quench the gen'rous flame, the ardent / love / Of liberty in Servia's freeborn sons." Then, in reference to the play's title, the villainous leader says he must seek out the "adulating tongues" of his inner circle to relieve the pangs of his "phantom conscience."[1] Patriot readers of *The Spy* quickly recognized the item as a mock advertisement for a fictional dramatic performance and the character Rapatio (the rapacious one) as a representation of the hated Massachusetts Royal Governor Thomas Hutchinson. *The Adulateur* was the first of a series of dramatic sketches by Mercy Otis Warren, a member of a prominent Patriot family, and their novel approach to satire electrified the emerging revolutionary movement.

Before taking up arms, the American Patriots launched a war of words against Britain in colonial legislatures and newspapers. At a time when women were largely excluded from the public sphere, publishing anonymous pieces in the newspapers offered Warren a way to contribute to the cause. The pieces also established her as America's first female playwright.[2] Warren's writing reflected a worldview shaped by radical political and social ideas that first appeared during the

1. Mercy Otis Warren, extract from *The Adulateur* published in *The Massachusetts Spy*, March 26, 1772, Massachusetts_Spy_published_as_The_Massachusetts_Spy___March_26_1772__1_of_1___1_.pdf, 3.
2. Jeffrey Richards, *Mercy Otis Warren* (New York: Twayne Publishers, 1995), 84.

English Civil Wars and Commonwealth of the mid-1600s, contributed to the Glorious Revolution of 1688, and forcefully reemerged in the works of opposition political thinkers of the early 1700s. Writers such as John Trenchard and Thomas Gordon saw the gains of the Glorious Revolution, which set new limits on the monarchy and enshrined parliament as England's ruling power, as insufficient to protect personal freedoms. Their *Cato's Letters*, a series of essays published from 1720-1723, warned of the dangers of corruption and creeping authoritarianism.[3]

Mercy Otis was born in 1728 in Barnstable, a Massachusetts town on Cape Cod, to James Otis and his wife Mary, the descendent of a Mayflower passenger. A successful farmer and lawyer, Otis entered politics and won a seat in the Massachusetts House of Representatives. Unusually for the time, he allowed his daughter to attend tutoring sessions with her brothers, who were preparing to attend Harvard College. She studied history and literature spanning from ancient Greece and Rome to the eighteenth century. In 1754, Mercy married James Warren, a friend of her brother James, and had five sons in quick succession. Early in her marriage, Mercy focused on running the household, first at her husband's family's farm and then at a new home in Plymouth, and caring for her children. In her spare time, she wrote poetry.[4] A 1763 portrait by John Singleton Copley showed her as a young woman with a pale forehead, dark eyes, and hair pulled tight under a bonnet.[5]

During those years, Warren's family started to clash with British officials. In 1757, James Otis, Sr., thought he would win a vote in the House of Representatives for a place on the Governor's Council, the legislature's upper chamber. When he unexpectedly lost, he blamed Hutchinson, then the lieutenant governor, for influencing members to vote against him. A few years later, Hutchinson edged Otis out for the position of Massachusetts Superior Court chief justice. The Otises viewed these developments not only as personal setbacks but also as a worrisome sign of consolidation of power. In addition to his positions as chief justice and lieutenant governor, Hutchinson was a probate court judge and member of the Governor's Council. Moreover, he was related

---

3. Bernard Bailyn, *The Ideological Origins of the American Revolution* (London: Belnap Press of Harvard University Press, 2017), 35; Edmund S. Morgan, *American Slavery, American Freedom* (USA: W.W. Norton & Company, Inc., 1975), 369.

4. Rosemarie Zagarri, *A Woman's Dilemma: Mercy Otis Warren and the American Revolution* (Chichester, West Sussex, UK: John Wiley & Sons, 2015), 44.

5. John Singleton Copley, Portrait of Mrs. James Warren, collections.mfa.org/objects/32409m.

by marriage to the powerful Oliver family, whose members held several other key government posts.[6]

In 1761, James Otis, Jr., who had become a successful Boston lawyer, argued the landmark writs of assistance case. The writs gave customs inspectors broad powers to search any property at any time for smuggled goods, prompting a legal challenge from a group of Boston merchants. Arguing on behalf of the merchants in court, Otis called the writs the "worst instrument of arbitrary power ... ever found in an English law-book," and rejected the authority of parliament to impose such legislation on the colonies.[7] He lost the case but capitalized on the excitement generated by his courtroom performance to win a seat in the House of Representatives. Then, when the British parliament suddenly started levying taxes on the colonies, Otis penned some of the most influential critiques of the new measures. In his 1764 pamphlet *Rights of the British Colonies Asserted and Proved*, Otis formulated the first arguments against taxation without representation.[8]

James Warren, who had inherited his father's position as high sheriff of Plymouth, joined the protest against Britain's new taxes and won election to the House of Representatives. The Warrens' home on North Street in the heart of Plymouth, strategically located on the road between Boston and the communities of Cape Cod, became a meeting place for prominent Patriots such as Samuel and John Adams.[9] In 1769, amid escalating tensions with the mother country, tragedy struck and the family lost its leading spokesman. Otis encountered a customs official with whom he had been trading public insults, fought with him, and suffered a severe blow to the head. Already prone to manic behavior before the incident, Otis became increasingly mentally unstable and was forced to abandon his work for the Patriot cause.[10] His sister would pick up his mantle a few years later.

Mercy Otis Warren wrote *The Adulateur* in 1772 partly in response to the case of Ebenezer Richardson, a customs informer who had fired birdshot into a Patriot mob that was attacking him, killing a young boy. At Richardson's trial, Superior Court Chief Justice Peter Oliver — whose brother Andrew was married to Hutchison's sister-in-law — argued the mob's actions were to blame for the incident and advised

6. Zagarri, *A Woman's Dilemma*, 32.
7. James Otis, *Collected Political Writings of James Otis* (Indianapolis: Liberty Fund, 2015), 13.
8. Ibid., 148.
9. Zagarri, *A Woman's Dilemma*, 43.
10. J.L. Bell, "What Was James Otis's Problem," boston1775.blogspot.com/2006/09/what-was-james-otiss-problem.html.

Richardson's acquittal. Yet the jury, under pressure from a raucous public in the courtroom, found him guilty of murder, punishable by death. The court responded by applying for and obtaining a royal pardon for Richardson, a brazen act of corruption in the Patriots' eyes. The March 26, 1772, edition of *The Spy* led with a long piece of political commentary by an author writing under the pseudonym of "The CENTINEL." The piece warned the citizens of Massachusetts to be "watchful" of "tyranny" and then commented on the Richardson case: "When the execution of a man legally convicted is suspended twenty-two months, and the murderer is then discharged in an unusual manner, society ought to be alarmed."[11]

The dramatis personae included in the purported advertisement for *The Adulateur* quickly established a link to the characters in the real-life drama playing out in Massachusetts. Warren chose names that also evoked the plight of once-free societies struggling against oppression in other places and times, a common theme in eighteenth-century political writing. In addition to Rapatio, bashaw of Servia, the dramatis personae listed Limpet, married to the sister of Rapatio; Lord Chief Justice Hazlerod, brother to Limpet; Ebenezer, a friend to the government; Cassius, a virtuous senator; waiters, pimps, and parasites. Servia (Serbia) was then occupied by the Ottoman Turks, and a bashaw (pasha) was a high-ranking Turkish official.[12] Cassius was the leader of the plot to kill Roman dictator Julius Caesar. In the closing soliloquy of the March 26 sketch, Cassius appeals for divine assistance in the fight against Rapatio and his associates: "If ye powers divine / Ye mark the movements of this nether world / And bring them to account, crush / crush these vipers."[13]

On April 23, 1772, *The Spy* published another extract from *The Adulateur*, this one more directly focused on the Ebenezer Richardson affair. The first scene opens with Ebenezer languishing in a jail cell, lamenting his fate, when in sweeps Hazlerod. The chief justice says, "What loss to grief? Dejected? Can it be? / Can the verdict of some half-formed peasants, / Unmeaning dull machines, thus damp your courage?" He pledges Ebenezer, "Shall one day leave this dreary tenement, / Again with pleasing scenes of blood and carnage / To glut our vengeance."

11. *The Massachusetts Spy*, March 26, 1772, https://chroniclingamerica.loc.gov/lccn/sn83021193/1772-03-26/ed-1/seq-1/.

12. Richards, *Mercy Otis Warren*, 165.

13. Mercy Otis Warren, extract from *The Adulateur* published in *The Massachusetts Spy*, March 26, 1772, Massachusetts_Spy_published_as_The_Massachusetts_Spy___March_26_1772__1_of_1___1_.pdf.

Though Warren chose a dramatic format for her satires, she had almost certainly never seen a play at the time she was writing them. The authorities in Massachusetts considered theatrical productions immoral and prohibited them. Nonetheless, educated people read plays and were fond of using stage metaphors in speaking and writing. For Warren, this format allowed her to put emotionally charged speeches in the mouths of characters clearly delineated as heroes and villains. Other articles in the newspaper provided real-world context. It was effective propaganda that made "Rapatio" a household name in revolutionary Massachusetts and spawned numerous imitators.[14] In early 1773, an anonymous author took the excerpts from *The Adulateur* published by Warren and expanded them into a full-length play in pamphlet format. Warren would later refer to it as a "plagiary."[15]

In addition to writing for public consumption, Warren penned hundreds of letters to a wide network of family and friends, including prominent Patriots such as John and Abigail Adams. Her correspondence employed similar literary flourishes to her newspaper pieces and explored many of the same themes. In a February 1773 letter to her friend Hannah Winthrop, Warren began with a discussion of her motivations for writing poetry but soon pivoted to the political situation in Massachusetts. "The reflections of your compassionate heart on the impending ruin which threatens the whole are spirited and just, every uncorrupt mind must spurn the rod of oppression held over this once happy people," Warren wrote. She then lashed out at Jonathan Sewall, a prominent Loyalist propagandist writing under the pseudonym Philalethes ("lover of truth," in Greek). "It is my opinion that [Philalethes's] prostituted pen can give little consolation to the cankered bosom of the betrayer of his country," Warren wrote to Winthrop.[16]

Loyalist defenses of British policies prompted redoubled Patriot criticism, further inflaming the war of words in colonial Massachusetts.

14. Sandra J. Sarkela, "Freedom's Call: The Persuasive Power of Mercy Otis Warren's Dramatic Sketches, 1772-1775," *Early American Literature*, Vol. 44, No. 3 (2009): 544; Richards, *Mercy Otis Warren*, 85.

15. Mercy Otis Warren, 1728-1814, Plays and poetry: manuscript, Houghton Library, Harvard University, 7, fromthepage.com/harvardlibrary/colonial-north-america-houghton-library/warren-mercy-otis-1728-1814-plays-and-poetry-manuscript-17-ms-am-1354-1-houghton-library-harvard-university-cambridge-mass/display/1045665.

16. Mercy Otis Warren, "Letter from Mercy Otis Warren to Hannah Winthrop," Correspondence of Mercy Otis Warren and Hannah Winthrop, Massachusetts: Massachusetts Historical Society, www.masshist.org/database/viewer.php?item_id=3367&img_step=1&noalt=1&br=1&mode=transcript#page1.

In early 1773, the two sides focused on a controversy over paying British officials' salaries. Patriots had been upset to learn a couple of years earlier that the British crown would be taking over the payment of the governor's salary from the local assembly, depriving it of a check on his power. They were further enraged in late 1772 when the crown also took over the payment of superior court justices' salaries, undermining what they had hitherto viewed as an independent judiciary. Patriot outrage prompted speeches in defense of the measure by Hutchinson and dueling newspaper essays for and against it by militia general William Brattle (a former Patriot who had switched allegiances) and by John Adams. Drawing on this context, Warren published extracts from a new play called *The Defeat* in the *Boston Gazette* on May 24, 1773.

In an opening scene crafted to conjure an image of Hutchinson drafting his recent speeches, Rapatio declares, "I've travers'd o'er the records of the land, / Ransack'd the musty volumes of the dead, / Research'd the deeds of former infamy, / And trac'd each monument of early days, / Nor unexplored have left one useful line." The next scene opens with a character named Proteus, the shape-shifting god of Greek mythology, and described as Rapatio's "general"—a reference to Brattle. Proteus offers a full-throated defense of the hated Rapatio: "Did mortal e'er behold such worth abus'd? / Rapatio sure is virtue's first born son, / (Tho' I his slave at humble distance kept) / No sordid views contaminate his soul, / No rank ambition sucks within his breast."[17]

The scandal over the judges' salaries still reverberated when another broke out, triggered by the discovery of letters written by Hutchinson and Andrew Oliver to British officials years earlier in which they urged a strong response to the unrest created by the Stamp Act. Benjamin Franklin, serving as the American postmaster and agent for Massachusetts in London, obtained the letters and sent them to Patriot leaders back in Boston in 1773, prompting a fresh bout of indignation. The missives contained one particularly inflammatory statement by Hutchinson: "There must be an abridgment of what are called English liberties." Sewall, using the Philalethes pseudonym, wrote a couple of essays in Hutchinson's defense, arguing that the Patriots were deliberately misconstruing the meaning of the governor's comments.

The episode prompted Warren to write another sketch, published as a second extract from *The Defeat* in the *Boston Gazette* on July 19,

---

17. Mercy Otis Warren, excerpt from *The Defeat* published in *The Boston Gazette*, May 24, 1773, Boston_Gazette_published_as_THE_Boston-Gazette_AND_COUNTRY_JOURNAL.___May_24_1773__1_of_1_.pdf, 2.

1773. It consisted of a long exchange between Rapatio and Limpit, the character from *The Adulateur* representing Oliver. In an apparent reference to the discovery of the Hutchinson letters, Rapatio says: "Hah—Betray'd—Dear Limpit can it be? / Originals! / The Hand! The Signature." He worries his evil plans have been exposed. "Is the Game up? Can I deceive no more?" To defend themselves, Limpit suggests they call on "Some wretched Scribler," someone capable of "Confounding all Things with the Sceptics Art." Then, invoking Sewall with the same language Warren used in the earlier letter to Winthrop, Limpit says, "And what so fit for such a base Design, / As Philalethes prostituted Pen."[18]

The revolutionary struggle reached a key milestone later that year. To undercut the smuggling that allowed the colonies to skirt a tax on tea, and to help the ailing East India Company, parliament in late 1773 reduced the taxes on tea it shipped to the colonies. Angered by what they saw as a devious ploy to get the colonies to pay the tea tax, the Patriots organized a campaign to prevent half a dozen East India Company ships sailing to Massachusetts and other colonies from unloading their cargo. On December 5, Abigail Adams wrote to commiserate with Warren, suggesting that the recent developments were likely particularly distressing for her friend who had "so thoroughly looked thro the Deeds of Men, and Develloped the Dark designs of a Rapatio Soul." She added, "The Tea that bainfull weed is arrived. Great and I hope effectual opposition has been made to the landing of it."[19]

A few days later, a group of Patriots dressed as Indians forced their way onto the East India Company ships docked in the Boston harbor and threw 342 chests of tea overboard. The daring act thrilled the Patriots. "The Spirit of Liberty is very high in the Country and universal," John Adams wrote in a December 22 letter to James Warren. He asked that Mercy Warren write a poem about the Boston Tea Party. "I wish to See a late glorious Event, celebrated, by a certain poetical Pen, which has no equal that I know of in this Country," Adams wrote.[20] Mercy Warren was happy to oblige with a long poem about a fight over tea involving Indians and Greek mythological figures that came to be known as "The Squabble of the Sea-Nymphs." It filled the entire first page of the *Boston Gazette* on March 21. The second stanza read: "The Hero's of the Tuskarora Tribe, / Who scorn alike, A Fetter,

18. Ibid.

19. Abigail Adams, "Letter from Abigail Adams to Mercy Warren," *Warren-Adams Letters, Vol. 1, 1743-1777* (Boston: The Massachusetts Historical Society, 1917), 18.

20. John Adams, "Letter to James Warren," *Papers of John Adams, Volume 2* (Cambridge: The Belknap Press of Harvard University Press, 1977).

or a Bribe: / In order rang'd, and waiting Freedom's Nod, / To make an off'ring to the wat'ry God."²¹

In addition to galvanizing the revolutionary movement, the Boston Tea Party also stiffened Britain's resolve to stamp it out. A few months after receiving news of the shocking event, parliament passed the so-called Coercive Acts, which closed the port of Boston, stripped the House of Representatives of the ability to appoint the members of the Governor's Council, transferred the trials of British officials and soldiers to Britain, and enabled the quartering of troops among the local population. The crown appointed Gen. Thomas Gage, commander-in-chief of British forces in North America, to do double duty as Massachusetts governor, replacing Hutchinson. War was starting to appear inevitable.

"I tremble for the event of the present commotions; — there must be a noble struggle to recover the expiring liberties of our injured country; we must re-purchase them at the expence of blood, or tamely acquiesce, and embrace the hand that holds out the chain to us and our children," Warren wrote in a letter to Winthrop in the spring of 1774.²² Later that year, Warren wrote Catharine Macaulay, a radical English historian who supported the American Patriots, to warn her that war would result if the House of Commons (Parliament) did not change course: "If the Majority of the Commons still continue the Dupes of Venality and Corruption, they will soon see the Genius which once Animated their Hambdens, Haringtons, & Pyms, has taken up her Residence on these Distant shores."²³ The references are to John Hampden, James Harrington, and John Pym, republican theorists and political figures who played important roles in the English civil wars of the mid-1600s.

In September 1774, the First Continental Congress convened in Philadelphia with representatives from all thirteen colonies to coordinate a response to the latest British actions. Around the same time, towns and counties throughout Massachusetts held conventions to discuss the same issue. One of these, Suffolk County, outlined a nineteen-point resistance strategy and sent it to the delegates in Philadelphia, who approved the so-called Suffolk Resolves in their first official act. The eighth point focused on the issue of appointments to

21. Mercy Otis Warren, "The Squabble of the Sea Nymphs," *Boston Gazette*, March 21, 1774, Boston_Gazette_published_as_THE_Boston-Gazette_AND_COUNTRY_JOUR NAL.___March_21_1774__1_of_1_.pdf, 1.

22. Mercy Otis Warren, "Letter to Hannah Fayerwether Toman Wintrhop," *Mercy Otis Warren Selected Letters*, eds. Jeffrey H. Richards and Sharon M. Harris (Athens, Georgia: University of Georgia Press, 2009), 27.

23. Mercy Otis Warren, "Letter to Catharine Sawbridge Macaulay," ibid., 37.

the Governor's Council, which would now be made by the governor himself. The text stated that those who accepted these appointments would be considered "obstinate and incorrigible Enemies to this Colony."[24] Under the threat of violence from Patriot mobs, only a handful of the new governor's proposed appointees did so. Those who lived outside Boston relocated to the city where the British army could protect them. Warren took aim at the new council in *The Group*.

Printed on page 2 of the *Boston Gazette* on January 23, 1775, *The Group* interrupted an essay by "Novanglus" (John Adams) refuting the arguments of a pro-British writer calling himself "Massachusettensis." Mirroring the new appointments to the council, *The Group* has just a handful of characters from previous plays: Hazlerod (Peter Oliver), Meagre (Foster Hutchinson), and Dupe (Thomas Flucker). These old characters and a series of new ones discuss their mercenary motivations. In one exchange, Hum Humbug tells Beau Trumps he "wonder'd much to see thy patriot name / Among the list of rebels to the state." Beau Trumps — who represented Daniel Leonard, an old friend of John Adams newly turned Loyalist and unbeknownst to Adams and Warren the author of the Massachussetenis essays—replied that the Patriot cause was "a poor unprofitable path / Nought to be gain'd, save solid peace of mind. / No pensions, place or title there I found."[25]

In new scenes added for a pamphlet version of *The Group* published a couple of months later, the Loyalist characters plumb new depths of depravity. Simple Sapling says he would be happy to host British troops in his home and suggests his wife would be willing to tend to their every need. "Silvia's good natur'd, and no doubt will yield, / And take the brawny vet'rans to her board, / When she's assur'd 'twill help her husband's fame," Sapling says.[26] The play ends with a description of the actors leaving the stage and the curtain rising to reveal "a Lady nearly connected with one of the principal actors in the / Group, reclined in an adjoining sleeve, who in mournful accents / accosts them." The lady in this striking image delivers some of the first lines

24. Delegates from the towns and districts of the county of Suffolk, "Suffolk Resolves," *The Massachusetts Gazette*, September 15, 1774, www.masshist.org/database/viewer.php?item_ id=696&pid=2.

25. Mercy Otis Warren, *The Group*, published in *The Boston Gazette*, January 23, 1775, Boston_Gazette_published_as_THE_Boston-Gazette_AND_COUNTRY_ JOURNAL.__January_23_1775__1_of_1_.pdf.

26. Mercy Otis Warren, 1728-1814, Plays and poetry: manuscript, 34, fromthepage.com/ harvardlibrary/colonial-north-america-houghton-library/warren-mercy-otis-1728-1814-plays-and-poetry-manuscript-17-ms-am-1354-1-houghton-library-harvard-university-cambridge-mass/display/1045692.

given to a woman in an American play:[27] "What painful scenes are hov'ring o'er the morn / When spring again invigorates the lawn! / Instead of the gay landscape's beautious dies, / Must the stain'd field salute our weeping eyes . . . Till British troops shall to Columbia yield, / And freedom's sons are masters of the field."[28]

The publication of *The Group* likely marked the end of Warren's work as a revolutionary propagandist. With the shots fired at Lexington and Concord a few months later on April 19, 1775, the armed phase of the conflict began. Though a handful of other satirical plays appeared in Boston in the following years that some scholars have attributed to Warren—one of these, *The Blockheads*, has characters with names taken from previous Warren works—others argue they were more likely the work of one or more Warren imitators. The author left no manuscript evidence of these plays, which have abundant stylistic differences to her known works.[29] Warren went on to write a series of historical dramas such as *The Ladies of Castile* and then returned to the political fray with a 1788 pamphlet arguing against the ratification of the U.S. Constitution.[30] Like other anti-federalists, Warren believed the new charter proposed a system of government as oppressive as the one the country had just thrown off. In 1805, Warren published the first of three volumes of her *History of the Rise, Progress and Termination of the American Revolution*. Though praised by then-President Thomas Jefferson, the work failed to attract much public interest and incited a barrage of criticism from John Adams, who felt it undervalued his achievements. Warren responded spiritedly to Adams's letters.[31] By then, her eyesight failing, Warren confined herself to writing poetry and letters and enjoying the company of a reduced family circle. Three of her sons had died, but her son Henry had settled nearby to start a family of his own, and James had come to live with his elderly parents at their Plymouth home. Warren's husband died in 1808, and she followed him in 1814, at the age of eighty-six.

27. Sarkela, "Freedom's Call," 561.

28. Mercy Otis Warren, 1728-1814, Plays and poetry: manuscript, 41, fromthepage.com/harvardlibrary/colonial-north-america-houghton-library/warren-mercy-otis-1728-1814-plays-and-poetry-manuscript-17-ms-am-1354-1-houghton-library-harvard-university-cambridge-mass/display/1045699.

29. Richards, *Mercy Otis Warren*, 103.

30. Mercy Otis Warren, "Observations on the New Constitution," 1788, National Constitution Center, constitutioncenter.org/the-constitution/historic-document-library/detail/mercy-otis-warren-observations-on-the-new-constitution-1788.

31. Letters between John Adams and Mercy Otis Warren, July-Aug. 1807, about her *History of the Rise, Progress and Termination of the American Revolution, Massachusetts Historical Society Collections*, 5th ser., vol. 4 (Boston: printed for the Socity, 1878), 341.

# John Hancock's Politics and Personality in Ten Quotes

## ❧ BROOKE BARBIER ❧

Nearly every American knows the name of John Hancock, but often for little more than his signature on the Declaration of Independence. Hancock was one of the most popular men in eighteenth-century North America, winning people over with his style, personability, and generosity. These ten quotations offer a fuller picture of the character, political temper, and personality of the man behind the pen and help expand our understanding of the leadership of the American Revolution.

1. "Come in Revere, we're not afraid of you."—John Hancock to Paul Revere, April 19, 1775[1.]

This breezy line from Hancock came at a pivotal moment in US history, when Hancock felt calm despite the peril swirling around him. Hancock and Samuel Adams were staying in Lexington, Massachusetts, in April 1775 because Boston, with its occupying soldiers, had become too dangerous. The countryside wasn't a safe haven either, however. Rumors spread that the redcoats were marching to Lexington to seize Hancock and Adams.

On April 18, Paul Revere set off on his famous midnight ride to warn the two rebel leaders that they were in danger. He arrived at the Hancock-Clarke House and demanded that the men guarding it let him in. He was asked to quiet down, which enraged Revere, who told them, "The regulars are coming out!" Hancock was awakened by the noise, peered out a window, and saw Revere. He told him to come into the house and share his news.

---

1. Elias Phinney, *History of the Battle at Lexington, on the Morning of the 19th April, 1775* (Boston: Phelps and Farnham, 1825), 16–17.

After Revere disclosed that British soldiers were on the march, Hancock sent a warning to Concord and then readied himself to personally take on the redcoats by polishing his sword. It took a lot of coaxing before he eventually agreed to flee to a nearby town, just before the deadly confrontation on Lexington Green.

2. "to Appear in Character I am Obliged to be pretty Expensive."— John Hancock to Thomas Hancock, August 22, 1761[2.]

Despite fashion often being derided as insignificant or simply a feminine whimsy, Hancock knew that clothes can make the man. While on his first trip overseas, Hancock spent a lot of money in London on the trendiest styles and justified the expense to his uncle, who was paying the bill, writing that he did it to "appear in character." Suitable clothing gave the inexperienced twenty-three-year-old a more confident air. If he dressed like a successful merchant, then he would feel like one, and others would think he was one too. He frequently used clothing and accessories—including a powdered wig, gilded jackets, and rich fabrics—to communicate how he felt about himself and project power and status. Despite wearing such obvious signs of wealth, he had a gift for connecting with all orders of people, and this made him one of the most popular men in Massachusetts.

3. "I hope the same Spirit will prevail throughout the whole Continent." *and* "The Injury that has been Done the Lieut. Govr. was quite a different Affair & was not done by this Town, & is what I abhor & Detest as much as any man breathing . . . but an opposition to the Stamp Act is highly commendable."—John Hancock to Jonathan Barnard, August 22, 1765 and January 25, 1766[3.]

These two quotations about the Stamp Act riots in Boston in August 1765 are best examined together because they explain Hancock's mixed feelings about the protests. When a mob destroyed parts of stamp tax collector Andrew Oliver's home and warehouse and forced him to resign shortly after, Hancock was pleased and hoped that others throughout North America would follow Boston's lead. And they did. Rhode Island, New York, New Jersey, and Maryland similarly intimidated their tax collectors to stand down.

2. John Hancock to Thomas Hancock, January 14, 1761, *Proceedings of the Massachusetts Historical Society (MHS-P)* 43 (October 1909-June 1910): 196.

3. John Hancock to Jonathan Barnard, August 22, 1765; January 25, 1766, Hancock Letterbook (business), Hancock Family Papers (HFP), Baker Library Special Collections (BLSC); Pauline Maier, *From Resistance to Revolution: Colonial Radicals and the Development of American Opposition to Britain, 1765–1776* (New York: W. W. Norton & Company, 1991), 62–64.

But when a mob of Bostonians went after Lieutenant Governor Thomas Hutchinson's house two weeks after the attack on Oliver, Hancock condemned it. He wanted to create further distance from it, claiming it wasn't done by his fellow townspeople. The second mob had violated the careful orchestration of group violence in eighteenth-century America, which allowed people to protest government policies they disagreed with. When the group got their way, as they had when Oliver resigned, they were to stop their disorder.

Hancock wanted people to oppose the Stamp Act but loathed the unnecessary violence against Hutchinson, with good reason. A mob indiscriminately targeting a man of privilege like Hutchinson could easily turn on him, the wealthiest man in Boston. As a result, Hancock worked hard to earn the trust of the lower orders, which paid dividends a few years later when he got in trouble with the customs board.

4. "I do not stand at any price, let it be good, I like a Rich Wine."— John Hancock to partners in London, July 23, 1765[4.]

As an affluent man, John Hancock could afford a luxury that most could not: madeira, a fortified wine made on the North Atlantic island of the same name. He was exacting when placing this particular order, specifying several times in the same letter that he wanted the highest quality. It had a steep price tag because it was imported and subject to higher taxes, but cost was not an issue for Hancock—except when it came to paying taxes on the wine. Hancock's desire to avoid them led to one of the most memorable mobs of the American Revolution.

In May 1768, one of Hancock's ships docked in Boston, and the captain claimed to customs commissioners that there were twenty-five casks of madeira on board. The ship could hold at least double that, but the bureaucrats accepted the suspiciously low number. Other officials were sure that Hancock had smuggled in more madeira, so a month later, they used a technicality to seize *Liberty*, one of Hancock's ships, and its cargo, branding the vessel with the king's mark and tying it to a British warship.

Over the previous few years, Hancock had courted the favor of men from the lower orders with alcohol-filled hospitality, and those efforts were rewarded when *Liberty* was taken. A mob gathered at the waterfront, savagely attacked the customs officials, and then dragged one of their pleasure boats out of the harbor, hauled it through town, and

---

4. John Hancock to Hill, Lamar, and Bissett, July 23, 1765, Hancock Letterbook (business), HFP, BLSC; G. G. Wolkins, "The Seizure of John Hancock's Sloop 'Liberty,'" *MHS-P* 55 (Boston, 1923): 240.

dropped it on Boston Common, the town's public park. There, they set it on fire. This stunning event solidified Hancock's reputation as an influential town leader, inspiring all orders of men while enraging crown officials.

5. "I am almost prevail'd on to think my letters to my Aunt & you are not read, for I cannot obtain a reply, I have ask'd [a] million questions & not an answer to one . . . I Really Take it extreme unkind . . . I want long Letters."—John Hancock to Dorothy Quincy, June 10, 1775[5.]

Hancock pleaded with his fiancée, Dorothy "Dolly" Quincy, to write him letters, but she never seemed to care much for Hancock, even after they were married. Her epistolary neglect was especially difficult for a man prone to feeling loss acutely. When Hancock was seven years old, his father died suddenly, and despite being adopted by his wealthy uncle and aunt, he searched for connection and love throughout his life.

He didn't only nag his wife; he frequently chided friends and loved ones about not writing to him. He sent gifts, promised warm receptions, told them about his life in letters, and asked many questions about theirs. He expended a great deal of energy to gain people's affection, with mixed success. He was popular and beloved in Massachusetts with the masses, but it was not enough. He wanted to feel he belonged with those closest to him.

6. "I am Glad, as it will afford you some Relaxation from Business w[ch] is absolutely necessary for the preservation of Health that best of Blessings."—John Hancock to George Hayley, February 21, 1769[6.]

Hancock's business partner in London, George Hayley, hired an employee and Hancock hoped it might help Hayley step away from his business and relax. Hancock had experienced firsthand the toll stress can take on one's health. Throughout his life, Hancock's body failed him when matters were demanding or particularly serious. He was rarely physically well and often suffered from painful fits of gout, which swelled his legs and hands and sometimes prevented him from walking or holding a quill.

Political pressure made this condition worse, and, unfortunately for his delicate disposition, there were plenty of times in the United States in the 1770s and 1780s to feel uncertainty and anxiety. Both supporters and critics accused Hancock of using his poor health to avoid messy

5. John Hancock to Dorothy Quincy, June 10, 1775, *Letters of Delegates to Congress, 1774–1789*, ed. Paul H. Smith, *et al.*, vol. 1 (Washington, DC: Library of Congress, 1976), 472.
6. John Hancock to George Hayley, February 21, 1769, Hancock Letterbook (business), HFP, BLSC.

political fights, which seemed to be true at times. His body did not handle contention well, and he ultimately died young, at fifty-seven, a body sacrificed to the turmoil of the late eighteenth century.

7. "I am persuaded you will join with me in the sentiment that this unhappy occurrence cannot be considered as a certain mark of the indisposition to good order & government."—John Hancock to the General Council, October 18, 1787[7.]

Hancock's political moderation calmed his home state after an uprising in 1786 and 1787. Farmers in western Massachusetts had forcibly closed courts in protest of the state's devastating taxes and to prevent debtors from being imprisoned. Governor James Bowdoin assembled an extralegal body of men to crush what had become known as Shays's Rebellion and then took extraordinary measures to punish the participants, including suspending their voting rights and sentencing many to death. In the 1787 Massachusetts gubernatorial election, Bowdoin became the first incumbent governor of the state to be voted out of office, and Hancock was elected by an overwhelming margin of three to one.

For most of his political life, Hancock had sought a moderate path, which was exactly what the state needed at the time. He pardoned almost all of the rebels and worked to restore peace and trust among inhabitants of the countryside. He told his legislature that the rebellion should not brand the participants as being forever incapable of living under the new government. The state was fragile—having only adopted its constitution in 1780—and Hancock's temperance provided stability. Thereafter, voters rewarded him with the governorship every year until he died in 1793.

8. "We must all rise or fall together."—John Hancock to the US Constitution Ratification Convention of Massachusetts, February 6, 1788[8.]

7. John Hancock Speech, October 18, 1787, Paul D. Brandes, *John Hancock's Life and Speeches: A Personalized Vision of the American Revolution, 1763–1793* (Lanham, MD: The Scarecrow Press, Inc., 1996), 301; Woody Holton, *Unruly Americans and the Origins of the Constitution* (New York: Hill and Wang, 2007), 76; Leonard L. Richards, *Shays's Rebellion: The American Revolution's Final Battle* (Philadelphia: University of Pennsylvania Press, 2002), 119.
8. John Hancock Speech, February 6, 1788, Brandes, *John Hancock's Life*, 328; Pauline Maier, *Ratification: The People Debate the Constitution, 1787–1788* (New York: Simon & Schuster, 2010), 166; "From George Washington to James Madison, 5 February 1788," founders.archives.gov/documents/Washington/04-06-02-0074; "From George Washington to Benjamin Lincoln, 31 January 1788," founders.archives.gov/documents/Washington/04-06-02-0059.

In 1788, Hancock was governor of Massachusetts and president of the state's constitutional convention when he proclaimed these words in one of the most important speeches of his life. The proposed national constitution had been sent to the states for ratification, and as the Massachusetts convention began, five states had already approved it. The new government framework was more than halfway to securing the necessary votes for approval.

While Americans think of the Constitution as an inevitable part of the country's fabric today, it faced considerable pushback from states concerned about an overreaching federal government. Massachusetts was considered a swing state for ratification. Because of its strong revolutionary credentials, other states might be inclined to follow its lead. New Hampshire was waiting to see which way their neighbor went, and George Washington was worried their decision could also sway Virginia and New York.

Hancock himself was skeptical about the new Constitution, and as the most powerful political figure in Massachusetts, he would no doubt influence others. Just before the vote was taken, Hancock gave a speech supporting the Constitution but asked everyone to recognize that it was a divided issue. As such, no one should rejoice that half of the population would be disappointed with the outcome. He hoped everyone would be conciliatory and eventually unite together. This was a sentiment rarely heard from leaders during such a contentious time, and it showed Hancock's power. The Constitution narrowly passed in Massachusetts.

9. "In short no Person could possibly be more Notic'd than myself."— John Hancock to Dorothy Quincy, May 7, 1775[9.]

On his way to Philadelphia for the Second Continental Congress, Hancock traveled with delegates from Massachusetts and Connecticut who were greeted on the roads and enthusiastically cheered by well-wishers. In one instance, a crowd offered to act as horses and pull Hancock's carriage for the final stretch into town. Hancock was thrilled and proudly wrote to his wife about the attention that the delegation received. He also declared that he was the most noticed of all.

Rivals frequently charged Hancock with vanity, a claim historians often repeat today. It is true that Hancock loved attention and appreciation. It was a deep need of his to have both. But even the dour Adams cousins, John and Samuel, who accompanied Hancock, noticed

9. John Hancock to Dorothy Quincy, May 7, 1775, HFP, Massachusetts Historical Society.

the flattering reception during their trip. The Massachusetts delegates' reputations as leaders of the resistance had preceded them, and it set up their future influence in the Second Continental Congress.

10. "The important Consequences to the American States from this Declaration of Independence, considered as the Ground & Foundation of a future Government, will naturally suggest the Propriety of proclaiming it in such a Manner, that the People may be universally informed of it."—John Hancock to Certain States, July 6, 1776[10.]

In the months leading up to July 1776, Hancock had been reluctant to separate from the British Empire. He and his uncle had made a sizeable fortune under crown rule, and he and other wealthy delegates questioned whether the colonies would really be better off on their own. The Massachusetts delegation of John and Samuel Adams and Elbridge Gerry, however, had been pushing for independence and eventually rallied enough delegates to support it, including many moderates. As president of the Second Continental Congress, Hancock went along and authorized it with his confident signature.

He wrote to "certain states" and enclosed the Declaration of Independence, asking that its recipients spread the word. Notably, he acknowledged that the document might be the basis of a future government—presciently recognizing that the words hold an enduring promise for Americans. The Declaration's assurance that all men are created equal was unfulfilled for many for centuries, but the ideal forms a foundation Americans still look to—and demand—today.

10. John Hancock to Certain States, July 6, 1776, *Letters of Delegates to Congress, May 16, 1776 to August 15, 1776*, ed. Paul H. Smith, *et al.*, vol. 4 (Washington, DC: Library of Congress, 1979), 396; Jack Rakove, *Revolutionaries: A New History of the Invention of America* (Boston: Houghton Mifflin Harcourt, 2009), 73-75.

# Charles Lee's First Inklings of Fractious American Political Battles

**GENE PROCKNOW**

Unique among the Continental Army generals, Charles Lee expressed prescient insights into the upcoming political issues dividing Americans during the Early Republic era. Born and educated in England, Lee espoused pre-Revolution British Whig views seeking to moderate the monarchy's powers and engender a more representative government. As a recent immigrant, Lee brought his radical republican ideas to America and fought for them in the American Rebellion. However, Lee's controversial military command decisions and attempts to supplant George Washington greatly overshadowed his fervent advocacy for expanded democracy. Additionally, historians emphasize Lee's quarrelsome military leadership and attack on Washington; a closer look at Lee's writings reveals keen insights into the coming highly contentious Early Republic era electoral battles. In the late eighteenth and early nineteenth centuries, two partisan factions would clash over issues raised by Lee in 1779, including the creation of political parties, the establishment of a standing army, political rights, suffrage, and the role of the president. Lee's anti-Washington and republican political philosophies would re-emerge publicly during the 1800 presidential election campaign.

After Maj. Gen. Charles Lee's 1778 court-martial conviction for insubordination and unauthorized actions during the Battle of Monmouth, the suspended general engaged in a concerted public relations campaign to regain his military stature at the expense of Gen. George Washington. As part of this self-promotion effort, Lee convinced William Goddard, a friend and editor of the *Maryland Journal* (Baltimore), to anonymously publish a series of twenty-five pointed questions making his case that the court-martial verdict was biased and a miscarriage of justice.[1] Initially, the publication of Lee's queries generated a firestorm of criticism, and violent mobs forced Goddard to retract them publicly.[2] A few days later, after receiving legal and Maryland governmental support, Goddard retracted the retraction.[3] While the initial public reaction was violently adverse, the first nine queries later commanded more respect from the American public.

The initial nine queries examined Congressional policies and actions, raising vexing issues to be resolved many years later. Demonstrating Lee's command of political theory and British history, he started his queries by invoking the actions of King George I, the first Hanoverian King of Great Britain and Ireland.

> Whether George the First did not, on his accession to the Throne of Great-Britain, by making himself King of a Party, instead of a whole nation, sow the seeds not only of the subversion of the liberties of the People, but of the ruin of the whole empire?
>
> Whether, by proscribing the class of men to which his Ministry were pleased to give the appellation of Tories, he did not, in the end, make them not only real Tories, but even Jacobites?

Lee contended that King George I made himself "king of a party," bestowing benefits on a small class of people and giving them the appellation of Tories.[4] Lee asserted that creating a favored party led to several pernicious effects, including diminished parliamentary powers and a loss of liberty, which "overturned the mighty fabric of the British Empire."[5] Lee further stated that Congress was following the first Hanoverian monarch's example by creating favored and unfavored groups that would engender party politics.

In query three, Lee warned against the "enormous additional weight and pecuniary influence of a large standing army."

> Whether the consequence of this distinction, now become real, was not two rebellions—and whether the fruit of those rebellions, although

---

1. Anonymous and Charles Lee, "Some Queries, Political and Military, Humbly Offered to the Consideration of the Public," *Maryland Journal*, July 6, 1779. Also reproduced in Charles Lee, *The Lee Papers*, ed. Henry Edward Bunbury, 4 vols. (New York: New York Historical Society, 1872), 3:341-45.

2. William Goddard, "A True Copy of an Acknowledgement most nobly exhorted by a Band of Ruffians," *Maryland Journal*, July 27, 1779.

3. Goddard published the retraction of the retraction in the *Maryland Journal* on July 20, 1779. For a description of the controversy resulting from the publication of Lee's twenty-five queries, see Ward L. Miner, *William Goddard - Newspaperman* (Durham, NH: Duke University Press, 1962), 168–74.

4. Anonymous and Lee, "Some Queries," 1.

5. Ibid., 1.

defeated, were not septennial Parliaments, a large standing army, an enormous additional weight and pecuniary influence through into the seal of the Crown, which in a few years have born down not only the substance, but almost the form of liberty, all sense of patriotism, the morals of the people, and, in the end, overturned the might fabric of the British Empire?

Revolutionary War historians have well-documented the military strategy dispute in which Washington sought a large, professional Continental Army equipped and trained to fight massed European-style open terrain battles. Lee favored a smaller central army supplemented by the highly motivated militia to lure the British away from port cities and defeat them through many small actions. While Washington's military strategy won the day (and the war), the existence and role of a standing army became a highly contested political issue in the Early Republic.[6]

In query four, Lee alleged that Congress was following the example of the "pernicious" British ministry "by proscribing and disenfranchising so large a proportion of citizens as those men whom they find it their interest to brand with the denomination of Tories."[7]

> Whether the present men in power in the State do not tread exactly in the steps of this pernicious Ministry, by proscribing and disenfranchising so large a proportion of citizens as those men whom they find it in their interest to brand with the denomination of Tories?

Lee believed that treating a particular group differently from others was an abuse of power and led to quarrelsome class conflict. He particularly called out the government of Pennsylvania for disenfranchising individuals for political and tyrannical reasons. The aggressive Rebel Pennsylvania government arrested and exiled prominent Quaker leaders who refused to swear an oath of allegiance to the Rebel government.[8]

In queries five and six, Lee offered his most egalitarian and democratic assertions.

---

6. Two excellent examples of military strategy disputes are Jonathan Gregory Rossie, *The Politics of Command in the American Revolution* (Syracuse, NY: Syracuse University Press, 1975) and Stephen R. Taaffe, *Washington's Revolutionary War Generals* (Norman: University of Oklahoma Press, 2019).

7. Anonymous and Lee, "Some Queries," 1.

8. For an overview of the treatment of Quakers and others by the Pennsylvania Revolutionaries see Aaron Sullivan, *The Disaffected: Britain's Occupation of Philadelphia during the American Revolution* (Philadelphia: University of Pennsylvania Press, 2019), 23–44.

Whether liberty, to be durable, should not be constructed on as broad basis as possible?—and whether the same causes, in all ages, and in all countries, do not produce the same effects?

Whether it is not natural, and even justifiable; for that class of people (let the pretext be ever so plausible) who have been stripped of their rights as men, by the hard hand of power, to wish for and endeavor to bring about, by any means whatever, a revolution in that State, which they cannot but consider as an usurpation and tyranny?

He rhetorically asked, "Whether liberty, to be durable, should not be constructed on as broad basis as possible?"[9] In this question, Lee pointed to the startling contradiction between the words of the Declaration of Independence, "All men are created equal," and actual suffrage rights. During the American Revolution, all states had property and, in some cases, tax-paying restrictions on men eligible to vote and hold office. As a result, a tiny minority of citizens cast votes in the first ten presidential elections. Universal white male suffrage emerged after the Civil War, and female and Native American voting would only occur in the early twentieth century.[10] While Lee posited his question broadly, he likely was not advocating extending the franchise to women and non-white men. As evidence of his gender and racial views, he owned enslaved people and never brought women into the political sphere.

In query seven, Lee posited the Rebel retribution policy against Loyalists as an anathema to liberty and a just society.

Whether a subject of Morocco is not (when we consider human nature) a happier mortal than a disenfranchised citizen of Pennsylvania, as the former has the comfort of seeing all about him in the same predicament with himself; the latter, the misery of being a slave in the specious bosom of liberty—the former drinks the cup, but the latter alone can taste the bitterness of it?

To illustrate his point, Lee argued that a subject of Morocco was happier than a disenfranchised Pennsylvanian as all in Morocco knew that society treated them poorly but equally. The unequally treated Pennsylvanian knew that he was subservient to others similarly situated.

Further, query eight offered a politically charged contention that many contemporary readers viewed as an attack on a friendly ally. He

---

9. Anonymous and Lee, "Some Queries," 1.

10. For a detailed table of suffrage rules and changes by state, see Stanley L. Engerman and Kenneth L. Sokoloff, "The Evolution of Suffrage Institutions in the New World," *The Journal of Economic History* 65, no. 4 (2005): 898.

analogized the juxtaposition of a Russian serf and a member of the French Parliament to the treatment by Congress of those who disagreed with its pronouncements.

> Whether an enlightened member of a French Parliament is not a thousand times more wretched than Russian cirf [*sic*] or peasant—as to the former, the chains, from his sensibility, must be extremely galling; and on the latter, the fit as easy as the skin of his back?

Lee posited that a French member of parliament was "a thousand times more wretched than a Russian cirf [sic] or peasant" as the chains "fit as easy on the skin of his back."[11] Lee pointed out that peasants were often resigned to their fate with low expectations, while more politically privileged people felt more profound injustice when unfairly treated.

In the last of Charles Lee's nine political queries, he aimed directly at the wisdom of granting broad powers to Washington. Lee asserted that it was hazardous to "inculcate and encourage in the people an idea that their welfare, safety, and glory depend upon one man."

> Whether it is salutary or dangerous, consistent with, or abhorrent from the principles and spirit of Liberty and Republicanism, to inculcate and encourage in the people an idea, that their welfare, safety, and glory depend on one man: Whether they really do depend upon one man?

Lee argued that the Rebels possessed too much faith in Washington, which was dangerous as Lee regarded Washington as a flawed general and an ineffectual military commander.

Demonstrating his keen political instincts, Charles Lee's republican and liberty-seeking political views, as expressed in Goddard's publication, re-emerged in the highly energized partisan environment of the new republic almost a generation after his death. In the first nine queries, Lee raised four hotly contested issues in the Early Republic era—the creation of political parties, the establishment of a standing army, political rights and suffrage, and presidential powers.

In queries one and two, Lee forewarned the creation of political parties, a development that emerged in the 1790s. Ironically, at the end of his second presidential term, Washington would also warn the nation about the ill effects of political parties, stating, "the common and continual mischiefs of the spirit of party are sufficient to make it the interest and duty of a wise people to discourage and restrain it." Invoking

---

11. Anonymous and Lee, "Some Queries," 1.

comparable sentiments, Lee and Washington similarly concluded that governmental-favored parties lead to the "ruin of the whole empire" and the "ruin of Public Liberty," respectively.[12]

As expressed in query three, Lee's opposition to a standing American Army became a highly disputed issue between the Federalists and the Democratic-Republicans. Under President Washington, Congress initially created a tiny professional army to defeat the Native Americans. However, at the turn of the nineteenth century, the establishment and size of a Federal army became a hotly contested political question. In 1798, the threat of war with France engendered the Federalist Congress and President John Adams to authorize an increase in the army's size to ten thousand soldiers. The Democratic-Republicans and Thomas Jefferson opposed war with France and the massive Federal Army expansion. Newly-elected President Thomas Jefferson sought to reverse the military enlargement. Jefferson wrote to Congress in his first annual message, "Nor is it conceived needful or safe that a standing army should be kept up, in time of peace."[13] Jefferson's views became the prevailing public opinion. During his first term, he significantly reduced the army's size to three regiments (one artillery and two infantry).[14] Consistent with Jefferson's policies and Charles Lee's admonitions, Americans would remain wary of large, peacetime armies for the next hundred and fifty years.

As prognosticated in queries four through eight, politically motivated disenfranchisement re-emerged as an issue between Federalists and Jefferson's Democratic-Republicans. The Federalists sought to limit suffrage and disproportionately exclude the opposition to maintain their slipping grip on power. In 1798, the Federalist Congress and President John Adams enacted four Alien and Sedition Acts.[15] The Alien Friends Act extended the naturalization period from five to fourteen years, depriving the Jeffersonians of likely voters. Additionally, under the Sedition Act, the Federalists could prosecute the Demo-

12. Farewell Address, September 19, 1796," founders.archives.gov/documents/Washington/05-20-02-0440-0002.

13. Fair Copy, First Annual Message, [by November 27, 1801]," founders.archives.gov/documents/Jefferson/01-35-02-0497-0014.

14. "An Act fixing the Military Peace Establishment of the United States, 16 March 1802" reprinted in Robert K. Wright and Morris J. MacGregor, Jr., *Soldier-Statesmen of the Constitution* (Washington, DC: Center of Military History, US Army, 1987), 251–52.

15. "Alien and Sedition Acts (1798)," Government, *US Archives - Milestone Documents* (blog), November 30, 2022, www.archives.gov/milestone-documents/alien-and-sedition-acts#transcript.

cratic-Republicans for espousing competing political beliefs.[16] Issues over expanding and restricting suffrage exploded during the Civil War and in the early twentieth century and continue to vex the American electorate.

As raised by Lee in query nine, the issue of how much power to bestow on the president would fester throughout the Federalist/Anti-Federalist Constitutional ratification debates and during the following Federalist/Democratic-Republican political contests. Many Democratic-Republicans believed that George Washington and John Adams sought to re-create a monarchical presidency. First, Senate adversaries opposed Vice President Adams's purported desire for a presidential title akin to a European king. As a result of Adams' suggested royalty-sounding presidential titles, legislators mockingly referred to Adams as "his rotundity."[17] More seriously, the Democratic-Republicans widely alleged that Washington and Adams sought to amass monarchial powers within the presidency. Federalist opponents cited Washington's predilection for social levees, birthday celebrations, and a hereditary Society of the Cincinnati as evidence of steps towards creating an American royalty. Eventually, Americans became comfortable with Washington's presidency as he demonstrated respect for Congress's prerogatives and power and twice resigned from commanding positions.

Although Charles Lee did not live to see America's constitution, his reputation and ideas returned to public discourse. During the run-up to the hotly contested presidential election of 1800, Democratic-Republican-leaning newspaper editors reprinted articles extolling Charles Lee's virtues as a proxy for attacking Washington and the Federalists. A widely reprinted article throughout Northern and Western states characterized Lee as "well-remembered among us ... besides his military qualities, he was a man of education, taste, and experience in the world." The article continued by quoting a 1776 Lee correspondence with Patrick Henry objecting to using Washington's wartime title "His Excellency." Sarcastically, Lee concluded, "If, therefore, I should sometimes address a letter to you without His Excellency tacked, you must not esteem it a mark of personal or official disrespect, but the reverse."[18] By invoking the Lee narrative, the Jeffersonians could attack iconic Washington indirectly.

---

16. Ibid.

17. "Philadelphia," *Aurora General Advertiser*, November 7, 1797.

18. Reprinted in New York City, Philadelphia and Connecticut, Virginia, and Massachusetts newspapers, including "General Lee," *Western Telegraphe and Washington Advertiser*, November 25, 1797.

A farcical anecdote attributed to Lee circulated in Democratic-Republican-leaning newspapers in another veiled attack in the same period. The concocted story recounted a discussion between Frederick II (the Great) and Lee in which Lee predicted that people "will dispense with the service of MONARCHS," and Frederick purportedly responded, "I am a royalist by profession and am determined to live by my trade."[19] Perceptive readers would conclude that Frederick II was a stand-in for John Adams and Thomas Jefferson averred Charles Lee's opinions.[20] Lee's citations circulated widely in the Early Republic period. Political writers continued to invoke Lee's writings and beliefs into the antebellum period to make political points for broad expressions of liberty and equality.[21]

Lee's republican and democratic views, as expressed in the first nine queries, have been overlooked by recent historians who focus on the remaining sixteen self-serving queries that stress purported deficiencies in Washington's generalship. These other sixteen queries highlight the long-simmering Lee-Washington power tussle focusing on Lee's criticisms of Washington, including the commander-in-chief's mistakes (by not abandoning Fort Washington), poor battle leadership (the overly complex Germantown battle plan), a penchant for blaming others for his failures (Maj. Gen. John Sullivan at Brandywine), and misrepresenting the facts (Lee's battlefield performance at Monmouth).[22]

Dismissing Charles Lee as merely a rude, insubordinate, self-serving military officer who inappropriately sought to displace George Washington as commander-in-chief overweights one dimension of his Revolutionary War participation. While interpersonal and behavioral issues limited his fitness for supreme command, Lee possessed excellent po-

---

19. Reprinted in at least eight newspapers, including "Anecdote," *Albany Chronicle*, October 16, 1797.

20. Charles Lee reported in an April 3, 1765 letter to his sister, Sidney Lee, that he discussed the American situation with Frederick II. However, Lee does not reveal any specifics nor anything reported in the 1797 newspaper reports. Charles Lee, *The Lee Papers*, ed. Henry Edward Bunbury (New York: New York Historical Society, 1872), 1:37-39.

21. Three newspaper articles represent the types of Lee citations in the Antebellum press. His supporters periodically republished the proceedings to demonstrate the unfairness of Lee's court-martial conviction (See *Daily National Intelligencer*, Washington, DC, November 12, 1823). Others republished Lee's correspondence with famous politicians (see "Letter from Edmund Burke to Lee" reprinted in the *Albany Gazette*, July 7, 1803). Finally, newspapers published flattering accounts of Charles Lee's life (for example, *Independent Inquirer*, Brattleboro, VT, January 18, 1834).

22. For example, John Richard Alden, *General Charles Lee Traitor or Patriot?* (Baton Rouge: Louisiana State University Press, 1951), 279–82.

litical theory acumen and genuinely unwavering republican beliefs. As demonstrated by his nine queries, Lee offered unusually perceptive prognostications of the coming partisan issues of democracy, citizenship, and individual rights. As an outsider, Lee offered a de Tocqueville-like lens to describe the emerging American political environment. Neglecting his outside-in perspectives and unwavering radically democratic philosophies oversimplifies his character, contributions, and political influence on America's Founding Era.

# William Walker Crossed the Ferry

❦ MICHAEL J. F. SHEEHAN ❦

On the second day of 1780, Capt. Silas Burbank of the 12th Massachusetts Regiment sat down to record a deposition from William Walker, a private soldier in the 2nd Massachusetts Regiment. Walker wasn't sure if he was in trouble, but after losing £2,561 worth of clothing destined for the Continental Army wintering in Morristown, he certainly had to explain himself.

Walker had been in the army for three years, enlisting in January 1777 for the duration of the war. As he left no pension application and only late-war muster rolls remain that record his name, it is difficult to determine what he did from 1777 to 1780, but the tale he told Captain Burbank would certainly rank among his most unique wartime experiences.

Walker left Fishkill Depot on Christmas Day 1779, taking "one two horse Sleigh for General Greene QMG [Quartermaster General] to carry to Morris Town" clothing for the troops. He was to travel south to Verplanck Point "and to go the route of Kings Ferry between the hours of nine & Ten oClock in the forenoon." Walker loaded the "Baggage, Sleigh and Horses in the Boat to cross the River, where Liuet. Grant ordered" them to take their goods out again, to instead load the boat with oxen. Frustrated, Walker obeyed orders "when the Boatmen turned everything on Shore [and] I was obliged to wait until evening when Mr. Grant then ordered me to cross the River."

The crossing went routinely enough until they neared the Stony Point side of the ferry, when "a body of Ice came down the river against the Boat." The ferryman "jumped on shore in order to save the Boat," but Walker "was obliged to save my own life and Horses." He jumped or was knocked into the icy Hudson River, "driving with the ice near to my arm pitts and jumped the Horses out of the Boat by which means I saved my own life and my Horses but also my Sleigh & Harness and

Baggage went off in the Boat which we could not save and further saith not."[1]

Just like that, Walker, through no fault of his own, lost all the baggage intended for Morristown. He made it back to Fishkill a few days later where he delivered his deposition. What exactly was lost among the baggage? Before Walker left Fishkill on Christmas Day, Lt. Col. Udny Hay, the Deputy Quartermaster General, had an invoice drawn up. The baggage included:

| | £ | S | d |
|---|---|---|---|
| 1 Ps [Piece] Green Broad Cloth Containing | | | |
| 26 yds at 32£ pr yd | 832 | | |
| 1 Ps Claret do [ditto] Containing | | | |
| 32 ¼ yards at 32£ pr yd | 1032 | | |
| 1 Ps Mixt do Containing | | | |
| 18 ½ yds at 32£ pr yd | 592 | | |
| 3 ¾ do French Thread at 12£ pr do | 45 | | |
| 2 do Colored do at 20 pr do | 40 | | |
| 11 oz White do at do do | 13 | 25 | |
| 10 oz Twist at 10£ do | 6 | 5 | |
| | 2561 | 0 | 0 |

Walker gave his mark (as he was likely illiterate) and affirmed he would deliver the clothing to General Greene. As we know, it drifted down the Hudson, and we don't know that it was ever recovered.[2]

Lt. Col. Hay enclosed the receipt and Walker's account in a letter to General Greene on January 3, 1780, noting that "the misfortune that happened in its transportation across at Kings Ferry as will appear by the enclosed affidavit is as far as I can yet totally owing to the accident, a more accurate enquiry how ever shall be made." Days later, Hay wrote back to Greene after receiving some of Greene's letter written the week before. Hay had told Greene "some days ago of the misfortune which attended the cloathing . . . in its passage across Kings Ferry."

Luckily for Walker, Hay was unable to "find it was in any degree owing to negligence or design." William Walker was off the hook. Hay continued that he "had several complaints from Kings Ferry lately,

1. Return of Burr's Company, 2nd Massachusetts Regiment, September 9, 1778, fold3.com/image/17240186; Deposition of William Walker, January 2, 1780, Papers of the Continental Congress: Letters from Nathaniel Greene, with Various Papers Relating to the Quartermaster's Department, 1778-1780, fold3.com/image/352034. Hereafter noted as PCC (Papers of the Continental Congress). The author was unable to identify Lieutenant Grant.
2. Invoice of Clothing forwarded by Udny Hay DQMG to the Honorable M. General Greene QMG, December 25, 1779, PCC, fold3.com/image/352036.

many of them I am afraid to be well grounded, the ferrymen there are without doubt a sett of as great banditte as ever existed." He explained this behavior as "for want of better men we were under the necessity of enticing them again to reinlist and for that purpose allow them many liberties which at any other time would by no means have been granted."

William Walker returned to duty as a waggoner out of Fishkill, a job he maintained consistently without joining his regiment through the rest of 1780 and as least as late as April 1781, where muster records for him end. Hopefully, the rest of Walker's deliveries were more routine.[3]

3. Udny Hay to Nathaniel Greene, January 3, 1780, PCC, fold3.com/image/352031; Udny Hay to Nathaniel Greene, January 9, 1780, PCC, fold3.com/image/352041. The author was unable to determine what unit was operating King's Ferry during Walker's episode, nor whether they were Continental, state levies, or militia units. William Walker January-June 1780 Muster Roll, fold3.com/image/1724023; William Walker April 1781 Muster Roll, fold3.com/image/17240214.

# Emily Geiger's Fabulous Ride

❀❧ C. LEON HARRIS, HARRIET IMREY,
CONNER RUNYAN ❧❀

Fabulous: *adj.* 1) wonderful; 2) existing only in fable. Emily Geiger is celebrated in numerous books and articles, memorialized on monuments, and portrayed in videos.[1] Her fame rests on the story that as a teenager she volunteered to carry a message from Gen. Nathanael Greene to Gen. Thomas Sumter in South Carolina when no man would dare to do so. As the story goes, Miss Geiger was stopped by enemy scouts who put her in a room and sent for an older woman to search her, and while waiting, she ate the message, the contents of which Greene had told her. Her mission undetected, she completed her journey and recited the contents of the message to Sumter.

Over time the tale acquired layers of conflicting ornamentation, mainly from writers who valued style over accuracy, but also from some serious historians. Benson J. Lossing, respected author and illustrator of *Pictorial Field Book of the Revolution*, gave the above account of Emily Geiger's ride in that work published in 1859.[2] In 1881, however, he gave a different version that he claimed was told to him in 1849 by a Mrs. Buxton. In that version not one, but two women searched Emily Geiger—Mrs. Buxton as a young girl, and her mother.[3] Lyman C.

---

1. For examples see "Emily Geiger: a set of source documents," sciway3.net/clark/revolutionarywar/geigeroutline.html.

2. Benson J. Lossing, *Pictorial Field Book of the Revolution*, vol. 2 (New York: Harper Brothers, 1859), 488-489.

3. Benson J. Lossing, "Fair Messenger," *Harper's Young People: An Illustrated Weekly* II no. 86 (June 21, 1881), 530-531. Lossing stated that he "lodged at the house of a planter not far from Vance's Ferry, on the Santee, where I passed the evening with an intelligent and venerable woman (Mrs. Buxton)." In the version in *Pictorial Field Book of the Revolution*, Lossing stated that he "passed the night at Mr. Avinger's," and he did not mention Mrs. Buxton. We have not found a Mrs. Buxton in census or other records. Also missing is a man surnamed Simons, who Mrs. Buxton said was a grandson of Emily Geiger living a few miles away.

Draper, author of *Kings Mountain and Its Heroes*, was informed by sixty-six-year-old "Maj. Theodore Starke" of Columbia, South Carolina, that Emily Geiger did not ride alone, but was accompanied by his aunt, Rebecca Starke, then about seventeen years old. "The girls [were] put in a room, & women sent for to search them. The girls at once opened & read the letter, so as to know its contents, tore in two, each agreeing to eat one half of it. Emily soon made way with her portion; the other failed—when Emily, the good hearted, & frank Dutch girl, exclaimed, 'Blast your dainty stomach, Rebecca Starke; give it to me, & I'll eat it,' & did so."[4]

The story of Emily Geiger would be much different if the accounts attributed to Buxton or Starke had been better known, but it happened that a version by Elizabeth F. Ellet published in 1848 in *The Women of the American Revolution* became the most popular.[5] As others have noted, Ellet enclosed her account of Emily Geiger's exploit in quotation marks and stated that it had previously "appeared in several of the journals." After much searching we found that Ellet quoted a version by Judge William Dobein James printed first in the Charleston *Mercury* on July 21, 1824, and subsequently reprinted in other newspapers.[6] Unfortunately Judge James did not name his sources. As a youth James had served with Francis Marion, but he did not mention Geiger's ride in his *Sketch of the Life of Brig. Gen. Francis Marion* published in 1821. By 1824 he had written a biography of Sumter that was never published,[7] and he may have heard about Geiger while researching that book.

Judge James began his account as follows:

> At the time General Greene retreated before Lord Rawdon from Ninety-Six, when he had passed Broad River he was very desirous to send an order to Gen. Sumter who was on the Wateree, to join him, that they might attack Rawdon, who had now divided his force.

---

4. Notes by Lyman C. Draper on information from "Maj. Theodore Starke," Draper Manuscript Collection, Wisconsin Historical Society, Thomas Sumter Papers, 11VV525, copy provided by the Southern Revolutionary War Institute, McCelvey Center, York SC. Transcribed at sciway3.net/clark/revolutionarywar/draper.html. "Maj. Theodore Starke" was more likely Mayor Theodore Stark (1805-1882), who was mayor of Columbia from 1866 until July 1868. localhistory.richlandlibrary.com/digital/collection/p16817coll10/id/13/. "Dutch" generally meant German, but the Geiger's were German-speaking Swiss.
5. Elizabeth F. Ellet, *The Women of the American Revolution*, vol. 2 (New York: Baker and Scribner, 1848), 295-297.
6. We have been unable to find a copy of the original article from the Charleston *Mercury*. The version quoted here is from The Raleigh, North Carolina *Register*, August 10, 1824.
7. Charleston *Mercury*, July 3, 1824, page 2. We do not know if the manuscript of James's biography of Sumter survives.

This passage by James is accurate, except that Greene's original plan was to attack Fort Granby near Friday's Ferry on Congaree River before Lt. Col. Francis, Lord Rawdon arrived there. On June 19, 1781, the approach of Rawdon had forced Greene to lift his siege of Ninety Six. Greene retreated northeast with Rawdon in pursuit until June 24, when Rawdon turned back to Ninety Six. Greene continued across Broad River, and on June 25 he decided to attack the British post at Fort Granby. He sent letters to Sumter and Marion urging them to join him near Friday's Ferry for the planned attack.[8] Apparently anticipating Greene's plan, Rawdon marched from Ninety Six to Fort Granby, arriving in the evening of July 1. In the following two days Greene marched toward his objective, stopping at Winnsboro on July 3 and 4, as shown on the accompanying map. At the same time, Sumter marched eastward across Catawba River, then southward toward Camden on Wateree River to check on the manufacturing of arms for his troops, arriving there on July 5. Thus according to James's account, it would have been on July 4 or 5 that Greene needed to send a message to Sumter on Wateree River.

James continued his account by stating that Greene "could find *no man* in that part of the State who was bold enough to undertake so *dangerous* a mission." Here the story of Emily Geiger's ride begins to fall apart. Greene had already ordered Sumter to join him in the letter dated June 25, ten days before Sumter arrived on the Wateree River. Greene and Sumter exchanged several other letters on the subject before, during, and after Emily Geiger supposedly made her perilous ride, and all the letters appear to have reached their recipients within a day of being sent. On July 2 Sumter wrote to Greene that he intended to join him. On July 3 Greene wrote two letters to Sumter, one stating that Sumter's "letter of yesterday overtook me on the march for the Congaree," and the other stating that he had been informed that Rawdon arrived at Friday's Ferry at about 11 PM on July 1. Both letters reached Sumter by the following day, as Sumter acknowledged in a letter to Greene written "near the Hanging Rock" on July 4. On July 6 Sumter wrote to Greene that he had arrived at Camden on the previous day, and that he would proceed a short distance and await further orders. There is no mention in this letter of anyone having conveyed a message orally to him from Greene. On July 7 Greene wrote to Sumter informing him that Rawdon was leaving Fort Granby, and on the next

8. Nathanael Greene to Thomas Sumter and Greene to Francis Marion, June 25, 1781, in Dennis M. Conrad, ed. *The Papers of Nathanael Greene* vol. 8 (Chapel Hill: University of North Carolina, 1995), 457-458.

day Sumter acknowledged receipt of that letter.[9] Sumter was then at Russell's Ferry on Congaree River, and on the following day he, as well as Marion, finally joined Greene. In the meantime Rawdon had gone to Orangeburg about thirty miles south of Fort Granby, where he remained until at least July 16.

It is apparent that the premise of Emily Geiger's ride is baseless. We are not the first to observe that Greene did not need Emily Geiger to send a message to Sumter. Almost a century ago Alexander Samuel Salley, Jr. (1871-1961), secretary of the South Carolina Historical Commission, commented on it in a scathing article that opened with, "Some of the absurdities that are offered in support of spurious history would be amusing if so many people did not take them seriously."[10]

Judge James's account continues as follows:

> The country to be passed through for many miles was full of blood-thirsty tories, who on every occasion that offered imbrued their hands in the blood of the whigs. At length Emily Geiger presented herself to General Greene, and proposed to act as his messenger; and the General, both surprised and delighted, closed with her proposal. He accordingly wrote a letter and delivered it, and at the same time communicated the contents of it verbally, to be told to Sumter in case of accidents. Emily was young, but as to her person or adventures on the way, we have no further information except that she was mounted on horseback upon a side-saddle, and on the second day of her journey she was intercepted by Lord Rawdon's scouts.

This passage should have raised questions. Did Greene know Emily Geiger well enough to trust that she was not a Tory spy who would warn the defenders of Fort Granby of the planned attack? If Greene knew she was a true Patriot, would he really have been so callous as to expose her to "blood-thirsty tories, who on every occasion that offered imbrued their hands in the blood of the whigs?" The last clause in the passage quoted above tells us that Geiger's journey occurred over a period of at least two days and brought her within reach of Rawdon's scouts. The shortest route between Greene and Sumter (highlighted on the map) would have taken her no closer than twenty miles from Rawdon's base at Fort Granby. It is unlikely that Rawdon would have had scouts that far distant, pinned between the two armies of Greene and Sumter.

---

9. *Papers of Nathanael Greene* 8:482-486, 493, 503, 504, 511.
10. A. S. Salley, Jr., "Grave of Emily Geiger: Myth Worshipers' Mecca," *The State* (Columbia, South Carolina), November 6, 1927.

Dr. W. T. Brooker, after "patient and untiring research extending over a period of several months" but without citing evidence, proposed a route that would have brought Geiger within range of Rawdon's scouts.[11] He asserted that Emily first crossed Saluda River at Lorick's Ferry about thirty-five miles southwest of Winnsboro, then went eastward toward Fort Granby another thirty-five miles distant. Along the way, according to Brooker, she was "accosted by three British troopers and learned for the first time that Rawdon had passed down the river on the south side the night before." Rawdon had in fact arrived on the evening of July 1, but as seen above, Greene knew that already and should have warned Geiger to stay away.

James's account continues:

> Coming from the direction of Greene's army, and not being able to tell an untruth *without blushing*, Emily was suspected and confined to a room; and as the officer in command had the modesty not to search her at the time, he sent for an old tory matron as more fitting for that purpose. Emily not wanting in expedient, and as soon as the door was closed and the bustle a little subsided, she *ate up the letter* piece by piece. After a while the matron arrived, and upon searching carefully nothing was to be found of a suspicious nature about the prisoner, and she would disclose nothing. Suspicion being thus allayed, the officer commanding the scouts suffered Emily to depart for where she said she was bound.

According to Brooker, the Tory woman who conducted the search was named Hogabook, and she was assisted by her daughter (Lossing's Mrs. Buxton?). According to James, after being searched, Geiger

> took a route somewhat circuitous to avoid further detention, and soon after struck into the road to Sumter's camp, where she arrived in safety. Emily told her adventure and delivered Greene's verbal message to Sumter.

According to Brooker, Geiger's route was indeed somewhat circuitous: she proceeded thirty miles southeast to cross Congaree River at McCord's Ferry the following morning, then rode another thirty miles northward to cross Wateree River, and at last recited the message to Sumter at Camden on the afternoon of July 4. A total of 130 miles in three days, in the July heat of South Carolina! We single out Brooker's story simply to illustrate the lengths to which defenders of the story have gone in attempting to reconcile its incongruities.

---

11. W.T. Brooker, "Emily Geiger's Ride," Orangeburg *Times and Democrat*, December 18, 1913, 6.

According to James, in consequence of Emily Geiger's ride, Sumter "soon after joined the main army at Orangeburg." In fact, of course, the message would have been about Fort Granby, since Greene did not know that Rawdon had left for Orangeburg until July 7.[12] James concluded his account as follows:

> Emily Geiger afterwards married Mr. Threrwits [sic: Threewits], a rich planter on the Congaree. She has been dead thirty five years; but it is trusted her name will descend to posterity among those of the patriotic females of the Revolution.

Often cited as proof of Emily Geiger's existence is an invitation to her wedding to John Threewits on October 18, 1789. The original invitation is said to have been kept in a box with other relics, including "the set of jewels presented by General Greene to Emily on her wedding morning."[13] Greene must have regarded her highly to have gone to such expense and trouble after being dead three years. If, as Judge James stated, Emily Geiger had been dead thirty-five years at the time he wrote about her, then she would also have been dead at the time of her wedding. Another encumbrance to the marriage would have been that John Threewits already had a wife.[14]

In addition to John Threewits, his brother Lewelling and another man have been proposed as Emily Geiger's husband. "I will have to indict Emily for bigamy yet," Salley sarcastically joked.[15] Lewelling Threewits did, in fact, marry a Geiger, but her name was Ann Mary (Anna Maria).[16] It is possible that Judge James got the name wrong, or

12. Greene eventually decided not to attack because Rawdon was too well defended at Orangeburg.

13. "Relics of Emily Geiger," sciway3.net/clark/revolutionarywar/geiger21.html.

14. A deed in Fairfield County, South Carolina Deed Book I, 165, dated June 25, 1782, indicates that John Threewits was married to Mary Thomas. Fairfield County SC Deed Records 1789-1797, image 418, www.familysearch.org. She was still the wife of John Threewits as late as February 27, 1802, as shown by a deed in Edgefield County SC Deed Book 22, 282-285. Edgefield County SC Deed Records 1802-1803, image 339, www.familysearch.org.

15. "Insists 'Emily Geiger's grave' is invention by myth builders," *The State*, November 20, 1827, 10. Lyman C. Draper was told by Jacob and Abram Geiger of Lexington District that Emily Geiger married Lewelling Threewits. Sumter Papers 11VV529. "Lewelling" is the spelling given by his brother, John Threewits, and Lewelling Threewits signed his name as Lew'g Threewiits in the audited account for his Revolutionary War services. revwarapps.org/sc3039.pdf.

16. Charleston County SC Deed Book Z-5, 352, September 27, 1787. Charleston, Charleston County SC Land Records 1787-1788, image 586, www.familysearch.org. Anna Mary Geiger apparently died soon after signing the deed, because Lewelling Threewits and his second wife, Eleanor Fitzpatrick, had a son, Llewellen Williamson Threewits, who reached legal age shortly before January 8, 1810 (thus born in 1788).

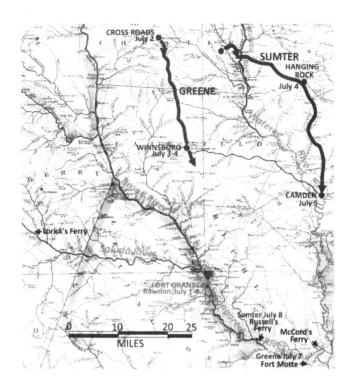

Emily may have been a nickname for Ann Mary Geiger, but we have found no evidence for that. In any case, even if Ann Mary Geiger was Emily Geiger, it would not change the fact that the ride attributed to Emily Geiger was unnecessary and unsupported by any evidence.

Emily Geiger could simply have gestated in Judge William Dobein James's mind at a time when it may have been in a precarious state. Two years after publishing his account of her, Judge James was accused of "habitual intoxication and drunkennness ... *daily, openly* and *publicly*, and thereby hath often rendered himself from indisposition of body and imbecility of mind ... unfit for understanding and correct decision of cases brought on for trial before him.[17] In 1827 he was impeached and removed from the bench.

Judge James did get one thing right: in spite of the lack of evidence, Emily Geiger's name has descended to posterity among patriotic females of the Revolution. Emily Geiger's fabulous ride might best be viewed as symbolic of the actual services performed by numerous unnamed women in the American cause.

17. "Proceedings of the General Assembly of South Carolina in the Matter of the Impeachment of Judge William Dobein James, November-December, 1827, and January, 1828," page 6, dc.statelibrary.sc.gov/handle/10827/20769.

# "Earned by Veteran Intrepidity": Spencer's Ordinary, June 26, 1781

#### ❦ CONOR ROBISON ❦

Captain Johann Ewald had much to thank the Almighty for.[1] Five years' service in America had endowed him with the "confidence . . . a partisan needs for his ticklish trade" even in the face of an Virginia bullet that nearly took his leg. Three months recovery left him without a limp, strong enough to return to his beloved Jägers who trudged through the summer heat with "pieces of cowhide around their feet in place of shoes," a grim reality his men endured with laughter. "How the German soldier," Ewald marveled "makes the best of everything."[2]

Now, taking post near a crossroads on the road to Williamsburg, the weary captain longed only to sleep. But no sooner had he closed his eyes than gunfire erupted to his left front. Springing upward, Ewald demanded to know the source of it. Hushed back to sleep by assurances that it needn't worry him, Ewald closed his eyes once again only to rise as the volume of fire intensified. Rousing his Jägers, Ewald rode with two men into a nearby orchard and stumbled upon a startled blue-coated Frenchmen of Armand's Legion, who reported the Americans to be "Very near, sir!" Confirmation came as no more then "three hundred paces away, just on the point of moving forward," a battle line ma-

---

1. Johann Ewald, *Diary of the American War. A Hessian Journal*, trans. Joseph P. Tustin (New Haven: Yale University Press, 1979), 289-291. In the action at Scott's Creek on March 19, 1781, Ewald was "wounded in the knee" and feared that "the bone and large tendon must have been injured." Ibid., 290. Ten days later he rejoiced after having been able to sleep for the first time in over a week after pus was drained from his wound. "Up to now," he reported "I ran the risk of losing my leg, since the upper part of the bone . . . was damaged, and the main tendon of the large muscle in the knee hung only by a thread." Ibid., 294. His patience paid off, enabling him to lead his Jägers to their destiny at Yorktown.
2. Ibid., 303.

terialized.[3] The Marquis de Lafayette's advance guard was before him in force, readying to sweep Ewald and his men from the crossroads of Spencer's Ordinary, Virginia. What followed this day, June 26, 1781, gave the Hessian even more reasons to count his blessings.

MOVEMENT TO CONTACT, JUNE 1781

This clash of arms in the morning dawn came unexpectedly to the country round Virginia's ancient capital. The high summer of 1781 saw Gen. Charles, Earl Cornwallis's army withdrawing down the peninsula towards Williamsburg. His enemy's retrograde movements after so many weeks of advancing left Lafayette justifiably perplexed about Cornwallis's intentions. "In this country," he complained to Alexander Hamilton, "there is no getting good intelligences," a problem which plagued him well into June. Caution guided his movement, even after a brigade of Pennsylvania Continentals under Brig. Gen. Anthony Wayne arrived in the middle of the month to bolster his numbers. "Lord Cornwallis has not, as yet, explained himself clearly enough," the twenty-three-year-old Lafayette confessed on June 25, "to determine upon his immediate objectives."[4]

Guessing Williamsburg as Cornwallis's destination, Lafayette turned to Wayne to head the advance against him, recommending—on June 22—the formation of an advanced corps under Col. Richard Butler's command.[5] The Dublin born Butler was to be the spear in Wayne's hand. Second in prestige only to Wayne himself among the warrior sons of Pennsylvania, Butler had helped Daniel Morgan forge the feared riflemen of Saratoga and carried the leftward column over the palisades at Stony Point. To contemporaries Butler remained an "officer of superior talent" from his first commissioning in 1776 to the day he left his bones on the banks of the Wabash.[6] So it was that he

---

3. Ibid., 308.

4. Marquis de Lafayette to Alexander Hamilton, May 23, 1781, founders.archives.gov/documents/Hamilton/01-02-02-1175; Charles Cornwallis to Henry Clinton, May 26, 1781, *Correspondence of Charles, First Marquis Cornwallis*, ed. Charles Ross (London: John Murray, 1859), 1:100-101.

5. Lafayette to Anthony Wayne, June 21, 1781, *Lafayette in the Age of the American Revolution. Selected Letters and Papers, 1776-1790. Volume IV, April 1, 1781-December 23, 1781*, ed. Stanley J. Idzerda (Ithaca: Cornell University Press, 1981), 206-207; Richard Butler to William Irvine, July 8, 1781, *in The Pennsylvania Archives. Fifth Series, Volume III*, ed. Thomas Lynch Montgomery (Harrisburg: Harrisburg Publishing Company, 1906), 5.

6. On Richard Butler see: Simon Gratz, "Biography of General Richard Butler," *The Pennsylvania Magazine of History and Biography. Volume VII* (Philadelphia: The Historical Society of Pennsylvania, 1883), 7-10; Anthony Wayne to George Washington, February 27, 1781, in Charles J. Stille, *Major General Anthony Wayne and the Pennsylvania Line in the*

wrote, "on the 24th I was sent out with a small Advanc'd light Corps, to try to strike the British rear." About forty-eight hours later, a sleep deprived Butler finally caught up with the enemy.[7]

SIMCOE'S DETACHMENT, JUNE 24-26, 1781

That enemy found itself detached from the main army, ordered out by Cornwallis the same day Butler began his march, to scour the banks of the Chickahominy river and torch any rebel foundries and boats they found lurking in the vicinity. Neutralizing these assets walked hand in hand with the herding of cattle from local farms to Williamsburg for the nourishment of Cornwallis's army. For the task the Earl turned to two officers, old friends who had made themselves masters of partisan warfare.[8]

Command of the detachment fell on the shoulders of the twenty-nine-year-old lieutenant colonel of the Queen's Rangers: John Graves Simcoe. An officer of the regular army at the war's outset, Simcoe grew into the rough and tumble role of a partisan commander whilst maintaining the gentlemanly decorum instilled within him by the masters of Eton and Oxford. "A man of letters," one American adversary noted, "enterprising, resolute, and persevering"; a commander who carefully planned his missions, and when in the field seized "upon every advantage which offered in the course of execution." He assumed command of the Queen's Rangers in the fall of 1777 and set about grafting them to his will. Raised by the famed Robert Rogers, these loyalists in arms bore upon their backs distinctive green jackets and boasted eleven companies, replete with grenadiers and light infantry on the flanks, and a cadre of highlanders bedecked in bonnets with a piper to play them pibrochs around the campfire.[9] Under Simcoe's hand they added a mounted element for greater tactical mobility, a crucial asset in the war of outposts upon which they were frequently engaged and infused them with a tactical doctrine that favored an aggressive "use of the bayonet."[10]

---

*Continental Army* (Philadelphia: J. B. Lippencott, 1893), 262; Alexander Garden, *Anecdotes of the American Revolution, Illustrative of the Talents and Virtues of the Heroes and Patriots, who Acted the Most Conspicuous Parts Therein* (Charleston: E. Miller, 1828), 2:72.

7. Butler to Irvine, July 8, 1781. *Pennsylvania Archives*, 5.

8. John Graves Simcoe, *Simcoe's Military Journal. A History of the Operations of a Partisan Corps, called the Queen's Rangers, commanded by Lieut. Col. J. G. Simcoe, during the War of the American Revolution* (New York: Bartlett & Welford, 1844), 225. Ewald, *Diary*, 306. Both Ewald and Simcoe's units had been acting as Cornwallis's left rear since June 22; Tarleton's legion formed the same service on the right, his flank inclined towards the Pamunkey River. Banastre Tarleton, *A History of the Campaigns of 1780 and 1781, in the Southern Provinces of North America* (1787; reis., New York: New York Times, 1968), 308.

9. Simcoe, *Military Journal*, 19-21.

10. Ibid., 21.

Simcoe's companion was a one-eyed captain of a company of Hessian Jägers whose first taste of combat in America was almost his last. Captain Johann Ewald had "wished for nothing more then to get to know the enemy" and within twenty-four hours of first setting foot on American soil he met them. Courting ruin by stumbling with a single company into several American battalions, the captain quickly wised up to the ways of this new war. His Jägers were literal hunters, rifle-armed woodsmen renowned for their accuracy and individualism, who donned green coats and marched to war with the blast of the hunting horn ringing in their ears.[11]

The offensive minded Simcoe worked well with Ewald whose own dictums on partisan warfare stressed that if a commander "be forced . . . to give battle . . . one must not hesitate for long but speedily make one's dispositions and attack" the enemy "with saber in hand and bayonet mounted even if the enemy be twice as strong;" for "he who attacks first," Ewald reasoned, "has the victory already half in his hands," and fortune—the soldier's friend—"is usually on the side of the most decisive and courageous."[12]

Courageous and decisive—two attributes most needed now. As Cornwallis hastened towards Williamsburg, Simcoe's command hovered along the banks of the Chickahominy, finding "little . . . to destroy," but plenty of cattle. Disappointed, Simcoe soon had greater worries. The bridge spanning Diascund Creek, a tributary of the river, was no more. Rebuilding it would be a time-consuming process with the exact whereabouts of the Americans unknown. Like Lafayette, Cornwallis's "general intelligence," Simcoe "knew to be very bad."[13] Still, Cornwallis promised his subordinate that should he come to trouble the army would decamp from Williamsburg in full array, to pounce on their pursuers.

11. Rodney Atwood, *The Hessians* (Cambridge, MA: Harvard University Press, 1980), 45; Ewald, *Diary*, 56. See note 170 on page 388 for further information on the Jäger hunting horns. Throughout the war, however, casualties would reduce the quality of Ewald's personnel. As early as November 1777 he was to write that reinforcements for the Jagers "consisted partly of deserters from all nations, partly of ruined officers and nobleman, students . . . bankrupts, merchants, and . . . adventurers." Ewald. *Diary*, 105. These would have to be molded through hard experience on the firing line.

12. Simcoe, *Military Journal*, 21; Johann Ewald, *Treatise on Partisan Warfare*, trans. Robert A. Selig and David Curtis Skraggs (Westport: Greenwood Press, 1991), 79-80. Ewald and Simcoe and their units had often operated together, so that a brotherly bond had developed between the Rangers and Jägers by the summer of 1781. That bond was further strengthened by their stand at Spencer's Ordinary.

13. Simcoe, *Military Journal*, 226.

Crossing the creek after some hasty repairs, Simcoe consolidated his command and reordered the line of march. Ewald pressed on to the crossroads at Spencer's Ordinary with his Jägers and the flank companies of the Rangers. The main body followed under the command of Maj. Richard Armstrong—"a very good man and nothing more," as Ewald described him, while the cattle herders pressed their burdens forward, hurried on by the ever-vigilant Simcoe who held the rear with his cavalry and highlanders.[14]

The British came at last to the crossroads of Spencer's Ordinary around 7 o'clock on the morning of June 26, 1781. Fifteen hours earlier, Wayne had decided to cast Butler's spearhead against those very same crossroads, informing Lafayette that "Colo. Butler will advance to the fork of the road leading to James Town and Williamsburg, as the only chance of falling in with this Cattle Drove. I shall advance to support him."[15] The die, it seemed, was now cast.

THE SKIRMISH BEGINS

Spencer's Ordinary was a quaint tavern nestled upon an open expanse of ground abutting the angle forged by the divergence of the highway from Norell's Mills, Virginia. Dense woods cloaked the high ground north of the tavern before spilling in scattered clumps eastward either side of the divergent road surging eastward towards Williamsburg and the beckoning safety of Cornwallis's army some six miles away. Upon this thoroughfare Ewald and Armstrong's infantry companies "camped in platoons ... breakfasted, and rested." Surveying the open ground to their front, Simcoe dubbed it "an admirable place for the chicanery of action."[16] The main road carried on southwestward towards Jamestown and the river James; to its left farms nestled amidst scattered hills where Simcoe allowed his horsemen to graze. The fences lining either side of the road were torn down, allowing greater access to the avenue should the need arise.[17] That need came when the Americans suddenly burst down the lane.

"After three days and night successive march," Butler remembered "I got up with Simcoe." His ad hoc command consisted of all elements of Lafayette's army: Pennsylvanians and Continental Light infantry, and veteran Virginia riflemen eager to meet the enemy "who were rob-

14. Ibid., 226-227; Ewald, *Diary*, 306-308.
15. Wayne to Lafayette, June 25, 1781, *Lafayette in the Age of the American Revolution*, 211.
16. Ewald, *Diary*, 308; Simcoe, *Military Journal*, 227.
17. Simcoe, *Military Journal*, 227-228.

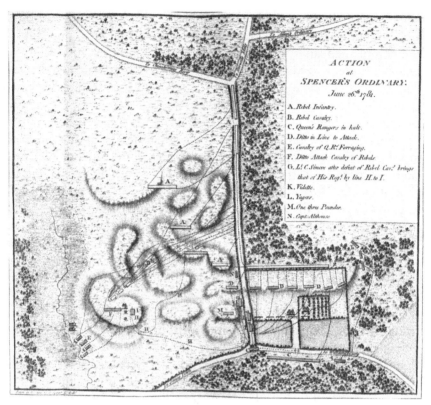

"Action at Spencer's ordinary : June 26th, 1781," "taken on the spot by G. Spencer Lt. Q. Rs." (*From* A Journal of the Operations of the Queen's Rangers *by John Graves Simcoe, 1787*)

bing the country of cattle."[18] Chasing them had been an exhausting and gruesome business, [19] and as the Americans feared that Simcoe was moving too fast for them, it was thought the British could only be brought to heel by Maj. William MacPherson's dragoons. These last

18. Benjamin Colvin Pension Statement, in J.T. McAllister, *Virginia Militia in the Revolutionary War* (Hot Springs, VA: McAllister Publishing Co., 1913), 108.

19. *Journal of Lieut. William Feltman, of the First Pennsylvania Regiment, 1781-1782* (Philadelphia: The Historical Society of Pennsylvania, 1853), 6. Thousands of blacks had attached themselves to Cornwallis's army, seeking refugee from bondage. Those who could not keep up with Simcoe were left behind. "A negro man with the small pox," a Pennsylvanian recalled, was left "lying on the side of the road." Others "in that condition starving and helpless" begged the Americans "to kill them." Simcoe's treatment of the infected may seem harsh, but smallpox could easily spread and ravage his humble command. Moreover, he had a mission to complete and with the enemy so near could not afford to be merciful towards those who slowed him down.

remnants of the mounted legions of Pulaski and Armand, "were not only in number entirely inadequate for reconoitring duty," one Virginian complained, and "were worn down by incessant fatigue." But they were all Butler had to hand. Strengthening their numbers by mounting some fifty continentals behind them, they went forward boldly.[20] And consequently, outstripped their infantry support, coming into action prematurely. Their sudden appearance was announced by an eruption of shots from the ranks of Simcoe's highlanders, standing sentinel amidst the trees bordering the roadside, with the sudden burst of Trumpeter Bernard Griffiths' trumpet adding to the tumult. Wheeling his mount around, Griffiths hurried to alert his mounted comrades, bellowing frantically for them to "Draw your swords, Rangers, the rebels are coming!"[21] Galvanized, the Rangers countercharged and burst among their enemies with a ferocity that shattered them. MacPherson was dismounted in the first instance and evaded capture only by hiding in a nearby swamp. Butler's infantry it seemed would now have to carry the day alone.[22]

The cavalry fight off to the left startled Ewald from his blankets. Jumping up, he hastened his men to arms before embarking upon the personal reconnaissance that nabbed him the equally startled French dragoon. Simcoe, meanwhile, riding furiously westward, arrived just in time to see his cavalry chasing MacPherson's troopers back up the road. Bringing them under his control, Simcoe dispatched what remained of the cattle down the road towards Williamsburg, simultaneously ensuring that a line of retreat toward Jamestown remained opened to him by deploying his one remaining cannon. To the east, holding the right wing of their paltry army, Ewald swung his three-company command into action at the battle's outset with dauntless skill. "While Ewald lives," Simcoe pronounced to those around him "the right flank will never be turned."[23] Such confidence was not misplaced.

20. John F. Mercer to Col. Simms, in *Fragments of Revolutionary History*, ed. Gaillard Hunt (Brooklyn: The Historical Printing Club, 1892), 36; Butler to Irvine, July 6, 1781, *Pennsylvania Archives*, 5; *Journal of Lieut. William Feltman*, 6.

21. Simcoe, *Military Journal*, 228.

22. Lafayette, probably on information received from Butler, claimed that MacPherson "overtook Simcoe, and regardless of numbers made an immediate charge." Lafayette to Tomas Nelson, June 28, 1781, *Lafayette in the Age of the American Revolution*, 217-218. American prisoners told Ewald after the fight of their firm belief that MacPherson's charge was "responsible for our misfortune. He had showed himself too early and been unhorsed by our cavalry." Ewald, *Diary*, 312.

23. Simcoe, *Military Journal*, 232.

By this time of the war, Capt. Johann Ewald had seen and done it all. In snow and heat he had marched and fought and won and lost and suffered wounds in a war the Landgrave deemed worthy of his service. Friends had fallen in bloody heaps before his eyes, generals had ridiculed his conduct and exulted him as amongst the bravest in the army, and through it all he had honed his art to a blinding sheen. Yet in this supreme moment he acknowledged the difficulties of remaining calm. "Thank God I did not lose my head," he remembered, as the enemy emerged in line of battle to his front. Sword in hand Ewald placed himself at the head of Simcoe's flankers, his own Jägers scurrying into the woods to the right in a bid to hammer the American flank just as their captain met it head on. The opening salvo from the Americans dropped "two-thirds of" the men about Ewald, but the survivors rushed on, following the Hessian "like obedient children" until "we came among them . . . hand to hand."[24]

The sudden rush from front and flank drove the Americans from the tree lined slope. It was but a momentary success. "Had we taken one backward step," Ewald knew, "the courage of the enemy would have redoubled while that of the soldiers on our side would have forsaken them." There was nothing left to do but press forward. Regrouping his companies, Ewald received reinforcements as Major Armstrong's Rangers came into action on his left, "advancing as fast as the ploughed fields they had to cross would admit," Simcoe noted proudly.[25]

With his left secured, Ewald probed deeper into the woods just as one of his Jägers "whispered softly in my ear that an entire column of the enemy was approaching" up a footpath. Of his own accord the bold captain went several paces ahead—and suddenly ran into the column. "I could not help myself" he remembered "and cried 'Fire! Fire!'," igniting a firefight that scorched the trees and riddled men's bodies.[26]

The burst of fire all along his infantry's line of battle impressed upon Simcoe the desperate situation his meager force was in. Eyes fixed upon the enemy to their front, Simcoe's infantry could not perceive the growing threat emerging down the roadside to their left. The Americans were once again pressing down the road, beyond Armstrong's leftmost company; survivors among the American officers engaged would later insist that the Rangers had "begun to give way" and that a decisive push

24. Ewald, *Diary*, 308-309.
25. Ibid., 312; Simcoe, *Military Journal*, 231.
26. Ewald, *Diary*, 309.

round the flank would seal the deal. That opportunity never came, for Simcoe's riders once again threw themselves into the fray, sabers in hand, crashing into the oncoming enemy, just as those in contact with Armstrong and Ewald's infantry broke contact.[27]

Simcoe did not waste the precious lull that settled over the field. Having fulfilled his original intention of "checking the enemies' advance till such times as the convoy was in security" Simcoe hastily gathered his wounded in Spencer's tavern and hurried down the road towards Williamsburg where within two miles they met Cornwallis's leading elements and returned to the field to collect their wounded. By day's end Cornwallis's army was secured within Williamsburg, feasting off the prime beef of Virginia.[28]

The skirmish at Spencer's Ordinary was a soldier's fight, brought about to the surprise of all. Both sides claimed victory. Butler himself boasted that he had given Simcoe "a handsome stroke, with little loss myself." But his recollection of the skirmish is unfortunately nowhere near as detailed as his adversaries, for the fatigue of the march and the subsequent action left him overcome with "a violent fever and diarrhea, which had like to take me off" had his constitution failed him.[29] Thus we know little enough of the decision making from the American side.

For Simcoe and Ewald however, the affair that day was far more memorable. Surprised though they had been, the pair had fought off ruin with levelheaded coolness and Spartan bravery, and with the intuitive understanding of each other's abilities and the capabilities of their men forged through a long operational partnership and personal friendship. Though out of personal contact for most of the action, Ewald and Simcoe were able to launch a relatively coordinated and aggressive counterattack that parried, retarded, and ultimately checked the American advance. Butler's ad hoc command, by comparison, though drawn from veteran elements had only come together as a combined force in the days immediately before the action, and though it went forward bravely, it did not possess the long-standing relationship of the Queen's Rangers and Hessian Jägers. In staving off disaster, Simcoe could justifiably claim Spencer's Ordinary as "an honorable victory earned by veteran intrepidity."[30]

27. Mercer to Simms, *Fragments*, 42-43; Simcoe, *Military Journal*, 232-233.

28. Ewald, *Diary*, 312.

29. Butler to Irvine, July 8, 1781, *Pennsylvania Archives*, 5.

30. Simcoe, *Military journal*, 234-235.

# The French Army in Williamsburg, Virginia, 1781–1782

## MICHAEL CECERE

For most of 1781, the inhabitants of Williamsburg lived in a constant state of anxiety. Already economically devastated by the loss of the state capital, which was moved to Richmond in April 1780, city residents lived under threat of British attack for most of 1781. The arrival of the infamous American traitor, Benedict Arnold, at the start of the year with a small British force prompted the first alarm. He threatened to march on Williamsburg, but failed to carry through and instead, sailed on to Richmond.

A brief British occupation of Williamsburg in April was followed in late June and early July by another occupation that lasted ten days and involved thousands of British and German troops. The anxiety continued after they left, when Gen. Charles Cornwallis moved his army from Portsmouth to Yorktown, just twelve miles from Williamsburg, in August and established a fortified post there.

The situation improved considerably for Williamsburg in early September when several thousand French troops under General St. Simon arrived in the city.[1] They were part of a French force from the Caribbean under Admiral de Grasse, and they were the first of thousands of French and American reinforcements destined for Williamsburg and ultimately Yorktown.

General Marquis de Lafayette, who commanded an American force in Virginia only half the size of the British under Cornwallis, led his

---

1. E. Lee Shepard, ed., *Marching to Victory: Capt. Benjamin Bartholomew's Diary of the Yorktown Campaign, May 1781 to March 1781* (Richmond: Virginia Historical Society, 2002), 21, and Stanley J. Idzerda, ed., "General LaFayette to the Chevalier de La Luzerne, September 8, 1781," *LaFayette in the Age of the American Revolution: Selected Letters and Papers, 1776-1790*, Vol. 4 (Ithaca and London: Cornell University Press, 1981), 391.

continentals and militia into Williamsburg on September 4, and just like that, the allied army of French and American troops in Williamsburg presented a formable challenge to General Cornwallis in Yorktown.

On September 8, Lafayette informed the Chevalier de La Luzerne, who was still aboard a French naval ship, that nearly 6,000 French and American troops were in and around Williamsburg.[2] Most were encamped on the outskirts of town. A grand camp was located about half a mile west and northwest of the Wren Building at the College of William and Mary and east of present day Matoaka Lake. The American camp was located on ground that is part of the college campus of William and Mary. Some of the French troops also encamped on part of today's campus, but the bulk of the French encamped north of the road to Richmond (Route 60) in what is now a mixed residential and commercial neighborhood.[3] It appears that Williamsburg was off limits to most of the troops. They spent an uneventful week waiting for Generals Washington and Rochambeau to arrive with reinforcements from the north.

The arrival of the American and French commanders ahead of their troops created a frenzy of excitement in Williamsburg. Lt. William Feltman with the Pennsylvania continentals noted that, "In the evening about four o' clock twenty-one pieces of cannon were fired on the arrival of his Excellency, General George Washington. There was a universal joy amongst our officers and soldiers, especially the French troops, on his arrival,"[4] Another officer, St. George Tucker, provided a more detailed account of the reaction to their arrival.

> About four o' clock in the afternoon [Washington's] approach was announced. He had passed our camp, which is now in the rear of the whole army, before we had time to parade the militia. The French line had just time to form. The Continentals had more leisure. He approached without any pomp or parade, attended only by a few horsemen and his own servants. The Count de Rochambeau and General [Edward] Hand, with one or two more officers were with him. I met him as I was endeavoring to get to camp from town, in order to parade the brigade; but he had already passed it. To my great surprise he rec-

2. Idzerda, ed., "General LaFayette to the Chevalier de La Luzerne, September 8, 1781," *LaFayette in the Age of the American Revolution*, 4:391.

3. *Armee de Rochambeau, 1782, Carte des environs de Williamsburg en Virginia ou les armees froncoise et americaine ont camps en Septembre 1781*, Library of Congress.

4. William Feltman, *The Journal of Lt. William Feltman, 1781-82*, (New York: New York Times & Arno Press, 1969), 13.

ognized my features and spoke to me immediately after. General Nelson, the Marquis, etc., rode up immediately after. Never was more joy painted in any countenance than theirs. The Marquis rode up with precipitation, clasped the General in his arms, and embraced him with an ardor not easily described. The whole army and all the town were presently in motion. The General, at the request of the Marquis de St. Simon, rode through the French lines. The troops paraded for the purpose and cut a most splendid figure. He then visited the Continental line. As he entered the camp the cannon from the Park of Artillery and from every brigade announced the happy event. His train by this time was much increased; and men, women and children seemed to via with each other in demonstrations of joy and eagerness to see their beloved countryman. His quarters are at Mr. Wythe's house. Aunt Betty [the wife of the late Peyton Randolph] has the honor of the Count de Rochambeau to lodge at her house. We are all alive and so sanguine in our hopes that nothing can be conceived more different than the countenances of the same men at this time and on the first of June. The troops which were to attend the General are coming down the bay. . ... Cornwallis may now tremble for his fate, for nothing but some extraordinary interposition of his guardian angels seems capable of saving him and the whole army from captivity.[5]

The first of the American and French troops from New York arrived at Burwell's Landing on September 22.[6] They continued to arrive over the next four days, some landing at Burwell's, others College Landing, and still others at Jamestown. They then marched into Williamsburg and encamped near the capitol on the east end of town.[7] Jean-Francois-Louis, Comte de Clermont-Crevecoeur, an artillery officer and French nobleman, recorded his impressions of Williamsburg in his journal.

> Williamsburg is situated on a charming plain between two creeks that flow into the James and York rivers. The town itself is not particularly pretty and consists of a single very long street at either end of which are very handsome buildings. . . . The streets are not paved and are very rough in both summer and winter.[8]

5. Lyon G. Tyler, "Col. St. George Tucker to his Wife, September 15, 1781," *Williamsburg, the Old Capital* (Richmond, VA: Whittet & Shepperson, 1907), 83-84.
6. Feltman, *The Journal of Lt. William Feltman, 1781-82*, 14, and Shepard, ed., *Marching to Victory*, 22.
7. Shepard, ed., *Marching to Victory*, 22.
8. Howard C. Rice and Anne S.K. Brown, trans. and eds., "Clermont-Crevecoeur Journal, September 26, 1781," *The American Campaigns of Rochambeau's Army, 1780-83*, Vol. 1 (Princeton, NJ and Providence, RI: Princeton University Press, Brown University Press, 1972), 56.

On September 27, General Washington repositioned the troops encamped west of Williamsburg; they marched through town and joined
the newly arrived northern troops camped near the capitol. Rations of
bread or flour and meat for four days were issued to all the American
troops. The allied march to Yorktown commenced the next day at 5
a.m.[9] To protect the supply magazines established in Williamsburg as
well as the city itself, Washington left nearly eight hundred troops behind. He explained to Admiral de Grasse, the French naval commander, that he could ill afford to lose the men for the siege, "but unless
this detachment is made, the Enemy might in the greatest security land
above Queen's Creek to cover his left flank, and by a very short march
effect the most destructive purposes."[10]

Over the next three weeks the allied army besieged the British at
Yorktown. Most of the allied sick and wounded were sent to Williamsburg, the French used the college as a hospital and the Americans used
the former Governor's Palace. On October 19, the British surrendered.
Most of the British and Hessian prisoners were marched to Winchester, Virginia. General Washington sent some of his troops to the Carolinas and led the rest north to New York, while Admiral de Grasse
returned to the Caribbean with his naval squadron. The French army
under General Rochambeau, however, stayed in Virginia for the winter.

THE FRENCH IN WILLIAMSBURG

General Rochambeau posted his French army in several locations in
Virginia. He left one regiment at Yorktown, posted another in Hampton, ordered a detachment of artillery to the small town of West Point
at the head of the York River, and ordered the remaining two French
regiments, with several companies of artillery, to Williamsburg.[11]
Rochambeau and his staff took up residence at George Wythe's home,
General Washington's former headquarters on Palace Green.[12]

To at least one French officer who recorded his experience in
Williamsburg, the city's inhabitants were thrilled to host the French
for the winter.

---

9. John C. Fitzpatrick, ed., "General Orders, September 27, 1781," *The Writings of George Washington*, Vol. 23 (U.S. Government Printing Office, 1937), 146-148.

10. Fitzpatrick, ed., "General Washington to Comte De Grasse, October 1, 1781," *The Writings of George Washington*, 23:160.

11. Rice and Brown, trans. and eds., "Journal of Jean-Baptiste-Antoine de Verger," *The American Campaigns of Rochambeau's Army*, 1:152.

12. "General Rochambeau to General Washington, December 24, 1781," *House History File, George Wythe House Historical Report*: Colonial Williamsburg Foundation Library Research Report Series 1484 (1938), 16-17.

One could not be more hospitable than are the inhabitants of Williamsburg to all the army officers; they receive them very cordially in their homes and do all in their power to provide entertainment for them . . . In this city, the fair sex, although they are not the prettiest I have seen, form a very agreeable and, in general, very well bred society.[13]

It is not difficult to understand why Williamsburg's residents embraced the French army in their city. The departure of the state government to Richmond eighteen months earlier, the city's economic engine, was a severe blow to Williamsburg's merchants and inhabitants. Months of disruption caused by two British occupations and the constant threat of another attack also brought economic hardship to the city in 1781.

The arrival of the American and French armies in the fall offered some relief to the commerce-starved city; the needs of thousands of troops and hundreds of draft animals had to be met. Although the paper currency offered by the Americans was nearly worthless, the French offered hard specie (coin) for payment. Their arrival and continued stay in Williamsburg was thus an economic blessing to many of the city's inhabitants.

Based on the journals of several French officers, the French were fascinated with both the natural wonders of Virginia as well as the character and custom of the people. One officer posted at West Point over the winter recorded candid observations of Virginians that likely described those in Williamsburg as well.

These people are very hospitable and receive you in a most cordial manner, but they are exceptionally lazy. The gentlemen, as well as those who claim to be but are not, live like lords. Like all Americans they are generally cold, but the women are warmer. They have the advantage of being much gayer by nature than the northern women, though not so pretty. They love pleasure and are passionately fond of dancing, in which they indulge in both summer and winter. When a gentleman goes out of his house—something he does rarely—he is always followed by a negro groom who rides behind him.[14]

13. Jane Carson, ed., "Diary Entry of Baron von Closen, November 24, 1781," *We Were There: Descriptions of Williamsburg, 1699-1859* (Charlottesville: The University Press of Virginia, 1965), 50.
14. Rice and Brown, eds., "Clermont-Crevecoeur Journal," *The American Campaigns of Rochambeau's Army*, 1:66.

Detailed description of Virginia's wildlife, plants, terrain, and climate, appear in many of the French journals. One officer noted that General Rochambeau, like General Washington, thoroughly enjoyed fox hunts and went several times a week whenever conditions allowed.[15] One can imagine that, given the propensity of Virginians to dance and entertain, the general and his officers also found plenty of opportunity to enjoy the favorite pastime of most Virginians.

Although both the French and their hosts in Williamsburg seemed satisfied with their stay in the city, their presence in Williamsburg was not incident free. On November 23, the residence of Reverend James Madison, the president of the college who had allowed the building to be used as a hospital for French soldiers, was damaged by fire. Rochambeau conveyed the news to General Washington in late December following yet another fire that destroyed the governor's palace.

> The Wing of the College where we Lodged our wounded officers had begun to be burnt down, we carried away all the sick, and all the furniture, but could only think about hindering the communication of the fire with the main building. Last night, the same accident happened to the Palace, in which was the American hospital, all the sick were saved as well as the greatest part of the effects, and we hindered the fire from communicating to the neighbouring houses, to mine [the Wythe House] especially; it is the one occupied by your Excellency, it was covered all the night long with a rain of red hot ashes. We have put all your sick in the Capitol, and today have had all which was possible for us to furnish them with. At Colonel Menzies's requisition I have ordered a guard to be set around it to prevent the same accident, and I have caused the precaution to be tripled [at] our hospital at the College.[16]

General Rochambeau agreed to pay £12,000 for the damage caused to the college building as well as the loss of a significant part of Reverend Madison's library and several pieces of physics equipment.[17] There was no French compensation for the governor's palace, which lay in ruins for years after the fire. That was the responsibility of the American government.

The French remained in Williamsburg and the surrounding posts through June 1782. Unaccustomed to Virginia's summer, many suffered

15. Rice and Brown, trans. and eds., "Journal of Jean-Baptiste-Antoine de Verger," *The American Campaigns of Rochambeau's Army*, 1:158.
16. "General Rochambeau to General Washington, December 24, 1781," *House History File, George Wythe House Historical Report*, 16-17.
17. Carson, ed., "Diary Entry of Baron von Closen, November 24, 1781," *We Were There*, 50.

through the heat and humidity. An officer posted in West Point observed in his journal that,

> We suffered greatly from the heat. The nights seemed even hotter than the days. We did not know where to turn. Added to this discomfort was an invasion of gnats, whose bite is far more venomous than those of Europe . . . During the summer it is impossible to go out of the house in the daytime. The houses are designed to stay cool, being built round a large hall or vestibule with a cross draft running through it. This serves as a sitting room during the day. In the evening you go out, but you do not stay long outdoors since the dampness of the night air is dangerous. The Americans stand the heat better than we do, or at least they are less sensitive to it.[18]

When orders to march back to New York were issued in late June 1782, they no doubt came as a relief to many of the French soldiers who wished to escape Virginia's searing summer. The bulk of the French army marched north on July 1. Their departure marked the end of an era for Williamsburg, which completed its transformation into a sleepy Virginia town. The city would, of course, rise from obscurity one hundred and fifty years later, much to the joy of history enthusiasts everywhere. But that is another story.

---

18. Rice and Brown, eds., "Clermont-Crevecoeur Journal," *The American Campaigns of Rochambeau's Army*, 1:71.

# Eutaw Springs and the Ambiguity of Victory

## ♦♦♦ DAVID PRICE ♦♦♦

The Battle of Eutaw Springs, South Carolina, on September 8, 1781 was the last major open-field battle of the Revolutionary War and per-haps its most savage. The close-quarter fighting that occurred there ranks among the bloodiest and most intensely contested military en-counters in young America's quest for independence.[1] It has, however, been eclipsed in historical memory by the climactic military event of the conflict—the siege at Yorktown, Virginia, and subsequent surrender of Maj. Gen. Charles, Earl Cornwallis's army that overshadowed the struggle in South Carolina.

OVERVIEW

Eutaw Springs Battleground Park, near today's Eutawville in Orange-burg County, was added to the National Register of Historic Places in 1970. The site is some fifty miles northwest of Charleston, which at the time of the battle had been occupied by British troops for well over a year. Here some 2,200 Americans—Continental regulars from Mary-land, Virginia, North Carolina, and Delaware; state troops from South Carolina; and militia from North and South Carolina; supported by two cavalry units and four cannon—under Maj. Gen. Nathanael Greene, a Rhode Island Quaker-turned-Patriot warrior, collided with the last of His Majesty's field armies operating south of Virginia. The latter comprised about two thousand British regulars and Loyalists under Lt. Col. Alexander Stewart—the 63rd and 64th Regiments of Foot; the 84th Regiment of Foot (Royal Highland Emigrants);

---

1. Theodore P. Savas and J. David Dameron, *A Guide to the Battles of the American Revolution* (Eldorado Hills, CA: Savas Beattie LLC, 2013), 329.

grenadiers and light infantry drawn from the 3rd, 19th, and 30th Regiments of Foot; Loyalist units from New York and New Jersey; a single cavalry unit; and five cannon.[2] The combatants were bathed in blistering heat during an engagement that lasted between three and four hours, one of the longest of the war, and over 1,400 were killed, wounded, captured, or missing—consuming about 40 percent of Stewart's army and a quarter of Greene's.[3]

Shortly before this encounter, Greene had written, "we must have victory or ruin, nor will I spare anything to obtain it."[4] As soon as it was over, each side professed to be the victor, and the question of who won has been a source of contention ever since.[5] A confluence of factors underlay Greene's decision to withdraw from the battlefield: his men's increasingly urgent thirst for water after their extended march preceding the action and several hours of fighting that carried the threat of heat stroke; and the need to reorganize his force in the wake of heavy losses to his officer corps, even as he intended to further challenge the enemy by attempting (unsuccessfully, as it would turn out) to cut off

2. Most historians maintain that the opposing armies in this battle were at about equal strength and that the number of soldiers on each side was between 1,800 and 2,400. See John Buchanan, *The Road to Charleston: Nathanael Greene and the American Revolution* (Charlottesville, VA: University of Virginia Press, 2019), 218. For a discussion of troop estimates on both sides at Eutaw Springs as suggested by various primary and secondary sources, see *The Papers of General Nathanael Greene*, ed. Dennis M. Conrad (Chapel Hill, NC: The University of North Carolina Press, 1997), 9:333n2.

3. "Eutaw Springs," American Battlefield Trust, www.battlefields.org/learn/revolutionary-war/battles/eutaw-springs. This site characterizes the result as a British victory and indicates total casualties of 1,461, including 882 British and Loyalists, and 579 Americans killed, wounded, and missing (including captured). By comparison, the losses reported by Greene and Stewart of 522 and 692, respectively, were quite conservative, especially the latter. See Robert M. Dunkerly and Irene B. Boland, *Eutaw Springs: The Final Battle of the American Revolution's Southern Campaign* (Columbia, SC: The University of South Carolina Press, 2017), 112-113. Captain Robert Kirkwood of the Delaware Continental Regiment reported 525 American casualties. See Robert Kirkwood, *The Journal and Order Book of Captain Robert Kirkwood of the Delaware Regiment of the Continental Line*, ed. Rev. Joseph Brown Turner (Wilmington, DE: The Historical Society of Delaware, 1910. Reprint: Sagwan Press, 2015), 24. To put these tallies in perspective, Robert Middlekauff notes the notorious unreliability of Revolutionary War casualty statistics, in *The Glorious Cause: The American Revolution, 1763-1789* (New York: Oxford University Press, 2005), 502. The Battle of Eutaw Springs was no exception, according to William Johnson in *Sketches of the Life and Correspondence of Nathanael Greene, Major General of the Armies of the United States in the War of the Revolution* (Charleston, SC: A.E. Miller, 1822), 236.

4. Nathanael Greene to Henry Lee, August 22, 1781, in *The Papers of General Nathanael Greene*, 9:223.

5. Dunkerly and Boland, *Eutaw Springs*, xi.

their anticipated retreat to Charleston.[6] Sergeant Major William Seymour of the Delaware Regiment echoed these concerns when he recounted that the rebel soldiers "were so far spent for want of water, and our Continental officers suffering much in the action, rendered it advisable for General Greene to draw off his troops, with the loss of two 6-pounders."[7] For the British, the battle arguably yielded a tactical success because they held the field, but it was a strategic setback. It sliced deeply into their limited troop presence in the Carolinas and failed to neutralize Greene's army or rally public support for the royal cause. The same could be said of Greene's earlier confrontations with the King's forces that year—at Guilford Courthouse (March 15), Ninety Six (June 19), and Hobkirk's Hill (April 25).[8]

THE COST

To General Greene, who had a horse shot from under him at Eutaw Springs, this was "the most obstinate fight" and "by far the hottest action I ever saw."[9] Col. Otho Holland Williams of Maryland, who commanded a brigade and was wounded in the battle, described "the field of battle" as being at one point "rich in the dreadful scenery which disfigures such a picture."[10] Capt. John Hughes of the South Carolina militia, a veteran of numerous engagements, avowed that "This was the severest action I was ever in."[11] Jim Capers, an enslaved drum major (who would be freed after the war) serving in the South Carolina Militia under Brig. Gen. Francis Marion (known to future generations as "the Swamp Fox"), "was wounded, in four different places, one on the head & two on the face with a sword and one on the left side with a ball."[12] The loss of American officers may have exceeded that in any

6. Christine R, Swager, *The Valiant Died: The Battle of Eutaw Springs, September 8, 1781* (Westminster, MD: Heritage Books, Inc., 2006), 115-118.

7. William Seymour, "A Journal of the Southern Expedition, 1780-1783," *The Pennsylvania Magazine of History and Biography*, 7:4 (1883): 386.

8. Matthew H. Spring, *With Zeal and with Bayonets Only: The British Army on Campaign in North America, 1775-1783* (Norman, OK: University of Oklahoma Press, 2008), 279.

9. Greene to George Washington, September 17, 1781. *Founders Online*, National Archives, founders.archives.gov/documents/Washington/99-01-02-06976.

10. Otho Holland Williams, "Battle of Eutaw," in R.W. Gibbes, ed., *Documentary History of the American Revolution . . . Chiefly in South Carolina* (Columbia, SC: Banner Steam-Power Press, 1853), 3:152.

11. Dunkerly and Boland, *Eutaw Springs*, 12.

12. Pension Application of Jim Capers, R1669, transcribed and annotated by C. Leon Harris, posted on Southern Campaigns Revolutionary War Pension Statements & Rosters, http://revwarapps.org/r1669.pdf. See also Jim Piecuch, "Francis Marion at the Battle Of Eutaw Springs," in *Journal of the American Revolution*, June 4, 2013, allthingsliberty.com/2013/06/francis-marion-at-the-battle-of-eutaw-springs/.

other engagement of the war, with sixty out of one hundred killed, wounded, or captured,[13] while Colonel Stewart reported seventy casualties among his officers.[14] Lt. Hector Maclean, with the 84th Foot, wrote of his first battlefield experience that day: "Were I a veteran I would venture to say never was battle fought with a more strenuous, a more laboured obstinacy, but as this was my first it might with propriety be answered I only thought so having never seen any other."[15]

WHO WON?

After this slugfest, the civil war raging between Loyalists and Whigs in the South continued into the following year, but the Patriot faction controlled the countryside and limited the redcoats' activity in the interior to raids for food and forage.[16] Throughout the Carolinas and Georgia, British authority was now limited to the major seaports of Charleston, Savannah, and Wilmington; the troops occupying them— who had entertained visions of crushing all resistance in this region just the year before—would evacuate all three ports by the end of 1782. According to Lt. Col. Henry "Light Horse Harry" Lee (father of Confederate general Robert E. Lee), who led the mixed cavalry and infantry of the 2nd Partisan Corps or Lee's Legion, "The battle of the Eutaws evidently broke the force and humbled the spirit of the royal army; never after that day did the enemy exhibit any symptom of that bold and hardy cast which had hitherto distinguished them."[17]

Be that as it may, we are told by one study of the battle that most historians credit the British with a win at Eutaw Springs.[18] Modern-day chroniclers have differed on this point. For example, one asserts that the results of this contest and the others fought by Greene as commander of the Southern Department of the Continental Army were decisively in favor of the Americans.[19] Another argues that this affair began and ended in utter confusion with both sides devastated by the

---

13. Theodore Thayer, *Nathanael Greene: Strategist of the American Revolution* (New York: Twayne Publishers, 1960), 380.

14. Alexander Stewart to Charles Cornwallis, September 9, 1781, in *Documentary History of the American Revolution*, 139.

15. Hector Maclean, September 12, 1781 (*Maclean of Lochbuie Muniment*. GD174/2154/7. Scottish Records Office, Edinburgh), in Dunkerly and Boland, *Eutaw Springs*, 78.

16. Buchanan, *The Road to Charleston*, 234.

17. Henry Lee, *Memoirs of the War in the Southern Department of the United States* (New York: University Publishing Company, 1870), 540.

18. Swager, *The Valiant Died*, 135.

19. Theodore Thayer, "Nathanael Greene: Revolutionary War Strategist," in George Athan Billias, ed., *George Washington's Generals* (New York: William Morrow and Company, 1964), 132.

magnitude of their losses, a large share of them officers, and that Greene won none of his battles in the Carolinas.[20] A third contends that a clearer example of a draw could not be had, as the rebels took several hundred prisoners and pushed their adversary back but did not break Stewart's army, which was too enfeebled to pursue its opponent and barely held its position.[21] Another simply terms the result of this and Greene's other battles indecisive.[22] And yet another tries to have it both ways, observing that Greene was denied a victory at Eutaw Springs that would have crowned his Southern campaign with the laurels he richly deserved, but then later claiming the Americans had clearly prevailed.[23]

Colonel Williams of Maryland argued that the "evidence [of victory] is altogether on the American side"; it regrouped after evacuating the field on the 8th, and the following day Greene dispatched Marion's and Lee's units in a fruitless pursuit of the retreating enemy. The latter "relinquished the country it commanded" and withdrew to Charleston Neck.[24] Still, Williams acknowledged that Greene's effort to score an unambiguous success was foiled by devastating fire from a formidable defensive position that the British established in a large, two-story brick house, whose owner remains unknown.[25]

## THE BRICK HOUSE

In a field to the west of Eutaw Springs stood the brick dwelling with its garden and a palisaded fence extending to Eutaw Creek, a tributary of the Santee River. (The creek was submerged under Lake Marion, the largest lake in South Carolina, when the Santee was dammed in the 1940s.) This sturdy building resisted small-arms fire and commanded an open field extending to the west, south, and east.[26] Once

20. Christopher Hibbert, *Redcoats and Rebels: The American Revolution through British Eyes* (New York: W.W. Norton & Company, 1990), 312-313.

21. Dunkerly and Boland, *Eutaw Springs*, xii.

22. Henry Steele Commager and Richard B. Morris, eds., *The Spirit of 'Seventy-Six: The Story of the American Revolution as Told by Participants* (New York: Harper & Row, Publishers, 1967), 1185.

23. Page Smith, *A New Age Now Begins: A People's History of the American Revolution* (New York: McGraw-Hill Book Company, 1976), 2:1691, 1825.

24. Otho Holland Williams, in *Documentary History of the American Revolution*, 3:157.

25. Dunkerly and Boland, *Eutaw Springs*, 28.

26. Otho Holland Williams, in *Documentary History of the American Revolution*, 3:147. For a discussion of geographic interpretation issues relating to the battlefield and adjacent roads at the time of the battle, see Stephen John Katzberg, "Mapping the Battle of Eutaw Springs: Modern GIS Solves a Historic Mystery," in *Journal of the American Revolution*, March 2, 2020, allthingsliberty.com/2020/03/mapping-the-battle-of-eutaw-springs-modern-gis-solves-a-historic-mystery/.

"Battle of Eutaw Springs," the Brick House, 1850. (*Anne S. K. Brown Military Collection, Brown University Library*)

barricading themselves inside, a Loyalist detachment—the New York Volunteers under Maj. Henry Sheridan—fusilladed any exposed rebels, taking particular advantage of the upper windows. According to Colonel Williams, "The enemy were defeated and obliged to retire to their camp, which had the advantage of a large brick house in which many of them found refuge from our fire and annoyed us from the windows, which circumstances alone saved them from a total rout, and in all probability, the whole of them from being made prisoners."[27] This improvised fortress played a role similar to the Chew Mansion at the Battle of Germantown in thwarting an attack.[28]

In many cases, the Americans taking fire from the house were officers who had advanced through the British camp where tents were still standing, even as most or all of their men hung back and sought refreshment from whatever temptations they could find in those tents or concealment therein from enemy volleys.[29] Colonel Williams reported that when the officers "proceeded beyond the encampment, they found

27. Otho Holland Williams to Elie Williams, September 11, 1781 (General Otho Holland Williams Papers, Baltimore: Maryland Historical Society), in Dunkerly and Boland, *Eutaw Springs*, xiv.
28. Smith, *A New Age Now Begins*, 2:1691.
29. Buchanan, *The Road to Charleston*, 229-230.

themselves nearly abandoned by their soldiers, and the sole marks for the party who now poured their fire from the windows of the house."[30] One of the soldiers there that day, James Magee, explained that "the British were driven beyond their baggage, when our men commenced rummaging their tents, drinking rum, etc., which the enemy discovering, came back upon us and drove us back into the woods."[31]

THE BLACKJACK

John Chaney, serving with a cavalry contingent composed of the 1st and 3rd Continental Light Dragoons under Lt. Col. William Washington (George's distant cousin), recalled the maelstrom of combat into which he plunged when the colonel was captured during a charge against the three hundred or so elite light infantry and grenadiers defending the British right flank under Maj. John Majoribanks (pronounced "marshbanks"). The latter were posted behind a thicket of blackjack (a dense formation of scrub oak) lining Eutaw Creek, which proved impenetrable to Washington's horsemen as well as to Col. Wade Hampton's cavalry from the South Carolina State Troops who joined the charge. "Washington jumped his horse into the midst of the enemy and was suddenly taken prisoner," as Chaney described it. "A British soldier appearing to be in the posture of attempting to stab Colonel Washington, one of his men rushed forward and cut him down at one blow." He continued, "Washington being a prisoner, and his men mingled in confusion with the enemy, and not knowing what else to do, this applicant with about twenty-five retreated and left the field." Chaney related that "Afterwards, they were joined by five of Washington's other soldiers, stating that they only escaped out of a great many who attempted to charge through the enemy's lines."[32] Few visual representations of this engagement have come down to us, and the one by the noted artist Don Troiani of a sword-wielding Colonel Washington leading his brave but futile charge is probably the most widely known modern-day image of the battle.[33]

Writing to Gov. John Rutledge of South Carolina on September 9, Greene referenced the twin obstacles of topography—the brick house

---

30. Otho Holland Williams, in *Documentary History of the American Revolution*, 3:154.

31. Pension Application of James Magee, S1555, http://revwarapps.org/s1555.pdf.

32. John Chaney, Military Pension Application Narrative, in John C. Dann, ed., *The Revolution Remembered: Eyewitness Accounts of the War for Independence* (Chicago: University of Chicago Press, 1980), 232.

33. *Battle of Eutaw Springs*, 2006 (oil on canvas), Bridgeman Images, www.bridgemanimages.com/en/noartistknown/title/notechnique/asset/3026974. See "William Washington's Charge at Eutaw Springs," in Don Troiani and James L. Kochan, *Don Troiani's Soldiers of the American Revolution* (Guilford, CT: Stackpole Books, 2007), 168-169.

and the thicket of blackjack—that in his opinion had enabled the other side to avert a catastrophic defeat. According to the rebel commander, "We took between three and four hundred prisoners, and had it not been for the large Brick Building at the Eutaw Spring and the peculiar kind of brush that surrounds it, we should have taken the whole army prisoners."[34] The resistance offered by Sheridan's Loyalists occupying the house, as well as Majoribanks's light infantry and grenadiers on the British right flank and Maj. John Coffin's cavalry unit on their left flank, gave Stewart the time he desperately needed to organize a successful counterattack in the center.[35]

KIRKWOOD'S ACCOUNT

Capt. Robert Kirkwood of the Delaware Continental Regiment, whose men were in the "Corps de Reserve" on this day, explained that they were positioned behind a front line of militia from the Carolinas led by General Marion and Brig. Gen. Andrew Pickens, with Colonel Henry Lee's cavalry on their right flank and mounted infantry on their left, and a second line "with North Carolina regulars, Virginians, and Marylanders." He reported that "we arrived within [a] mile of [the British] encampment, where we met their front line, which soon brought the action general." The Delawares pushed back the opposing "first, and second lines, [and] took upwards of five hundred prisoners." Ultimately, "our men were so far spent for want of water, and our Continental officers suffering much in the action, rendered it advisable for Genl. Greene to draw off his army, with the loss of two 6 pounders . . . found our army had withdrawn from the field, [which] made it necessary for us likewise to withdraw." Although Greene's soldiery retired first, the Delawares gained a measure of redemption when they "brought off one of the enemy's three pounders, which with much difficulty was performed through a thick wood for near four miles, without the assistance of but one horse. We got to the encamping ground, which we left in the morning, about two in the evening."[36]

THE BRITISH PERSPECTIVE

Even before this affray, Greene had encapsulated his troops' combat experience during their remarkable Southern campaign in one famously memorable sentence. Reflecting on his performance in wearing down their adversary by making British victories so costly while preserving

---

34. Greene to John Rutledge, September 9, 1781, in *The Papers of General Nathanael Greene*, 9:308.

35. *The Papers of General Nathanael Greene*, 9:336-337n14.

36. Kirkwood, *Journal and Order Book*, 22-23.

the integrity of his army, the wily strategist wrote, "We fight, get beat, rise and fight again."[37] Colonel Stewart insisted that the rebel general had been beaten once more on September 8, reporting to General Cornwallis the following day that he had "totally defeated" Greene.[38] However hyperbolic that judgment may have been, given that his battered force was too weak to risk another engagement, the colonel's reasoning was plausible to the extent that Greene, not he, had broken off the fight and largely ceded the field by withdrawing to the Americans' starting point that morning at Burdell's Plantation, seven miles from the battlefield.[39] According to Stewart, the rebels, once repulsed by Majoribanks's counterattack on their left flank, "gave way in all quarters, leaving behind them two brass 6-pounders, and upwards of two hundred killed on the field of action, and sixty taken prisoners, amongst which is Col. Washington, and from every information, about eight hundred wounded, although they contrived to carry them off during the action." The colonel added that his foe "retired with great precipitation to a strong situation, about seven miles from the field of action, leaving their cavalry to cover their retreat."[40] Even Greene conceded that the other side had "really fought worthy of a far better cause."[41]

Stewart's missive to Cornwallis complimented the efforts of his officers, in particular those of "Major Majoribanks [who was mortally wounded and today lies buried in the battleground park], and the flank battalion under his command, [to whom] I think the honor of the day is greatly due." Claiming to have fought off nearly four thousand Americans—almost twice the size of Greene's actual strength—Stewart, "a good deal indisposed by a wound which I received in my left elbow," commended the performance of his supposedly outnumbered contingent:

> I hope, My Lord, when it is considered such a handful of men, attacked by the united force of Generals Greene, [Thomas] Sumter [he was not actually at the battle but the South Carolina State Troops, whose command he had recently relinquished, were], Marion, [Brig.

37. Greene to Chevalier de La Luzerne, April 28, 1781, in *The Papers of General Nathanael Greene*, 8:167.
38. Stewart to Cornwallis, September 9, 1781, in *Documentary History of the American Revolution*, 136.
39. Buchanan, *The Road to Charleston*, 233.
40. Stewart to Cornwallis, September 9, 1781, in *Documentary History of the American Revolution*, 138.
41. Greene to Thomas McKean, September 11, 1781, in *The Papers of General Nathanael Greene*, 9:329.

Gen. Jethro] Sumner, and Pickens, and the legions of Colonels Lee and Washington, driving them from the field of battle, and taking the only two 6-pounders they had, deserve some merit.[42]

And British Maj. Frederick Mackenzie remarked that Greene's report to Congress on the engagement "seems principally designed to gloss over a defeat by bestowing great praise on all the officers and troops under his command. Greene is, however, entitled to great praise for his wonderful exertions," for according to MacKenzie, "the more he is beaten, the farther he advances in the end. He has been indefatigable in collecting troops and leading them to be defeated."[43]

ACCOLADES

While overseeing the siege of Yorktown, Washington acknowledged Greene's claims of success at Eutaw Springs by congratulating him "upon a victory as splendid as I hope it will prove important."[44] John Adams, writing more than a month after Cornwallis's surrender, opined that "General Greene's last action in South Carolina . . . is quite as glorious for the American arms as the capture of Cornwallis. The action was supported, even by the militia, with a noble constancy. The victory on our side was complete."[45] Not to be outdone, Congress awarded the presumed victor a gold medal—one of only six medals authorized by Congress for battles or campaigns of the Revolutionary War.[46] And today, the bronze doors of the House of Representatives in the U.S. Capitol Building include as one of their six panels of history the presentation of the medal and a flag to Greene by the Continental Congress

42. Stewart to Cornwallis, September 9, 1781, in *Documentary History of the American Revolution*, 139.
43. Frederick Mackenzie, *Diary of Frederick Mackenzie* (Cambridge, MA: Harvard University Press, 1930), 2:673.
44. Washington to Greene, October 6, 1781, in *The Papers of General Nathanael Greene*, 9:429.
45. John Adams to John Jay, November 28, 1781, in *The Works of John Adams*, ed. Charles Francis Adams (Boston: Little, Brown and Company, 1852), 7:487.
46. South Carolina General Assembly, Committee to Study the Advisability of Establishing a Bicentennial Commission of the American Revolution for South Carolina to Be Known as the "Spirit of 1776 Commission" (1971), *Liberty and Independence, South Carolina and the Founding of the Nation: Second Report of the Committee to Study the Advisability of Establishing a Bicentennial Commission of the American Revolution for South Carolina to Be Known as the "Spirit of 1776 Commission"* (Columbia, SC), 6. The Continental Congress authorized medals to be struck in honor of the following battles or campaigns: the Siege of Boston in 1776, Saratoga in 1777, Stony Point in 1779, Paulus Hook in 1779, Cowpens in 1781, and Eutaw Springs. In lieu of a medal, Congress directed that a marble obelisk be erected in recognition of the victory at Yorktown.

for the Battle of Eutaw Springs.[47] Although such adulation may be exaggerated given the engagement's ambiguous outcome, it conferred upon the enterprising Rhode Islander the recognition he had long sought as a battlefield commander.[48] He yearned to win an illustrious victory that would earn him the plaudits of his contemporaries and posterity; and when circumstances denied him such a triumph, he lay claim to it anyway at Eutaw Springs.[49] Brig. Gen. (soon to be Maj. Gen.) Henry Knox's approbation of Greene's efforts in the South perhaps rang the loudest, noting that he had "performed wonders" without "an army, without means, without anything."[50]

The common soldier who became embroiled in this clash of arms received no such acclaim, for as Joseph Plumb Martin noted in his memoir of service in the Connecticut militia and the Continental Army, "Great men get great praise, little men nothing."[51] Even so, Philip Freneau, in his second volume of *Poems Written and Published During the American Revolutionary War*, memorialized the Americans who fell on that September day. His elegy begins, "At Eutaw Springs the Valiant Died" and ends with this verse: "Now rest in peace, our patriot band; Though far from nature's limits thrown, We trust they find a happier land, A brighter sunshine of their own."[52]

FINAL THOUGHTS

Regardless of who won, the story of the ferocious brawl that enveloped this South Carolina battleground graphically illustrates the brutality of war during a grueling contest for American independence. In particular, it gives vivid testimony to the deprivations suffered by the common

47. "House Bronze Doors," Architect of the Capitol, www.aoc.gov/explore-capitol-campus/art/house-bronze-doors. The bronze doors were designed by the American sculptor Thomas Crawford in Rome in 1855-1857. Upon Crawford's death, William H. Rinehart executed the models from the sculptor's sketches in 1863-1867. The models were shipped from Leghorn, Italy, in 1867 and stored in the Crypt of the Capitol Building until 1903, when they were cast by Melzar H. Mosman of Chicopee, Massachusetts. The doors were installed in 1905 at the east portico entrance of the House wing.

48. Terry Golway, *Washington's General: Nathanael Greene and the Triumph of the American Revolution* (New York: Henry Holt and Company, LLC, 2006), 286.

49. Ibid., 302.

50. Theodore Thayer, *Nathanael Greene: Strategist of the American Revolution*, 381.

51. Joseph Plumb Martin, *Memoir of a Revolutionary Soldier: The Narrative of Joseph Plumb Martin* (Mineola, NY: Dover Publications, Inc., 2006), 54.

52. Philip Freneau, "To the Memory of the Brave Americans, under General Greene, in South Carolina, who fell in the Action of September 8, 1781," in *Poems Written and Published During the American Revolutionary War*, 3rd ed. (Philadelphia: From the Press of Lydia R. Bailey, no. 10, North-Alley, 1809), 2:71.

soldiers on each side, the horrors of civil war that befell Patriots and Loyalists alike, and the enormous sacrifice in blood and treasure incurred by Great Britain in its ill-fated quest to defeat a colonial insurrection in a distant land from which many of its sons would never return.[53] The specter of carnage on this and other fields was foreseen by Edmund Burke, the great British orator and Member of Parliament, when he warned his fellow lawmakers in 1775 of the consequences for America—and implicitly for those fighting on both sides—likely to ensue from Britain's military action against her recalcitrant subjects: "The thing you [will have] fought for, is not the thing which you [will] recover; but deprecated, sunk, wasted, and consumed in the contest."[54]

Perhaps the stone marker that was erected by the Daughters of the American Revolution at Eutaw Springs Battleground Park in 1912 provides the most succinct and accurate assessment of the outcome there: "Neither side was victorious, but the fight was beneficial to the American cause." To any history buff's dismay, the ultimate triumph at Eutaw Springs belongs to the tide of residential and commercial development that has encroached upon, and in some cases engulfed, many a Revolutionary War and Civil War battlefield. Most of where the action occurred on that long-ago September day has been overtaken by a modern neighborhood dating largely from the 1960s. Except for the small roadside park with its verdant canopy, there is little to see of the site where the last major battle of the War for Independence was fought.[55]

53. By at least one estimate, Great Britain suffered forty thousand casualties and expended fifty million pounds in the course of the war. See Joseph Ellis, *Revolutionary Summer: The Birth of American Independence* (New York: Alfred A. Knopf, 2013), 178.
54. "The Speech of Edmund Burke, Esquire, on Moving his Resolutions for Conciliation with the Colonies, March 22d, 1775," in *The American Revolution: Writings from the Pamphlet Debate*, Gordon S. Wood, ed. (New York: The Library of America, 2015), 2:544.
55. Dunkerly and Boland, *Eutaw Springs*, 98.

# British Soldiers Wounded at Eutaw Springs

**꧁ DON N. HAGIST ꧂**

After the Battle of Eutaw Springs in South Carolina on September 8, 1781, the commander of the British forces reported, among other casualties, 313 rank and file (that is, corporals and private soldiers) wounded and another 224 missing.[1] While surviving muster rolls can be used to determine which men were killed in a battle, it is rare to be able to identify individual British soldiers who were wounded—which in turn makes it impossible to know how many of those wounded men returned to fight another day.

A seldom-used source for this type of information is the discharge documents for British soldiers who received army pensions. When a soldier was discharged from the army, he obtained a document—usually a printed form with details written in—to prove that he was legally released from his service obligation. Included on the discharge was the man's name, age, place of birth, the trade he practiced before enlisting (if any), length of service, sometimes some descriptive information such as height and hair color, and the reason that he was no longer fit to serve in the army. When a man received an army pension, the pension office retained a copy of the discharge; today, many of these documents survive for men discharged after 1785.

Among the thousands of surviving discharges for British soldiers who served in America are a few that tell the place and date where the man was wounded. And among these, ten have been found that record wounds received at the Battle of Eutaw Springs.

---

1. Alexander Stewart to Charles Cornwallis, September 9, 1781, in *Documentary History of the American Revolution . . . Chiefly in South Carolina*, ed. R.W. Gibbes (Columbia, SC: Banner Steam-Power Press, 1853), 1:139.

The youngest among the ten known wounded soldiers was William Long of the 3rd Regiment of Foot. At the age of seventeen, he enlisted on April 28, 1778, and three years later found himself disembarking with his regiment in Charlestown, South Carolina in March 1781. Although he was "wounded in the left leg at the Battle of the Eutaws 8th Septr 1781," he continued in the regiment until 1792, when he was discharged and obtained a pension. His discharge records his birthplace as Castle Durrow in Kilkenny, Ireland, but Castle Durrow is just over the border to the north in County Laois. Long signed his own name on his discharge; having no trade, he was listed with the catchall term "labourer."[2]

Most of the soldiers known to have been wounded in this battle were from the 3rd Regiment of Foot. Michael McCann enlisted on April 18, 1780, making him the least experienced of the known wounded. The native of "Drumaree" in County Armagh, Ireland had been a weaver before enlisting in 1780 at the age of twenty. He received a wound in the thigh at "the Eutaws," but remained in the army for another ten years. When he was discharged in 1792, an officer wrote that, besides his wound, he was "lame from rheumatism contracted in 1790 on board ship while serving as a Marine." Unable to sign his own name, McCann marked his discharge with an X.[3]

Another new enlistee was John Brown, a laborer from "Drumrow" in County Tyrone, Ireland. He served from May 1778 through 1791, when he was awarded a pension because of "Lameness occasioned from Wounds received in America at the Battle of Eutaw Springs on the 8 Septr 1781 in the left Groin & Right leg." He, too, put his mark on his discharge rather than signing his name.[4]

William McCreally—whose name appears on the 3rd Regiment's muster rolls as McCawley—was another Irishman. From Desertmartin in Londonderry, he worked as a blacksmith before joining the regiment on July 26, 1778 at the age of eighteen. At Eutaw Springs he received "a ball in his leg." When the war ended in 1783, the 3rd Regiment went south to Jamaica where they remained for several years. During that time, perhaps in September 1786, a hurricane struck the island and McCreally, in unknown circumstances, had both of his arms broken.

2. The National Archives of Great Britain (TNA): Discharge of William Long, WO 121/13/127; muster rolls, 3rd Regiment of Foot, WO 12/6699.
3. TNA: Discharge of Michael McCann, WO 121/13/129; muster rolls, 3rd Regiment of Foot, WO 12/6699.
4. TNA: Discharge of John Brown, WO 121/10/7; muster rolls, 3rd Regiment of Foot, WO 12/6699.

He nonetheless served for two more years, signing his name on his discharge in September 1788.[5]

James Keating enlisted in the 3rd Regiment on October 10, 1777 at the age of twenty-three after working as a weaver in his native Dublin, Ireland. In spite of being wounded in the head at Eutaw Springs, he remained in the 3rd Regiment until about 1789, then spent another six years in two other regiments before putting his name on his discharge in January 1796.[6]

That all of these new recruits were Irish is a reflection of the 3rd Regiment having been posted in Ireland for several years before serving in America. Like most British regiments during this era, the 3rd included men from all over Great Britain and Ireland. Edward Allen, for example, was from Chislet in County Kent, England. When he enlisted in the 3rd Regiment on June 4, 1775, he was nineteen years old. By the time he wrote his name on his discharge on February 23, 1792, he had been "wounded in the right ancle at the Eutaws 8th Septr 1781; also considerably weakened from severe service on the Mosquito shore."[7]

It bears noting that all of these wartime enlistees were volunteers. When the war ended in 1783 and the 3rd Regiment of Foot went to Jamaica, where they encamped at a place called Up Park, they received orders for a reduction in size to a new peace-time establishment; men who had enlisted after December 16, 1775 were entitled to be discharged, after which they could return to their homeland rather than remaining in the hostile tropical climate. All of ten of the men discussed here, in spite of having been wounded in battle, chose to re-enlist, as did dozens of their comrades, continuing in the regiment until they were deemed no longer fit for service.

Thomas Crooks, from North Waltham in Norfolk, England, enlisted in the 3rd Regiment on March 20, 1769, and remained in its ranks until 1789 when he was discharged, having attained the rank of corporal during his twenty years of service. He was recommended for a pension due to "a Wound he recd in his breast, at the battle of Eutaw Springs South Carolina & an ulcerated leg, which was contracted at Black River Musquito Shore." In spite of these infirmities, he returned

5. TNA: Discharge of William McCreally, WO 121/5/117; muster rolls, 3rd Regiment of Foot, WO 12/6699.
6. TNA: Discharge of James Keating, WO 121/25/94; muster rolls, 3rd Regiment of Foot, WO 12/6699.
7. TNA: Discharge of Edward Allen, WO 121/13/112; muster rolls, 3rd Regiment of Foot, WO 12/6699.

to the army in 1797, spending five years in a corps called the Plymouth Invalids before returning to the pension rolls in 1802.[8]

James Flint was a weaver from the city of Manchester in Lancashire, enlisted in the 64th Regiment of Foot early in 1776 at the age of twenty-one, and soon joined his regiment in America. He was "wounded through the right thigh at the Battle of Brandywine [in 1777], & right breast at the Eutaw Springs in 1781." When the 64th Regiment went to Jamaica and discharged him, instead of going home he opted to join the 3rd Regiment and stayed with them until 1791.[9]

Michael Kelly was a "nailor" (nail maker) from the town of Shinrone in County Offaly. He, too, enlisted in in the 64th Regiment in 1776, joining them in America in December of that year. At the Battle of Germantown in 1777 he was wounded in the left leg. At Eutaw Springs he was wounded again, this time in the left arm, and taken prisoner. In spite of having endured these hardships, he, too, chose to re-enlist in 1783, serving in the 3rd Regiment until 1792.[10]

The only British soldier known to have been wounded at Eutaw Springs who had no connection to the 3rd Regiment of Foot is Samuel Wright, a five-foot six-inch tall Englishman with brown hair and grey eyes. A gardener from Austrey in Warwickshire, England, he enlisted at the age of twenty-one into the 19th Regiment of Foot in 1770. His regiment, like the 3rd, landed in Charlestown, South Carolina in early 1781 and was soon deep in the war. Although he was wounded in the left thigh, he remained with his regiment until 1792 when he was discharged because of "Length of service and being wounded during the war in America at the Eutaw Springs." He quickly re-enlisted, this time in a regiment called the West Lowland Fencibles, where he served another four years. In 1803 he went into the army one last time, spending four years and two months 6th Royal Veteran Battalion, taking his leave for the last time in 1807 at the age of fifty-eight. By then, besides being "wounded through the left thigh," he was, quite aptly, "worn out."[11]

8. TNA: Discharges of Thomas Crooks, WO 121/6/33 and WO 121/153/146; muster rolls, 3rd Regiment of Foot, WO 12/6699.

9. TNA: Discharge of James Flint, WO 121/11/282; muster rolls, 64th Regiment of Foot, WO 12/7313; muster rolls, 3rd Regiment of Foot, WO 12/6699.

10. TNA: Discharge of Michael Kelly, WO 121/13/126; muster rolls, 64th Regiment of Foot, WO 12/7313; muster rolls, 3rd Regiment of Foot, WO 12/6699.

11. TNA: Discharges of Samuel Wright, WO 121/15/23, WO 121/145/163; WO 121/65/120.

# Clark vs. Livingston: Pettiness, Paper Money, and Elections

#‽ ERIC WISER ‽#

John Adams said of his Whig contemporaries that they had views as "various as the Colors of their Cloths."[1] Such was the paradigm in the civil yet often contentious political relationship of Abraham Clark and William Livingston. Both men were, as the saying goes, cursed with being born in interesting times. They were the top political leaders of New Jersey during the tumultuous years of the American Revolution. Hailing from the "second tier" of Founding Fathers, they nonetheless made significant contributions to the establishment of the United States. Livingston believed in strong central government, and Clark believed it tyrannical. However, the shared struggle of asserting America's rights, defending New Jersey, and winning the war forced them to work together in a common cause. Their differences in the beginning were petty but grew more substantive as time progressed.

Clark was a perennial legislator who served in the Continental Congress and New Jersey state legislature. His ideological opponent Livingston was a member of the First and Second Continental Congresses and the longest serving governor of the Revolution. Clark signed the Declaration of Independence, and Livingston, the Constitution of 1787. Their political rivalry, which started poorly, began as the British were delivering their massive military counterstroke in the vicinity of New York City during the summer of 1776.

In the last days of June 1776, Abraham Clark, surveyor, farmer, and self-styled advocate for the people, and nicknamed the "poor man's counselor," packed necessities for an eighty-mile journey from Elizabethtown, New Jersey to Philadelphia to take his seat in the Third

---

1. John Adams to Joseph Hawley, June 27, 1774, *Founders Online*, National Archives.

Continental Congress. Middle-aged, frail, and with seriousness chiseled on his face, Clark knew Congress's agenda for the first days of July was to be of a weight and significance not seen in his many years in government. Clark's small house west of Elizabethtown's center housed his large family. From there, he wrote to his neighbor Elias Dayton, colonel in the Continental Army, "Our Congress have determined upon a new form of government, and are drawing it up. The Continental Congress are to determine next Monday upon Independency. I am going among them tomorrow."[2] Clark and three other members of the New Jersey delegation were instructed by the legislature to support declaring Independence if necessary to preserve "the just Rights and Liberties of America."[3]

A French diplomat described Abraham Clark as a "Man of the people . . . despised by gentlemen and returning the sentiment to them with interest." Clark was an only child, from an old Elizabethtown family of civic leaders who were devout Presbyterians. Modestly educated, he was a surveyor during a boom time for the profession. Despite being sole inheritor of substantial landholdings from his father, Clark nonetheless considered himself a yeoman farmer. He blamed the King for the crisis gripping the colonies, and his primary focus during his years in politics was twofold: advocate for common citizens and fight centralized power in all government institutions.

Clark's political career started with a clerkship in the colonial general assembly. His transformation into a Revolutionary started with his being chosen by Elizabethtown's freeholders in December 1774 to direct the town's boycott of British goods. Clark represented Essex County in the New Jersey legislature in the summer of 1776.[4] The legislature was controlled by members swept into power on a wave of populism fired by an expanded franchise. Its members were inexperienced in government but motivated to public service by the emerging crisis.[5] Clark was serving with them when the call came to go to Philadelphia. He wrote Colonel Dayton on July 4, "Our Congress is an August As-

2. Abraham Clark to Elias Dayton, June 26, 1776, *Jared Sparks Collection*, Harvard University.

3. Samuel Tucker to Richard Stockton, Clark, John Hart, and Francis Hopkins, in Worthington Chauncey Ford, et al., eds. *Journals of the Continental Congress 1774-1789* (Washington, DC: Library of Congress, 1906), 5:490 (JCC).

4. Ruth Bogin, *Abraham Clark and the Quest for Equality in Revolutionary America* (East Brunswick: Associated University Press, 1982), 42, 142, 163-166; Clark to Dayton, June 26, 1776.

5. James Gigantino II, *William Livingston's American Revolution* (Philadelphia: Penn, 2018), 42.

sembly, and can they support the Declaration now on the Anvil, they will be the greatest Assembly on Earth." Clark's signature is preserved for posterity on the Declaration at the bottom of the New Jersey delegation.[6]

Living north of Elizabethtown in a palatial home built in 1772 for his retirement, New York ex-pat William Livingston was incensed by Abraham Clark. Tall, long faced, and hawkish nosed, the Dutch- and Scottish-mixed Livingston was fifty-three years old and hailed from a powerful upstate New York family that ran a mercantile empire. The former lawyer was supposed to be enjoying an early retirement immersed in books, but was instead serving New Jersey as representative in the Continental Congress. Livingston believed Clark conspired with allies in the legislature to replace him in Congress. Clark told his close friend Dayton that Livingston, "seems much Chagrined at his being left out of Congress, and there is not wanting some who Endeavor to persuade him that it was through my means to Supplant him, which was far from true."[7]

As a consolation prize to the aggrieved Livingston, the New Jersey legislature offered him command of the militia being assigned to the defense of New York. This Livingston declined, and he instead fell back on a brigadier generalship of militia overseeing East Jersey secured the previous October.[8] None of this healed his wounded pride, and Livingston endured the humiliation of receiving a letter dated July 5 from Clark, informing him of the Declaration of Independence's passage. This was by no means malicious on Clark's part; Congress recommended that commanders in the field receive the Declaration. Clark told his rival, "I have no doubt you will Publish in your Brigade."

The measure Livingston feared was now a reality.[9] He had fallen out of favor with the legislature due to his hesitancy to back independence. Livingston whole-heartedly supported economic boycotts in addition to voting yes on *The Declaration of the Causes and Necessity of Taking Up Arms* resolution passed by the Second Continental Congress. His trepidation, and those of like mind, stemmed from a fear that independence would unleash mob rule and violence.

In public life, Livingston was introverted and seldom sought public attention. This trait outwardly concealed his effectiveness and killer in-

---

6. Clark to Dayton, July 4, 1776, in Paul H. Smith, et al., eds. *Letters of the Delegates to Congress, 1774-1789, May 16-August 15, 1776* (Washington, DC: Library of Congress, 1979), 4:378-379 (LOTDC).
7. Clark to Dayton, June 26, 1776.
8. Gigantino, 57, 68.
9. Clark to William Livingston, July 5, 1776, LOTDC 4:391.

stinct toward political opponents. His letters to friends and family were exceptionally heartwarming, but his political correspondence was serious and confrontational. His favorite end-around weapon was the satirical polemic, which he started writing as a hobby during his law apprenticeships.

Livingston, a Yale graduate, eschewed religion, and embraced the ideas of The Enlightenment. Consequently, he undertook a lifelong crusade against the establishment of religion and the Anglican Church in particular. In 1752, Livingston along with two young lawyers practicing in New York City, known as "The Triumvirate," published a weekly newspaper called *The Independent Reflector*. In short, the *Reflector*'s fifty-two issues of satirical propaganda attacked the establishment of a particular religion in the colonies. The paper used ample word space on the Anglican Church and the DeLancey political faction which supported it. Livingston avidly worked to prevent nascent King's College (Columbia University) from falling under the influence of the church.

The countryside of northern New Jersey was introduced to Livingston through his wife Suzannah French. In theory, Elizabethtown was far enough away for a peaceful retirement, and the ferry to New York City would keep him connected to Manhattan's bustle. This fell by the wayside as his natural proclivities won out and the crisis with Britain expanded. Unlike Clark, Livingston was a conservative who blamed Parliament for the crisis rather than the King. He formed political associations with like-minded men on Clark's turf. One such alliance was with future Congress president and Elizabethtown resident Elias Boudinot.

Livingston directed the defense of East Jersey with vigor and competence despite deep personal misgivings as to his own competence as a soldier. Clark was in Philadelphia and feared that his hometown would be "laid to ashes," and a rival, Livingston, headquartered there was charged with protecting it. Livingston oversaw the construction of redoubts and fortifications along the coast. He positioned troops at strategic points, and adeptly managed issues of supply and manpower; in the process, he established a rapport with Gen. George Washington. Boudinot was Livingston's aide-de-camp, and he had a solid Continental Army connection in the person of Gen. William "Lord Stirling" Alexander, his brother-in-law and old friend from New York City.

As the calendar turned from August to September 1776, the man who showed little promise in his father's eyes and had lost his first law apprenticeship for cause was chosen governor of New Jersey under its first constitution. The legislature chose Livingston on the second ballot of voting, for reasons that are uncertain. If Livingston had a modern resume, his introduction would read "received promotions of increased responsibility." He was chief executive alongside a legislature comprising a Legislative Council, and a lower house, the Assembly. The New Jersey constitution made the governor commander-in-chief of the state's armed forces. Livingston, as such, faced enormous challenges as a wartime governor including stopping "London Traders" from supplying the enemy. The main concentration of British forces in America was nearby at New York City; and Staten Island, with its disaffected garrison of Royal Provincials and Refugees, was perilously close to Elizabethtown. Elizabethtown itself was the gateway to New Jersey, and thus, his home, and much of the state, was in the direct path between the British army and the rebel capital at Philadelphia.[10]

Clark and Livingston had a professional and prickly relationship. Few of Clark's letters survive, but Livingston's ample record sheds light on some of their squabbles. On July 26, 1776, a month after Livingston was relieved from Congress, and no doubt still nursing his wounded pride, he sarcastically offered up Clark as a candidate to command New Jersey soldiers in the Flying Camp. Livingston wrote to New Jersey legislator Samuel Tucker:

> As every private Gentleman has a right humbly to submit his opinion to Superiors for the public good, & as the reason why I was so strongly pressed to take command of Brigadier Heards Brigade now ceases by my being superseded as a Member of Congress, I would with all Deference recommend Jonathan Sergeant or Abraham Clark Esqrs. to that Post—as those Gentleman have always shewn the warmest Patriotism in the Cabinet, I doubt not they will with equal Alacrity venture their lives in the field.[11]

In November 1779 Clark was serving in Congress when he learned that an officer named Silvanus Seely was a suspected London Trader. Seely, a colonel in a New Jersey regiment, was supposedly running supplies to the British from Elizabethtown. Clark reported the matter to Governor Livingston. Livingston wrote to Seeley, "I hope Mr. Clark's Information as far as it respects itself not well founded." Seely challenged Clark's claim and insisted on a court of inquiry, and Livingston promised to submit his counterclaim to Clark. Clark continued pursu-

---

10. Gigantino, *William Livingston's American Revolution*, 22-23, 31, 70-71, 74-77, 84.
11. Livingston to Tucker, July 26, 1776, in Carl Prince, et al., eds. *The Papers of William Livingston, June 1774-June 1777* (Trenton: New Jersey Historical Commission, 1979), 1:107 (PWL).

ing Seely and was unhappy that Livingston did not press matters further, accusing him of "sporting with the Laws." Livingston replied, "If
therefore it is of any Consequence, or concerns the Dignity of Government, that I should know the particulars from which you have
drawn this charge against me, you will occasion to explain the Matter
more fully." It was but one of a number of scrappy exchanges between
the two.[12]

The matter of Cornelius Hatfield, Jr. illustrates the commitment
Clark had regarding the priority civil authority had over military authority, while at the same time highlighting the family ties of small
colonial communities. The Hatfield family of Elizabethtown, like the
Clarks, were highly respected and went back to the town's founding.
Abraham Clark's wife Sarah was a Hatfield and cousin to a young man
caught loading a ship with supplies for the British. Cornelius Hatfield,
Jr. was arrested and incarcerated in Elizabethtown's provost to await
his fate while under the care of General Maxwell.

The Essex County Supreme Court issued a writ of habeas corpus
for Hatfield's release. General Maxwell, who claimed he was waiting
for more clarity on how to proceed, verbally and physically abused a
handful of unlucky deliverers of the writ. On December 21, 1778, Clark
wrote Continental Congress President and William Livingston's son-
in-law John Jay, pointing to Hatfield's guilt but that the latter "is an
inhabitant of this state and entitled to the privileges of the same, where
the civil authority is fully competent for the trial and punishment of
offenders, I believe fully competent for the apprehending General
Maxwell for the contempt shown to it in the present case."[13]

Clark followed up his letter with one to Livingston pressing his case
for Hatfield's release and accusing him of wanting Hatfield executed.
Livingston responded that Clark's case was "founded on mistakes of
both fact & of law." During wartime, "the military had a right to take
up & secure persons guilty of practices that endangered the army till
they could be delivered up to the civil power." Livingston was caught
between a community he recently became a part of and governed with
limitations, and Congressionally empowered General Washington who
implored governors to squash London Trading. The governor paid a
fruitless visit to Maxwell's headquarters to get his side of things, and
wrote to Clark, "I do not think to myself vested with any judicial au-

12. Livingston to Silvanus Seeley, November 26, 1779, PWL 3:233; Livingston to Seeley,
December 7, 1779, PWL 3:255; Livingston to Clark, February 1, 1780, PWL 3:294.
13. Clark to John Jay, December 21, 1778, *Papers of the Continental Congress*, Letters Addressed to Congress 1775-1789, Roll 93, M247, p. 287-289 (POTCC).

thority" and that the "officer in charge to whom [the writ] is directed is punishable by Law, but not responsible to the Governor."

Livingston punted the issue to Washington. Clark never refrained from challenging the military, Washington included, and a refusal from the general to release Hatfield surely would have triggered more protests. Washington assented to Hatfield's release, which was irrelevant because he had escaped to Staten Island. Hatfield guided a nighttime raiding party from Long Island to Elizabethtown just days after his flight. Burning buildings on their way, they marched to Liberty Hall with an intent to capture the governor. Livingston was away, but was shocked at the audacity of the venture and wrote with sardonic humor, "General Clinton thought proper to send an Express for me to Elizabeth Town."[14]

After the war, New Jersey and its political class struggled to meet its obligations in the Federalist program to pay the national debt. The United States was in an economic depression and New Jersey's economy was especially hard hit. Abraham Clark was serving in the New Jersey General Assembly in the Fall of 1785 when he lamented the state's shortage of hard currency due the Federal government. "To Attempt to raise by Taxation the Sum required in Specie will be vain and fruitless; in this State it cannot be done." New Jersey, unlike its wealthier neighbors New York and Pennsylvania, did not possess a bustling large port for imposing import duties, and also lacked large reserves of western lands to sell.

Clark's concerns stemmed from a game-changing law passed by Congress on September 27, 1785. New Jersey was assigned a quota of $166,716 toward the national debt with one third required in hard currency. The dollar figure was based on a pre-war population estimate which Clark felt outdated and inaccurate. The specter of centralized government abuse haunted Clark's mind:

> This is a burden too unequal and grievous for this State to Submit to. We are ready to bear our part in the defense, and also of the expense necessary in Support of the Union, provided the same can be done in a just equal and practicable way, but Oppression will make even a Wiseman mad.

The Articles of Confederation governing the United States prevented Congress from directly taxing the states. The September 1785 act contained a clever mechanism to ensure that each state legislature approved the requisition, and that United States' domestic debt was ef-

14. Livingston to Nathaniel Scudder, December 24, 1779, PWL 3:278.

fectively cancelled. To settle this, Congress agreed to reduce a state's liability to the federal treasury by the amount of domestic debt the federal government owed a state's citizens.

Under the new law, New Jerseyites could take a Continental note to a federal loan officer and receive an interest-bearing certificate that could be used to pay taxes imposed on them by the state to pay for the requisition. This circular arrangement shifted tax collection to the state legislatures. The legislatures redeemed a citizen's interest-bearing certificate to Congress—not for cash, but for cancellation of a portion of its requisition liability to the federal treasury. The plan circumvented the Articles of Confederation, driving Clark to call it a "scheme," and he determined a course of action to resist it.[15] On November 8 Clark, then serving as an Essex County Assemblyman, introduced a resolution delaying a vote on the federal requisition until the legislature's next session.[16] Peacetime Gov. William Livingston was being pressured by the federal government to get the legislature in line.[17]

The fuss over the requisition ran concurrently with Clark's push to assist New Jersey's yeomanry by issuing paper money. Shortage of currency stimulated waves of petitions to the legislature from farmers across several counties. Fortunately for the petitioners, the incoming legislative class of New Jersey Assemblyman elected in October 1785 held several paper emission champions.[18]

The recess of the legislature in the fall provided Clark time to prosecute his information campaign to dissuade the electorate against the requisition. Clark also took up the cause of greasing New Jersey's economic engine by placing non-specie paper currency into circulation. Livingston was a member of the creditor class exposed to the danger of inflationary paper currency and, like many, was turned off to the idea from experience with the Continental dollar in the Revolution. Livingston could not resist the temptation to unleash his polemic writing skills on Clark.

Clark chose Elizabethtown printer Shepard Kollock and his *The Political Intelligencer and New Jersey Advertiser* as his delivery device. He chose "A Fellow Citizen," and "Willing to Learn," as his pseudonyms. Isaac Collins' Trenton-based *New Jersey-Gazette* published Livingston's

---

15. Richard P. McCormick, "New Jersey Defies the Confederation: An Abraham Clark Letter," *The Journal of the Rutgers University Libraries*, vol. 13, no. 2 (1950), 47-50; Report of Congressional Committee, September 27, 1785, JCC 29:765-775.

16. Bogin, *Abraham Clark*, 125.

17. Benjamin Thompson to Livingston, October 22, 1785, PWL 5:208-209.

18. *"To tarnish the glory,"* National Virtue and the Constitutional Convention September 21, 1784—October 1787, PWL 5:151-152.

"Primitive Whig" series to answer Clark. Other authors of unknown identity, mostly on Livingston's side, published pieces jabbing at the pro-paper, anti-requisition supporters.

On December 14, 1785, Abraham Clark, as "Willing to Learn," launched the opening salvo in *The Political Intelligencer*. The 1,200-word piece was an emotional appeal in support of the paper money. Clark promulgated that the soul of the American Republic was the guarantee of equality for common people, and that:

> By misfortune or otherwise, [they] owe money which it is not now in their power to pay, many of whom are obliged to submit to prosecutions, and to have their estates sold far below the value to the breaking of families and increase of poverty, and to the promoting that inequality of property which is dangerous in a republican government ... without a doubt, that is in the power of our legislature at their next sitting to remedy all those grievances and put a new aspect on our affairs.

Willing to Learn asked for the immediate printing of 200,000 pounds to be placed in New Jersey's loan office and made immediately available.[19]

One week later Clark published his second piece under Willing to Learn. Clark's essay confronted the elephant in the room—the nightmarish experience of paper money during the Revolution. Clark offered that the legislature could tame inflation by interest rate manipulation. He issued a challenge in a way that inspired Livingston and others to action by way of attacking the gentleman-creditor class of New Jersey:

> Behold the farmer with his head uncovered saying, Sir, I am in necessity for the three shillings in hard cash to pay my tax; I have paper money, but that will not do, can you help me to that sum? I will suppose two different answers to be given in such cases, and your imaginations may paint as many more as you think may be given.

Clark's hypothetical gentleman responded to the farmer:

> D—n you and your paper rags, you have got it made and you may wipe your a-s with it, for you see the assembly won't take it for their wages, and I'll see you all d—d together before you shall have any had money for me ... Yes I have a little hard money, but it is hard for you get it; but I believe I must let you have it. I saw some cleaver shoats near your house the other day, I supposed were yours, if you will fetch me a likely barrow, I will give you three shillings for it.[20]

19. *The Political Intelligencer and New Jersey Advertiser*, December 14, 1785.
20. *The Political Intelligencer*, December 21, 1775.

On January 9, 1786, the first essay in Livingston's "Primitive Whig" series appeared in the *New Jersey-Gazette*. The governor tackled the requisition, questioning the patriotism of those "Americans who promised to stand by Congress and General Washington with their lives and fortunes in opposing the mediated tyranny of Britain, now grumbling about paying the taxes." And on the paper money issue and attack of creditors like himself, the Primitive Whig commented:

> To see a lazy, lounging, lubberly fellow sitting nights and days in a tippling house, working perhaps but two days in the week, and receiving for that work double the wages he earns, and spending the rest of his time in squandering those his non-earnings in riot and debauch, and then complaining, when the collector calls for his tax, of the hardness of the times, and the want of a circulating medium-Ingrate!

Livingston characterized non-requisition supporters as London Traders and conflated the position with disloyalty. For Clark's hypothetical destitute farmer, the Primitive Whig remarked, "But who is that yonder honest looking farmer, who shakes his head at the name of taxes, and protests that he cannot pay them! Why, he is a man whose three daughters are under the discipline of a French dancing-master."[21]

Clark answered with two pieces in the January 11, 1786 *Political Intelligencer*, one under the pseudonym, "A Fellow Citizen." A Fellow Citizen's tone was sober and simple, short in length, and without any satire attacked the all-at-once approach of the federal requisition:

> The general policy of most nations, either from the impracticability of inexpediency of the measure, doth not attempt to said the supplies necessary for the annual expense of government, by the ordinary mode of taxation only; it is done principally by the imposts and excises, which collects a revenue gradually, and almost imperceptibility, and at the same time voluntary from the consumers in equal proportion to their circumstance and abilities.[22]

The impost mentioned by Clark was a committee brainchild of Congress in the middle years of the war to pay the confederation's debts. In 1781, a five percent tax was proposed on all imports into the United States. This nationalized mechanism for raising revenue was supported by Clark despite its inherent violation of his principles. The positive for New Jersey was that the federal treasury would be topped off by states with larger ports while poorer states paid their respective

---

21. *New Jersey-Gazette*, January 9, 1786.
22. *The Political Intelligencer*, January 11, 1786.

smaller portion. This failed along with a similar impost measure in 1783.[23]

The "Primitive Whig" reappeared in the January 16 *New Jersey-Gazette*. Livingston attacked paper money as "hocus pocus" and tied the effort to enact it as a reelection gimmick:

> The mischiefs to be apprehended from so fatal a measure are almost innumerable; and as all of them are not likely to occur to one man . . . Who are the men that are in favor of paper money? They are, generally, debtors; and debtors, by their own confession, utterly irretrievable without this iniquitous device . . . It is therefore their hopes of the depreciation of this money, that is the whole burden of the song. And thus the business is eventually to terminate in the shifting the creditor instead of paying the debt, or the finally sham payment of it in depreciated currency, to their great consolation indeed as to the saving their bodies from imprisonment, but to the evident exposition of their souls to eternal perdition for such bare-faced knavery.

Livingston confronted the interests of creditors including himself, asking:

> who are against emission of paper money, being creditors and men of property, are also self-interested in their opposition to it. Granted. But great is the difference between the self-interest and honesty of these and that of the debtors in question. The interest of the creditor coincides with that of the community. Not so the interest of the debtor. The former desires no more than his own. The latter wants to pocket the property of another.[24]

Livingston's last Primitive Whig essay appeared in the *New Jersey-Gazette* on February 13. On February 8, Shepard Kollock had published Abraham Clark's pamphlet *The True Policy of New-Jersey, Defined*. Published under Clark's *A Fellow Citizen* pseudonym, it was a summary of his newspaper arguments.[25] In *The True Policy*, Clark summoned his ideology, stating that artisans, farmers, and mechanics were the backbone of New Jersey, and that republicanism would triumph with the printing of currency. Clark believed in grass roots campaigns, and A Fellow Citizen asked the people of New Jersey to

23. Bogin, *Abraham Clark*, 78-83.
24. *New Jersey-Gazette*, January 16, 1786.
25. Bogin, *Abraham Clark*, 160-161.

pressure their representatives with "humble petitioning only, and no doubt you may be heard."[26]

Clark returned to the General Assembly after its winter recess. He introduced the kill shot to Congress's tax requisition on the floor of the legislature in Trenton on February 20. The information campaign, along with any unseen pressures, yielded a harvest of yeas that rebuffed the federal government's debt program.[27] On March 7, a panicked Congress responded by dispatching envoys to Trenton to "represent to them, in the strongest terms, the fatal Consequences that must inevitably result to the said State, as well as to the rest of the Union, from their refusal to comply with the requisition of Congress."[28] In addition, Clark and the populists were victorious on paper currency when, on March 9, the legislature approved the printing of money and bills of credits.[29]

The failures of the federal imposts of 1781 and 1783, and the requisition of 1785, exposed the fiscal weakness of the United States under the Articles of Confederation. Governor Livingston supported all three, while Clark supported only the imposts. Clark was never comfortable with the end product of the Constitutional Convention of 1787, yet in some way he helped create it by defeating the requisition. Clark and Livingston were chosen to represent New Jersey at Philadelphia:

> To His Excellency William Livingston, and the Honorable Abraham Clark, Esquires, Greeting. The council and assembly reposing especial trust and confidence in your integrity, prudence and ability, have at a joint meeting, appointed you . . . to meet such commissioners in as have been appointed by other states in the union at Philadelphia . . . for the purpose of taking into consideration the state of the union, as to trade and other important objects, and of devising such other provisions as shall appear to be necessary, to render the constitution of the federal government adequate to the exigencies thereof.[30]

26. "The True Policy of New Jersey, Defined," in Howard L. Green ed., *Words That Make New Jersey: A Primary Source Reader* (Trenton: New Jersey Historical Commission, 1995), 67-69.

27. General Assembly Meeting, February 20, 1786, in Isaac Collins, ed., *Journal of the Votes and Proceedings of The Tenth General Assembly of the State of New-Jersey*, 2nd sitting (Trenton: Isaac Collins, 1786), 12-13. (JV&P).

28. Meeting of Congress, March 7, 1786, JCC 30:96.

29. General Assembly Meeting, March 9, 1786, JV&P 43-44.

30. Credentials of the State of New Jersey, *Journal of the Acts and Proceedings of the Convention, Assembled at Philadelphia* (Boston: Thomas B. Wait, 1819), 26.

Clark had been re-elected to Congress (then meeting in New York), and therefore declined his invitation citing a conflict of interest. Livingston was enjoying life as a peacetime governor, spending more time with his family and books in Elizabethtown when the call to Philadelphia came. In Philadelphia, Livingston was his usual introverted self, and James Madison did not mention him making any speeches in the debates. Livingston did, however, serve as chairperson for two committees that waded through state debts, the militia, and the importation of slaves. Livingston's signature can be found on the Constitution of the United States.[31]

Abraham Clark wrote to a fellow New Jersey assemblyman expressing his displeasure in the Constitution: "I never liked the System in all its parts. I considered it from the first, more a Consolidated government than a federal, a government too expensive, and unnecessarily Oppressive in its Operation; creating a judiciary undefined and unbounded." Despite his misgivings, he hoped it would be ratified by the states and believed that the amendment process would cure its weaknesses. In the end, Clark, fearful that smaller and less wealthy New Jersey was being exploited by Congress under the Articles of Confederation, swallowed his idealism, believing taxation would be more equitable with the new Constitution. His expressed critiques of the Constitution came back to haunt him in the first federal election under the nation's new charter.[32]

William Livingston helped decide Clark's fate in an election so fraught with problems, New York merchant Walter Rutherfurd remarked, "Poor Jersey, is made a laughing stock of." Historian Richard P. McCormick extensively studied the New Jersey election of 1789 and concluded:

> Loose franchise requirements . . . poorly distributed polling facilities, partial election officials, lax balloting regulations, and ambiguous provisions for closing the election and counting the votes were but some of the flaws in the mechanism. There existed every opportunity for determined political managers to pile up votes in a brazenly calculated manner. Because the machinery was faulty, it cannot be said that the election represented the popular will of the people of New Jersey.

New Jersey had four seats in the House of Representatives to fill. Under the new federal Constitution, selection of House representatives

---

31. Gigantino, *William Livingston's American Revolution*, 189-191.
32. Clark to Thomas Sinnickson, July 23, 1788, in John P. Kaminski, et al., eds. *The Documentary History of the Ratification of the Constitution Digital Edition* (Charlottesville: University of Virginia, 2009).

bypassed the state government, going to the majority choice of eligible voters. The legislatures, however, established the ground rules for the election. An act of the New Jersey legislature established voter qualifications, polling locations, oversight and also established the governor and his Privy Council (chosen from the Legislative Council) as certifiers. Most importantly, the election of the representatives consisted of a statewide four-person slate.

New Jersey was politically bifurcated as a "result of historical, geographic, social, cultural, and economic differences between the two regions" of East and West Jersey. Both sections were united in their widespread support for the new Constitution and the belief that federal import tariffs would ease the tax burden of less wealthy New Jersey. To the chagrin of West Jersey, Abraham Clark and his fellow East Jersey representatives dominated the legislature. West Jersey's leaders and sympathizers looked to the election of 1789 to seize back the government. In this effort, they had a Federalist ally living in Elizabethtown, Livingston's friend Elias Boudinot. A veteran, former Continental Congress President, and Federalist, Boudinot emerged as the leader of the four-person slate preferred by West Jersey. "The Junto," as Boudinot's ticket was known, also included James Shureman, Thomas Sinnickson and Lambert Cadwallader. All three had experience in government and were against the major policies advocated by Clark. East Jersey was unable to produce a unanimous four-person slate. Clark and Jonathan Dayton, the son of his friend Elias Dayton, were the two leading East Jersey candidates appearing on several four person slates.

The West Jersey faction branded the election as a choice between those who favored the Constitution and those who favored the old government. Substantive policy took a backseat to personal attacks. An organized effort to discredit and smear Abraham Clark emerged from several quarters. Just days before the polling started on February 11, Clark published a piece in the *Political Intelligencer* defending himself against published accusations that he was anti-Constitution. Seen as the strongest candidate, Clark was the number one target of The Junto and was also accused of feeling contempt for George Washington. Quakers were planning to sit out the election, and The Junto convinced them that Clark and Dayton were planning to impose a Presbyterian tyranny on them. Clark's East Jersey compatriot Dayton was accused by The Junto of being a London Trader. Clark-Dayton allies fought back by spreading word that Boudinot was a corrupt politician who had stolen from the national treasury while in Congress.

The election turned into a confused hotly contested affair due to the mistake of not having a hard date for counties to report their results.

The election statute only required that counties submit results when they were finished counting. This not surprisingly led to unscrupulous efforts to win. The West Jersey Junto's operatives in East Jersey relayed ongoing vote totals to the campaign back home. Boudinot's slate sent election inspectors around friendly counties with ballot boxes to rake in more votes, which was illegal because exact polling locations were specified by election law.

On March 3, with polling one month-old, Governor Livingston summoned a meeting of the Privy Council to sort out the election. At the time of Livingston's meeting, county returns were still outstanding with Clark and Dayton leading the West Jersey Junto. Two of the Privy Council members favored giving them the victory with limited results reported. The other two members supported waiting until all counties reported. Livingston chose to keep the counting going. Here was the benefit of holding power. Livingston was a referee for an election involving his friend and partisan ally Boudinot.

Livingston reconvened the Privy Council on March 18, at which time Boudinot's ticket moved into a lead with all West Jersey counties reporting. Essex county was still open, however. Clark and Dayton's supporters, despite not having favorable math, wanted to buy more time and accordingly took to the newspapers. The East Jersey ticket was countered by published articles appealing to the patriotism of Essex County to close the polls. The Governor and Privy Council were again divided on when to call the election. Despite this, on March 19, Livingston declared the Boudinot ticket winners. He certified the results, publicly declaring that Essex County was preventing New Jersey from having representation in the incoming Congress.[33]

The contentious election was not over. James Madison wrote to George Washington who was about to start his first term as President of the United States, "In New Jersey the election has been conducted in a very singular manner . . . by a rival jealousy between the Eastern & Western divisions of the State . . . an impeachment of the election by the unsuccessful competitors has been talked of."[34]

Essex County did not close it polls until April 27, and the day after, the "impeachment" arrived in Congress as a bundle of numerous petitions from "citizens of New-Jersey, complaining of the illegality of the

---

33. Richard P. McCormick, "New Jersey's First Congressional Election, 1789: A Case Study in Political Skullduggery," *The William and Mary Quarterly*, vol. 6, no. 2 (1949), 238-250.

34. James Madison to George Washington, in Gillard Hunt, ed., *The Writings of James Madison* (New York: G.P. Putnam's Sons, 1904), 5:329-330.

election of the members holding seats in this house." The House referred the matter to its Committee of Elections which was charged with interviewing petitioners to "receive such proofs and allegations, as the petitioners shall judge proper to offer, in support of said petition," and those "in opposition to said petition." On July 14, the House received the Committee of Elections report. Read and debated the next day, it was not until September 2 that the House officially declared "upon full and mature consideration, that James Schureman, Lambert Cadwalader, Elias Boudinot, and Thomas Sinnickson, were duly elected and returned to serve in this House."[35]

35. House of Representatives, April 18-19, 1789, *Journal of the House of Representatives* (Francis Childs & John Swaine: New York: 1789), 25-28, 54, 105, 120

# Thomas Paine on Popular Government in America: The Evolution of a Radical's Thinking

## ❦ JETT CONNER ❦

It would be hard to find a more strident, vocal supporter of popular government during America's founding period than Thomas Paine. The proposals put forth in his January 1776 pamphlet *Common Sense* for an "unmixed" and unchecked democratic scheme for America, designed to replace the British arrangement of balanced and mixed powers of King, Lords and Commons, were radical.[1] Remarkably, the pamphlet appeared just over a year after Paine had immigrated to America from England. But while his ideas helped push the colonies toward separating from British rule, they rattled at least one leading voice for independence in the Second Continental Congress. John Adams asserted that Paine's ideas were too "democratical."[2] A decade later Paine agreed, at least on several important points.

Believing that the true source of legitimate power was to be found only in the sovereignty of the people and not in any governmental institutions or claims to higher authority, Paine set out in *Common Sense*—following forceful arguments urging Americans to separate themselves from Great Britain—to outline what kind of government the colonies should create: a new, more egalitarian, democratic scheme of representative government. "Let the assemblies be annual, with a president only. The representation more equal, their business wholly

---

1. Corinne Comstock Weston, *English Constitutional Theory and the House of Lords* (New York: Columbia University Press, 1965), 179.
2. John Adams Autobiography, Part 1, "John Adams," through 1776, sheet 23 of 53, *Adams Family Papers: An Electronic Archive*. Massachusetts Historical Society, www.masshist.org/digitaladams/.

domestic, and subject to the authority of a Continental Congress."[3] Although many welcomed Paine's vigorous call for independence, his simple formula for "a government of our own" in *Common Sense* must have elicited a sardonic smile or two at the time. It still does.

At the heart of Paine's proposals was his advocacy of a unicameral legislative body with no independent executive, no mention of a judiciary and no internal balanced powers or checks anywhere to be found. Instead, he envisioned separate roles for the colonial assemblies and the national Congress to play, divided along the lines of domestic and international duties. And he hinted at a fundamental principle of a federal structure: any such a division of delegated powers between the states and national government should tilt in the direction of the latter.

But *Common Sense* found no room for royalty, aristocracy, or clerical absolutism. These were relics of the Old World, Paine advised. There was no place in Paine's recommendations for America for the venerated "balanced" powers in the British constitution that French thinker Montesquieu so admired in the British model.[4] For there was nothing left to balance. The only institution that Paine found useful in the British system of government was the Commons. But it was corrupted by the allegiance-owing king's ministers. So, Paine did away with the foundations of British authority and representation and grounded both instead in the people.

One who did not find Paine's ideas so attractive was Adams, a kindred rebellious spirit and powerful voice for independence in the Congress. Alarmed by Paine's radical recommendations for government in *Common Sense* (though supportive of the pamphlet's call for independence and envious of its popular appeal), he rushed to counter Paine's proposals for forming a government by publishing a pamphlet of his own later that spring: *Thoughts on Government: Applicable to the Present State of the American Colonies.*[5] Holding that the only valuable thing about the British constitution was its republican features (a republic is an "empire of laws, and not of men") Adams set out in his pamphlet to build a better republican model than Paine's democratic prescriptions offered.

---

3. Thomas Paine, *The Complete Writings of Thomas Paine*, 2 vols., ed. Phillip S. Foner (New York: Citadel Press, 1969), 1:28.
4. Montesquieu, *The Spirit of Laws*, ed. David Wallace Carrithers (Berkley: University of California Press, 1977), 196-214.
5. John Adams, "III. Thoughts on Government, April 1776," founders.archives.gov/documents/Adams/06-04-02-0026-0004.

Adams made no bones about his skepticism of Paine's single-chamber, all-powerful legislature, wondering whether all powers of government, legislative, executive, and judicial, should be contained in a single legislative body. He answered no, because such an assembly would be "liable to all the vices, follies and frailties of an individual."[6] Paine did not possess this insight, at the time.

The Second Continental Congress meeting in Philadelphia that spring and summer had two competing, widely read pamphlets informing delegates of what sort of republican government ought to replace British rule, should independence be declared. Many colonies were already in the process of building their own new governments, drawing on ideas from these and other sources.

After the Declaration of Independence was promulgated in July, Congress moved to create America's first national constitution by proposing the Articles of Confederation. Paine's recommendations for a single-house legislative body, devoid of separation of powers and checks and balances, contrary to Adams' proposals, prevailed and was formally put into place at the successful conclusion of America's War for Independence. Adams paid little attention to the structure of the national government when writing down his proposals in *Thoughts on Government* for new colonial constitutions.[7]

Differing from Paine's thinking, the new states' powers remained superior over those meager few delegated by the Articles to the Congress. But many of Adams' recommendations, though he supported the creation and ratification of the Articles, informed several of the new state governments being created at the time and eventually were incorporated in the proposals for a new Constitution in 1787.

Pennsylvania's first constitution had more similarities to Paine's democratic proposals found in *Common Sense*. Though he worked for a while as a clerk to the Pennsylvania Assembly, he was never a delegate, just as he never was to the Continental Congress. But his influence was certainly apparent in the structure of both the Articles and Pennsylvania models from the start. Notably however, both constitutions were short lived. Both were flawed, but for different reasons: A lack of power for national government and unbridled legislative powers in a single-chamber assembly in Pennsylvania where the powers of a partisan majority could be wielded unchecked. The Articles were replaced by the ratification of the Constitution, the Pennsylvania constitution, soon after.

6. Ibid.
7. Jett B. Conner, *John Adams vs Thomas Paine: Rival Plans for the Early Republic* (Yardley, PA: Westholme Publishing, 2018), 35.

At least one Paine scholar has questioned the notion that Pennsylvania's constitution of 1776 was the most democratic of all the states. Pointing out that the constitution was never approved by a vote of the people, that representation was not based on "per head" but on counties (giving the western back-country counties an advantage over the Assembly from the beginning), and that it disenfranchised most of the eligible electorate in the state, J.C.D. Clark argued that the idea was a myth. He also pointed out that Paine had no objections to the constitution's arrangements.[8]

In his last published pamphlet prior to heading off to Europe on the eve of the Constitutional Convention (both Paine and Adams were in Europe during the Convention), Paine confronted the stresses and cracks in the functioning of the Pennsylvania model: the problem of an overbearing majority. His *Dissertation on Government: The Affairs of the Bank: And Paper Money*, 1786, came about because of actions taken by "back-country" Pennsylvania farmers and the Constitutionalist Party they controlled in the Pennsylvania Assembly beginning in 1785.

The most important problem that Paine addressed in his pamphlet as well as in letters and articles in the local papers at the time, was that the state assembly revoked the Pennsylvania charter of Robert Morris's Bank of North America, chiefly over its preference for paper money.[9] Rural debtors feared that the value of paper money, which the state had attempted to regulate to help, among other things, keep the farmers afloat, would not be accepted on par with money, based on specie, issued by the national bank. They believed the bank unfairly favored the urban, mercantilist class. The conflict began about the same time as Shay's Rebellion, a similar battle, though one much more threatening and violent, between debtors and creditors, that broke out in Massachusetts.

The Pennsylvania dispute tested Paine's majoritarian principles, for he also favored the national bank. Originally aligned with the Constitutionalist Party, he broke with it over the issue. Paine was an early nationalist: he believed that a national bank was necessary to tie the colonies (and then states following Independence) together, in order

8. J.C.D. Clark, *Thomas Paine: Britain, America & France in the Age of Enlightenment and Revolution* (Oxford: Oxford University Press, 2018), 78n45.
9. Samuel B. Harding, *Party Struggles over the first Pennsylvania constitution* (Trustees of Indiana University: 2002), 389n1, purl.dlib.indiana.edu/iudl/inauthors/VAC1009. The charter was restored after pro-bank factions won the elections of 1786. Harvey J. Kaye, *Thomas Paine and the Promise of America* (New York: Hill & Wang, 2005), 69. See Thomas Paine National Historical Association, www.thomaspaine.org, for additional writings on the matter, based on the years 1785 and 1786.

to fund and win the war, and then to establish an independent nation. A national debt, he declared in *Common Sense*, is a national bond. Conflicts over national and state monetary policies such as those arising in Pennsylvania and Massachusetts amounted to existential threats to the new nation.

He also earlier had worked for a time for Robert Morris, a point not lost on the farmers who accused Paine, after publishing his articles and *Dissertation on Government*, of abandoning the common man by defending the bank. They accused him of being a hired pen.[10]

But Paine's pamphlet revealed that he was beginning to explore limits to the principles of majority rule. His solution to limiting an overbearing majority was found in the idea of fundamental law. An enabling charter, such as that of the national bank, was the kind of law, like a constitution, that could not, he argued, be overridden by routine legislation.

> For admitting a question of law to arise, whether the charter, which that act attempts to repeal, is a law of the land in the manner in which laws of universal operations are, or of the nature of a contract made between the public and the bank . . . the repealing act does not and cannot decide the question, because it is the repealing act that makes the question, and its own fate is involved in the decision. It is a question of law and not a question of legislation, and must be decided on in a court of justice and not by a house of assembly.[11]

In a rudimentary way, Paine anticipated Alexander Hamilton's *Federalist 78* essay on the necessity for judicial review. Though he had not mentioned an independent judiciary in *Common Sense* (assuming, following the English model, that it would reside in the legislative body), Paine began to understand that courts might have to step in to mediate disputes between a charter and a politically motivated legislative majority. Fundamental law was superior to ordinary law as he and many others understood it. As Pennsylvania had granted a perpetual charter to Morris' bank, mere legislation could not repeal it. A founding charter constituted a "higher law," a doctrine echoed thirty years later by Chief Justice John Marshall in *Dartmouth College v. Woodward*, 17 U.S. 518 (1819).[12]

---

10. Harding, *Party Struggles*.

11. Paine, *Complete Writings*, 2:403-404.

12. For an interesting comparison of Paine's and Marshall's ideas on constitutional law, see Robin West, "Tom Paine's Constitution," *Virginia Law Review* 89 (2003): 1413-1461, scholarship.law.georgetown.edu/cgi/viewcontent.cgi?article=1285&context=facpub.

Paine also took Adams' concern about a majority in the legislature, capable of acting just as ruthlessly as an individual could, to a new level: "despotism may be more effectually acted by many over the few, than by one man over many."[13] In short, the potential tyranny of the majority, especially a party majority, was worse. That forced him to rethink his position on bicameralism:

> My idea of a single legislature was always founded on a hope, that whatever personal parties there might be in the state, they would all unite and agree in the general principles of good government—that these party differences would be dropped at the threshold of the state house, and that the public good, or the good of the whole, would be the governing principle of the legislature . . . But when party operates to produce party laws, a single house is a single person, and subject to the haste, rashness and passion of individual sovereignty. At least, it is an aristocracy.[14]

Adams, if he read the piece (he was in Europe), must have grinned. Perhaps Paine rethought the advice offered in Adams' *Thoughts on Government.* Furthermore, James Madison had yet to pen his famous *Federalist 10,* a piece that directly confronted this problem of popular government: the problem of a majority faction acting in its own self-interest against the common good, a potential problem of the era that bore serious consideration.

One Paine scholar and historian, Eric Foner, remarked that "Paine on popular sovereignty did not get along easily with Paine on charter contracts."[15] But at the very least, Paine's *Dissertation on Government* demonstrated the evolution, and the necessity for an accommodation, in the political philosophy of one of early America's most radical voices for popular government.

13. Paine, *Complete Writings,* 2:374.
14. Ibid., 2:409.
15. Eric Foner, *Tom Paine and Revolutionary America* (New York: Oxford University Press, 1976), 199.

# The "Western Forts" of the 1783 Treaty of Paris

**RICHARD WERTHER**

The Revolutionary War was formally ended by the Treaty of Paris in early 1783. Problems with compliance arose on both sides nearly immediately on several issues. One was the continued occupation by Great Britain of the so-called "Western Forts." These forts should have reverted to American hands according to the terms of the Treaty. The breach this represented was a problem that lasted all the way until 1796, when the United States finally ratified the Jay Treaty of 1794 and Britain turned over the forts. What forts comprised these "Western Forts"?

Identifying the forts included in "Western Forts" proved to be less straightforward than I expected. Counts of the number of forts involved vary depending on which sources you consult. Much contemporary correspondence suffered from the same problem that interested me in researching this in the first place: They simply refer to "Western Forts" (or Outposts, or Garrisons). They covered three general areas: The Northwest Territories, Upstate New York, and Lake Champlain (the latter a little more Northern than Western). The consensus among the various sources leads me to the following list:

NORTHWEST TERRITORIES
> Fort Michilimackinac/Fort Mackinac
> Fort Lernoult/Fort Detroit
> Fort Miami

UPSTATE NEW YORK
> Fort Niagara
> Fort Oswegatchie
> Fort Oswego/Fort Ontario

LAKE CHAMPLAIN
Fort Au Fer
Fort Dutchman's Point

Some of this needs further explanation. Several forts had multiple names. Lernoult and Oswego became Detroit and Ontario – same forts, new names. Alternatively, Michilimackinac and Mackinac are two different forts, the former located in Mackinac City in Michigan's Lower Peninsula, the latter located on Mackinac Island, close by in the straits between lakes Michigan and Huron. Mackinaw was built in 1781, and shortly thereafter Michilimackinac was destroyed. Mackinac is the one the British occupied, though the prior appellation was sometimes used in the correspondence from the time.

The list changes a bit depending on whether you are looking backward from the perspective of John Jay's 1794 treaty, or forward from the Paris Treaty of 1783. For example, the Fort Miami in Ohio was constructed (by the British!) on American territory in the period between the two treaties. It was not in existence for the Paris Treaty, though it was included in what was handed over in the Jay Treaty (however, see the next point).

The British-built Fort Miami was built on U.S. soil, in direct violation of U.S. sovereignty, in 1794. Its purpose was to obstruct Gen. Anthony Wayne's march toward Fort Detroit, and to rally Indian support to do it. The resulting Battle of Fallen Timbers was won by Wayne in short order as the tribes which included the Shawnee, Miami, and Ottawa, among others, quickly dispersed. The resulting Treaty of Greenville (Indiana) opened much of Ohio to white settlement.

Just to complicate things further, some of the Paris perspective lists did include a Fort Miami. The only explanation I can find for this was that there was a second Fort Miami (Fort Saint Phillipe or Fort Miamis), located in Indiana. The French constructed this much earlier and it eventually became Fort Wayne.

Fort Erie (or Presque Isle) was mentioned in a letter from Thomas Jefferson to the British demanding Treaty compliance though, by one source at least, it was not in American territory. Yet another source indicated it was on American land. The latter proved correct, but was somehow not involved in the controversy.

Finally, I also have a list of what I call "orphan forts" as they appear in one source. These include the Great Sodus Fort (referenced in a letter from Secretary of State Edmund Randolph to Jay), Fort Recovery (built by Gen. Anthony Wayne during the time between the Treaty of Paris and the Jay Treaty but never British occupied), and Fort Sandusky (burned down in Pontiac's Rebellion in 1763 and long gone by 1783). All these forts will be set aside for the remainder of this discussion.

Article VII of the Treaty of Paris of September 30, 1783, stipulated that "his Britannic Majesty shall with all convenient speed … withdraw all his armies, garrisons, and fleets from the said United States, and from every post, place, and harbor within the same; leaving in all fortifications."[1] When final ratification of the treaty was completed in early 1784, the British continued to hold all these outposts.

What followed was a fruitless series of U.S. attempts to take back the forts. In August 1783, Gen. George Washington had dispatched Gen. Friedrich von Steuben to Canada to arrange details of evacuation with British Gen. Frederick Haldimand. Von Steuben was soon sent packing with two letters, one to Washington explaining how Haldimand had instructions about the cessation of hostilities but nothing about turning over forts, and one to Von Steuben himself explaining the same. In reporting the incident to his superiors, Haldimand admitted he was playing for time.[2] In May 1784, Lt. Col. Nicholas Fish arrived representing Gov. George Clinton of New York, only to be similarly dispatched by Haldimand, who added that Britain would discuss the subject only with Congress, not with individual states. This excuse evaporated when Lt. Col. William Hull arrived in July 1784 bearing a letter from Henry Knox, America's Secretary of War. Having since received impossibly vague instructions from London, Haldimand elected to rebuff Hull and sent him away empty-handed.

Strike one, strike two, and strike three. It was clear by now that the British were not interested in surrendering the posts. Their motives for doing so were several, complicated, and to some extent overlap. The major ones were:

TREATY LEVERAGE. The British wanted leverage to force American compliance with the treaty terms. The U.S. had not complied with several portions of the treaty, most critically not making good on pre-Revolution debts owed to British merchants and subjects, and their continued confiscation of Loyalist properties. Britain still held American territory, they asserted, as a gauge for the proper performance of its treaty obligations by the Americans.[3]

---

1. *The Paris Peace Treaty of September 30, 1783*, The Avalon Project, avalon.law.yale.edu/18th_century/paris.asp.
2. A.L. Burt, "A New Approach to the Problem of the Western Posts," *Report of the Annual Meeting of the Canadian Historical Association*, Volume 10, Number 1 (1931), 66.
3. Samuel Flagg Bemis, *Jay's Treaty: A Study in Commerce and Diplomacy* (New York: The Macmillan Company, 1923), 3.

Legitimate complaints about the U.S. treaty violations, however, were a smokescreen as it is now known that the day before formal ratification of the Treaty of Paris, the British Home Secretary Lord Sydney secretly decided to instruct its governor general in Canada to maintain control over all the forts.[4] The British strategy going forward would be to hide behind the debt issue to disguise their continued imperial ambitions and the resulting non-compliance with the treaty. If Britain had made a move to turn over the forts and then pulled back, the debt and loyalists arguments might have held water. But no such move was ever made.[5]

The courts of some states had declared that the Revolution, as a social upheaval, had broken all previous contracts and engagements; hence, American debtors were not responsible for the interest on their debts incurred during the conflict. Two states particularly presenting problems were New York and Virginia. It was a nice try but was not going to cut it with the British. In its impotence, the Confederation Congress could not overrule state actions, making resolution of the debt issue even more difficult. One British official was heard to quip that Britain needed to send not one but thirteen envoys to the States![6]

The American government's weakness was resolved with the new Constitution and the assumption of the presidency by Washington in 1789. One of the first tasks for Washington was to establish control of the hinterlands where the British still controlled the forts. This proved to be a harder task than envisioned due to some of the other factors listed below.

THE FUR TRADE. Despite British misdirection on the debt issue and the treatment of loyalists, America maintained that the real issue for holding the posts was to retain control of the fur trade. Despite British protestations to the contrary, the British National Archives contains reams of documents which provide fine ammunition for the American charge.[7] The fur trade was at that time the greatest and most profitable single industry in North America.[8] Exactly how profitable was a question.

---

4. Howard Jones, *Crucible of Power: A History of American Foreign Relations to 1913* ( Lanham, MD: Rowman & Littlefield, 2001), 23.

5. Burt, "A New Approach," 70.

6. N.A. Graebner, R.D. Burns, and J.M. Siracusa, *Foreign affairs and the founding fathers: From confederation to constitution, 1776-1787* (Santa Barbara: ABC-CLIO, LLC., 2011), 35.

7. Burt, "A New Approach," 70.

8. Bemis, *Jay's treaty*, 5.

The forts, though comprising little land by themselves and widely dispersed, controlled the fur trading routes. Estimates of the worth of this trade vary greatly. One source put it at as much as £200,000 annually (roughly $240,000),[9] while another put it closer to between £20,000 and £60,000 per annum.[10] A third source indicates Fort Detroit and Mackinac generating £40,800 and £60,400 per year, respectively.[11]

The counterpoint is the cost of controlling the forts. It is estimated that at just one fort, Fort Detroit, the bill for merchandise, rum and provisions purchases for the period June 1779 to October 1780 (pre-treaty) was nearly £90,000.[12] Further, at stake was not the sales price of the furs, but the profits, a far lower number than the gross sales. It is likely that holding the forts to maintain the fur trade was a losing proposition financially. From purely business considerations, it was probably in Britain's interest to turn over the forts.[13] In fact, the British Prime Minister in 1782, Lord Shelburne, stated that the treaty would save the British £750,000 annually, at least part of this due to not having to provision the forts.[14]

Lord Dorchester (formerly Sir Guy Carleton), the governor general of British North America, was instructed by the British government five months later that the posts must be held at all costs, and recaptured if taken; that this was preferable to the loss of the fur trade and the endangering of Quebec.[15] Over time, the fur trade shifted in anticipation of the eventual loss of the posts, such that when the British actually turned them over via the Jay Treaty, there was little perceptible impact on the industry. The British had held the posts until they were no longer of value from a fur trade perspective.[16]

INDIGENOUS RELATIONS. The thorniest issue in the mix was relations with the Native Americans. They represented a delicate matter for both the British and the Americans, exacerbated by the high unpredictability of the Indian reaction to the Paris Treaty and the differing reactions among the different tribes. The primary sore point with the Indians

9. Graebner, et al, *Foreign affairs*, 31.
10. Celia Barnes, *Native American Power in the United States 1783-1795* (Cranbury, NJ: Rosemont Publishing & Printing Corp., 2003), 79.
11. Frank E. Ross, "The Fur Trade of the Western Great Lakes Region," *Minnesota History Magazine* Vol. 19 No. 3 (1938), 299.
12. Barnes, *Native American Power*, 79.
13. Burt, "A New Approach," 72.
14. Louise Phelps Kellogg, *The British Régime in Wisconsin and the Northwest* (Madison: State Historical Society of Wisconsin, 1935), 190.
15. Bemis, *Jay's treaty*, 17.
16. Burt, "A New Approach," 71.

was the lack of their inclusion at the table in the Paris Treaty negotiations. But this would have not been the issue it was had the Treaty not drawn the borders as it had. The Treaty had assigned the region south of the Great Lakes and between the Ohio and Mississippi Rivers to the United States, a region the Indians had considered theirs since the 1768 Treaty of Fort Stanwix. The British had bargained the Indian land out from under them, leaving them to work it out with the Americans.

The American stance was quite clear from the beginning as expressed by Richard Butler, one of the emissaries designated to make the Paris Treaty terms a reality through negotiations with the Indians:

> You joined the British King against us, and followed his fortunes; we have overcome him, he has cast you off, and given us your country; and Congress, in bounty and mercy, offer you country and peace. We have told you the terms on which you shall have it; these terms we will not alter.[17]

In other words, American and Indian representatives would need to conclude their own peace in North America, but it would hardly be a negotiation.[18] Technically, the United States remained at war with the King's Indian allies in 1783.[19] This war would play out in conflicts too numerous to discuss in the scope of this article, running all the way to the 1794 Jay Treaty and beyond.

By 1786, the United States had signed peace treaties with all the important northern and western tribes. These paper agreements had little value, however, when compared to the realities on the ground. Events soon spiraled out of the control of the conciliators, as militants from various tribes vowed resistance and followed their own courses. The frontier was embroiled in an unofficial but quite real war, such was the intensity of Indian hostility.[20]

The British had put themselves in a tough position. They felt a certain responsibility toward the tribes—if not as a matter of honor, then certainly as a matter of security. It was up to Canadian officials, therefore, to regain their trust and allegiance with promises of continued support.[21]

17. Barnes, *Native American Power*, 69.
18. Lawrence B. Hatter, *Citizens of Convenience: The Imperial Origins of American Nationhood on the U.S.-Canadian Border* (Charlottesville and London: University of Virginia Press, 2016), 17.
19. Hatter, *Citizens of Convenience*, 40.
20. Barnes, *Native American Power*, 74.
21. Ibid., 76.

Holding the forts illustrated the tightrope Britain was trying to walk—keeping on good terms with the tribes but avoiding conflict with the United States. Evacuation of the posts would be a sure sign of betrayal of the Indians. British officials even feared that the Indians, because of the treaty terms, would vent their rage on the still British-held garrisons.[22] To reconcile the Indians with the Americans while at the same time recovering the confidence of the natives proved an impossible needle to thread.[23]

LACK OF COMMERCIAL AGREEMENT. The inability to strike a comprehensive commercial agreement between Britain and the United States also led to failure to resolve the standoff. Negotiations between the parties continued after the initial 1783 agreement to reach a comprehensive trade agreement between the two, an agreement that would deal with issues such as the fur trade and resolve the border disputes. In sum, a treaty that would resolve many of the questions the Treaty of Paris left unanswered about the relationship between the peoples of the British Empire and the United States. Surely it was simply a matter of time before the final pieces of the border settlement fell into place.[24]

Well, no. Several problems with this approach arose. First was the American "take it or leave it" stance with the Indians, described in the previous point. When the Indians chose not to back down, the tiny and underfunded U.S. Army, an extension of the weakness of the Confederation government, could not back up the diplomatic bullying of American policymakers with armed force.[25]

Further, to codify future British-American trade relations, British negotiator David Hartley came to Paris in 1783 with a series of proposals written by Canadian merchants. These included a provision that British troops would continue to garrison the western posts for three years, primarily because the merchants did not believe that the United States was currently capable of protecting the lives and property of traders.[26]

The American peace commissioners, John Adams, Benjamin Franklin and John Jay, tentatively agreed to this, in exchange for trade reciprocity between the U.S. and the British West Indies. This last part may be where things broke down. A change in the British ministry to one much less sympathetic to the Americans resulted in a less concil-

22. Graebner, et al, *Foreign affairs*, 31.
23. Burt, "A New Approach," 73.
24. Hatter, *Citizens of Convenience*, 17.
25. Ibid., 18.
26. Ibid., 34.

iatory stance toward the U.S. and a desire to remain true to the Navigation Acts. Among other restrictions, the Acts required goods to be transported between Britain and the (now former) colonies on British ships and restricted what types of goods could be carried. The result was that the proposed language was not included in the final agreement. With no commercial agreement reached, the forts and commerce situations remained at status quo.

The Americans were convinced that the inability to spell out commercial details and the functioning of the border beyond what was fashioned in the initial treaty was due to the perception (unfortunately largely accurate) that the Confederation Congress would be unable to enforce the treaty provisions with all the states. American policymakers would need to prove that the United States could act like a unified national state if it ever expected to strike a deal with Great Britain.[27] The border situation remained in limbo, not only between the U.S. and British Canada but between both and the Indians.

REASSUMING CONTROL? Lastly, some attributed an even more opportunistic spin on British policy, believing that they were waiting for the nascent republic to disintegrate so that they could re-assume their possession of the country. Congress's inability to control the states, as exemplified by the debt and loyalist issues, its ineffectiveness in collecting taxes from the states, and its difficulties in solving the Western lands issues, all signaled its tenuous hold on power. This lack of control indicated a real possibility of disunion and collapse. As Benjamin Franklin observed, "she desired to postpone as long as possible the final surrender of a valuable region. She hoped that the new Union would not hold together and that a coveted territory would thus revert to her."[28] But this was a mirage, one that ultimately persuaded Britain to sign Jay's Treaty in 1794.[29]

The establishment of a new constitutional government in 1789 changed the dynamics of many of these factors that were predicated on the weakness of the American government, though even then it would take some time for the new government to establish its bona fides and remedy the weaknesses of the Confederation. The new government was soon much more actively engaged, as exemplified by one Thomas Jefferson missive to the British government cataloging all the

27. Ibid., 38.
28. John Bigelow, *Breaches of Anglo-American Treaties A Study in History and Diplomacy* (New York: Sturgis & Walton Company, 1917), 8.
29. Burt, "A New Approach," 76.

treaty violations that ran some thirty-plus pages (modern typed!) along with sixty enclosures. Things like this started to prepare the ground for the Jay Treaty.

When the sides finally tried again, the issue of the forts was settled by Article II of the Jay Treaty in 1794. Reminiscent of the failed Treaty of Paris, it read in part:

> His Majesty will withdraw all His Troops and Garrisons from all Posts and Places within the Boundary Lines assigned by the Treaty of Peace to the United States. This Evacuation shall take place on or before the first Day of June One thousand seven hundred and ninety-six, and all the proper Measures shall in the interval be taken by concert between the Government of the United States, and His Majesty's Governor General in America, for settling the previous arrangements which may be necessary respecting the delivery of the said Posts.[30]

The Jay treaty, though famously hotly debated in America, was eventually signed by President Washington on May 6, 1796. Most of the outposts were formally handed over by the end of the summer, with the last, Fort Mackinac, handed over on October 2.[31] The long episode of the Western forts was over, at least for now. Some would come back into British hands the War of 1812, but that's another story for another day.

30. *The Jay Treaty, November 1794,* The Avalon Project, avalon.law.yale.edu/18th_century/jay.asp.
31. Bigelow, *Breaches of Anglo-American Treaties,* 15.

# Attended with Disagreeable Consequences: Cross-Border Shopping for Loyalist Provisions, 1783–1784

## ❧ STUART LYALL MANSON ❧

In the months following the end of the American Revolutionary War, British authorities in Canada desperately required supplies for refugee Loyalists slated to be resettled in that northern colony. The cross-border market that they targeted to meet these supply demands was ironic. They looked southward to a region of the United States that, during the recent military conflict, British, Loyalist and Indigenous troops had recently raided and ravaged.

By 1783 the war and its effects had turned tens of thousands of American Loyalists into landless refugees. They were no longer welcome in the Thirteen Colonies—now the newly-minted United States of America—where they formerly made their homes and where they had lived for years or decades. In the case of Indigenous Loyalists such as the Haudenosaunee (Iroquois), their wartime displacement disrupted a history that spanned centuries. Many factors contributed to the Loyalists' plight: siding with the Crown during the conflict in general; enlistment and service in Loyalist military regiments; and indirect acts such as supporting raiding parties or gathering intelligence for the British war effort against their rebellious neighbours. Moreover, throughout the war, Loyalist lands and possessions in the thirteen colonies were seized and sold by their enemies. In some areas, both sides waged vicious campaigns in which vast amounts of property and numerous lives were destroyed.

In particular, during the previous eight years of war, detachments of

Loyalist regiments and allied Indigenous war parties based in Canada (also known as Québec) launched destructive raids into the northern colonies. Originating from British posts on the Great Lakes, the upper St. Lawrence River, and the settled parts of Québec, the Loyalists were often joined in these raids by British regular regiments and sporadically by German auxiliary troops. Their objectives focussed on the fertile regions of the Mohawk River valley in central New York. Occasionally targeted were the communities nestled among the green mountains along the eastern shoreline of Lake Champlain in what is now known as western Vermont. One such raid against the latter was commanded by Major Christopher Carleton, the nephew of Guy Carleton who was an earlier Governor of Québec and who would soon to become its governor once again.[1]

Major Carleton's force scoured the shores of Lake Champlain in 1778, destroying Rebel infrastructure along both sides of the lake, including the east side which would later become the State of Vermont. Major Carleton's journal describes how the use of fire was essential in this operation: on November 6, 1778, in reference to the planned destruction of a Rebel-owned mill, Carleton wrote that he "sent a mattross with a fireball least they should not have time to fire it in the usual way."[2] A mattross was an artilleryman. A fireball, also known as a carcass, was an incendiary projectile usually fired from artillery. It was used to set fire to buildings or vessels and was made from a metal frame filled with a flammable mixture of gunpowder, pitch, saltpetre, sulphur, turpentine and tallow. Its vent holes spewed forth inextinguishable flames for several minutes.[3] In total, Carleton's raid resulted in the destruction of ninety-five structures, including twenty-one barns full of wheat, as well as dozens of sacks of wheat and stacks of hay.[4]

Another raid was led by Loyalist leader Sir John Johnson in 1780. His force included a large detachment of Johnson's military unit, the

1. Guy Carleton was also and the commander-in-chief of the British army in America during the latter part of the American Revolutionary War. See G. P. Browne, "Carleton, Guy, 1st Baron Dorchester," in *Dictionary of Canadian Biography*, Vol. 5, University of Toronto/Université Laval, 2003–, www.biographi.ca/en/bio/carleton_guy_5E.html.

2. Carleton's 1778 journal, reproduced in Ida H. Washington and Paul A. Washington, *Carleton's Raid* (Canaan, NH: Phoenix Publishing, 1977), 90.

3. David McConnell, *British Smooth-Bore Artillery: A Technological Study to Support Identification, Acquisition, Restoration, Reproduction, and Interpretation of Artillery at National Historic Parks in Canada* (Ottawa, ON: Environment Canada, National Historic Parks and Sites, 1988), 307-309.

4. "Return of Buildings &ca destroyed by the Detachment under Major Carleton in November 1778," reproduced in Washington and Washington, *Carleton's Raid*, 95.

King's Royal Regiment of New York, which was the largest loyalist regiment to serve out of Québec during the war.[5] It targeted Johnson's former stomping grounds in the Mohawk Valley of New York. Many of his regiment's soldiers and officers hailed from the region. Johnson's post-raid report to Québec Governor Frederick Haldimand noted that his party had been busy "laying waste to everything before them." His men destroyed 120 houses, barns and mills in which, according to Johnson, "vast quantities of flour, bread, Indian corn and other provisions were burnt ... many cattle were killed and about seventy horses brought off."[6] These and other raids have received attention in print, in detailed historical books such as Gavin K. Watt's *The Burning of the Valleys* and *Fire & Desolation,* and also in fictional works such as Walter D. Edmond's 1936 novel (and 1939 movie) *Drums Along the Mohawk*.[7] The ferocity of these raids renders it surprising that, only a few years later, British authorities would look to both New York and Vermont as possible sources of post-war seed and livestock for the Loyalists newly settled in Québec.

In 1783 the Treaty of Paris brought an official end to the conflict. Article VI of the treaty seemingly protected the future interests of Loyalists. It stated that:

> there shall be no future confiscations made, nor any prosecutions commenced against any Person or Person, for or by reason of the part which or they may have taken during the present War; and that no person shall on the account suffer and future loss or damage either in his person, liberty, or property.[8]

These words were evidently difficult to enforce among a war-weary populace; the victorious were disinclined to entertain the notion of *status quo ante bellum.* Instead, the Loyalists became landless refugees who were unwelcome in their former communities.

5. Mary Beacock Fryer, *King's Men: The Soldier Founders of* Ontario (Toronto, ON: Dundurn Press, 1980), 63.

6. Library and Archives Canada, MG 21, Add. Mss. 21661-21892 (hereafter Haldimand Papers), Vol. B158, 129-30.

7. Gavin K. Watt, *The Burning of the Valleys: Daring Raids from Canada Against the New York Frontier in the Fall of 1780* (Toronto, ON: Dundurn Press, 1997); Gavin K. Watt, *Fire & Desolation: The Revolutionary War's 1778 Campaign as Waged from Québec and Niagara Against the American Frontiers* (Toronto, ON: Dundurn Press, 2017); Walter D. Edmonds, *Drums Along the Mohawk* (Boston, MA: Little, Brown, and Company, 1936).

8. Adam Shortt and Arthur G. Doughty (eds.), *Documents Relating to the Constitutional History of Canada, 1759-1791. Part II* (Ottawa, ON: J. de L. Taché, King's Printer, 1918), 729.

After much thought about the landless Loyalists' plight, Québec Governor Frederick Haldimand eventually recommended that lands on the north shore of the upper St. Lawrence River, west of Montréal, become a landing spot for a portion of these displaced people. Situated adjacent to New York State and not far from the area that would soon become the State of Vermont, this region had been inhabited and hunted by the Haudenosaunee (Iroquois) and other Indigenous people for centuries. It had also been navigated by French traders, explorers and soldiers during decades prior to 1763 when it was part of New France. In 1783 the area had not yet received permanent European set-tlements. Immediately prior to the Loyalists' arrival in this region, gov-ernment surveyors subdivided the lands into farming lots to permit an orderly distribution of lands for settlement. Simultaneously, British government officials recognized that these settlers would require assis-tance in the form of provisions and agricultural supplies; with time run-ning out, they urgently required a procurement plan for those necessities and decided to look southward to meet the demand.

The first step in this cross-border shopping excursion occurred on March 4, 1784, only a few months before the scheduled movement of Loyalists from refugee camps around Montréal, Trois Rivières, and Québec City, to the undeveloped lands on the upper St. Lawrence River. On that day Governor Haldimand, through his military secretary Maj. Robert Matthews, authorized Loyalist officer Capt. Justus Sher-wood to investigate a full range of supply possibilities in Vermont. Sherwood was a Connecticut and Vermont Loyalist and an officer in the Queen's Loyal Rangers. He was also famously the Crown's wartime secret service expert in that neighborhood. He took part of the bold late-war attempt to lure Vermont back into the Crown fold, away from its rebellious predilections.[9] In reference to the search for agricultural supplies, Matthews explained to Sherwood that it was necessary to ex-amine this area within the United States for these commodities because Canadian-sourced wheat was "not only very dear, but scarce and indif-ferent in its quality." He proposed that wheat, potatoes, and cattle could be procured from Vermont.[10]

In reply to Matthews, Sherwood instead advocated obtaining wheat from another source: the Mohawk Valley of New York State. He sug-gested that suppliers in that region of the United States could deliver the grain to Oswego, a lakeside community at the eastern end of Lake Ontario. He considered Oswego to be an excellent location that offered

9. Fryer, *King's Men*, 264-9.
10. Robert Matthews to Justus Sherwood, March 4, 1784: Haldimand Papers, Vol. B65, 2-6.

easy water access to the new Loyalist settlements along the upper St. Lawrence River. Sherwood advised a "seasonable application" of effort along these lines and suggested that the low purchase price—five livres per bushel—made this a particularly attractive option.[11] A livre was an old French unit of currency which persisted into the British Regime, roughly equivalent to the British pound.[12] Governor Haldimand, upon being advised of this shift in geographic focus, quickly approved the plan and agreed with Sherwood's rationale. Haldimand summarized that "the conveyance from Oswego will be more convenient and more expeditious."[13]

Several months later and mere weeks before Loyalists were scheduled to pitch their wedge tents on their newly granted lands, little progress had been made on the provision procurement front. Perhaps the volume of other tasks associated with this demanding period interfered with the provisioning project. On May 20, 1784, Haldimand discussed the matter with the aforementioned Sir John Johnson, who had remained in Québec at the end of the war. Johnson had lost his vast Mohawk Valley estate during the war, originally amassed by his famous father, Indian Superintendent Sir William Johnson. Johnson the younger was an ardent Loyalist. Even before the war had begun he publicly declared his loyalty to the Crown when he received a request for support from the Tryon County Committee of Safety, a prominent Rebel organization in the Mohawk Valley. The committee wanted Johnson's assistance in embodying local militiamen against the British. Johnson replied: "Concerning myself, sooner than lift my hand against my King, or sign any association with those who would, I should suffer my own head to be cut off."[14] Moreover, when his regiment, the King's Royal Regiment of New York, was first formed in 1776 he described it as "a force sufficient to enable me to stand upon my legs and look my enemies in the face" and he portrayed these adversaries as "ingrateful Rebellious Miscreants."[15] In early 1784 Johnson had a new role: he was involved in the resettlement plan for the new "Royal Townships" on the St. Lawrence River upstream from Montréal. Haldimand told Johnson that, in addition to seed, livestock could also be sourced from

---

11. Sherwood to Matthews, March 12, 1784: Haldimand Papers, Vol. B162, 200-4.

12. Walter S. Avis, (ed.), *A Dictionary of Canadianisms on Historical Principles* (Toronto, ON: Gage, 1991), 432.

13. Matthews to Sherwood, March 22, 1784: Haldimand Papers, Vol. B63, 137-8.

14. Quoted in Richard Berleth, *Bloody Mohawk: The French and Indian War & American Revolution on New York's Frontier* (Delmar, NY: Black Dome Press, 2010), 174.

15. John Johnson to Daniel Claus, January 20, 1777: LAC, MG 19, Series F1, Vol. 1, 230-3.

the Mohawk Valley.[16] Time was running out and the project was further delayed, likely by the continued heavy demands of British and Loyalist authorities at the time.

The western Mohawk Valley of New York State was in no state to consider agricultural exports in 1784. Peter Sailly was a recent immigrant from France who travelled through the area that year. He described in his travel journal its bleak economic plight. For example, his entry dated May 29, 1784 describes the ravages perpetrated on German Flats during the late war, to which he noted:

> it would seem that Nature itself were in league with the enemy to desolate the country, for the land, naturally fertile, has been unproductive the present year. The most beautiful country in the world now presents only the poor cabins of an impoverished population who are nearly without food and upon the verge of starvation.[17]

Eastern portions of the valley, close to Johnstown, were not much better off. In his entry dated July 5, 1784, Sailly noted there was "but little commerce upon the Mohawk. The inhabitants are poor since the war."[18] In the northern colony of Québec, the Loyalists disembarked from their batteaux and stepped onto their newly allotted lands along the upper St. Lawrence River in June 1784, starting the work of transforming forest and bush into productive farmland. Despite this migration, again little progress had been made with the supply missions south of the border. By July of that year, Captain Sherwood and his men continued to investigate sources of supplies. During this period of continental transition, some Loyalists returned temporarily to their old homesteads in the former thirteen colonies, taking personal risk in attempts to settle their affairs. Sherwood informed Governor Haldimand, through Major Matthews, that Conrad Best planned to make such a trip in the near future. Best was a former ensign in the Loyal Rangers. He had offered to make enquiries while he was in the Mohawk Valley, to explore the availability of exporting wheat northward for use by the newly settled Loyalists.[19] Conrad Best was one of five brothers who joined Crown forces during the war, one of whom (Jacob Best Jr.) was a member of the King's Royal Regiment of New York and who died in the final year of the war. Their father, Jacob Best Sr., was "an old man, not able to bear arms" and stayed on the family

16. Frederick Haldimand to Johnson, May 20, 1784: Haldimand Papers, Vol. B65, 31-5.
17. Don Snow, Charles T. Gehring and William A. Starna (eds.), *In Mohawk Country: Early Narratives About a Native People* (Syracuse, NY: Syracuse University Press, 1996), 297.
18. Ibid., 299.
19. Sherwood to Matthews, July 23, 1784: Haldimand Papers, Vol. B162, 339-41.

homestead in the Hoosick region of New York, part way between Saratoga, New York and Bennington, Vermont. Best the elder was nonetheless "well attached to British Government" and had been fined by the Rebels for assisting Loyalist scouts from Québec. He had remained in Hoosick after the war and his location there was likely part of the reason why Conrad wished to visit the area in 1784, in addition to collecting debts owed to the family.[20]

Several days later Major Matthews also asked Sir John Johnson to despatch a trusted man to the Mohawk Valley "to learn to a certainty if any and what quantity may be procured, at what price, how soon, and what place it can be delivered for the most convenient and most expeditious transport of it to Cataraqui and downwards."[21] Cataraqui was the location of the town site of Kingston, at the head of the St. Lawrence River on Lake Ontario, and "downwards" referred to the Loyalist townships situated downstream from that site. Evidently this duplication of effort was necessary to ensure rapid progress on the much-delayed project. Johnson promptly replied, stating he had "great hopes" for the success of this mission.[22]

Governor Haldimand eventually accepted Captain Sherwood's manpower recommendation of Conrad Best as the man for this covert mission into the Mohawk Valley of New York State. Best received special instructions directly from Haldimand, which underscored the importance of discretion: "Do not impart to any person whosoever that this purchase is ordered to be made by Government," Haldimand advised, "but on account entirely of the settlers." He also requested that these written instructions should be left in Canada to prevent them from "falling into improper hands." Haldimand wisely hedged his bets by issuing similar instructions to Elijah Bottum, another former member of the Loyal Rangers, whose procurement mission targeted Vermont.[23] It is likely that Bottum had also been recommended by Capt. Justus Sherwood: The two men served together during the war, they were brothers-in-law, and Bottum had recently participated in an exploration of the north shore of the St. Lawrence to determine the lands' suitability for Loyalist resettlement.[24]

---

20. Loyalist financial claim: The National Archives, AO13, Series II, Piece 011, 264, 267, and 271; Loyalist financial claim: The National Archives, AO12, Series I, Piece 031, 64.

21. Matthews to Johnson, July 26, 1784: Haldimand Papers, Vol. B64, 93-5.

22. Johnson to Matthews, July 29, 1784: Haldimand Papers, Vol. B115, 279-80.

23. Matthews to Conrad Best, August 5, 1784: Haldimand Papers, Vol. B65, 44-6.

24. Haldimand Papers, Vol. B178, 311-312; Ian Pemberton, "Sherwood, Levius Peters," in *Dictionary of Canadian Biography*, Vol. 7, University of Toronto/Université Laval, 2003– www.biographi.ca/en/bio/sherwood_levius_peters_7E.html.

Prior to Best's return from the Mohawk Valley Sir John Johnson continued to be optimistic about the possibilities of acquiring wheat from these portions of the United States. He also predicted that Mohawk Valley wheat would be much cheaper than that procured from Vermont.[25] This was an important factor for a government whose purse had been drained by nearly a decade of war, on many fronts, and by the huge costs of maintaining the disbanded Loyalist soldiers and their families.

Finally, in early September 1784, Best provided an update on his mission. The information was disappointing. He reported, via another officer, that alarming intelligence forced him to abort his trek into the Mohawk Valley: "He was informed that his appearance upon the Mohawk River would be attended with danger to his person." Best therefore decided that the risk was too great; he sent another man into the valley in his stead. His alternate learned what British administrators ought to have known from the start: "No wheat would be permitted to go from that country, and that any proposals to the inhabitants upon the subject would be attended with disagreeable consequences."[26]

Attention then turned back to Vermont, despite the higher price tag and greater transport costs. Best and Bottum, now both tasked to that region, together secured 480 bushels of wheat for distribution to the Loyalists of the upper St. Lawrence River.[27] The man on the ground in the Loyalist settlements, Sir John Johnson, reported that this quantity, supplemented by smaller amounts available at Montréal, "will very near answer any demand that might be made."[28] The seeds were sent to the settlements for placement in warehouses known as the "King's Stores" for methodical distribution to Loyalist settlers.

Governor Haldimand was optimistic about the agricultural potential of the new Loyalist settlements and their occupants. He boldly estimated that "their industry will in a very few years raise in that fertile tract of country great quantities of wheat and other grains and become a granary for the lower parts of Canada."[29] Several years would pass before these Loyalist settlements would attain Haldimand's lofty projections of plenty. According to Thomas Gummersall Anderson, a boy soldier in his father Capt. Samuel Anderson's company in the King's Royal Regiment of New York, the settlers on the St. Lawrence had to

25. Johnson to Matthews, August 30, 1784: Haldimand Papers, Vol. B115, 294.
26. Campbell to Matthews, September 3, 1784: Haldimand Papers, Vol. B134, 349-50.
27. Matthews to Johnson, September 9, 1784: Haldimand Papers, Vol. B64, 233-4.
28. Johnson to Matthews, September 7, 1784: Haldimand Papers, Vol. B115, 295.
29. Haldimand to North, November 6, 1783: LAC, CO42, Q-Series, Vol. 23, 13-19.

"suffer many privations before they could raise crops to support their family." Anderson described the basic meal of this time, which consisted of "Indian corn, ground, and boiled for several hours, then eaten with milk, butter, sugar, etc., to suit the taste. It is very wholesome, nourishing and cheap food."[30] Loyalists also supplemented their diets through local hunting and fishing.

The British government provided rations to the Loyalists for three years after their resettlement along the St. Lawrence River. These rations consisted of flour, peas, meat such as pork or beef, and butter, distributed on a descending scale. In the first year, a full daily ration was provided, which was reduced to two thirds in the second year, and to one third in the third year.[31] The end of this rationing coincided with what is known as "The Hungry Year," a period of low crop yields that caused a near famine in 1788-1789. Almost a century later the memory of this trying time persisted. Early historian William Canniff noted in 1869 that:

> The period of famine is even yet remembered by a few, whose memory reaches back to the immediately succeeding years, and the descendants of the sufferers, speak of that time with peculiar feelings, imbibed from their parents.

Canniff referred to the Hungry Year as the "sad first page in the history of Upper Canada."[32] As noted by Canniff, the Loyalist settlements on the north shore of the St. Lawrence River became part of the founding townships of Upper Canada, a new colony created through British legislation in 1791. Upper Canada was officially renamed as Canada West in 1841. It later became the Province of Ontario, in the new nation called Canada, in 1867.

How did our cross-border shoppers—Conrad Best and Elijah Bottum—fare in the post-war period? Conrad Best survived the possibility of "disagreeable consequences" in his investigation of agricultural supplies in the Mohawk Valley in 1784, but not for long. He was one of the Loyalists who insisted on settling in the Missisquoi Bay area of southern Québec, much to the dismay of Governor Haldimand who preferred the upper St. Lawrence valley and elsewhere. Best, a widower,

30. Thomas Gummersall Anderson, "Reminiscences of Captain Thomas Gummersall Anderson," in James J. Talman (ed.), *Loyalist Narratives from Upper Canada* (Toronto, ON: The Champlain Society, 1946), 2.

31. Norman K. Crowder, *Early Ontario Settlers: A Source Book* (Baltimore, MD: Genealogical Publishing Co.), n.p.

32. William Canniff, *History of the Settlement of Upper Canada* (Toronto, ON: Dudley & Burns, 1869), 196.

died there in June 1785 leaving his two daughters orphaned.[33] Elijah Bottum, on the other hand, lived a long and prosperous life in what became the British colony of Upper Canada. There he settled in Augusta Township, which is now part of the United Counties of Leeds and Grenville on the north bank of the St. Lawrence River where he "settled and improved" several hundred acres of land.[34] In 1792, Bottum had the honour of delivering an address to John Graves Simcoe and his wife on behalf of "the loyal provincial corps" of the area. Simcoe was a prominent veteran of the American Revolutionary War and the newly-appointed Lieutenant-Governor of Upper Canada, who was on his way westward to take up his new vice regal appointment. A report of the proceedings described Bottum as "a large portly person, having at his side a formidable, basket-hilted claymore," who delivered the speech to Simcoe "in brief, military phrase, and gave one of the old war slogans."[35] He died in 1825 at sixty-eight years of age and is buried in the Blue Church Cemetery near Prescott, Ontario.[36]

33. Loyalist financial claim: The National Archives, AO13, Series II, Piece 011, 262-263; Loyalist financial claim: The National Archives, AO12, Series I, Piece 031, 64-65; Sherwood to Mathews, 1 March 1784: Haldimand Papers, Vol. B162, 190.
34. Land petition: LAC, RG 1, Series L3, Volume 29, Bundle B-3, Petition 37, Reel C-1619; Land petition: LAC, RG 1, Series L3, Volume 67, Bundle "B Misc. 1788-1795," Petition 147, Reel C-1635.
35. J. Ross Robertson, *The History of Freemasonry in Canada from its Foundation in 1749*. Volume 1. Toronto: George N. Morang & Co., 1900), 292.
36. Find A Grave, Elijah Bottum: www.findagrave.com/memorial/241915607/elijah-bottum.

# How the (First) West Was Won: Federalist Treaties that Reshaped the Frontier

## ❦ BRADY J. CRYTZER ❦

From November 1794 to October 1795, President George Washington's administration brokered three separate treaties with Britain, Spain, and the Confederated Tribes of the Ohio Country. Besides establishing America's place on the global stage, these treaties served to fundamentally alter the fortunes of the nation's western frontier. Since the era of the Seven Years War, the primary obstacles to western expansion and the region's overall economic health centered around the lack of access to the Mississippi River, foreign soldiers operating in disputed territory, and hostile relations with Native nations throughout the western backcountry. In that single, eleven-month period, President Washington's diplomats addressed and resolved each of these problematic situations. As a result, the American West experienced an age of unprecedented growth and expansion that set the stage for future dreams of its own "Manifest Destiny."

NO GATEWAY TO THE WEST

Since the earliest days of settlement in the Ohio River valley, the region had been one of unrealized potential. Although it was rich in natural resources, it had been considered limited by the realities of contemporary geopolitics. When British settlers first began moving into Western Pennsylvania, they were immediately stymied by hostile economic competition with the agents of New France. Despite the region being claimed by Britain's allies, the powerful Iroquois Confederacy, that reality rarely manifested as a benefit. In their highly competitive villages, the Iroquoian subjects of the Ohio Country often favored trade terms set forth by Quebec, and the "Covenant Chain" that bonded the British and Iroquois was superficial at best. At the outbreak of the Seven Years War in 1756, the previously unspoken alliance between the Ohioans and King Louis became official, and the Ohio River valley swiftly transformed from a trade zone to a war zone in spectacular fashion.[1]

Although the French were defeated in 1763, the war revealed one of the most glaring obstacles to Britain's financial exploitation of the west—they were not alone. France's prior control of the Ohio Country was a major step in a vast plan to control the whole of the American frontier. With its occupation of the region, France had unified it into a pre-existing sector of influence that included the St. Lawrence River valley, Great Lakes, Illinois Country, and Louisiana. To be truly realized, Britain's fortunes in the west required an accessible outlet for the raw materials that it harvested there. When France connected its continent-wide network, it linked the Mississippi River, Ohio River, and Great Lakes in a way that effectively blocked any of Britain's potential future growth. Without controlling those rivers and their treasured outlet to the Atlantic Ocean, Britain was forced to lug its wares over the Appalachian Mountains to the major cities of the coast. This cumbersome and expensive system was profitable, but not *nearly* as much as simply shipping them west and south along the Ohio and Mississippi Rivers.[2]

In the aftermath of the Seven Years' War these problems were not removed, only slightly altered. With the expulsion of New France, the Treaty of Paris (1763) declared that the entire eastern bank of the Mississippi River, and all of the Ohio River, was ceded to Great Britain. As an unexpected wrinkle, the western bank and New Orleans had been furtively given to Spain a year earlier. When the American Revolution began Spain proved itself to be a strong ally of the Patriots, and their aid proved essential for victory in the western theater. Following the brokered peace between the warring sides, Spain flexed its diplomatic muscles in 1784 by closing New Orleans to American commercial traffic flowing from the west. In response, western residents prepared for violent reprisal against Spain, writing:

> There now seems a greater call for the people here to appeal to justice and to arms, for the defence of their just rights, than was ever known in America. The five western counties of Pennsylvania are sensibly affected ... In Kentucky, Liberty or Death are in every one's mouth!—

---

1. David L. Preston, *Braddock's Defeat: The Battle of the Monongahela and the Road to Revolution* (Oxford: Oxford University Press 2015), 81.

2. Fred Anderson, *Crucible of War: The Seven Years' War and the Fate of Empire in British North America* (New York: Vintage Books, 2000), 72.

all is in confusion—and God only knows where it will end . . . America is ruined! inevitably ruined! "Blow ye the trumpet—sound it aloud—spare not—for wo is come upon Israel![3]

In short, twenty years after the Seven Years War, the economic future of the frontier remained uncertain for many of the same reasons as before it: a foreign adversary dominated the west. Without access to the Mississippi River, the economy of the Trans-Appalachian frontier was locked in a perpetual stall.[4]

WAR AND TRADE

Foreign policy had always been a critical component to the economic viability of the western frontier. At first glance, the Trans-Appalachian West appeared to be far removed from the global geopolitics of the Atlantic World. In truth however, the constant grappling and jockeying of the Old World was ever-present in the backcountry. While European settlers often blurred the lines of national identity, the west's indigenous peoples were adept at capitalizing on the competing ambitions of the superpowers in the region. For most of the 1750s, the Great Lakes and Ohioan peoples kept the British and French at bay by playing the sides off one another in a continual cycle of trading negotiations. As the natives sold their valuable furs to the highest bidders, colonial administrators in the east were racked with anxiety over the true nature of their loyalties. The French enticed native traders with abundant, albeit lesser quality, trade goods, and the British recoiled at the imminent danger presented by the transactions. Hoping to turn the tide of the competition that was slipping away from them, English-speaking agents traversed the backcountry laden with mass-produced ceremonial wampum belts promising not just trade opportunities, but natural and perpetual alliances. By 1755 the realities of war and trade had convinced the Great Lakes and Ohioan nations to align with New France, and Britain determined that relying on their traditional native alliances with the Iroquois were the most practical course of action.[5]

As British and French agents negotiated the Treaty of Paris in 1763, influential sachems such as Pontiac in the Great Lakes and Guyasuta

---

3. Responses to the Spanish closure of the Mississippi, including calls for violent reprisal, can be read in *Maryland Journal, 3 July, 1786,* in *Commentaries on the Constitution, Volume XIII: Commentaries on the Constitution, No. 1.*
4. Colin G. Calloway, *The Scratch of a Pen: 1763 and the Transformation of North America* (Oxford: Oxford University Press, 2006), 8.
5.Brady J. Crytzer, *War in the Peaceable Kingdom: The Kittanning Raid of 1756* (Yardley: Westholme Publishing 2016), 64-70.

in the Ohio Country preached that colonial influence should be contested at all costs. Although the French had made peace, their native
allies had not, and the frontier was destabilized by the conflict. In 1763
and 1764 the west was ravaged by organized raids on colonial settlements and fortifications in an event known colloquially as "Pontiac's
Rebellion." As native warriors attacked, hundreds of British settlers
were slain, and thousands more fled for the safety of the east in a mass
refugee crisis. The rebellion would eventually flame out, but it became
very clear that any economic future in the west would require peaceful
relations with native peoples to reach its full potential.[6]

For a decade after Pontiac's Rebellion, a relative peace prevailed over
the backcountry. Many settlers enjoyed lucrative trade with their Native
neighbors, and the economic potential of the west was visible for the
first time. It was a small sample, but the results were undeniable; barring
an unforeseen and dramatic turn in the politics of North America, it
seemed that *Pax Britannica* was the key to future prosperity on the
frontier. With the coming of the American Revolution, however, those
gains were soon erased and the region was hit with a geopolitical earth-
quake of almost unseen magnitude. Just as before, America's native peoples adeptly played the British and their Patriot counterparts against
one another, and soon took sides in the conflict. With the weight of
recent history on their side, the agents of King George were able to
broker alliances with many of their traditional Indian allies. With all
the heft of a global empire, the British made promises of land and concessions that the fledgling American revolutionaries could not match.
War engulfed the west yet again, and once more the region was torn
apart. Homes were burned, families destroyed, and entire settlements
were razed in a devastating scorched earth strategy employed by
Britain's Indian allies.[7]

Throughout the duration of the war the United States faltered in
its efforts toward Indian diplomacy. Most attempts were marred by violent assaults and soured by distrust, and any success was tepid at best.
The Patriots had not proven themselves to be trustworthy allies in the
eyes of the west's native peoples, and raids scarred the frontier for the
duration of the war. While the victory at Yorktown was celebrated as a
dramatic "final act" of the war, British allied Indians continued to vio-

---

6. For a detailed study of Pontiac's Rebellion, see David D. Dixon, *Never Come to Peace
Again: Pontiac's Uprising and the Fate of Empire in North America* (Norman: University of
Oklahoma Press, 2005), 118-120.
7. Eric Sterner, *Anatomy of a Massacre: The Destruction of Gnaddenhutten, 1782* (Yardley:
Westholme Publishing 2020), 88-90.

lently contest western settlements for another two years. The war may have been over in the east, but it was as fiery as ever across the frontier.

At the conclusion of the American Revolution, the major issues between native peoples and their American counterparts had not been resolved. There was never a brokered peace of any consequence, and the Indian warriors of the Great Lakes and Ohio Country had little reason to hope for one. While citizens of the east attempted to embrace their new identity as free peoples, Americans in the west grappled with the same realities that their parents had a generation prior. The west was believed to be America's by right of conquest, and the British had given it over to them as part of the Peace of Paris, but the reality on the ground proved to be very different. The new "Northwest Territory" was no more American than it had been British or French, and the great prosperity that was promised seemed a distant fantasy. Until the United States could reconcile its differences with the native nations of the west, it would never be so.

NEW NATION, OLD CHALLENGES

In the years immediately following the American Revolution, the nation's western frontier remained in doubt. Policy makers in Philadelphia took measured steps to ensure its viability, most notably by a policy of transferring land to war veterans. Known as "Donation Lands" and "Depreciation Lands," the system was designed to both compensate veterans for their service and jumpstart settlement in the west. Citizens happily accepted these Pennsylvania land deeds but were mostly reticent to begin investing in the region due to the factors previously discussed. They could certainly grow abundant crops in the west's fertile soil and harvest its many natural resources, but with the Spanish closure of the Mississippi they struggled to make ends meet. Moving their resources eastward would be expensive and cumbersome, and the ever-present threat of attack by hostile native warriors loomed large in their minds.[8]

Policy makers made attempts at settling these Indian-American disputes through a number of treaties. In 1784 they signed the Treaty of Fort Stanwix, a year later the Treaty of Fort Macintosh, and finally in 1786 the Treaty of Fort Finney. Each was designed to transfer land peacefully from Native control into American hands, but they all suffered from the same undeniable weakness. The agreements were signed by aging sachems or Indian leaders of waning influence. Though they

8. John E. Wimer, "The Depreciation and Donation Lands," *Western Pennsylvania Historical Magazine*, Vol. 8, No. 1, 2.

claimed to speak for all their respective peoples, few Indian leaders of *actual* influence recognized their legitimacy. In short order a resistance movement arose in the Ohio Country to push back against these feeble treaties, and its leaders were determined to plunge the west into violent chaos once again.[9]

The resulting conflict has become known as "The Northwest Indian War," but in so many ways it was merely a continuation of a conflict that was already decades old. This new phase was led by a wave of ambitious leaders like Little Turtle, Blue Jacket, and Buckongahelas who valued Pan-Indianism over loose alliances, and the resulting victories were stunning in their brutal effectiveness. As Ohioan warriors razed settlements along the frontier, an American force under the command of Gen. Josiah Harmar responded by marching deep into modern Ohio in the fall of 1790. Over a series of three days, October 19 through 21, Harmar's men engaged the confederated tribal warriors and were soundly defeated. Fearing that the resistance movement would spread, President Washington responded a year later by sending Gen. Arthur St. Clair into the west to subdue the warring Ohioans. On November 4, 1791 St. Clair suffered one of the worst defeats in the history of the American military at the Battle of the Wabash. Of the 1,400 men that St. Clair marched into battle, approximately 918 were killed and 276 were wounded in the affair. The result was a humiliating disaster for the Washington Administration that led to the resignation of St. Clair and the first congressional investigation in United States history.[10]

Further complicating the deteriorating situation in the west was that, contrary to the Treaty of Paris, the British had not fully evacuated the frontier. With a strong base of support in Canada, British agents continued to operate in America's Northwest Territory and actively supported the confederated tribes by providing the material support necessary for war. Although the British adopted an official stance of neutrality, they regularly supplied gunpowder, shot, weapons, and intelligence to Little Turtle and his warriors throughout the duration of the conflict. Frontier settlers balked at the notion of British troops operating with impunity on American soil, and they clamored for the Federal Government to remove the threat and even the scales. As the war dragged on it seemed to Westerners that George Washington's administration was unable, or unwilling, to respond.

9. Brady J. Crytzer, *Guyasuta and the Fall of Indian America* (Yardley: Westholme Publishing, 2013), 228-230.

10. Colin G. Calloway, *The Victory with No Name: The Native American Defeat of the First American Army* (Oxford: Oxford University Press, 2015), 129-139.

BREAKING THE WEST

In the spring of 1790 Treasury Secretary Alexander Hamilton published his *Report on the Public Credit* that laid out his visionary new plan to correct America's failing economy. Among his many recommendations was an unprecedented excise tax on whiskey designed to raise funds by taxing goods produced domestically on the frontier. While Hamilton framed the tax as a mere revenue stream, he also specifically crafted the law to bring the backcountry to heel and impose federal sovereignty over the region in which it proved so elusive. Since its earliest settlement decades prior, pioneering families across the west had expressed an affinity for localized self-determinism and a distaste for government intrusion into their lives. It was this sentiment which made the Ohio Country settlers strong supporters of the Patriot cause, and this same feeling which proved so frustrating to Washington's administration.[11]

Farming in the Ohio Country was an exercise in patience and disappointment. The fields of western Pennsylvania and western Virginia were rich and grew an abundance of corn and grain. While farmers could often produce a bountiful crop, the only meaningful way to transfer their harvest was by carting it on a weeks' long voyage over the Allegheny Mountains. An entirely impractical and expensive exercise, western farmers soon found that manufacturing their crop into whiskey made the system much more efficient. Whiskey was a valuable commodity, and could be transported to distant, thirsty markets with ease. Whiskey production became a reliable means of scratching out a living in the face of enormous obstacles, and Hamilton's new tax was viewed as an intentionally harmful attack on the frontier's way of life.

The new excise, on top of the government's seeming inability to protect frontier families from Indian attacks, led to a collusion of events that history has recorded as "The Whiskey Rebellion." As a direct challenge to the sovereignty of the United States lasting from 1791 into 1794, the event was one of the most persistent threats to the young nation during the Federalist Era. Known in its time as "The Western Insurrection," the event was about far more than whiskey and taxation. The unique challenges of frontier life swirled together to produce a period of terrible unrest, and soon led to talks of open sedition and separation across the western frontier. All the factors previously discussed coalesced in the minds of western citizens that led to an extraordinary distrust of the federal government. Just as the government could not

11. Report Relative to a Provision for the Support of Public Credit, January 9, 1790, founders.archives.gov/documents/Hamilton/01-06-02-0076-0002-0001.

open the Mississippi River for trade, it likewise could not defend its citizens from Indian war. To exacerbate matters, the passage of the Whiskey tax appeared to be a targeted piece of legislation designed to attack the very core of their economic structure.[12]

At the outset of the resistance, farmers petitioned Congress via prescribed channels as set forth by the new constitution. Local officials signed petitions and delivered passionate speeches in their assemblies, but their efforts mostly failed. Except for a one cent reduction of the Whiskey Tax, Federalist representatives seemed disinterested in the woes of the poor westerners living hundreds of miles away. By the end of 1791 local militants comprised of mostly Revolutionary War veterans began assaulting tax collectors with boiling tar, hot branding irons, and razor blades. Treasury agents saw their homes burned and their families terrorized, and in the ensuing months extra-legal courts developed across the west as well as unsanctioned, armed militias. By the summer of 1794 the rebels threatened to destroy Pittsburgh, the west's largest federal city, prompting President Washington to respond militarily. Amassing an army of over thirteen thousand men, Washington led troops himself into the west as commander-in-chief; it was the first and only time in American history that a sitting president ever personally commanded troops in the field. No great battle ever came, and the rebel leadership of "the Western Insurrection" fled into the wilderness as fugitives upon the arrival of Washington's federal army.[13]

1794 was a banner time for President George Washington in his quest to bring order to the American frontier. One year prior, Washington sent peace commissioners to negotiate with the Western Confederated tribes. As insurance, he also ordered Gen. Anthony Wayne to prepare a military force to engage the warriors if negotiations failed. Originally operating out of Pittsburgh during the tenuous Whiskey Rebellion, Wayne moved his troops approximately eighteen miles up the Ohio River due to the raucous nature of city life. Here he drilled his army for months and succeeded in creating a cohesive strike force known as the Legion of the United States. While Wayne drilled his troops, government agents saw diplomacy with sachems of the west disintegrate. Those discussions would break down, and Wayne mobilized his Legion for combat along the distant western edges of the Ohio Country. By the summer of 1794 Wayne had begun a full-scale military

---

12. Leland D. Baldwin, *Whiskey Rebels: The Story of a Frontier Uprising* (Pittsburgh: University of Pittsburgh Press 1967), 69.

13. William Hogeland, *The Whiskey Rebellion: George Washington, Alexander Hamilton, and the Frontier Rebels Who Challenged America's Newfound Sovereignty* (New York: Simon and Schuster, 2006), 220-221.

occupation of the west by constructing a line of forts that penetrated deep into the Confederacy's home territory including Fort Greenville and Fort Recovery. Much like Gen. John Forbes had done during his conquest of Fort Duquesne in 1758, Wayne created a permanent line of communication into the frontier that would keep future uprisings at bay and enforce federal sovereignty over the backcountry. In August 1794 Wayne's Legion battled Little Turtle's warriors on a field strewn with trees and debris from a storm known as "Fallen Timbers." Relying on the training of his men and strength of his position, Wayne delivered a convincing defeat to the confederated warriors. As the Indian forces fled in retreat, they hurried for the gates of nearby British Fort Miami, only to find them locked; they were denied entry. With this victory Wayne fractured the Confederacy's resistance and set the stage for an agreement that would fundamentally transform the racial and ethnic composition of the Ohio Country.

The defeat of the Western Confederated tribes and the submission of the Whiskey Rebels were among President Washington's most impactful achievements. "The Whiskey Rebellion" still stands as the second largest domestic rebellion in American history, topped only by the Confederate Secession of 1861. While it is often treated as an epilogue of sorts to the Revolutionary Period, many of its participants were Patriot veterans fighting for the same issues that were contested over the previous four decades. For policy makers in Philadelphia it had become clear that until the matters of Indian conflict, trade on the Mississippi, and foreign occupation were addressed, the violence was likely to manifest again in the years to come.

With those two victories George Washington's administration succeeded in taming the violent, reactionary instincts of the Ohio Country, and allowed for the forceful implementation of federal sovereignty over the area. Although it calmed the region, it did not yet fully address the problems that made it so volatile, and Washington relied on his diplomats to ease those burdens.

THE TREATIES THAT WON THE WEST: THE JAY TREATY

In November 1794 Washington sent his trusted ally John Jay to Britain to negotiate what was called "The Treaty of Amity, Commerce, and Navigation, Between His Britannic Majesty and the United States of America." As Britain warred with Revolutionary France, so too did America take sides. Alexander Hamilton and George Washington saw a treaty of friendship with the Crown as the best way to avoid conflict, while Thomas Jefferson and his Democratic-Republican allies tended to sympathize with France. As part of the treaty negotiations, Jay pur-

sued a variety of concessions from the British Empire with mixed results. He sought relief from Revolutionary debts, a more clearly defined
Canadian border, and a halt to the impressment of American sailors,
but he achieved none of those. Overall, the British seemed to gain more
from the agreement in the form of valuable trading rights, but Jay did
achieve one meaningful compromise: the abandonment of western
posts. Since the end of the Revolution the British had retained a strong
military presence in America's Northwest Territory and aided Little
Turtle's warriors both politically and materially. With the ratification
of "The Jay Treaty," the native nations of the west lost a valuable ally
that hampered their future attempts at waging war against American
settlers along the frontiers of the Ohio Country.

In accordance with the treaty, Britain relinquished its posts in Forts
au Fer, Niagara, Ontario, and Oswegatchie (New York), Fort Miami
(Ohio), and Forts Lernoult and Mackinac (Michigan). In an effort to
codify the rights of Americans, Canadians, and Natives in the continent's border regions, Article III of the treaty stated that

> It is agreed, that it shall at all times be free to His Majesty's subjects,
> and to the citizens of the United States, and also to the Indians dwelling
> on either side of the said boundary line, freely to pass and repass, by
> land or inland navigation into the respective territories and countries
> of the two parties on the continent of America . . . and freely carry on
> trade and commerce with each other.[14]

With the removal of the British threat and all the intrinsic destabi-
lizing forces that came with it, the frontier saw one of its greatest obstacles to growth eliminated. While the Jay Treaty was a reasonable
compromise between the two contentious powers, American partisans
balked at its passage. Washington saw it as a positive alternative to war,
but the agreement was viewed by Democratic-Republicans as too favorable to Britain, and deleterious to America's standing in the world.
Resistance to Federalist policies hardened in the wake of its passage.
Even in the west, it was widely criticized across the frontier despite the
inherent benefit that it provided. Despite being a point of major contention in the hyper-partisan realm of American politics, the passage
of the Jay Treaty cleared the way for a period of major expansion across
the Ohio Country and its neighboring regions.

---

14. "Treaty of Amity Commerce and Navigation, between His Britannick Majesty; and
The United States of America, by Their President, with the advice and consent of Their
Senate," *Treaties and Other International Acts of the United States of America*, Volume 2, Doc-
uments 1-40: 1776-1818 (Washington, DC: Government Printing Office, 1931).

## THE TREATIES THAT WON THE WEST: THE TREATY OF GREENVILLE

In the aftermath of Wayne's victory at Fallen Timbers and Washington's suppression of the Whiskey Rebellion, calm was restored to the Ohio Country. Many of the most prominent leaders of the insurrection were arrested and released, and their previously seditious grievances were legitimized into the platforms of Thomas Jefferson's new Democratic-Republican Party. The core of their complaints was central to Jefferson's major political theme: the Federalist Party was intrusive and overbearing and needed to be restrained. Likewise, the political motives that drove Little Turtle's Western Confederacy were also changing. While the aging sachems of the west advocated peace with the United States, younger warriors demanded that the war continue. Men like the Shawnee Tecumseh advocated a continuation of the struggle and would eventually become the voice of a new generation of resistance along the frontier.

Despite this divide, peace was defined on a generational level. The elder sachems of the Ohio Country had fought for decades dating back to the 1770s and saw conflict as a political dead end. Against the protests of their younger warriors, the aging power brokers agreed to treat with Gen. Anthony Wayne in the summer of 1795 and sealed the fate of the Ohio Country. Meeting at Fort Greenville in modern Ohio, Wayne orchestrated negotiations with dozens of native leaders from seventeen confederated tribes of the frontier. Included in their ranks were the Miami Little Turtle, the Shawnees Black Hoof and Blue Jacket, and the Ottawa Egushawa. Among the other nations represented were the Kickapoo, Kaskaskia, Wyandot, and twenty-three members of the powerful Potawatomi nation. As per their agreement, the warring parties agreed to "put an end to a destructive war, to settle all controversies, and to restore harmony and friendly intercourse between the said United States and Indian tribes." Per Wayne's demands the sachems ceded all Indian lands east and south of a line stretching from the Cuyahoga River to Fort Recovery, and southward to the Kentucky River. Along with this cession, the Confederated leadership also waived any native rights to strategic parcels of real estate including modern Detroit, Fort Wayne, Chicago, Toledo, and Mackinac Island.[15]

The Treaty of Greenville forever altered the ancient demographic composition of the Ohio Country. While most of its signatories were relative newcomers to the region, the cession brokered by Wayne guaranteed that they would be the last generation of natives to inhabit it.

---

15. "Treaty of Greenville," *Indian Affairs: Laws and Treaties* Vol II (Treaties) ed. Charles J. Kappler (Washington, DC: Government Printing Office, 1904).

In the wake of Fallen Timbers, an older generation of defeated sachems signed away the lands that many younger warriors believed to be theirs. By 1796 the native families of the Ohio Country flooded towards the Mississippi River in a mass migration, and their vacated lands were made available for American settlement. Over the next two decades a new wave of Indian nationalists would rise and begin the war again, but the fight would be for an entirely new frontier in the Indiana Territory. Because of the Treaty of Greenville, an Indian Ohio Country became a distant memory of the eighteenth century, long lost and never to return.

THE TREATIES THAT WON THE WEST: PICKNEY'S TREATY

By 1794, the Spanish Empire found itself at a crossroads. While it still hoped to maintain its status as a global superpower, economic stresses and European war had greatly weakened its position. In North America, Spain had hoped to combat American expansion, but the venture was proving to be increasingly problematic. To hem in the United States' zone of influence, Spanish officials restricted trade on the Mississippi River. Along with this limitation, the waning empire also maintained forts in disputed territory along the Gulf Coast in the lands of present-day Mississippi and Alabama. As a final measure, Spanish agents also empowered local Indian nations to resist the encroachment of American settlers through strategic raids on their settlements.

As the French Revolution rocked the European continent, Spain joined alongside many neighboring nations to combat its rise to prominence. Even though the war forced Spain into an alliance with its traditional enemy of Great Britain, Spain saw dramatic defeats in the Caribbean and European Theaters. After months of losses, the Spanish monarchy empowered Prime Minister Manuel de Godoy to manage its foreign affairs, and a new sense of urgency became the driving force of the empire's scattered political activities. For Godoy, the newfound alliance with Britain was proving to be an albatross around Spain's neck. By 1794 he immediately sought to divorce the two superpowers and restore the alliance traditionally reserved for France. That fall word reached the Prime Minister that the American diplomat John Jay had arrived in England to begin negotiations with the Crown, and Godoy sprang into action.

Shortly after Anglo-American discussions began, Godoy requested a new treaty with the United States. For the Spanish, the Jay Treaty could only mean that a new alliance between Britain and the United States was imminent, and such an agreement was certain to jeopardize all of Spain's colonial holdings in North America. President Washington selected the South Carolinian Thomas Pickney to serve as his chief diplomat, and he arrived in June 1795. In an unusual turn from America's previous negotiations in Europe, Pickney operated from a position of strength from the beginning of the discussions. Pickney insisted on the 31st parallel as the new border between the United States and Florida, as well as free navigation of the Mississippi River. Manuel de Godoy conceded to both with little argument, and only demanded an official alliance with Spain in return. In a show of diplomatic force, Pickney refused the alliance and threatened to abandon talks altogether; it was a gamble, but one that paid off spectacularly. The bluff was received as designed, and the Prime Minister waived his previous demand. As a final effort Pickney further asked that the Spanish dissolve any existing Indian alliances and eliminate any duties on American goods that passed through New Orleans.

The American terms presented by Pickney were diplomatically emasculating for the Spanish, but their urgency to ratify the treaty revealed just how far the once-mighty empire had fallen. With the signing of the Treaty of San Lorenzo on October 27, 1795 President Washington had completed a massive reorganization of the American frontier. The young nation scored a stunning victory on the world stage, and allowed for the full might of the western economy to be fully realized for the first time.[16]

THE SEEDS OF MANIFEST DESTINY

With the ratification of these three treaties, President George Washington solidified the gains that he had made along the Ohio frontier in 1794. While the suppression of the Whiskey Rebellion and the defeat of the Western Confederacy was a forceful showing of federal sovereignty, they alone did secure the west. The treaties with Britain, the Confederated tribes, and Spain revealed that America was still dependent on the greater geopolitics of the Atlantic World, and showed that its diplomats could adeptly engage with other superpowers at the highest levels. Prior to 1794 and 1795, the United States remained huddled along the eastern seaboard, unable to capitalize on the territory handed to it following the American Revolution. Several Old World powers viewed the young republic as fleeting, and unable to sustain itself if it could not even command its own lands and people. On November 1, 1794 Washington penned a letter to John Jay relating these same concerns, stating:

16. "Treaty of Friendship, Limits, and Navigation Between Spain and The United States; October 27, 1795," *Treaties and Other International Acts of the United States.*

the insurrection in the western counties of this State has excited much speculation, and a variety of opinions abroad; and will be represented differently according to the wishes of some, and the prejudices of others; who may exhibit it as an evidence of what has been predicted 'that we are unable to govern ourselves.' Under this view of the subject, I am happy in giving it to you as the general opinion, that this event having happened at the time it did, was fortunate, although it will be attended with considerable expence.[17]

Indeed, it *was* fortunate. In the months immediately following the Whiskey Rebellion, land speculators (including Washington) saw the value of their holdings increase by as much as fifty percent in the Ohio Country. With peace came prosperity, and new settlers flooded the region with aims of participating in the newly liberated western economy. Within seven years of these treaties' ratification, the bustling state of Ohio was granted full statehood. Although the Ohio Country had been home to pioneering families since the 1750s, those hardscrabble frontiersmen were quickly replaced by enterprising landowners from the eastern seaboard. Cities like Pittsburgh, Morgantown, and Wheeling soon emerged as regional commercial centers, and the days of cheap land disappeared.

The frontier did not vanish, it just moved west and south to Indiana, Illinois, Missouri, and beyond. The challenges of land, power, native war and native trade would always be hallmarks of American life in the west, but those obstacles been vanquished in the Ohio Country. By 1796 George Washington and his Federalist administration had succeeded in controlling the first frontier, and setting America on a permanent trajectory of westward expansion and manifest destiny.

17. George Washington to John Jay, November 1-4, 1794, founders.archives.gov/documents/Washington/05-17-02-0088.

# Captain Luke Day, A Forgotten Leader of Shays' Rebellion

### ❀ SCOTT M. SMITH ❀

While Daniel Shays (1747-1825) has basked posthumously in the glory of leading the 1786-87 populist rebellion that bears his name, Luke Day (1743-1801) was a co-commander of the forces on the ground that fateful winter. Both Shays and Day were battle-hardened Continental army captains who returned home to rural Massachusetts to find their fellow farmers squared off against the state legislature, financially more oppressive than the British Crown which they had just helped defeat. The newspapers of the day, overwhelmingly biased against the backwoodsmen, needed a rebel leader to demonize and somewhat randomly picked Shays, condemning Day to an eternity of ignominy. In his *History of Western Massachusetts*, published in 1855, Joshua Gilbert Holland noted: "Day was the stronger man in mind and will, the equal of Shays in military skill, and superior in the gift of speech."[1]

At the end of the Revolution, Day and Shays had many similarities; it was their differences, although slight at the time, that likely led to the vast divergence in their places in history. Both men were middle to upper class farmers living twenty-five miles apart, a full day's journey at the time, with large families to support. Day was the scion of a prominent bloodline in West Springfield, while Shays, born to landless Irish immigrants, married well, settling into a sixty-eight acre farm in Shutesbury.[2]

---

1. Josiah Gilbert Holland, *History of Western Massachusetts: The Counties of Hampden, Hampshire, Franklin, and Berkshire, Embracing an Outline, Or General History, of the Section, an Account of Its Scientific Aspects and Leading Interests, and Separate Histories of Its One Hundred Towns, Volume 1* (Springfield, MA: S. Bowles, 1855), 245.

2. Leonard Richards, *Shays's Rebellion: The American Revolution's Final Battle* (Philadelphia: The University of Pennsylvania Press, 2002), 6.

Both men volunteered immediately after the battles at Lexington and Concord in April 1775, fought with distinction, and were promoted to captains effective January 1, 1777. Most notably, Day slogged through the Adirondack forest with Benedict Arnold's ill-fated assault on Quebec,[3] while Shays was an elite light infantryman in Anthony Wayne's surprise attack at Stony Point in 1779.[4] Henry Hallowell, a soldier serving in the Hudson River region, noted: "Captain Shays . . . belonged to our regiment in the 3 years service and respected as a very good officer, was very good to his men."[5] Shays retired from the Army in October 1780,[6] while Day served until the end of the war, although he was furloughed home at times for medical reasons in its latter years.[7] Massachusetts records show privates, such as Ezekiel Wood, joining Day's company early in 1781,[8] and some accounts place him at Yorktown later that year.

Once home, Shays and Day became leaders of their local militia, training their fellow yeomen on their respective village greens. In 1782, Day sided with the state government, defending the courthouse during Ely's Rebellion, an uprising led by an itinerant preacher who "delighted in nothing more than sowing jealousies between the poor and the rich."[9] He joined the Society of the Cincinnati shortly after its inception in 1783, demonstrating his camaraderie with his fellow army officers, while Shays pointedly did not. Shays did join the Committee of Safety and was elected warden in the neighboring town of Pelham.

With the election of James Bowdoin as governor in 1785, the Massachusetts government was dominated by merchants who were determined to pay back the state's war debts in full—to their own personal benefit as bondholders. To this end, the state raised taxes to quadruple their pre-war levels.[10] The combination of this tax increase

3. Ibid., 43.

4. Daniel Bullen, *Daniel Shays' Honorable Rebellion* (Yardley, PA: Westholme Publishing, 2021), 63.

5. Howard Kendall Sanderson, *Lynn in the Revolution* (Boston: W.R Clarke and Company, 1909) 180.

6. Francis B. Heitman, *Historical Register of Officers of the Continental Army During the War of the Revolution* (Washington DC: Rare Book Shop Publishing, 1914), 492.

7. shaysrebellion.stcc.edu/shaysapp/person.do?shortName=luke_day.

8. *Massachusetts Soldiers and Sailors of the Revolutionary War: A Compilation from the Archives* (Boston: Wright and Potter, 1908), 735.

9. Reverend John H. Lockwood, ed., *Western Massachusetts: A History: 1636–1925*, volume 1. (New York: Lewis Historical Publishing Company, Inc., 1926), 116.

10. Scott M. Smith, *Insurrection and Speculation: A Farmer, Financier and a Surprising Sharper Seeded the Constitution* (Journal of the American Revolution, July 14, 2022), allthingsliberty.com/2022/07/insurrection-and-speculation-a-farmer-financier-and-a-surprising-sharper-seeded-the-constitution/.

with the national inflationary spiral following the war overwhelmed the meager coffers of the farmers of western Massachusetts. One third of the adult males in Worcester county, including Shays and Day, were hauled into court by their creditors.[11] Day was actually jailed for two months in Northampton during the summer of 1785 (although allowed out of his cell to work in town) before breaking his bond and going home.[12]

This incarceration likely proved the catalyst for Day to about-face and turn against his government. On August 29, 1786, a year to the day of his escape, Day effectively launched Shays' Rebellion by marching the twenty miles back to Northampton at the head of a column of one hundred armed men determined to prevent the court (which had ruled against him) to imprison any more of his neighbors. Hundreds of men from other towns, also led by veteran officers, joined the protest. Reminiscent of the war, the men wore green sprigs in their hats, a symbol of liberty,[13] and were accompanied by fife and drums. Shays was offered the captainship of the Pelham delegation but declined. While there is no written documentation of the reason, one supposition was that Shays was not yet prepared to anger his father-in-law who was staunchly pro-government.[14]

Events in Northampton were caustically summarized in the *American Mercury*:

> about one hundred men from West Springfield . . . commanded by Captain Luke Day whose private character and circumstances as well as his personal liberty made it very convenient . . . were joined by a number from various other towns and by a body of horse and foot from Amherst, Pelham, etc under the command of Captain Hinds and Lieutenant Billings . . . making in the whole about four hundred . . . but instead of calling upon the militia . . . the day was spent in frequent and idle conferences . . . the court complied with all the wishes of the insurgents and adjourned . . . without making the least attempt to do their duty.[15]

The court's action here confirmed the popular support the rebellion garnered, particularly outside of Boston. Unsurprisingly, every county

---

11. David Szatmary, *Shays Rebellion: the Making of an Agrarian Insurrection* (Amherst, MA: University of Massachusetts Press 1980), 29.

12. Marion Lena Starkey, *A Little Rebellion* (Alfred Knopf, New York 1955), 27.

13. Szatmary, *Shays Rebellion*, 69.

14. Bullen, *Daniel Shays' Honorable Rebellion*, 137.

15. "Northampton, Sept. 6," *American Mercury* (Hartford, Connecticut), September 11, 1786.

west of Boston voted in their local conventions to support the rebellion.[16] In fact, farmers closed courts in Concord, Taunton, and Great Barrington, where 80 percent of the town's militia actually crossed lines to join the rebels.[17]

Needless to say, Bowdoin and his fellow Bostonian bluebloods were not pleased with Day's success in Northampton. On September 2, the Governor issued a proclamation calling for "judges, justices, sheriffs, grand jurors, and constables . . . to suppress all riotous proceedings . . . prosecute and bring to condign punishment the ringleaders . . . of the atrocious violation."[18] To this end, the Massachusetts Supreme Judicial Court met in Worcester on September 19, indicting twelve of the rebels (but not Day for some unknown reason) on riot and sedition charges. Since Day and the other leaders were entirely focused on debt relief, they had not made any effort to close the Worcester court, believing correctly that it would be pursuing criminal matters.

This indictment shocked Day and others who fancied themselves "Regulators," a timeworn moniker for commoners trying to rein in the excesses of the wealthy, not "revolutionaries" trying to overthrow the government, and certainly not "criminals." Daniel Shays now stepped up to lead the next protest at the courthouse in Springfield on Sept 25, fearing that Day would get arrested if he appeared out front again (although he was present anyway[19]), and worse, bloodshed might ensue if this arrest happened on Day's home turf.

The indictments clearly aroused the countryside as two thousand men converged on Springfield, doubling the number of militia the state could muster to guard the courthouse.[20] For the first time, the newspapers highlighted Shays as the rebellion's leader while also noting: "the governmental party were men of property, virtue and consideration [while] half the insurgents were men of the vilest principles and desperate in their fortunes."[21] After much parading and parleying, but no gunfire, the court adjourned until December without issuing any rulings or warrants, a victory for the Regulators.

The conflict intensified over the course of the fall. Prodded by Samuel Adams, incensed that American citizens now appeared to be

---

16. Bullen, *Daniel Shays' Honorable Rebellion*, 117.

17. Richards, *Shays's Rebellion*, 12

18. "Legislative Acts/Legal Proceedings," *American Herald* (Boston, Massachusetts), September 4, 1786.

19. Holland, *History of Western Massachusetts*, 245

20. Bullen, *Daniel Shays' Honorable Rebellion*, 140.

21. "Hartford, October 2," *Connecticut Courant* (Hartford, Connecticut), October 2, 1786.

rebelling against their own *elected* government, the Massachusetts legislature undertook discussion of the Riot Act, which would allow militia and other officials to shoot rioters who failed to disperse, and the Militia Act, which could punish any soldier who left his post or joined or incited any riot with death.[22]

In response, a communication circulated to the western towns under Shays' signature calling on the farmers to turn out fully armed on a minute's notice. Shays disavowed writing this letter, claiming it was planted by bondholders to spur the legislature to action.[23] Regardless of the letter's true authorship, the government passed both acts in the last week of October and suspended *habeas corpus* (the right to a speedy trial) two weeks later. On November 30, a posse arrested Job Shattuck, a prominent rebel leader in central Massachusetts who had threatened to put all opposition to the sword, and carted him off to jail in Boston.[24]

While escalating the battle with the rebellious farmers, the legislature also passed several measures of relief for their dire circumstances. Massachusetts would now allow payment in kind (not just specie) for various taxes, extend the deadline for payments, rescind selected legal fees, impose a tax on imported luxury items such as jewelry, and sell off land in Maine to reduce the public debt. The state, however, would not yield to the rebels' demands to print paper money, move the seat of government out of Boston, or temporarily close the debt courts. Finally, on November 15, despite Samuel Adams continued harping that "the man who dares rebel against the laws of a republic should suffer death,"[25] the government offered amnesty to "rioters" who took no further actions against the state and signed an oath of allegiance by January 1.

Day, Shays and their fellow Regulators spent October and November back on the farm, likely tracking events in Boston, fifty miles away, as closely as possible with winter approaching. There is little surviving documentation of their actions during this period other than a record that only one Regulator accepted the legislature's offer of amnesty,[26] an indication of the countryside's palpable mistrust of the state government.

---

22. www.statutesandstories.com/blog_html/shays-rebellion-the-laws-that-provoked-and-suppressed-the-revolt-part-2/.

23. Starkey, *A Little Rebellion*, 91.

24. George Minot, *The History of the Insurrections in Massachusetts* (Boston: James Burdette and Company, 1810), 42.

25. Richards, *Shays's Rebellion*, 16.

26. Ibid., 17.

The lone protest occurred on November 21 when Adam Wheeler, another retired army captain, led 160 men to Worcester. After the sheriff read the newly enacted Riot Act to Wheeler's men blocking the courthouse steps, the judges met briefly in a local tavern before adjourning till the new year.[27]

In late November, Day and Eli Parsons, a veteran of Valley Forge who "bore all the earmarks of a dangerous character,"[28] hiked to Vermont to meet with Ethan Allen and offer him command of the Massachusetts rebellion.[29] They hoped to find common ground with the fabled leader of the Green Mountain Boys who were in their own conflict with the aristocracy in New York over land rights.

Was this meeting authorized by Shays or were the two captains acting on their own? The prevailing assumption is the former; however, documentation is slim. Based on Day's leadership at Northampton in August and in Springfield the coming January, it is entirely possible that he chafed under the attention Daniel Shays received and was seeking a new, more forceful, leader on his own, particularly one that could attract national attention. Regardless, Allen, whose priority was statehood for Vermont, chose not to risk further wrath of the establishment by supporting the Massachusetts insurrection. He summarily rejected the overture, booting Day and Parsons out of his colony.

Upon Day's return, the rebels more formally organized their forces, settling on a leadership committee of seventeen former Army captains who would command six regiments. Day had the second regiment, while Shays led the fourth. Notably, the rebels did not name a "general."[30]

The arrest and incarceration of Job Shattuck spurred the committee to action. Hoping for a massive show of support, Shays (and likely Wheeler and others) circulated a proclamation throughout the countryside calling for a massive show of volunteers to stop the court

---

27. Starkey, *A Little Rebellion*, 97. The leader of this minor action is in dispute, but was not likely Shays. Historian Marion Lena Starkey clearly implicates Wheeler, while Josiah Gilbert Holland leaves the leader nameless; Daniel Bullen places Shays in front "for the sake of narrative convenience," but also acknowledges that other historians "fail to see Shays as the 'generalissimo' the government saw and cast doubt on his participation in the court closings beyond the September 25, 1786 closing in Springfield." Bullen, *Daniel Shays' Honorable Rebellion*, 372, 375.
28. Starkey, *A Little Rebellion*, 114.
29. Greene, James M. "Ethan Allen and Daniel Shays: Contrasting Models of Political Representation in the Early Republic." *Early American Literature* 48, no. 1 (2013): 125-151.
30. Holland, *History of Western Massachusetts*, 257.

from sitting in Worcester on December 5.[31] The goal was five thousand men.

The scope of the rebellion was beginning to strike fear not only in Governor Bowdoin and the Massachusetts legislature but also in leadership throughout the new nation. Boston battened down, fearing the insurgents would launch an attack to break Job Shattuck from jail, while alarm spread down the Atlantic seaboard. The rich and powerful would not demonstrate much empathy with the insurgent cause, but rather chose to assail the motives of its leadership.

George Washington, retired from public office and residing at Mount Vernon, closely tracked events in Massachusetts through correspondence with his inner circle of former Continental Army generals. Henry Knox, now Secretary of War, wrote to him: "The people who are the insurgents have never paid any, or but very little taxes—But they see the weakness of government; They feel at once their own poverty, compared with the opulent, and their own force, and they are determined to make use of the latter, in order to remedy the former."[32] Benjamin Lincoln, the Massachusetts general who would ultimately lead the mercenary force that put down the rebellion, added: "In short the want of industry, economy, and common honesty seem to be the causes of the present commotions."[33] Washington, in turn, surmised: "They [the insurgents] may be instigated by British Councils—actuated by ambitious motives—or being influenced by dishonest principles."[34]

Intent on steering the United States towards a centralized federal government, the Founding Fathers needed to smash the farmers' revolt not only on the ground in Massachusetts but, more importantly, in the minds of citizens in every state. Their message would be much more forceful if they could blame a single leader, preferably an anarchistic madman manipulating the farmers, rather than a "committee of seventeen" veteran Army officers. Major newspapers throughout the country were only too happy to oblige, singling out Daniel Shays, rather than Luke Day, as their pinata of choice.

31. Starkey, *A Little Rebellion*, 101
32. Henry Knox to George Washington October 23, 1786, founders.archives.gov/documents/Washington/04-04-02-0274.
33. Benjamin Lincoln to George Washington, December 4, 1786, founders.archives.gov/documents/Washington/04-04-02-0374-0002.
34. George Washington to David Humphries, December 26,1786, founders.archives.gov/documents/Washington/04-04-02-0408.

Day was from a prominent landholding family, served in the Army until its very end, defended the courthouse against Ely's Rebellion, and joined the Society of the Cincinnati. Shays, on the other hand, had no such lineage and, more important, had retired early from the Army amidst a semi-scandal. After serving for five years with virtually no pay, Shays had sold a sword presented to him by General Lafayette, incurring the wrath of his fellow officers.

Lafayette fought with the Continental Army from his arrival in America in June 1777 until he chose to return to France in January 1779 for personal reasons. He witnessed firsthand the suffering of patriot troops at Valley Forge from the lack of proper food and clothing, as well as their meager weaponry. He sailed back to America in the spring of 1780, bringing with him a cache of swords and uniforms (including black and red feathers) for the men who would serve in his new command.

Because of his valor in the assault on Stony Point, Daniel Shays was selected for Lafayette's elite light infantry brigade set to patrol Westchester and New Jersey in the fall of 1780. Accordingly, he, among many officers, received one of these swords. Given his combat experiences, he undoubtedly sported a trusted sword at his side already. With six children at home to feed, Shays sold Lafayette's sword. Aghast at this "insult," his peers threatened a court-martial hearing.[35] Shays retired from the Army instead. Lafayette's unit was disbanded in November 1780 and the Marquis rode off to Philadelphia to await further assignments.[36]

While the award of the sword factored significantly into Shays' life story, it barely registered with Lafayette. The Marquis, born into nobility, expressed his global view of the farmers' insurrection in western Massachusetts in a letter to Washington: "the late disturbances in the Eastern States Have Given me Great deal of Concern and Uneasiness . . . [The people] hurt their Consequence in Europe to a degree which is Very distressing, and what glory they Have Gained By the Revolution, they are in danger of losing."[37] Knox had to remind Lafayette that "A Captain Shays who was in the light Infantry under your orders in 1780 & who was deranged at the latter end of that

---

35. Starkey, *A Little Rebellion*, 71.
36. David A. Clary, *Adopted Son - Washington, Lafayette and the Friendship that Saved the Revolution* (New York: Bantam Books, 2007), 242.
37. Lafayette to Washington, January 13,1787, founders.archives.gov/documents/Washington/04-04-02-0442.

campaign was the principal officer among the insurgents."[38] Knox continued on with his falsehood about the true masterminds of the rebellion: "Besides him [Shays] there were three or four others who had served as officers in the Continental army—But the insurrection originated from designing men who had never served."[39]

Clearly, the leading lights of the Continental Army, well-enough off in their own circumstances, refused to believe that the establishment of a strong central government (and assumption of all War debts), which they viewed as essential to the sustained success of America, could cause so much economic pain to the veterans who had fought alongside them. More importantly, and correctly, they feared that this pain extended well beyond the borders of Massachusetts, threatening the stability of the new nation.

The newspapers piled on to the Shays' story. On December 2, the *Massachusetts Centinel* blared: "from his youth he was remarkable for subtlety and duplicity . . . in the year 1780, the distinguished nobleman, the Marquis de la Fayette, presented the officers of the army, each with an elegant sword—this pledge of his affection, which a man of honor and spirit would have sacredly preserved, and handed down to his posterity as a jewel of high price, he was mean enough to dispose of for a trifling consideration."[40] The paper followed up with a likely falsified interview with Shays himself who supposedly claimed his army was going to "lay the town of Boston to ashes . . . [and] overthrow the present [Massachusetts] constitution."[41] The *Pennsylvania Gazette* bellowed: "every state has its Shays" and "should the federal government be rejected none other than Daniel Shays would seize control of Massachusetts."[42]

The *Centinal* pummeled Luke Day as well. A December 23 article recounted "Anecdotes" of Day swindling both his brother-in-law on the sale of a slave and his jailer with fraudulent government securities. The article concluded: "to such persons courts of all kinds will be grievances."[43]

38. Gilder Lehrman Collection; Henry Knox to Lafayette, February 13, 1787, www.gilderlehrman.org/collection/glc0243703451.

39. Ibid.

40. "Anecdotes of Daniel Shaise, Leader of the Insurgents," *Massachusetts Centinel* (Boston), December 2, 1786.

41. Ibid., January 17, 1787.

42. *Pennsylvania Gazette*, February 5 and 12, 1787; Richards, *Shays's Rebellion*, 139.

43. "Miscellany," *Massachusetts Centinel* (Boston), December 23, 1786.

In fact, Bowdoin and the legislature had little to worry about in early December as a road-choking blizzard scuttled most farmers' plans to reach Worcester, let alone Boston. Day and his men from Springfield could only get as far as Leicester, six miles away. All told, less than one thousand rebels arrived to close the court, most of them ill-provisioned for the weather. The force, however, was sufficient to convince the judges to adjourn without incident or ruling.

The next test came at Springfield just after Christmas. Captains Shays, Day and Tom Grover (6th regiment) took the lead. Gen. William Shepard, veteran of twenty-two battles of the Revolution,[44] led the government forces, smartly deploying his men to protect the federal arsenal in town, rather than the courthouse. With no militia to shield them, the judges adjourned without an argument. Shays headed home to Pelham, while Day and Grover actually dined with the judges.[45]

Governor Bowdoin was not going to rely on the weather, or local militias with divided loyalties, to put the insurgency down once and for all. Raising funds from the Boston elite, he assembled four thousand mercenaries under the direction of Benjamin Lincoln, the state's favorite son despite a checkered war record.[46] With this army marching their way and the death penalty hanging over their heads, the Committee of Seventeen began to waver.

Shays, who had literally been thrust into the spotlight by the newspapers, indicated in a clandestine conversation, likely with his old commander, Rufus Putnam, that he would accept a pardon if offered; but it never materialized.[47] The government wanted Shays to plead his case in Boston, while Shays feared he would be jailed, like Shattuck, if he showed his face anywhere near the state capital. Accordingly both sides girded for war, with Shays barracking his men in Rutland to maintain their unity of force.

The federal arsenal in Springfield would be the first battleground. While the Regulators had ignored the armory in December, an indication of their relatively benign intentions at the time, they knew they could not stand up against the mercenaries without better munitions. In fact, had the Regulators secured the arsenal, they would

44. Reverend John Lockwood, *Westfield and its Historic Influences 1669-1919* (Springfield, MA: Springfield Printing and Binding Company, 1922), 44.
45. Starkey, *A Little Rebellion*, 117
46. Smith, *Insurrection and Speculation*.
47. Holland, *History of Western Massachusetts*, 258; Bullen, *Daniel Shays' Honorable Rebellion*, 205.

have become the best-armed military force in North America. By late January, the armory was effectively surrounded: Day with 400 men in West Springfield, Parsons with a similar number to the north, and Shays commanding eleven hundred marching from the east.

Until General Lincoln arrived with his mercenary force, the Regulators would have roughly twice as many men in Springfield as the government. On January 19, with Lincoln still a week or longer away, Shepard wrote to Lincoln asking for money and arms:

> Let me urge you, Sir, to use your whole influence to process what is of the most importance to the speedy and effectual success, money . . . Two thousand pounds at least must be sent . . . failure . . . it appears to me, must defeat the plan of government, for the men can not be kept together long, unless they are pretty well supplied with rum, hay and a little money . . . no leave has been obtained from the Congress or General Knox to take any [arms] from the Arsenal of the United States . . . It will be very disagreeable to me to be defeated by such bandits, when I am guarding the arms of the union . . . because I had no arms to defend myself.[48]

Even at this late stage, Shays was still proselytizing for a peaceful solution. He sent a petition to Lincoln stating:

> Unwilling to be any way an accessory to the shedding of blood, and greatly desirous to restoring peace and harmony to the convulsed Commonwealth [Massachusetts], we propose that all the troops on the part of government be disbanded immediately, and that all and every person who has been acting, or in any way aiding or assisting in any of the late risings of the people, may be indemnified in their own person and property . . . on which conditions, the people now in arms, in defense of their lives and liberties, will quietly return to the respective habitations, patiently waiting and hoping for constitutional relief.[49]

Day likely surmised the government would never accept these terms. As Holland noted: "Day was not like Shays a tool of the rebellion but an active agent . . . [he] carried the boldest and most determined spirit."[50] Day drilled his men daily and instituted martial law in West Springfield, arresting and imprisoning several prominent locals who resisted.

---

48. William Shepard to Benjamin Lincoln, January 19, 1787, Massachusetts Historical Society, Lincoln Papers.
49. *Boston Gazette,* January 29, 1787.
50. Holland, *History of Western Massachusetts,* 295, 262.

When a reply from Lincoln, still on the march to Springfield, was not forthcoming, Shays relinquished his hope for peace. He sent a courier to Day informing him that he would launch his assault on the armory the next day, Thursday January 25. Day immediately penned a note indicating that he would not be ready to move until Friday.

Day's men were ready to fight, so why the delay? Perhaps Day wanted to establish his own control of the assault. To this end, he sent a militant proclamation to Shepard, demanding that "the troops in Springfield lay down their arms . . . and return to their homes on parole."[51] Regardless, Day's message never reached Shays. It was intercepted by government supporters (when the courier stopped at a tavern for a libation - or three) and delivered to Shepard instead.

Shays dragged his heels until late afternoon on Thursday, likely waiting for Day to appear, before at last ordering both his and Parsons' men forward, fearing Lincoln's imminent arrival. In fact, Lincoln was still more than a day away, and had just received Shays' petition, summarily rejecting it.[52] Shepard, now well armed, gave Shays every chance to stand down. He purposely sent two cannon volleys over the heads of the Regulators, but they still pressed forward in the dwindling winter light. Finally he ordered his artillerymen to lower their aim. The next three volleys ripped through the advancing Regulators, killing four. The rest turned and ran, despite Shays' cries to rally. At last, Shays had no choice but to follow his men into the darkness.

Luke Day likely heard the cannon blasts from his post in West Springfield but made no move towards the armory. Assuming his message was delivered, he had little reason to expect Shays to attack without him. By evening on the 25th, Day would certainly have learned of Shays' rout. Now outnumbered, however, he did not attack on the 26th; nor was there any communication from Shays. Since West Springfield was his home, Day did not make any attempt yet to flee, either.

Lincoln's mercenary army, including infantry, artillery and cavalry, arrived in Springfield on the morning of the 27th. Taking no chances that the two captains would unite their forces, the wizened general ordered an immediate assault across the frozen Connecticut River to Day's stronghold. The Regulators were completely surprised, breaking at the first onslaught of the invaders. Lincoln sent his horsemen in

51. "The following is a Copy of a Letter from Luek Day, at West-Springfield, to the Commanding Officer at Springfield," *Connecticut Courant* (Hartford,), January 29, 1787.
52. Benjamin Lincoln to James Bowdoin, January 26, 1787. Massachusetts Historical Society; Lincoln Papers.

pursuit, chasing the Regulators into the hills. He routed the bedraggled, and steadily dwindling, Regulator forces on February 3 in Petersham and again in Sheffield on February 27. Shays, Day, Wheeler and Parsons ran to Vermont (still not part of the United States) for their lives.

Without its leadership, the rebels lost any semblance of military discipline, looting and tormenting the local population as they fled through the countryside. Barns, warehouses and a factory owned by merchants who supported the government mysteriously burned to the ground; General Shepard's property was ransacked and two of his horses mutilated. In fact, the only two Regulators who were actually executed late in 1787 were condemned much more for their criminal actions after Springfield than their participation in the rebellion.[53]

To his death in 1830, Captain Parsons believed that the Regulators would have captured the armory had Day joined the assault on the 25th.[54] If so, what would have been the next step? A march on Boston? Based on the inability of all three Regulator regiments to stand up to battlefield pressure from government forces, it is hard to see how Day's presence would have achieved any lasting victory.

On February 4, Governor Bowdoin formally declared "a horrid and unnatural rebellion hath been openly and traitorously raised," setting a $750 bounty on the head of Shays and $500 for the other three leaders.[55] All four, as well as other Regulator leaders, faced execution if captured. Two weeks later, the Massachusetts legislature passed the Disqualification Act, empowering the governor to pardon privates and non-commissioned officers who delivered up their arms, took an oath of allegiance, and accepted disqualification from public office for three years.[56] Four thousand men took the oath, almost 10 percent of the free white men living outside of Boston.[57]

While the armed rebellion was effectively defeated, the people of western Massachusetts were not placated. The town elders of Colrain

---

53. Richards, *Shays's Rebellion*, 41.

54. Ibid., 28.

55. *Boston Gazette*, February 12, 1787.

56. shaysrebellion.stcc.edu/shaysapp/artifact.do?shortName=act_disqualification16feb87.

57. Richards, *Shays's Rebellion*, 43. According to the census of 1790, roughly half of Massachusetts (population 378,000) lived in the Boston metro area with legal voters (free white men) totaling 96,000. Assuming a similar 50/50 split between city and farmlands, there would have been 48,000 free white men residing outside of Boston. Population of States and Counties of the United States 1790-1990 (Department of Commerce; United States Bureau of the Census) 15, en.wikipedia.org/wiki/1790_United_States_census.

wrote: "However, it may be admitted that the cause of the assembled in arms is bad ... yet it must we think be admitted that many persons of valuable private character have embarked in that cause, and that taken collectively they are no despicable part of the community and their numbers great."[58] Williamstown leadership asked for: "a cessation of the effusion of the blood of our dear brethren may take place immediately for a time sufficient that the real grievances under which the people labor may be fairly stated and petition for redress thereof duly presented to our legislative body or the General Court."[59]

Before the year was out, Bowdoin would be overwhelmingly defeated by John Hancock in the 1787 gubernatorial election and 75 percent of the state legislators would be voted out of office.[60] These electoral victories occurred despite the fact that the signers of the Disqualification Act oath were not eligible to vote. Under Hancock, Massachusetts passed a moratorium on debts, cut taxes by as much as 90 percent, and pardoned the leaders of the rebellion, including Shays and Day.

More important than Massachusetts politics, the rebellion had a marked impact on the Constitution of the United States which would be drafted in the summer of 1787. Ninety percent of the towns in western Massachusetts initially voted against ratification, forcing the state's leadership to adopt amendments guaranteeing a grand jury review for capital cases and reserving powers for the states not expressly given to the federal government. Even then, the constitution only passed by a vote of 187-168 on February 6, 1788.[61] By reluctantly acquiescing to support these and other amendments, the Founding Fathers were able to convince voters in hesitant states to approve the Constitution, thereby ensuring its ratification by mid-1788. The ten amendments comprising the Bill of Rights were ratified on December 15, 1791.

In hindsight, whether the rebellion was, in fact, led by Daniel Shays or Luke Day (or Adam Wheeler or Eli Parsons or Job Shattuck or a Committee of Seventeen) is largely irrelevant. Day's absence from the Springfield assault, and the subsequent rout of Shays' forces, has enabled modern historians to recast the rebellion as "peaceful,"

58. Colrain to Benjamin Lincoln, January 29, 1787, Massachusetts Historical Society, Lincoln Papers.
59. Williamstown to Benjamin Lincoln, January 28, 1787, Massachusetts Historical Society, Lincoln Papers.
60. Richards, *Shays's Rebellion*, 118.
61. csac.history.wisc.edu/states-and-ratification/.

preserving the patina of martyrdom for Shays himself. Had Day joined the fight that January afternoon, it likely would have turned into a full-scale melee, the bloodshed staining the rebellion for all time. In the end, Luke Day's role in helping his fellow farmers of western Massachusetts organize, protest, and ultimately assert their rights at the ballot box is his lasting legacy.

EPILOGUE

Daniel Shays escaped to Vermont where he and his followers established a settlement on Egg Mountain, building a fort, inn, mill, dam and school.[62] While Vermont officially indicated it would not harbor the Regulators, it made no attempt to apprehend them. Shays was pardoned by Massachusetts in 1788, sold his property in Vermont shortly thereafter, and returned to Pelham. In the 1790s he migrated west to Sparta, New York where he settled into obscurity. In 1818 he was granted a military pension by the federal government for the five years he had served.[63] He died in 1825 at age seventy-eight.

Shays' stature grew steadily after his passing. Poems were written, ballads sung, monuments erected, and highways named in his honor.[64] On the two hundredth anniversary of the assault on the Springfield armory, President Ronald Reagan declared January 25, 1987 Shays' Rebellion Day, noting: "Shays' Rebellion was to have a profound and lasting effect on the framing of our Constitution and on our subsequent history."[65]

Luke Day's memory has been far less hallowed. Fleeing the sanctuary of Vermont, he was captured in New Hampshire in January 1788 and carted off to prison in Boston (after Massachusetts paid the promised bounty). Pardoned two months later, Day returned to Springfield where he lived meagerly until his death in 1801. The Society of the Cincinnati expelled him in July 1787 and his father left him out of his will in 1791. Luke Day's grave was unmarked until the local historical society added a headstone in 1987 after President Reagan's proclamation.

62. Stephen Butz, *Shays Settlement in Vermont* (Charleston SC: History Press, 2017), 24, 140.
63. *The Pension Roll of 1835* (Washington, DC: United States War Department; 1992), 294.
64. www.youtube.com/watch?v=1QssCPx8t5I.
65. www.reaganlibrary.gov/archives/speech/proclamation-5598-shays-rebellion-week-and-day-1987.

# The Purpose of the Electoral College: A Seemingly Endless Controversy

**♦♦ MARVIN L. SIMNER ♦♦**

In recent years the operation of the Electoral College, as specified in Article II of the Constitution, has come under repeated attack by Congressional representatives and others throughout the United States. The following material from Section 1 contains what are considered to be the most contentious provisions in this Article.

> Each State shall appoint, in such Manner as the Legislature thereof may direct, a Number of Electors, equal to the whole Number of Senators and Representatives to which the State may be entitled in Congress ... The Electors shall meet in their respective States, and vote by Ballot for two Persons, of whom one at least shall not be an Inhabitant of the same State with themselves ... The Person having the greatest Number of Votes shall be the President ... after the Choice of the President, the Person having the greatest Number of Votes of the Electors shall be the Vice President.

Beyond these words the only other time "Electors" is mentioned in a major way in any of the constitutional documents is in the twelfth amendment and here only for the purpose of clarifying how the occupants of the two offices are to be selected. How the electors themselves were to be chosen was left to the state legislatures to decide, which is what has given rise to the following course of action that today is of central concern.

> Electors are nominated in a different manner in different states, but they are most commonly elected at state party conventions or are otherwise appointed by the political parties. They obtain their positions because of their loyalty and hard work for the party.[1]

1. Tara Ross and Robert M. Hardaway, "The compact clause and the National Popular Vote:

The current outcry from the opposition to this process holds that the final decision for President and Vice President should be made not through electors chosen by political parties but through an open election in which the population as a whole is asked to decide.

As an illustration of the highly divisive nature of this issue, between 1889 and 2004 it has been estimated that the number of proposals for change in the operation of the College was approximately 600 and it has even been claimed that by 2017 the number may have reached as high as 752.[2] With regard to this need for change, the number that endorsed the replacement of Section 1 with what are referred to as direct election plans literally exploded during the 1980s and 1990s.[3] Between 1981 and 2010 of all the bills that dealt with the Electoral College, 86.8 percent called for the use of nation-wide popular election results in one form or another in deciding who should become the chief executive officers of the United States. In fact, as recently as 2016 Senator Barbara Boxer introduced a joint resolution in the 114th Congress to abolish the College and replace it with the direct election of the President and Vice President of the United States.[4] Her proposal was then followed by two others in the 115th Congress that addressed this same matter.[5] Over the years, however, Congress as a whole has repeatedly shown a decided unwillingness to endorse these initiatives. To explain this unwillingness, Thomas H. Neale, in his concluding remarks in a Congressional Research Service Report for Congress, drew upon the following comments by John F. Kennedy, who was a leading defender of the College.

> In the course of Senate floor debate on this question in 1956, he [Kennedy] paraphrased a comment by Viscount Falkland, a 17th century English statesman, declaring of the electoral college, "It seems to me that Falkland's definition of conservatism is quite appropriate [in this instance]—When it is not necessary to change, it is necessary not

---

Implications for the Federal Structure," *New Mexico Law Review*, Vol. 44 No. 2 (2014), 428n.

2. Anonymous, "The Electoral College: An overview and analysis of reform proposals," *CRS Report RL 30804* (November 5, 2004), 2; Anonymous, "The Electoral College: Reform Proposals in the 114th and 115th Congress," *CRS Report R44928* (August 24, 2017), 4.

3. Gary Bugh, *Electoral College Reform: Challenges and Possibilities* (Surrey, England: Ashgate Publishing, 2010), 88.

4. Anonymous, "A Joint Resolution Proposing an Amendment to the Constitution of the United States to Abolish the Electoral College and to Provide for the Direct Popular Election of the President and Vice President of the United States." *S.J. Res. 41* (November 15, 2016).

5. Anonymous, *CRS Report R44928* (August 24, 2017).

to change." This aphorism may offer a key to the future prospects of the electoral college. To date, policymakers have generally concluded that it has not been necessary to change the existing system, or perhaps more accurately, there has been no compelling call for change.[6]

Contrary to Neale's conclusion, and as the above review indicates, there is now a growing as well as a compelling call for change. In view the heated nature of the current debate, from an historical perspective, it may be helpful to consider the words and actions of the Framers of the Constitution when the method for choosing electors was first proposed and ask whether such a debate also would have been relevant during the early years of the republic.

BACKGROUND

The initial debate over the use of electors was launched on May 29, 1787 when Charles Pinckney of South Carolina "laid before the House for their consideration, the draught of a foederal government to be agreed upon between the free and independent States of America."[7] Pickney then elaborated on the many issues the representatives needed to address in the forthcoming days, one of which included the following resolution put forward by Gov. Edmund Randolph of Virginia: "that a National Executive be instituted; to be chosen by the National Legislature."[8] Four days later, and in opposition to Randolph's recommendation, James Wilson of Pennsylvania moved that a national executive should not be chosen in this manner but instead should be elected in the following manner.

> That the States be divided into Districts—and that the persons, qualified to vote in each District, elect Members for their respective Districts to be electors of the Executive Magistracy. That the electors of the Executive Magistracy meet and they or any of them shall elect by ballot, but not out of their own Body, a Person in whom the Executive authority of the national government shall be vested.[9]

Central to Wilson's view was his strong belief that if a true republic was to be established such a person needed to be elected by the people at large.[10] Although the procedure he recommended was certainly in-

---

6. Thomas H. Neale, "Electoral College Reform: 111th Congress Proposals and Other Current Developments," *CRS Report R40895* (September 13, 2010), 28.
7. *Records of the Federal Convention*, 2 (May 29, 1787), 16.
8. Ibid., 21.
9. Ibid. (June 2, 1787), 77.
10. Charles C. Thach, *Creation of the Presidency, 1775-1789* (Baltimore, OII: Johns Hopkins Press, 1922), 86-87.

direct and in opposition to a national public referendum, the reason he favored this approach stemmed from a belief, widely held at the time, that a public referendum was simply impractical.[11] Given the length and breadth of the newly formed country, coupled with the relatively slow and extremely poor means of communicating across vast distances, the average voter would have little if any knowledge of those who were best equipped to lead the country if such persons resided at a considerable distance from themselves. To circumvent this difficulty, according to Wilson's scheme, the voters in each state would select from an array of knowledgeable and worldly candidates within their own state, individuals who would then serve for the voters in that state, as proxies or intermediaries in a forthcoming election of the most qualified person to serve as the chief executive officer for the country at large.

While Wilson's motion was defeated by a vote of seven to two and Randolph's motion was approved by a vote of eight to two, for the most part, it was these two diametrically opposite and competing positions coupled with a number of other matters concerning the presidency, that dominated the Congressional deliberations throughout June, July, and much of August. The final meetings were held on August 24 and again on September 4-6 when the representatives were asked to approve, disapprove, or modify the overall wording in the initial version of the entire constitution prepared by an eleven-member committee appointed by Congress.

THE AUGUST 24 DEBATE

Among the items the representatives were asked to consider on August 24 was the following clause modeled after the original resolution put forward by Randolph on May 29:

> The executive power of the United States shall be vested in a single person . . . He shall be elected by ballot by the Legislature.[12]

Near the start of the debate Daniel Carrol of Maryland moved to eliminate "by the Legislature" and insert in its place "by the people," which was defeated by a vote of nine to two. Charles Pinkney then moved to keep "by the Legislature" but to insert after Legislature the words "and by a majority of the votes of the members [of the Legislature] present when the vote was called." Unlike Carrol's motion, Pinkney's motion was approved by vote of ten to one.[13] Upon learning

---

11. Robert M. Alexander, *Representation and the Electoral College* (Oxford, England: Oxford University Press, 2019), 51.
12. *Records of the Federal Convention*, 2 (August 24, 1787), 401.
13. Ibid., 402-403.

of this latter result Gouverneur Morris from Pennsylvania was out-ranged!

Morris argued that any person who now desired to become President and who also wished to seek re-election would become totally dependent on the wishes of the national legislature throughout his term and therefore would be unable to serve as an independent judge on matters that affect the welfare of the country as a whole. As recorded in the minutes:

> Mr. Govr Morris opposed the election of the President by the Legislature. He dwelt on the danger of rendering the Executive uninterested in maintaining the rights of his Station, as leading to Legislative tyranny. If the Legislature have the Executive dependent on them, they can perpetuate & support their usurpations by the influence of tax-gatherers & other officers, by fleets of armies &c. Cabal & corruption are attached to that mode of election.[14]

To guard against "all these evils," (to use Morris' terminology) and in keeping with Wilson's original motion, Morris then moved that "the President shall be chosen by Electors to be chosen by the people of the several States."[15] Unlike the previous motions by Carrol and Pinkney where definitive results were obtained, the outcome here showed a much less definitive outcome with six states voting in opposition, five voting in favor. Nevertheless, and when considered in relation to the original vote on Wilson's motion, these results indicate that the representative's opinions on the use of electors had clearly begun to shift. Whereas only two states voted in favor before, now five states did so, and previously seven voted against, while here six states were opposed. The states were then polled on the first part of Morris's motion: "shall be chosen by electors." The issue this time was whether his proposal contained an "an abstract question." Here the most that can be said is an indeterminant outcome occurred: four agreed, four disagreed, and two were divided.[16]

SEPTEMBER 4-6

Due to the uncertainly over Morris's motion, in the next iteration of the constitution the eleven-member committee recommended, on September 4, the following wording in the clause concerned with electors.

> Each State shall appoint in such a manner as it's Legislature may direct, a number of Electors equal to the whole number of Senators, and

14. Ibid., 403-404.
15. Ibid., 404.
16. Ibid.

Members of the House of representative to which the State may be entitled in the legislature.[17]

The following material from the minutes of September 4 not only summarize several remarks made by Wilson but also provides a general sense of the ordeal that the representatives faced when forced to resolve this issue.

> The subject has greatly divided the House, and will also divide people out of doors. It is in truth the most difficult of all on which we have had to decide. He [Wilson] had never made up an opinion on it entirely to his own satisfaction. He thought the plan on the whole [the use of electors] a valuable improvement on the former [having the national legislature alone decide on the presidency]. It gets rid of one great evil, that of cabal & corruption.[18]

On September 6 the principal focus of the debate was on the need to clarify and endorse the wording in the above clause. Closure was reached that day on the appointment of electors (nine voted in favor, two opposed) and the final version of the Constitution was then sent for ratification on September 10.[19]

OUTCOME

Although the overall concept of each state choosing their own electors had been approved by the representatives and ratified by Congress,[20] during the first presidential election in 1789 half the states preferred that the final choice of electors be made not by the public at large within the states, as had been suggested by Wilson, Carol, and Morris, but instead by the members of the state legislatures. Of the ten states that voted in 1789, five employed this method. With the introduction of widespread public voting for the office of president in 1828, however, this method changed. Based on information compiled by historian Thomas Hudson McKee at the end of the nineteenth century, from 1828 through 1900 all of the states, with the exception of South Carolina and Florida, made use only of the public within each state to choose the electors instead of the legislators.[21] A detailed assessment of McKee's information also

17. Ibid. (September 4, 1787), 493-494.
18. Ibid., 501.
19. Ibid. (September 6 and 10, 1787), 517, 572-273.
20. For more information on the debate that led to approval and ratification see Robert M. Alexander, *Representation and the Electoral College*, Chapter 3.
21. Thomas Hudson McKee, *The National Conventions and Platforms of all Political Parties, 1789 to 1905*. (Baltimore, MD: The Friedenwald Company, 1906; re-issued in 1971 by the Lenox Hill Publishing and Distributing Company in New York).

shows that when the electors were obtained in this manner, with the single exception of 1876, in eighteen of the nineteen elections that took place during this period, the outcome of the Electoral College vote was identical to the outcome of the popular vote.

Moreover, as early as 1828 and continuing throughout the rest of the century, widespread communication of political ideology was no longer hindered by time or distance and those who sought public office were clearly able to communicate, if not in person, then through the action of their supporters. For example, the presidential campaign organized on behalf of Andrew Jackson in 1828 was a highly effective forerunner of all future campaigns.

> In addition to planning meetings and devising and distributing campaign materials to newspapers and voters, Jackson's organizers created a precursor of the Democratic and Republican National Committees by establishing a Washinton-based central correspondence committee ... They founded newspapers ... issued pamphlets, broadsides, and biographies.[22]

In addition to this campaign material, as early as 1834 all of the political parties had developed extensive political platforms, the contents of which also would have been widely known.[23] Thus, there was no shortage of information that prospective voters could access. Indeed, many voters would have been inclined to take advantage of this information since all voters were property owners, and the outcome of an election could very well have influenced the value of their holdings and possibly even the success of their businesses.

CONCLUSION

By the end of the nineteenth century, it was known that for each state the outcome of the Electoral College vote merely duplicated the outcome of the popular vote. Also, because of the widespread availability of information on the nature of the candidates who were vying for office, as well as their political positions, there was no longer the need for electors to serve as proxies. Considered together both points indicate that if there were indeed members of Congress as early as 1889 who were willing to initiate procedures for abandoning the College, they would have had ample grounds for doing so.[24] Although why such an attempt would have failed is unknown, it could be that Viscount Falkland's reasoning might very well have held sway even back then.

22. Kathleen Hall Jamieson, *Packaging the Presidency*. (New York, NY: Oxford University Press, 1996), 7.
23. McKee, Ibid.
24. Anonymous, 2004, Ibid.

# Early Presidential Elections:
# The Questionable Use of Electors
# to Correct Voter Imbalances

✺ MARVIN L. SIMNER ✺

An important issue that the Congressional delegates faced when drafting the Constitution was how to create an equitable balance in voting rights between the larger states (Massachusetts, Pennsylvania, Virginia) and the smaller ones (Delaware, Georgia, New Hampshire). Although the delegates were sworn to secrecy throughout their debates (May through September 1787), once the debates were over the delegates were at liberty to freely express their views and many did so. On November 29, 1787, Luther Martin, a Congressional delegate from an intermediate size state, Maryland, delivered the following remarks to the Maryland House of Representatives.

> When I join'd the Convention I found that Mr. Randolph [Governor of Virginia] had laid before that Body certain propositions for their consideration ... one of which was that [as few as] seven States might proceed to Business, and therefor four States composing a Majority of seven, might eventually give the Law to the whole Union ... It must be remembered that in forming the Confederacy the State of Virginia proposed, and obstinately contended (tho unsupported by any other) for representation [in voting] according to Numbers [that is, population size] ... These Views in the larger States, did not escape the observation of the lesser [states] and meetings in private were formed to counteract them.[1]

---

1. *Records of the Federal Convention*, 3 (November 29, 1787), Appendix A, CXLVIb, 151.

Among the delegates' major concerns over this matter was how to elect a chief executive officer for the country as a whole and, at the same time, provide an appropriate means to cope with the vast population differences that existed among the several states. To address this matter, on July 19, 1787, Oliver Ellsworth suggested that the states should not be allotted votes based on population size alone but on a ratio system devised to reflect a proportional representation of each state's population. To begin the discussion, Ellsworth moved that the president should "be chosen by Electors appointed for that purpose by the Legislatures of the States . . . One person from each State whose numbers shall not exceed 100,000, Two from each of the others, whose numbers . . . shall not exceed 300,000, and Three from each of the rest."[2] On July 20 James Madison underscored the significance of Ellsworth's motion when he observed,

> that this would make in time all or nearly all the States equal. Since there were few that would not in time contain the number of inhabitants entitling them to 3 Electors; that this ratio ought either to be made temporary, or so varied as that it would adjust itself to the growing population of the States.[3]

While a vote on the first part of Ellsworth's motion (appointed by the Legislatures) was approved, a vote on the second part (the nature of the ratio) was postponed. As the debate continued, a further concern also arose "from the disposition in the people to prefer a Citizen of their own State, and the disadvantage this would throw on the smaller States."[4] To address this added concern, on July 25 Hugh Williamson suggested,

> that each man [elector] should vote for 3 candidates. One of these he observed would be probably of his own State, the other 2, of some other States; and as probably of a small as a large one.[5]

In agreement with Williamson, but to simplify his suggestion, Gouverneur Morris then proposed that "each man should vote for two persons [instead of three] one of whom at least should not be of his own State."[6] According to Madison the only objection to Morris's double-voting procedure would be that the elector,

2. *Records of the Federal Convention*, 2 (July 19, 1787), 50.
3. Ibid., July 20, 1787, 63.
4. Ibid., July 25, 1787, 111.
5. Ibid., 113.
6. Ibid.

after having given his vote for his favorite fellow Citizen, would throw away his second on some obscure Citizen of another State, in order to ensure the object of his first choice. But it could hardly be supposed that the Citizens of many States would be so sanguine of having their favorite elected, as not to give their second vote with sincerity to the next object of their choice.[7]

While neither Williamson's suggestion nor Morris's proposal were ever put to a vote, it was Morris's wording, with two clarifications, that eventually found its way into the following material in Article II Section 1 of the Constitution which was sent to the House in final draft form by the Committee of Revision on September 12, 1787:

> The electors shall meet in their respective states, and vote by ballot for two persons, of whom one, at least, shall not be an inhabitant of the same state with themselves . . . The person having the greatest number of votes shall be the President . . . In every case, after the choice of the President by the representatives, the person having the greatest number of votes of the electors shall be the Vice-President.[8]

The first clarification involved the phrase, "The electors shall meet in their respective states, and vote by ballot." These words were added to avoid the possibility of collusion if all the electors were to meet at the same time and in the same location when they nominated their candidates and cast their votes. The second clarification involved the term vice-president, which was added merely to provide a home for one of the two votes, since it was not initially clear what the duties should be for the person holding this office.[9] The vice-president's duties were eventually defined during the final stages of ratification.[10]

Despite the second clarification, without also specifying which vote should apply to which office, it remained unclear how the elector's votes should be tabulated. The only information in Article II Section 1 that addressed this matter stated that the final nominations along with their respective numbers of votes, would be recorded, sealed, and transmitted to the president of the Senate for final tabulation.[11] Unfortunately, this wording did not address the issue at hand. To rectify this situation, it was decided that the candidate with the greatest number of overall votes, based on one of the two allotted votes, would become president.

---

7. Ibid., 114.
8. *Elliot's Debates*, 1 (September 12, 1787), 302.
9. Ray Raphael, *Mr. President* (New York, NY: Alfred A. Knopf, 2012), 118.
10. *Records of the Federal Convention*, 2 (September 4, 1787), 498.
11. *Elliot's Debates*, 283.

The candidate with the next highest number, based on the other of the two allotted votes, would then become vice-president. When ties occurred, the House of Representatives would determine the outcome.

IMPLICATIONS

Because of the clause that permitted the electors to "vote by ballot for two persons, of whom one, at least, shall not be an inhabitant of the same state with themselves," the electors, in fact, were now totally free to cast one of their two votes for their state's favorite son, which is precisely what happened, and which, in turn, led to a series of results diametrically opposite to what the delegates initially had hoped to achieve. In essence, the endorsement of this clause had permitted the large states to dominate the outcome of many of the early presidential elections.

In 1797, for example, Massachusetts, using one of its allotted votes, gave all sixteen of its electoral votes to John Adams, the state's favorite son, which enabled him to win the presidency in 1797. The state then spilt the second of its allotted votes and gave a further sixteen electoral votes to candidates from Connecticut (Samuel Johnson two votes, Ellsworth one vote) and South Carolina (Thomas Pinckney thirteen votes). Similarly Virginia, using one of its allotted votes, gave all or nearly all of its electoral votes to its favorite sons: Washington in 1789 and 1793, and Thomas Jefferson in 1797 and 1801, then spread the same number of electoral votes during each of these years across several of the other states. Although Jefferson failed to win the presidency in 1797, he did win the vice-presidency that year but only with Virginia's help.[12]

The one exception to this procedure was Pennsylvania. Presumably, owing to the poor health and subsequent death of its favorite son, Benjamin Franklin in 1790, and the apparent lack of any other favorite sons who chose to run for office, Pennsylvania opted to support the favorite sons of Virginia in 1789, 1793, and 1797. Only in 1801 did its electors choose to split their votes equally between Jefferson from Virginia and Aaron Burr, the favorite son from New York.

Although this highly questionable procedure was finally brought to an end in 1801, the end occurred not because of this procedure, but because of a tie vote in the election that year when Jefferson and Burr each received an overall total of seventy-three electoral votes that required thirty-six ballots in the House to resolve. As a result, Article II Section 1, came under severe attack over what has since been labeled

12. Svend Petersen, *A Statistical History of the American Presidential Elections* (New York, NY: Frederick Ungar Publishing Co., 1968), 11-13.

"one small defect" in its construction, namely, its failure to designate a specific office for each of the two votes.[13] To correct this defect, the Twelfth Amendment, approved on June 15, 1804, mandated the assignment of one of the votes to the office of president and the other to the office of vice-president with the names of both to appear on the ballot in accordance with the following wording:

> The Electors shall meet in their respective states and vote by ballot for President and Vice-President, one of whom, at least, shall not be an inhabitant of the same state with themselves; they shall name in their ballots the person voted for as President, and in distinct ballots the person voted for as Vice-President

Despite this correction, a careful reading of the amendment shows that it contained words identical to those originally used by Morris, which meant that his procedure remained totally intact. If the electors did not allocate any votes to a candidate from their own state who was running for the office of vice-president, it was still possible for the state's electors to allocate all their votes to their state's favorite son who was vying for the office of president, which again is exactly what happened. Between 1805 and 1821 Virginia allocated all its electoral votes to Jefferson, Madison, and James Monroe, while Massachusetts, in 1817, cast all its votes for Rufus King, a resident of Massachusetts. Pennsylvania, as before, opted to allocate all its votes in the same manner as Virginia. Each of these states, also as before, then distributed their same allotment of votes to candidates from a number of other states who were vying for the office of vice-president.[14]

DISCUSSION

In spite of the lengthy debates that had taken place among the delegates with the aim of equalizing voting across the states, with Morris's provision in place the favorite sons of the larger states continued to play an important, if not a dominant role, in the choice of president for the United States in all the elections from 1789 through 1821. In view of this outcome, it is worth asking if a procedure other than Morris's could have led to a different result. On June 2, 1787, James Wilson introduced the following resolution.

> That the states be divided into districts—and that the persons, qualified to vote in each District, elect Members for their respective Dis-

---

13. Raphael, *Mr. President*, 227. For a full account of the origin of the controversy surrounding Article II Section 1 see Tadahisa Kuroda, *The Origins of the Twelfth Amendment* (Westport, CT: Greenwood Press, 1994).

14. Petersen, *A Statistical History*, 14-16.

tricts to be electors of the Executive Magistracy. That the electors of the Executive Magistracy meet and they or any of them shall elect by ballot, but not out of their own Body, a Person in whom the Executive authority of the national government shall be vested.[15]

The major difference between Morris's procedure and Wilson's was that the latter called for a single vote by the electors whereas the former required a double vote. Of equal importance, although neither allowed the states to vote for their own favorite sons, Wilson's explicitly eliminated this likelihood, whereas Morris's did not. Unlike Morris's procedure, which was never put to a vote, Wilson's was defeated by a vote of seven to two.[16] Nevertheless, it is instructive to consider what would have occurred if Wilson's had been approved.

By reporting the total electoral count under each procedure for the first four presidential elections, the following table permits a direct comparison in outcome between the two. Although the total count under Morris' procedure remained as before, under Wilson's approach the new count was obtained by subtracting the number of votes allocated by each state to the state's own candidate. For example, under Wilson's approach in 1793 the count allocated to Virginia for Washington was reduced by twenty-one, for Adams from Massachusetts, the count was reduced by sixteen, and for George Clinton from New York, the count was reduced by the twelve.[17]

| Election Year | Candidate | Morris's Electoral Vote Count | Wilson's Electoral Vote Count |
|---|---|---|---|
| 1789 | Washington | 69 | 59 |
|  | Adams | 34 | 24 |
|  | Jay | 9 | 9 |
| 1793 | Washington | 132 | 111 |
|  | Adams | 77 | 61 |
|  | Clinton | 50 | 38 |
| 1797 | Adams | 71 | 55 |
|  | Jefferson | 68 | 48 |
|  | Pinckney | 59 | 51 |

15. *Records of the Federal Convention*, 1 (June 2, 1787), 77; *Elliot's Debates*, 1 (June 2, 1787), 156.
16. *Records of the Federal Convention*, 77.
17. Petersen, *A Statistical History*, 3.

| 1801 | Burr | 73 | 61 |
|------|------|----|----|
|      | Jefferson | 73 | 52 |
|      | Adams | 65 | 49 |

While no changes resulted in the first two elections under either procedure because of the very large number of electoral votes that Washington had received in both, such was not the case for the next two elections. In 1797 under Wilson's approach, Pinckney from South Carolina, instead of Jefferson from Virginia would have become vice-president, and in 1801 Burr from New York instead of Jefferson would have become president without the need for the House of Representatives to intervene. While neither candidate was from a small state, using Wilson's approach both were elevated in their rank order positions and therefore both provided alternatives to the large state nominations.

CONCLUSION

Given that Wilson's approach was more in keeping with the delegates' desire to minimize the importance of the larger states than Morris's, it is reasonable to ask why Morris's procedure was endorsed whereas Wilson's was not. The most promising explanation that comes to mind stems from the remarks attributed to Luther Martin, as quoted above, as well as from Jefferson's summary of events that were unfolding at the time: "The larger colonies had threatened they would not confederate at all if their weight in Congress should not be equal to the numbers of people they added to the confederacy."[18] Because both of these remarks strongly suggest that the larger states were clearly in favor of maintaining their positions of authority in governing the country, it would not be unreasonable to assume that, by supporting Morris's approach and not Wilson's, such action by the larger states would have been to their advantage.

In line with this explanation, recall that two of the large states, Pennsylvania and Virginia, when making use of Morris's approach, assigned all or nearly all of their electoral votes to Virginia's candidates. Needless to say, their combined action not only skewed the overall results in favor of these states but also completely dwarfed the impact of the small states. By way of example, consider once again the election of 1797. Whereas Virginia allotted twenty of its twenty-one electoral votes to Jefferson, and Pennsylvania also gave fourteen of its fifteen votes to him, this total of thirty-four votes meant that even if the five small

18. Eli Merritt, *Disunion Among Ourselves* (Columbia, MO: University of Missouri Press, 2023), 147.

states (Delaware, Georgia, Kentucky, Tennessee, and Vermont) had also acted in concert, they would only have been able to accumulate a total electoral vote count of eighteen, well below the number needed to overcome the enormous lead of these two large states in their choice of Jefferson.[19] In view of the delegates' level of education, range of experiences and overall sophistication, coupled with the elementary mathematics involved, it is difficult to believe that this future scenario would not have been realized by the delegates when they opted to favor Morris's approach over Wilson's.

19. Petersen, *A Statistical History*, 3-12.

# Thomas Jefferson and the Conditions of Good History: Some Implications for Writing about the American Revolution and Early American History

**M. ANDREW HOLOWCHAK**

Thomas Jefferson has a Thucydidean, or fact-based, approach to the praxis of history. Evidence of that approach appeared early in his life, in his *Literary Commonplace Book*. There, Jefferson, quoted Henry St. John, Lord Bolingbroke (1678–1751), who wrote of history, rightly practiced. For history to be authentic, Jefferson, continuing to copy Bolingbroke, added that "these are some of the conditions necessary" (1–4, numbers mine):

1. it must be writ by a cotemporary author, or by one who had cotemporary materials in his hands.

2. it must have been published among men who are able to judge of the capacity of th[e] author, and of the authenticity of the memorials on whic[h] he writ.

3. nothing repugnant to the universal experience of mankind must be contained in it.

4. the principal facts at least, which it contains, must be confirmed by collateral testimony, that is, by the testimony of thos[e] who had no common interest of country, of religion, or of profession, to disguise or falsify the truth.

We may thus sum these needed conditions, according to Jefferson, for sound history:

1. (PROXIMITY CONDITION): a historian must either be living at the time of the events he describes or, if not, he must be privy to documents written of the time he describes by witnesses.

2. (AUTHENTICITY CONDITION): the author must be judged to be capable and ingenuous by others of his day who are capable and ingenuous and his materials must be judged authentic by such persons.

3. (CONSISTENCY CONDITION): what is described is consistent with what is universally experienced by mankind—e.g., there be no contraventions of the amply verified laws of physical nature.

4. (CONFIRMATION CONDITION): the axial facts of the testimony must be confirmed by qualified disinterested others.

Bolingbroke's principles, clearly driven by his empiricism, entail sufficient vetting of both persons and material. That Jefferson commonplaced the passage strongly intimates purchase of Bolingbrokean principles of proper history. Jefferson's inclusion of "some" indicates the likelihood of other conditions necessary, or at least desirable, not listed by Bolingbroke.

Let us look at each.

First, there is the proximity condition. To John Adams (10 Aug. 1815), Jefferson writes of his concern that the there can never be a definitive account of the American Revolution because none of the discussions of the Continental Congress has been left to posterity by members of that Congress. "On the subject of the history of the American Revolution, you ask who shall write it?" says Jefferson. "Who can write it? And who will ever be able to write it? Nobody; except merely its external facts; all its councils, designs and discussions having been conducted by Congress with closed doors, and no members, as far as I know, having even made notes of them. These, which are the life and soul of history, must forever be unknown."

To John Adams, Jefferson wrote of his notes on American independence:

> On the questions of Independence, and on the two articles of Confederation respecting taxes and votings, I took minutes of the heads of the arguments. On the first, I threw all into one mass, without ascribing to the speakers their respective arguments; pretty much in the manner of Hume's summary digests of the reasonings in parliament for and against a measure. On the last, I stated the heads of the arguments used by each speaker. But the whole of my notes on the question of Inde-

pendence does not occupy more than five pages, such as of this letter; and on the other questions, two such sheets. They have never been communicated to any one.[1]

Jefferson added, however, that there is an account, "the ablest work of this kind," of the debates over the Constitution at the convention in Philadelphia in 1788. "The whole of everything said and done there was taken down by Mr. Madison, with a labor and exactness beyond comprehension."

On June 12, 1823, Jefferson told William Johnson, "The opening scenes of our present government will not be seen in their true aspect until the letters of the day, now held in private hoards, shall be broken up and laid open to public view." On October 4 of the same year, he told Hugh Paul Taylor "every good citizen" must do what he can to preserve "documents relating to the history of our country." He was convinced that America, comprising liberty-loving people, has a privileged position in global history.

Next, there is the authenticity condition. In some notes he took on Christoph Daniel Ebeling (30 July 1795) and Ebeling's account of the history and geography of America in his *Erdbeschreibung und Geschichte von America* (first published in 1793), Jefferson commented on the American sources of Ebeling's work. There are President Stiles, Dr. Willar, Dr. Ramsay, Mr. Barlow, Mr. Morse, and Mr. Webster. The first was "an excellent man, of very great learning, but remarkable for his credulity." Ramsay, Barlow, and Morse were "men of respectable characters worthy of confidence as to any facts they may state, and rendered, by their good sense, good judges of them." Morse and Webster were "good authorities for whatever relates to the Eastern states, & perhaps as far South as the Delaware." Yet when they talked of states south of Delaware, "their information is worse than none at all, except as far as they quote good authorities." Each traveled once through the South so that they might be considered eyewitnesses. "But to pass once along a public road thro' a country, & in one direction only, to put up at it's taverns, and get into conversation with the idle, drunken individuals who pass their time lounging in these taverns, is not the way to know a country, it's inhabitants, or manners." And so, Ebeling was not entitled "to generalize a whole nation from these specimens."

What then of the newspapers of the country—such as John Fenno's *Gazette of the United States,* Noah Webster's *American Minerva,* Ben-

---

1. Thomas Jefferson to John Adams, August 10, 1815, founders.archives.gov/ documents/ Jefferson/03-08-02-0533.

jamin Russell's *Columbian Sentinel* (Boston), from which Ebeling drew? Those were each Federalist sources, and thus slanted.

Jefferson then recommended Philip Mazzei's *Recherches historiques et politiques sur les Etates-Unis de l'Amerique*—which could be got only from Paris—because "the author is an exact man."

The greatest illustration of inauthenticity is David Hume's *History of England*. Jefferson wrote of the enthusiasm with which he, unaware of its Tory slant, "devoured it when young." Hume, doing backwards history,[2] began with the Stuarts, "became their apologist, and advocated all their enormities," perhaps in some measure to gain fame. Jefferson wrote,

> He spared nothing, therefore, to wash them white, and to palliate their misgovernment. For this purpose he suppressed truths, advanced falsehoods, forged authorities and falsified records. . . . But so bewitching was his style and manner, that his readers were un-willing to doubt anything, swallowed everything, and all England became tories by the magic of his art. His pen revolutionized the public sentiment of that country more completely than the standing armies could ever have done, which were so much dreaded and deprecated by the patriots of that day.

He then turned to the Tudors, but then only "selected and arranged the materials of their history as to present their arbitrary acts only, as the genuine samples of the constitutional power of the crown.[3] "It is like the portraits of our countryman [Joseph] Wright, whose eye was so unhappy as to seize all the ugly features of his subject, and to present them faithfully, while it was entirely insensible to every lineament of beauty."[4]

Jefferson's gripe with Hume, he told George Lewis, was his pro-monarchy slant.[5] When discussing the reigns of the Plantagenets and Tudors, Hume wrote that "it was the people who encroached on the sovereign, not the sovereign who usurped on the rights of the people" and that "the grievances under which the English labored [i.e., whip-

---

2. Jefferson to George Lewis, October 1825, founders.archives.gov/documents/ Jefferson/98-01-02-5617.

3. Jefferson to William Duane, August 12, 1810, founders.archives.gov/documents/Jefferson/03-03-02-0001-0002.

4. Wright was known for his portraits of American patriots, like George Washington and Benjamin Franklin. He perished in 1793 with yellow fever in Philadelphia. Jefferson to Adams, November 25, 1816, founders.archives.gov/documents/Jefferson/03-10-02-0414.

5. Jefferson to George Lewis, October 25, 1825, founders.archives.gov/documents/Jefferson/98-01-02-5617.

ping, pillorying, cropping, imprisoning, fining, &c.], when considered in themselves, without regard to the constitution, scarcely deserve the name, nor were they either burthensome on the people's properties, or anywise shocking to the natural humanity of mankind." As a Tory historian, Hume derived his understanding of the British constitution from the provenance of the Norman Conquest, while Whig historians derived theirs from the era of the Saxons. (A critique of the cogency/uncogency of Jefferson's account of Hume is beyond the scope of this essay.)

Third, there is the consistency condition. In the manner of Leopold von Ranke (1795–1886) decades after him, Jefferson railed against writers who got right the "great outlines," though "the incidents and coloring are according to the faith or fancy of the writer." He had in mind Judge John Marshall's biography of George Washington. "Had Judge Marshall taken half your pains in sifting and scrutinizing facts, he would not have given to the world, as true history a false copy of a record under his eye." The nodus is amplified tenfold in subsequent biographies, which drew sustenance from the first. Historians must begin with facts. "When writers are so indifferent as to the correctness of facts," said Jefferson to William Wirt, who was in the process of a biography of Patrick Henry and enjoining Jefferson for information, "the verification of which lies at their elbow, by what measure shall we estimate their relation of things distant, or of those given to us through the obliquities of their own vision?" To allow for vetted material, it is incumbent on key players in a great historical drama to keep painstakingly records of events.[6]

In a later letter to Wirt, Jefferson lampooned his friend's finished biography of Henry. "You have certainly practiced vigorously the precept of 'de mortius nil nisi bonum.'[7] This presents a very difficult question,—whether one only or both sides of the medal shall be presented. It constitutes, perhaps, the distinction between panegyric and history."[8] Jefferson was clearly disappointed with the work. He would list the biography in his library under "Fiction."

It was imperative for Jefferson that chroniclers of persons and events do the digging, as it were, and get right their facts. Travelers to America—like d'Auberteuil, Longchamps, and Abbé Robin—crafted ac-

6. Jefferson to William Wirt, August 14, 1814, founders.archives.gov/documents/Jefferson/03-07-02-0403.
7. "Only say good things about the dead."
8. Jefferson to Wirt, November 12, 1816, founders.archives.gov/documents/Jefferson/03-10-02-0391.

counts of the Revolution or the jejune country, said Jefferson to the editor of *Journal de Paris*, that passed as genuine to contemporaries of the persons or events depicted. He wrote,

> How may we expect that future ages shall be better informed? Will those rise from their graves to bear witness to the truth, who would not, while living, lift their voices against falsehood? If cotemporary histories are thus false, what will future compilations be? And what are all those of preceding times?[9]

Jefferson cited a paragraph concerning John Dickinson's role in the American Revolution. Dickinson was said by a certain M. Meyer to be the sole driving force behind America's independence. Jefferson went on to give a thorough refutation of that account—a tissue of falsehoods with the exception of one claim. Meyer stated that there was a congressional split in the vote for independence; Jefferson noted that the vote was unanimous. After vigorous debate on Jefferson's Declaration, the final document was "approved by an unanimous vote and signed by every member, *except Mr. Dickinson*." Still, the journal claimed that Dickinson, and only Dickinson, declared the independence of the United States.[10]

Last, there is the confirmation condition, which required that even first-hand testimonies, if possible, be vetted by accounts of others. It is a condition of enumerative induction which sensibly states that the more testimony we have on behalf of some claim, so long as we do not stumble across disconfirmatory evidence, the more we can be convinced of its truth.

To William Short, Jefferson recounted a story which he was fond of relating. In a discussion with John Adams and Alexander Hamilton, the former stated that the British government would be "the most perfect model of government ever devised by the wit of man" if its imperfections were expunged. Hamilton corrected Adams, "With these corruptions it was perfect, and without them it would be an impracticable government." Jefferson added that the account was confirmable by Henry Knox and Edmund Randolph, who were then also present. Jefferson summed:

---

9. Jefferson to the editor of *Journal de Paris*, August 29, 1787, founders.archives.gov/documents/Jefferson/01-12-02-0073.

10. *Monsieur Mayer assure qu'une seule voix, un seul homme, prononça l'independance des Etats unis. Ce fut, dit il, John Dickinson, un des Deputés de la Pensilvanie au Congrés. La veille, il avoit vôté pour la soumission, l'egalité des suffrages avoit suspendu la resolution; s'il eut persisté, le Congrés ne deliberoit point, il fut foible; il ceda aux instances de ceux qui avoient plus d'energie, plus d'eloquence, et plus de lumieres; il donna sa voix: l'Amerique lui doit une reconnaissance eternelle; c'est Dickinson qui l'a affranchie.*

The true history of that conflict of parties will never be in possession of the public, until, by the death of the actors in it, the hoards of their letters shall be broken up and given to the world. I should not fear to appeal to those of Harper himself, if he has kept copies of them, for abundant proof that he was himself a monarchist. I shall not live to see these unrevealed proofs, nor probably you; for time will be requisite. But time will, in the end, produce the truth.[11]

In addition to the four needed conditions of right history, Jefferson also commonplaced a sentence on the worthlessness of circumstantial history.

A story circumstantially related, ought not to be received on the faith of tradition; since the last reflection on human nature is sufficient to shew how unsafely a system of facts and circumstances can be trusted for it's preservation to memory alone, and for it's conveiance to oral report alone; how liable it must be to all those alterations, which the weakness of the human mind must cause necessarily, and which the corruption of the human heart will be sure to suggest.

Thus, any report that is handed down through the years from mouth to mouth is historically unreliable. Reports must be first-hand. An excellent illustration of direct testimony occurs in a letter to James Madison, concerning Marquis de Chastellux's book, *Travels in North America, Through the Years, 1780, 1781, and 1782:* "He has visited all the principal fields of battle, enquired minutely into the detail of the actions, & has given what are probably the best accounts extant of them. He often finds occasion to criticise & to deny the British accounts from an inspection of the ground."[12]

There is more to say. Inspection of Jefferson's writings shows a commitment to other principles, not as needed principles, but as desiderata.

First, to be a fit historian, one must devote a lifetime to the discipline and write down one's experiences before one's faculties have decayed. In reply to an exceptional letter from Josephus Bradner Stuart wrote an exceptional letter to Jefferson, bidding him to write his account of his life and the times in which he had lived. Stuart wrote, "The American People, after all you have done for them, wish one more last & lasting favor from you: that is, that not withstanding your advanced

11. Jefferson to William Short, January 8, 1825, founders.archives.gov/documents/Jefferson/98-01-02-4848.
12. Jefferson to James Madison, February 20, 1784, founders.archives.gov/documents/Jefferson/01-06-02-0406.

age, your extensive correspondence, your numerous & important duties, you will yet favor them & the world with such history of your own life & times, as your leisure may permit you to compile. For such a work the voice of the nation, as far as I can ascertain it, seems to be loud & united."[13]

Jefferson replied that while a public servant, he had the cognitive resources but not the time, while now that he was retired, he had the time but lacked the cognitive resources:

> to write history requires a whole life of observation, of enquiry, of labor and correction. it's materials are not to be found among the ruins of a decayed memory. at this day I should begin where I ought to have left off. the 'solve senescentem equum' is a precept we learn in youth,[14] but for the practice of age; and were I to disregard it, it would be but a proof the more of it's soundness.[15]

Jefferson added that he would certainly lose the respect of his fellow citizens "by exposing the decay of [his] faculties," were he to attempt such a history. It was, thus, for Stuart and his "brethren of the rising generation to arraign at your tribunal the actions of your predecessors, and to pronounce the sentence they may have merited or incurred."[16]

Second, a historian must practice concision. On December 18, 1824, William Short wrote to Jefferson of the goings-on of the secret Hartford Convention, held by Federalists from late 1814 to early 1815.[17] Short remarked on his astonishment on a certain Harper who had writ-

---

13. Josephus B. Stuart to Jefferson, April 25, 1817, founders.archives.gov/documents/Jefferson/03-11-02-0204.

14. From Horace, who writes, "*Solve senescentem mature sanus equum, ne peccet ad extremum ridendus et ilia ducat*" ("Be wise in time, and turn loose the ageing horse, lest at the last he stumble amid jeers and burst his wind"). Horace, *Satires, Epistles, Art of Poetry*, trans. Rushton Fairclough (Cambridge, MA: Harvard University Press, 1926), Book I, Epistle I, lines 8–9.

15. Jefferson to Stuart, May 10, 1817, founders.archives.gov/documents/Jefferson/03-11-02-0287.

16. Ibid.

17. These were meetings at Hartford of Federalist from Massachusetts, New Hampshire, Connecticut, Rhode Island, and Vermont from December 15, 1814, to January 5, 1815, to discuss pressing political issues such as the dreadful War of 1812, the possibility of secession from the union of states, removal of the three-fifths clause, the legality of the Louisiana Purchase, the Embargo of 1807, a requirement to have two-thirds of congress approve declarations of war, restrictions of trade, and admission of new states. Three representatives from the secret meetings were subsequently sent to Washington to discuss their terms, but news of Andrew Jackson's stunning victory in the Battle of New Orleans preceded them. Thereby the representatives lost whatever leverage they might have had, and they returned to Massachusetts.

ten too little on the convention and had not consulted the pamphlet of Harrison Gray Otis. Jefferson replied: "It is impossible to read thoroughly such writings as those of Harper and Otis, who take a page to say what requires but a sentence, or rather, who give you whole pages of what is nothing to the purpose." Jefferson, though he lived in a time when prolixity of written expression was the norm—one sentence, especially in legal documents, could run on for pages—was remarkably economical when writing. Jefferson championed concision of expression for all manners of communicating through words.

Third, Jefferson militated for some degree of embellishment, so long as a historian does not depart from the facts. Given what I have mentioned of concision and given Jefferson's penchant for truthfulness, it might come as a surprise that he was not adamantly against any measure of embellishment to enliven the otherwise dreary, fact-based prose. He wrote to John Adams:

> I am now reading Botta's History of our own Revolution.[18] Bating the ancient practice which he has adopted of putting speeches into mouths which never made them, and fancying motives of action which we never felt, he has given that history with more detail, precision and candor, than any writer I have yet met with. It is, to be sure, compiled from those writers; but it is a good secretion of their matter, the pure from the impure, and presented in a just sense of right in opposition to usurpation.[19]

What exactly is Jefferson here saying? The second sentence seems to be a concession. Jefferson was likely asserting that despite having added speeches that were never uttered in the mouths of Patriots, Botta had still given the most detailed, precise, and candid account of the American Revolution. Drawing from other sources, he purified their impure accounts, because he explained the revolution from the perspective of right, not of insurgency for the sake of usurpation of power. If so, this is not a blanket endorsement of adding fictive speeches to enliven narrative, but Jefferson clearly did not object to the practice.

18. Carlo Giuseppi Guglielmo Botta, *History of the War of the Independence of the United States of America* (Philadelphia: 1820–1821).
19. Jefferson to Adams, May 5, 1817, founders.archives.gov/documents/Adams/99-02-02-6753.

# "The Modern American Wallace": Relics, Revolutions, and Revolutionaries

❈ SHAWN DAVID MCGHEE ❈

On Friday morning, December 30, 1792, Archibald Robertson, an ambitious painter from Aberdeen, Scotland, arrived at the doorstep of the executive mansion at Philadelphia.[1] David Steuart Erskine, 11th Earl of Buchan, entrusted him to deliver a wooden box to President George Washington.[2] Yet this was no ordinary box and Robertson's call no ordinary visit. For those of an early whig historical persuasion, both gift and guest reflected that timeless pursuit of liberty, dignity and human progress. And for Buchan, at least, Washington's disinterested leadership during the War for Independence not only liberated Americans from British oppression, it created a nation whose political mission prioritized private pursuits of happiness. From the earl's perspective, Washington continued a tradition that Scottish freedom fighter Sir William Wallace commenced some five hundred years earlier. The centuries may have changed, but for Buchan the circumstances revealed synergetic continuity.

Lord Buchan's earldom originated in 1469 (the second iteration of a 1374 creation) and, for more than two centuries, his family moved among Scotland's most elite circles.[3] His parents educated him at home

---

1. *National Gazette*, January 2, 1792.
2. Andrew Robertson, ed., *Letters and Papers of Andrew Robertson, A.M., Born 1777. Died 1845. Miniature Painter to His Late Royal Highness the Duke of Sussex: Also a Treatise on the Art of his Eldest Brother, Archibald Robertson, Born 1765. Died 1835, of New York* (London: Eyre and Spottiswoode, 1895), 9.
3. Ronald G. Cant, "David Steuart, 11th Earl of Buchan: Founder of the Society of Antiquaries

with the assistance of tutor James Buchanan, who later became Professor of Oriental Languages at Glasgow. Needless to say, Buchan developed a remarkable command of both English and Latin. At university, he studied jurisprudence and politics under Adam Smith and demonstrated a real interest in and talent for drawing and printing. In 1758, Thomas Pelham-Holles, 1st Duke of Newcastle, summoned Buchan to meet King George II at London; the earl remarked of that meeting, "The forms of the english court and its dullness disgusted me greatly."[4] In 1762, he accepted a commission in the 32nd Regiment of Foot offered by William Pitt, 1st Earl of Chatham but later declined to take a post in the British embassy at Madrid. Tellingly, the young aristocrat's real interests lay beyond the intrigue of court and desire for martial glory.[5]

Despite the expectation that Buchan would enter court politics, he felt a deep sense of public responsibility to preserve Scotland's cultural integrity and advance human knowledge.[6] Buchan's education and experience exposed him to sixteenth-century Scottish historians such as John Major, Hector Boece and George Buchanan.[7] Major and Boece produced patriotic pseudo-histories of ancient Scotland that recorded, in one historian's take, "the most implausible tales of Scottish antiquity."[8] Buchanan's controversial work advanced the claim that all political power originated from the people and any monarch broaching the bounds of their allotted authority deserved both resistance and retribution.[9] The earl hoped to investigate the Scottish past without relying on mythology. And he appears to have absorbed Buchanan's political radicalism: an outspoken critic of how Scottish representative peers advanced into Britain's House of Lords, he championed and se-

of Scotland," in A. Bell, AS, ed., *The Scottish Antiquarian Tradition: Essays to Mark the Bicentenary of the Society of Antiquaries of Scotland, 1780-1980* (Edinburgh: John Donald, 1981), 1-30.

4. David Erskine Steuart, 11th Earl of Buchan, as quoted in James Gordon Lamb, "David Steuart Erskine, 11th Earl of Buchan: A Study of his Life and Correspondence," PhD diss., University of St. Andrews, 1963, 16.

5. Cant, "David Steuart."

6. Lamb, "David Steuart Erskine," 58-67.

7. Cant, "David Steuart," 9.

8. John Major, *De Gestis Scotorum* (Paris: Badius Ascensius, 1521); Hector Boece, *Scotorum Historiae a Prima Gentis Origine* (Paris: Badius Ascensius, 1527); For a brief assessment and the quote, see Denys Hay, "The Historiographers Royal in England and Scotland," *Scottish Historical Review* 30, no. 109, pt. 1 (1951), 18.

9. Arthur H. Williamson, "George Buchanan, Civic Virtue and Commerce: European Imperialism and Its Sixteenth-Century Critics," *Scottish Historical Review* 199, no. 199, pt. 1 (1996):20-37.

cured freer and fairer elections for those positions.[10] And he embraced American defiance to king-in-Parliament's attempts at regulating British North America after 1763. In 1780 he formed the Society of Antiquaries of Scotland, hoping to recover lost customs, traditions and even languages. In the process, he expected to examine constitutional, military and ecclesiastical organization. These endeavors required the earl and his fellow antiquarians to locate and examine the remains of Scottish castles, weapons and churches among other lost artifacts. Each of these "noble and disinterested actions," Buchan claimed, inspired and motivated his continued efforts on behalf of the public.[11]

Lord Buchan referred to himself as an "Old acquaintance" of Benjamin Franklin and the Scottish earl kept a watchful eye on the American colonies as the imperial crisis intensified.[12] Buchan may have encountered Franklin in Scotland as early as 1759, but the two had certainly met at London by 1764. The earl criticized Britain's "foolish and oppressive conduct toward the colonies" and described America as a sanctuary for "truth and freedom."[13] According to scholar James Gordon Lamb, Buchan began to identify himself in spirit with the American cause. Lamb summarized Buchan's whiggish simplification of the empire's turmoil as a British "attempt to enslave a brave and industrious people fighting for the preservation of a simple and dignified way of life."[14] Once the United States secured its independence, Buchan contributed to American intellectual life by continuing to write letters of introduction for Scottish academics seeking appointments at American universities.[15]

In 1786, Lord Buchan purchased Dryburgh Abbey, a dilapidated estate once in the possession of his ancestors.[16] The earl hoped to bring that ancient property back to its former glory and live quietly as a country gentleman, attending to printing, publishing and curating a "Temple of Caledonian Fame." Buchan planned to dedicate this space to housing likenesses of "illustrious and learned Scots."[17] Drawing on George

---

10. Cant, "David Steuart," 8.

11. David Erskine Steuart, 11th Earl of Buchan, as quoted in ibid., 2.

12. Lord Buchan to Benjamin Franklin, April 22, 1772, in Leonard W. Labaree, et al, eds., *The Papers of Benjamin Franklin,* 43 vols. (New Haven: Yale University Press, 1959-2018), 22:203.

13. David Erskine Steuart, 11th Earl of Buchan, as quoted in Cant, "David Steuart," 13.

14. David Erskine Steuart, 11th Earl of Buchan, as quoted in Lamb, "David Steuart Erskine," 155.

15. Cant, "David Steuart," 15.

16. Ibid., 21.

17. David Erskine Steuart, 11th Earl of Buchan, as quoted in Lamb, "David Steuart Erskine," 83.

Washington's own Scottish ancestry, the earl sought to commission a portrait of the American president for his temple. In 1791, he found his opportunity to do so; the Goldsmiths Company of Edinburg presented Buchan with a gift in recognition of his services in preserving Scotland's cultural heritage and identity.[18] The offering, a lidded wooden box with "an elegant silver binding," put into the earl's hands a powerful connection to Scotland's past.[19]

The box harnessed the combined emotional power of Scottish history and folklore. In 1298, King Edward I's forces comprehensively defeated Scottish independence leader Sir William Wallace at the Battle of Falkirk.[20] The resistance warrior supposedly evaded capture by his English enemies by climbing up an oak tree with his broad sword and waiting out their watch. The Goldsmiths Company of Edinburgh used timber they believed came from the heart of that tree to fashion a relic commemorating both Scottish liberty and Wallace's spirit of defiance.[21] When the Goldsmiths Company delivered this token of appreciation to Buchan, the earl felt unworthy receiving what he described as such a "magnificently significant present." He requested and received the company's permission to gift the box to the one "Man in the World to whom I thought it was most justly due." The earl designed to send it to American president George Washington.[22] In doing so, Lord Buchan aimed to connect two revolutions and two revolutionaries through a political relic that represented, to the earl, humanity's common march toward liberty and dignity. Lord Buchan simply needed someone to deliver the box. In 1791, he found his opportunity.

In early 1791, Dr. Thomas Gordon, Professor of Humanity at King's College, Aberdeen, Scotland, secured an invitation for local artist Archibald Robertson to visit Columbia College in New York. Robertson initially balked at the idea of traveling to the United States, imagining that young nation as home to a race of uncivilized barbarians. When he finally agreed to cross the Atlantic he did so more in the spirit

18. Lord Buchan to George Washington, June 28, 1791 in Dorothy Twohig, et al., eds., *The Papers of George Washington: Presidential Series*, 21 vols. (Charlottesville: University of Virginia Press, 1998-2020), 8:305-8.

19. Archibald Robertson to Andrew Robertson, May 25, 1799, in Robertson, *Letters and Papers of Andrew Robertson*, 9.

20. Rachel D. Brewer, "'We will Drain our Dearest Veins, but We Shall Be Free!:' The Legend and Legacy of Sir William Wallace, Warrior, Martyr, and National Icon," *Legacy* 10, no. 1 (2010): 67-85.

21. Lamb, "David Steuart Erskine," 163.

22. The Earl of Lord Buchan to George Washington, June 28, 1791, in Twohig, *Papers of Washington: Presidential Series*, 8:305-8.

of curiosity than anything else.[23] Once Lord Buchan learned of the artist's impending departure, he requested the two meet at Edinburgh. After their appointment, the earl entrusted Robertson to deliver the "Wallace box" to President Washington.[24] Buchan wrote a letter of introduction for his new acquaintance to present to the president, describing Robertson as "an honest artist seeking for bread and fame in the New World."[25] Shortly after the painter arrived at New York on October 2, 1791, his former prejudices toward America began to evaporate. In fact, the nation impressed him so much that he resolved to take up a permanent residence.[26] Once settled, Robertson undertook the pilgrimage to the executive mansion at Philadelphia. Assistant Secretary of the Treasury Tench Coxe introduced the artist to the president in December 1791.[27]

This meeting and the purpose behind it briefly captured the American news cycle.[28] The *National Gazette* reported the president received a box "made of the celebrated *Oak Tree* that sheltered the *Washington* of Scotland, the brave and patriotic Sir *William Wallace*."[29] According to the *Gazette of the United States*, Buchan requested that Washington, upon his death, consign the box to an American who, in the president's judgment, merited ownership "upon the same considerations that induced [the earl] to send it to the present possessor."[30] Both papers printed a concise history of Wallace's pursuit of Scottish liberty, defeat at Falkirk and eventual betrayal and execution.[31]

In private correspondence between Lord Buchan and the president, the earl expressed hope that "providential aids" would assist Washington in securing the "Liberties and Happiness of the American People" through "Government instituted by themselves for publick and private security."[32] After offering a brief summary of the box's supposed prove-

23. Edith Robertson Cleveland, "Archibald Robertson and His Portraits of the Washingtons," *Century Illustrated Monthly Magazine* 18, no. 1 (1890) 2-13.

24. Robertson, ed., *Papers of Robertson*, 9.

25. The Earl of Lord Buchan to Washington, June 28, 1791 in Twohig, et al., *Papers of Washington*, 8:305-8.

26. Cleveland, "Portraits of the Washingtons," 2-13.

27. Ibid., 6.

28. *National Gazette*, January 2, 1792; *Gazette of the United States*, January 4, 1792; *Virginia Gazette and Alexandria Advertiser*, January 12, 1792.

29. *National Gazette*, January 2, 1792.

30. *Gazette of the United States*, January 4, 1792.

31. *National Gazette*, January 2, 1792; *Gazette of the United States*, January 4, 1792; *Virginia Gazette and Alexandria Advertiser*, January 12, 1792.

32. The Earl of Buchan to Washington, June 28, 1791 in Twohig, et al., *Papers of Washington: Presidential Series*, 8:305-8.

nance, Buchan labeled it "a relique of long endurance" and a "Mark of
... Esteem."[33] Washington responded, accepting, "with satisfaction, the
significant present of the Box." The president recognized the artifact
as memorializing mankind's deep appreciation for "patriotic and heroic
virtues" and thanked the earl "for the sentiments that induced the transfer."[34] It is impossible to know whether or not Washington saw any
connection between Wallace's resistance efforts and his own; he certainly detected in the Scot's defiance a timeless form of patriotism and
virtue.

Buchan then requested Washington sit for a portrait "from the pen-
cil of Mr. Robertson." Once completed, he asked the president to send
it to Dryburgh Abbey so "that I may place it among those whom I honour most" in his Temple of Caledonian fame.[35] Robertson's own account of his meeting with the president reveals just how intimidated
the recent arrival became in Washington's presence. Though Robertson
claimed to be comfortable in intimate settings with those of the highest
rank in his own country, he recorded that he had "never felt as he did
on his first introduction to the American hero." Washington, recognizing his guest's palpable anxiety, broke his customary silence and engaged in unguarded conversation with Robertson, but the president's
small talk failed to relax the painter. The commander-in-chief next
called for social backup: Martha Washington. Yet even her "polished,
and familiar gaiety, and ceaseless cheerfulness" (as described by Robertson), did not completely settle the Scotsman. Washington finally resorted to inviting Robertson to dinner the following evening and,
"contrary to his usual habits, [the president] engrossed most of the conversation" with humorous stories that, according to the portraitist, "repeatedly set the table in a roar." Sufficiently relaxed, the Scottish artist
finally felt prepared to begin his assignment. He successfully produced
an oil painting of Washington for what he described as Lord Buchan's
"collection of portraits of the most celebrated worthies in liberal principles."[36]

Of the finished image, Washington wrote to Buchan that the "execution does no discredit" to Robertson, "of whose skill favorable men-

33. The Earl of Buchan to Washington, September 15, 1791, founders.archives.gov/doc-
uments/Washington/05-08-02-0207.
34. Washington to Lord Buchan, May 1, 1792 in Twohig, et al., *Papers of Washington: Presidential Series*, 10:330-31.
35. Lord Buchan to Washington, June 28, 1791 in Twohig, et al., *Papers of Washington:
Presidential Series*, 8:305-8.
36. Cleveland, "Portraits of the Washingtons," 2-13.

tion has been made to me."[37] Robertson explained he sought to capture his subjects in "lines, bold, and free," a quite accurate description of his breezy Washington portraits.[38] The Scottish artist ultimately produced three pictures of the president and one of Martha. Indeed, Robertson's career took off in his new American home. He partnered with his brother, Andrew, to found the Columbian Academy of Painting which flourished for thirty years. Robertson enjoyed a career as an accomplished artist and lecturer and authored multiple manuscripts on artistic technique and theory.[39] Incredibly, he saw his American gamble pay off as he earned a respectable living in an honest pursuit.

George Washington kept the Wallace box for the duration of his presidency and brought it back to Mount Vernon upon his retirement in March 1797. There it rested under the same roof as another revolutionary relic: the Key to the Bastille.[40] When Washington finalized his will on July 9, 1799, the old warrior did not feel himself the appropriate judge to select another American worthy of the box so, upon his death, he directed the "valuable curiosity" back to Lord Buchan, thanking him for "the distinguishing honour."[41] After Washington's passing in December 1799, the relic found transport back to Dryburgh Abbey in 1800 by way of Sir Robert Lister, British minister to America. In the earl's own will, he designated the box to "Washingtons University of Columbia." He requested that students who made the "greatest progress in useful knowledge" and possessed principles most friendly to the "genuine liberties of Mankind" be awarded medals from that American university.[42] In his later years, the earl remained committed to advancing human knowledge while organizing his papers and publishing his work.

In 1814, Lord Buchan commissioned amateur sculptor Joannes Smith to craft a statue of William Wallace.[43] Smith carved a twenty-

37. Washington to the Earl of Buchan, May 1, 1792, in Twohig, et al., *Papers of Washington: Presidential Series*, 10:330-31.

38. Archibald Robertson to Andrew Robertson, May 25, 1799, in Robertson, *Letters and Papers of Andrew Robertson*, 11.

39. William Dunlap, *History of the Rise and Progress of the Arts of Design in the United States*, 2 vols. (New York: George P. Scott and Company, Printers, 1834), 1:425-26.

40. Washington to Lafayette, August 11, 1790, in Twohig, et al., *Papers of Washington: Presidential Series*, 6:233-35.

41. George Washington's Last Will and Testament, July 9, 1799, in W.W. Abbott, ed., *Papers of George Washington: Retirement Series*, 4 vols. (Charlottesville: University of Virginia Press, 1998-99), 4:479-511.

42. Papers of the Earl of Buchan, founders.archives.gov/documents/Washington/05-08-02-0207.

43. Brewer, "We Will Drain Our Dearest Veins," 75-76.

one-and-a-half foot Scottish colossus out of red sandstone and painted it white. On its almost ten-foot-tall pedestal, the extant plaque reads (in part) "Wallace: Great Patriot Hero!"[44] Somewhere on the same property sat the Robertson portrait of the American president. The Scottish Washington and the American Wallace, separated by both seas and centuries, finally rested together on the ancient acres of Dryburgh Abbey. Buchan's efforts at last joined the two revolutionaries together in time and space.

When Buchan died in 1829, his executors sent the Wallace box back to America as the earl's will stipulated. During transit, however, someone stole it.[45] The box supposedly resurfaced in a private collection in England during the 1950s but has officially been missing since the early nineteenth century.[46] And not long after the relic's disappearance, Dryburgh Abbey fell back into a state of disrepair.[47] Buchan's artwork filtered into various collections and the earl's Caledonian temple disappeared.

David Steuart Erskine, 11th Earl of Buchan, subscribed to a particular view of the past that scholars today define as whig history.[48] Though British historian Herbert Butterfield did not coin that term until more than a century after the earl's death, contemporary chroniclers had practiced this progressive-oriented narrative since at least the early eighteenth century.[49] Broadly speaking, whig historians endeavored to explain the present as a triumph over the past, celebrating, among other things, secularism, scientific inquiry and constitutional forms of government that promoted individual liberty and dignity.[50] In light of this dominant historical persuasion, Lord Buchan might be forgiven for claiming a connectivity between Wallace and Washington; through a glass darkly their struggles appear similar.

Naturally the political, social and material circumstances of William Wallace's Scotland and George Washington's anglosphere mirror each

44. "Detail of Inscription," *Royal Commission on the Ancient and Historical Monuments of Scotland*, November 21, 2022, canmore.org.uk/collection/1117782.

45. Cleveland, "Portraits of the Washingtons," 9.

46. *Country Life*, 123 (1958), 74.

47. Lamb, "David Steuart Erskine," 1-2.

48. Peter Novack, *That Noble Dream: The "Objectivity Question" and the American Historical Profession* (New York: Cambridge University Press, 1998), 12-13; William Cronon, "Two Cheers for the Whig Interpretation of History," *Perspectives on History*, September 1, 2012, www.historians.org/research-and-publications/perspectives-on-history/september-2012/two-cheers-for-the-whig-interpretation-of-history.

49. Herbert Butterfield, *The Whig Interpretation of History* (1931; reprinted, New York: W.W. Norton and Company, 1965).

50. Novack, *Noble Dream*, 13.

other in only the most tangential fashion. Wallace fought for Scottish independence against an English king, suffered a key betrayal and received the ultimate punishment; English authorities hanged and beheaded him before drawing and quartering his remains.[51] Washington fought for American independence against a British king, suffered a key betrayal yet managed to defeat George III and received the ultimate reward: American citizens offered him near-unanimous esteem, praise and trust.[52] In the laboratorial mindscape of whig thinker Buchan, the adjacency lies not in the negative but positive spaces. In the earl's cosmic drama, Wallace transformed into the "Washington of Scotland" just as Washington metamorphized into "the modern American Wallace," one completing the other.[53] Another nineteenth-century statue of Wallace bears the whiggish inscription, "From Greece rose Leonidas, from America Washington, and from Scotland Wallace, names which shall remain through all time the watchwords and beacons of liberty."[54] Despite their being separated by half a millennium, for antiquarian whig thinkers like Lord Buchan, the eternal longing for liberty and dignity echoed as but a song that remained the same.

51. Brewer, "We Will Drain Our Dearest Veins," 68.
52. Joseph Ellis, *His Excellency: George Washington* (New York: Alfred A. Knopf, 2004); John Ferling, *The Ascent of George Washington: The Hidden Political Genius of an American Icon* (New York: Bloomsbury Press, 2009).
53. For "Washington of Scotland," see *National Gazette*, January 2, 1792; For "modern American Wallace," see Lord Buchan as quoted in Martha J. Lamb, ed., *Magazine of American History with Notes and Inquiries* 19 (1888), 278.
54. Graeme Morton, *William Wallace: Man and Myth* (Gloucestershire: Sutton Publishing, 2011), 82.

# AUTHOR BIOGRAPHIES

**MARK R. ANDERSON** is an independent historian and retired U.S. Air Force officer. He earned his BA in history from Purdue University and his MA in military studies from American Military University. He is the author of *The Battle for the Fourteenth Colony: America's War of Liberation in Canada, 1774-1776*; *The Invasion of Canada by the Americans, 1775-1776: As Told through Jean-Baptiste Badeaux's Three Rivers Journal and New York Captain William Goforth's Letters*; and contributed an essay to *The 10 Key Campaigns of the American Revolution*.

**BROOKE BARBIER** received her PhD in American history from Boston College. She is the author of *King Hancock: The Radical Influence of a Moderate Founding Father* and *Boston in the American Revolution: A Town versus an Empire*. In 2013, she founded and operates Ye Olde Tavern Tours, a popular guided outing along Boston's renowned Freedom Trail.

**J. L. BELL** is the author of *The Road to Concord: How Four Stolen Cannon Ignited the Revolutionary War*. He maintains the Boston1775.net website, dedicated to history, analysis, and unabashed gossip about the start of the American Revolution in New England. His other historical writing includes *Gen. George Washington's Home and Headquarters—Cambridge, Massachusetts*, a comprehensive study for the National Park Service, and contributions to Todd Andrlik's *Reporting the Revolutionary War*, James Marten's *Children in Colonial America*, and many journals and magazines. He has been elected a Fellow of the Massachusetts Historical Society, a Fellow of the American Antiquarian Society, and a Member of the Colonial Society of Massachusetts.

**BENJAMIN L. CARP** is the Daniel M. Lyons Professor of American History at Brooklyn College and teaches at the Graduate Center of the City University of New York. He is the author of *The Great New York Fire of 1776: A Lost Story of the American Revolution*; *Defiance of the Patriots: The Boston Tea Party and the Making of America*), winner of the Society of the Cincinnati Cox Book

Prize; *Rebels Rising: Cities and the American Revolution*; and co-editor (with Richard D. Brown) of *Major Problems in the Era of the American Revolution, 1760–1791*). His work has also appeared in *Civil War History, Early American Studies*, and the *William and Mary Quarterly* as well as *BBC History, Colonial Williamsburg*, the *New York Daily News*, the *Wall Street Journal*, and the *Washington Post*.

MICHAEL CECERE is a retired history teacher who resides in Williamsburg, Virginia, with his wife, Susan. Originally from Maine, he taught high school and college level American history for thirty years in Fairfax County and Gloucester County, Virginia. The author of twenty-five books and numerous articles on the American Revolution and Revolutionary War, he continues to research and write in retirement. When he is not writing, Mr. Cecere volunteers and works at Colonial Williamsburg, sometimes as a tobacco farmer, other times as a soldier or colonial dancer. He also attends Revolutionary War reenactments and lectures at historic sites and gatherings.

WALT CHIQUOINE retired a few years ago after several career incarnations as a successful engineer, consultant, and business owner. He first learned to research the pre-internet archives and historical societies while building a family genealogy in the 1990s. Living near Hockessin, Delaware, Walt spent several thousand hours over many years researching local Mill Creek Hundred history as context for understanding and confirming the British movements of 1777. He has served on boards of the Hale-Byrnes House and the Hockessin Historical Society, and is a proud supporter of the 1st Delaware Regiment reenactors. Walt now lives on the Eastern Shore of Maryland.

JETT CONNER, PhD, is a retired political science professor, college administrator and academic policy officer for the Colorado Department of Higher Education. He studied the political thought of the American founding period during a National Endowment for the Humanities summer fellowship at Princeton University, and recently published *John Adams vs Thomas Paine: Rival Plans for the Early Republic* (Westholme, 2018). He's enjoying retirement in Denver while pursuing numerous interests including travel, wildlife watching and reading and writing about the history and political thought of the American Revolution.

BRADY J. CRYTZER teaches history at Robert Morris University. He is the recipient of the Donald S. Kelly and Donna J. McKee Awards for outstanding scholarship in the discipline of history. A specialist in imperialism in North America, he is the author of a number of books, including *War in the Peaceable Kingdom: The Kittanning Raid of 1756, Guyasuta and the Fall of Indian America*, and *Hessians: Rebels, Mercenaries, and the War for British North America*. He is also the host of Dispatches: The Podcast of the Journal of the American Revolution.

BENJAMIN M. GEORGE is a retired U.S. Marine. He served as an enlisted public affairs specialist and Marine Security Guard at U.S. diplomatic missions abroad, then commissioned as an officer after earning a BA degree in English from Pennsylvania State University. He spent twelve years as an intelligence officer, including a tour at Headquarters, Marine Corps with the Deputy Commandant for Information, where he helped develop new doctrine for integrating information into military operations. He holds an MA in history from George Washington University.

DON N. HAGIST is managing editor of *Journal of the American Revolution*. His historical studies focus on presenting an accurate picture of individual soldiers and their families, especially those of the British army who served in America. His books include *Noble Volunteers: the British Soldiers who fought the American Revolution*, *The Revolution's Last Men: The Soldiers behind the Photographs*, and *These Distinguished Corps: British Grenadier and Light Infantry Battalions in the American Revolution*. Don is an engineer for a major medical device manufacturer, and also writes for several well-known syndicated cartoonists.

LEON HARRIS earned a degree in physics at Virginia Tech and graduate degrees in biophysics at Penn State, then taught biology, wrote textbooks, and did neurobiological research at SUNY Plattsburgh for more than three decades. Since retiring, he has helped Will Graves at revwarapps.org transcribe pension and bounty-land applications and other documents of about thirty thousand Revolutionary soldiers who served from or in the South.

M. ANDREW HOLOWCHAK, PhD, is a retired professor of philosophy and history, who taught at institutions such as University of Pittsburgh, University of Michigan, and Rutgers University, Camden. He is editor of the *Journal of Thomas Jefferson and His Time* and author/editor of over fifty books and over two hundred published essays on topics such as ethics, ancient philosophy, science, psychoanalysis, and critical thinking. His current research is on Thomas Jefferson, and has published nearly 150 essays and twenty books on the subject. Like Jefferson, he has a passion for "putting up and pulling down," but his putting up and pulling down is not architectural, but done on a landscape or in a garden. He also enjoys lifting weights, bike riding, conferencing, and talking about Thomas Jefferson.

JONATHAN HOUSE, a California native and former *Wall Street Journal* foreign correspondent, discovered a passion for American history when he relocated to Washington DC. He is interested in researching and writing about the experiences of women during the American Revolution. In addition to Mercy Otis Warren, he has written about Grace Galloway, the author of a famous Loyalist diary, and the Baroness Frederika Charlotte Riedesel, who left a vivid memoir of her experiences during the Battles of Saratoga. Jonathan currently works as a research editor for a leading geopolitical risk firm in Washington.

CHIP LANGSTON is an Olympic-caliber farrier living in Palm Beach County, Florida, but has had a lifelong passion for chronicling the often untold and forgotten stories in American history. His works can be found in *Civil War Times Illustrated* and *Anvil Magazine*. His latest ebook, *Jamestown Odyssey: America's Untold History of Multiracial Families From its Founders* can be found on Apple Books. Based on his historical research on the life of the nearly forgotten abolitionist titan John Mercer Langston, he was recently invited to be a guest speaker at Howard University.

DOUG MACINTYRE is a retired business executive, community leader, and student of the American Revolution. His research led to creation of Thomson Park to commemorate the battle at the Breach (www.thomsonpark.org). He graduated from the U.S. Military Academy at West Point and served as an U.S. Army infantry officer. Doug earned an MBA with honors from Boston University and completed advanced management programs at Harvard, Wharton, and Stanford. He was chair, president, and CEO of public and private information technology companies and he has served on the boards of industry, civic, and historical organizations.

CHRISTIAN MCBURNEY is author of six books on the American Revolutionary War, including *Dark Voyage: An American Privateer's War on Britain's African Slave Trade*, *Kidnapping the Enemy: The Special Operations to Capture Generals Charles Lee & Richard Prescott*, and *The Rhode Island Campaign: The First French and American Operation in the Revolutionary War*. He is president of the George Washington American Revolution Round Table of the District of Columbia and is the founder of the online journal, Small State, Big History, devoted to the history of Rhode Island. He practices law in Washington, DC. For more information on his books, see christianmcburney.com.

SHAWN MCGHEE, PhD, Temple University, is author of *No Longer Subjects of the British King: The Political Transformation of Royal Subjects to Republican Citizens, 1774-1776*. His scholarly interests include the politics of eighteenth-century British North America and political identity formation. He is an educator and adjunct professor of history in the Philadelphia Metropolitan area. Beyond researching and teaching about the past, he enjoys hiking, scuba diving, kayaking and studying music. He resides in New Jersey with his wife and their three children.

STUART LYALL MANSON (stuartmanson.wordpress.com) is a professional independent historian based in Cornwall, Ontario, Canada. He is the author of the book series *Sacred Ground: Loyalist Cemeteries of Eastern Ontario* published by Global Heritage Press (globalgenealogy.com).

CURTIS F. MORGAN, JR. has taught world and US history at Laurel Ridge (formerly Lord Fairfax) since August 2000. He earned his PhD in Modern

European History from the University of South Carolina in 1998 and is the author of *James F. Byrnes, Lucius Clay and American Policy in Germany, 1945-1947.* His essay, "'A Merchandise of Small Wares': Nathanael Greene's Northern Apprenticeship, 1775-1780," appeared in the collection *General Nathanael Greene and the American Revolution in the South,* edited by Greg Massey and Jim Piecuch. He has three entries ("Lord Fairfax," Nathanael Greene," and "Winchester, VA") in the *Digital Encyclopedia of George Washington* which can be accessed at http://www.mountvernon.org/encyclopedia. He is presently working on a military biography of General Nathanael Greene.

LOUIS ARTHUR NORTON, professor emeritus at the University of Connecticut, has published extensively on maritime history topics that include *Joshua Barney: Hero of the Revolutionary War* and *Captains Contentious: The Dysfunctional Sons of the Brine.* Two of his articles were awarded the 2002 and 2006 and Gerald E. Morris Prize for maritime historiography in the Mystic Seaport Museum's LOG. Dr. Norton received the Connecticut Authors and Publishers Association's 2009–2010 and 2010–2011 awards for fiction and essay writing respectively.

DAVID OTERSEN is a history enthusiast with a particular interest in Constitutional Law. He studied at the University of Maryland, where he majored in Government and Politics and earned Dean's List distinctions.

DAVID PRICE has authored four books, including a pair about the "Ten Crucial Days" of the American Revolution—*The Road to Assunpink Creek* and *Rescuing the Revolution*—as well as *John Haslet's World* and *The Battle of Harlem Heights, 1776.* The latter was accepted into the permanent collection of the Connecticut Museum of Culture and History. His forthcoming *Winning the Ten Crucial Days: The Keys to Victory in George Washington's Legendary Winter Campaign* will be released in early 2025. He has been awarded the National Society of the Sons of the American Revolution Bronze Good Citizenship Medal in recognition of his work as an author, speaker, and historical interpreter at Washington Crossing Historic Park (PA) and Princeton Battlefield State Park (NJ). More information about David and his work can be found at dpauthor.com.

GENE PROCKNOW's passion for the American War of Independence emanates from living among Revolutionary War sites in Boston, New Jersey, and Vermont. His research includes interpreting "the politics of command" among the Continental Army major generals, and in Ethan Allen and the creation of Vermont. He is the author of two books—*William Hunter, Finding Free Speech: The Son of a British Soldier Who Became an Early American* and the *Mad River Gazetteer,* which traces the naming of prominent Vermont place names after Revolutionary War patriots. Procknow's website, Researching the American Revolution, aids students and researchers. Gene holds an MA in American History from Norwich University. He is married with two historian sons and lives in Washington, DC.

CONOR ROBISON is a creative writer and historian, with extensive earaches from dragging his mother around dormant battlefields, usually in the middle of nowhere, and being on the receiving end of her often-scathing remarks on warfare. He has published works in the *Journal of the Seven Years War, JAR,* and *History Ireland.*

MICHAEL J. F. SHEEHAN holds a BA in history from Ramapo College of New Jersey. He is the senior historian at the Stony Point Battlefield State Historic Site where he has been since 2008. Michael has spent most of his time studying the American Revolution with a focus on the role of the Hudson Highlands and Lower Hudson Valley, where he has lived his whole life. In his free time, he is currently working on a book about the history of King's Ferry during the American Revolution and he has been playing live traditional Irish music in the Stony Point area for ten years. Deeply involved in the Brigade of the American Revolution since 2008, Michael has reenacted and spoken at countless historic sites and societies in New York and New Jersey, and has served as a board member for Lamb's Artillery Company.

DR. MARVIN L. SIMNER retired after more than thirty years at Western University in London, Ontario. As a research psychologist throughout his academic career, his focus was on investigating many long held but rarely examined theories in the areas of School Psychology, Developmental Psychology, and Psychological Testing. His research reports have appeared in peer-reviewed national and international journals. In 2007 he was made a Fellow of the Canadian Psychological Association and in 2007 he received the Member of the Year award from the Association. Since his retirement his focus has been on an examination of many equally long-standing beliefs in the fields of Canadian and American history.

SCOTT M. SMITH retired in 2014 after a thirty year career on Wall Street to pursue a lifelong passion to write. His cybersecurity novel, *Darkness is Coming,* won Distinguished Favorite in the thriller category in the NYC Big Book Award competition. In 2017, he began researching the life and times of Nathan Hale, the official hero of his adopted home state of Connecticut. The effort resulted in a biographical novel, entitled *But One Life,* as well as whetted Scott's appetite to further explore this period in American history.

ERIC STERNER is a national security and aerospace consultant in the Washington, DC area. He held senior staff positions for the Committees on Armed Services and Science in the House of Representatives and served in the Department of Defense and as NASA's Associate Deputy Administrator for Policy and Planning. He earned a BA at American University and two MAs from

George Washington University. He has written for a variety of publications, ranging from academic journals to the trade and popular media. His idea of a good time is traipsing through historical sites with his family.

PHILIP D. WEAVER is a retired systems analyst. A living historian for nearly fifty years, he is a highly regarded tailor, presenter, author and independent researcher. Phil's articles on the colonial period and living history were first published nationally in 1979. An original member of the West Point Chapter, Company of Military Historians, he was elected a Fellow of the Company (May 2004). Phil's most recent book is *The 3rd New Jersey in New-York: Stories from "The Jersey Greys" of 1776*. He is also the editor and principal author of *The Greatest Hits of "The Colonial Chronicle" —The Rev-War Collection*.

RICHARD J. WERTHER is a history enthusiast living in Novi, Michigan. He studied business management at Bucknell University in Lewisburg, Pennsylvania and is a CPA by trade (though now retired).

ERIC WISER grew up on the northwest side of Chicago and earned a BA in history from Loyola University-Chicago and was a member of the Phi Alpha Theta National Honor Society in history. He is a certified secondary history teacher and a certified public accountant, having also studied accountancy at DePaul University. His fascination with the American Revolution started with a visit to Yorktown battlefield during college and increased when he learned of his family's heritage in the Revolution on a visit to Maryland and Virginia. Eric currently lives in Arlington Heights, Illinois, with his wife and daughter.

COLIN ZIMMERMAN is a devoted husband and father of three and currently resides in Southern New Jersey. He obtained an MA in military history from Norwich University and is currently working on a PhD specializing in the American Revolution through Liberty University. Mr. Zimmerman at present serves as the military historian for Washington Crossing Historic Park.

# INDEX